EMERGING CONVERSATIONS ON THEOFILIATION

ESSAYS IN HONOUR OF
ARCHBISHOP ANTHONY J. V. OBINNA

edited by

KENNETH AMEKE &
SAMUEL UZOUKWU

Emerging Conversations On Theofiliation

Essays In Honour Of Archbishop
Anthony J. V. Obinna

edited by

Kenneth Ameke & Samuel Uzoukwu

Library of Congress Control Number:		2019914780
ISBN:	Hardcover	978-1-7960-6112-3
	Softcover	978-1-7960-6111-6
	eBook	978-1-7960-6110-9

Rev. date: 10/10/2019

To order additional copies of this book, contact:
Xlibris
1-888-795-4274
www.Xlibris.com
Orders@Xlibris.com
798636

Contents

Pastoral, Mission, and Management

Philosophy, Politics, Postcolonial Reading and Psychology

Moral Theology, Human Life and Liturgical Music

To God the Father and the Son and the Holy Spirit
and Mother Mary, the Seat of Wisdom.

Abbreviations

ADF: Alaigbo Development Foundation
AG: Second Vatican Council, Decree on Missionary Activity, *Ad Gentes*, 1965
ATR: African Traditiona Religion
CA: John Paul II, encyclical letter, *Centesimus Annus*
CABAN: Catholic Biblical Association of Nigeria
CBCN: Catholic Bishops Conference of Nigeria
CCC: Catechism of the Catholic Church, 1994
CIWA: Catholic Institute of West Africa
CMS: Church Missionary Society
Cor.: 1Corinthians
CV: Benedict XVI, encyclical letter, *Caritas in Veritate*, 2009
Deut.: Deuteronomy
Eccles.: Ecclesiasticus
EG: Pope Francis, apostolic exhortation, *Evangelii Gaudium*, 2013
Eu Care: Eucharistic Care
Exod.: Exodus
Ezek.: Ezekiel
Gen.: Genesis
GS: Second Vatican Council, Pastoral Constitution, *Gaudium et Spes*, 1965
IPOB: Indigenous People of Biafra
Isa.: Isaiah
ITR: Indigenous/Igbo Traditional Religion
JDPC: Justice Development Peace and Caritas
Lev.: Leviticus
LG: Second Vatican Council, Dogmatic Constitution on the Church, *Lumen Gentium*, 1964
LS: Pope Francis, encyclical letter, *Laudato Si*, 2015
Matt.: Matthew
NA: Second Vatican Council, Declaration of Church Relation with Non-Christian Religions, *Nostra Aetate*, 1965
Neh.: Nehemiah

NT: New Testament

OT: Old Testament

PCID: Pontifical Council for Interreligious Dialogue

Prov.: Proverbs

RCM: Roman Catholic Mission

SC: Second Vatican Council, Constitution on the Sacred Liturgy, *Sacrosanctum Concillium*, 1963

Wisd.: Wisdom

UN: United Nations

UN CEDAW: United Nations Convention on the Elimination of All Forms of Discrimination against Women

UNDHR: United Nations Declaration on Human Rights

UR: Second Vatican Council, Decree on Ecumenism, *Unitatis Redintegratio*, 1964

Preface

Thank God, the twenty-fifth anniversary of the installation of the Most Rev. Anthony J. V. Obinna as the metropolitan of Owerri Ecclesiastical Province has given the impetus for this great treasure. This treasure *Emerging Perspectives on Theofiliation: Essays in Honour of Anthony J. V. Obinna* is a baby born at the right time. I feel greatly honoured to be asked to write this preface. Surely the desire to write essays on the quintessential first archbishop of Owerri Province by this galaxy of erudite scholars could never have come late. The title for the essays is *ad rem*. It is a good window into the thoughts of the jubilarian, which involve every human person as the son or daughter of God. Theofiliation as a concept gives room for a myriad of intellectual reflections and applications. Man is not just theofiliated; he is also confiliated. Because man has moved away from this filiation in God, man has become wolf to man.

The concomitant effect is a broken relationship with God, with one another, and with creation. That is the genesis of all forms of divisions: ethnicity, racism, nepotism, colonialism, and all other forms of prejudices. The archbishop has for long and in various fora demonstrated his unequivocal stand against any form of racial divide, both local and international. At the local level he has fought against the culturally clothed belief in the *osu, diala*, and *ume*. At the international level, he has carried this war against racial divide to the United States of America. In all, he has presented the reconfiliation dynamic as a veritable solution. According to him, there is need for our return together as sons and daughters of God. For him, humanity needs a reconfiliation. In the Igbo context, he once wrote, 'Thus the filiation of Jesus to our humanity has made it possible for us to be filiated to Jesus who is Chi-God. We thus become Chi-Christic as well as Christi-Chiic—created by God who is Christ and saved by Christ who is God. To be baptized in and converted to Christ tantamount to sharing the Godness of Christ and the Christness of God. It is within the Chi-Christic–Christi-Chiic communion that we live, flower and bloom to the full.'

This Festschrift in honour of Amarachi Obinna is a compendium of usable knowledge. The authors have dealt with various themes largely inspired by the theology and practice of the archbishop. The reflections of Amarachi run very deep into his religious conviction that God is for us all. This conviction leads to the reflections on theofiliation, the inGodment of all creation. This idea influences Vincent Onwukwe to reflect on what he calls reinGodment theology of A. J. V. Obinna in a disinGoded Christianity. The disinGoded Christianity needs to be reconfiliated and reinGoded. Since Jesus is God and became our Saviour by dying for us all on the cross of Calvary, theofiliation has given the thrust to Christifiliation. Thus, Amarachi Obinna has given us adequate terms for a broader intellectual reflection. This is precisely what this Festschrift is all about. Thus, Edmund Aku applies the Christifiliation idea towards the spiritual and pastoral care of the priest among the family of God's people. Being inspired by theofiliation dynamic, Boniface Anusiem examines how interpersonal communication can be seen in the pastoral context. Here the theofiliation dynamic can form the basis for vertical and horizontal dimensions of communication. Kingsley Ndubueze examines what he calls integral ecology and finds a nexus between the Odenigbo lecture series and the integration of the environment and cultural heritage, which creates Igbo identity through the Igbo language. Michael Konye finds in the theofiliation dynamic a good theological anthropology, which could help eradicate the obnoxious *diala-osu-ume* caste system. From the theofiliance, Bede Ukwuije takes the discussion to the reconfiliation dynamic in the service of healing humanity's division through the memory of the cross of Christ. This pastoral thrust finds expression in the contribution by Andrew Nkwocha, who sees the reconfiliation in Christ a challenge to Christianity in Nigeria. Donald Ude sees in Obinna's concept of filiation as the source of his politico-social philosophy. This philosophy makes Amarachi condemn the 'political jaywalking' evident in our society. We all can testify to his running battle with the political class. The leadership style of the archbishop is properly highlighted by Samuel Uzoukwu. He explores the model of confiliation dynamic as that which rectifies human dignity. Surely this will abhor any form of jiggery-pokery in human relations.

Furthermore, Stephen Egwim uses a biblical lens to capture the human person in the original filiation, the new filiation, and the ongoing filiation. He sees the filiation dynamic from Heigeschichte, which began at creation, then by blessing, by election, and by covenant, and ultimately, by adoption in Christ. Alexander Abasili uses the biblical story of Tamar (Gen. 38) to move the conversation to gender issues especially as it concerns childless marriage in the African context. Through the prism of confiliation, he makes a case for comparative study through African contextual hermeneutics. Patrick Mbarah' examines the Odenigbo Religious Cultural Project of the archbishop and finds its roots in his pastoral care for Ndigbo. The theofiliation dynamic comes alive in the context of ecumenism and interreligious dialogue and the practice of interculturality. Using the theme of reconfiliation and reinGodment, Emmanuel Obi and Kenneth Ameke take the conversation into the area of evangelization. According to them, the chifiliation theology of Amarachi Obinna makes for proper inculturated Christianity, which eliminates faith–culture conflict in mission work. In his 'From Colonialism and Slavery to Reconfiliation', Moses Chikwe examines the reconfiliation dynamic in the context of postcolonial Africa. This reconfiliation, according to him, will help heal the wounds of enslavement inflicted upon the African psyche. On the theme 'Evangelization: Locally and Globally: The Filiation Dynamic', Innocent Osuagwu and Bede Ukwuije see the theofiliation dynamic as an indigenous theological articulation with universal relevance. In his own contribution, Paschal Okpaleke argues from biblical point of view that we should advance from 'Right to Life' to 'Gift of Life'. For him we can better understand this from a theofiliated dimension.

Intellectually, Anthony J. V. Obinna is a Catholic humanist concerned with how individuals enhance or negate their humanity through interaction with one another. This is expressed in his theofiliation and chifiliation. As a theologian, he approaches Jesus Christ as the revelation of the fullness of humanity. This is expressed in the filiation of Jesus to our humanity, our sharing in the Godness of Christ and the Christness of God, and in this Chi-Christic–Christi-Chiic communion that we live, flower, and bloom to the full. As a poet, he celebrates the small victories of ordinary men and women. This is expressed masterfully by Stephen Egwim in his examination of Obinna's poems, putting them in context through a biblical framework. As a modern socioreligious thinker, he believes that creation needs a rebirth. This is expressed in the reconfiliation and reinGodment dynamic. This Festschrift is truly a treasure.

Rev. Fr Dr John Obilor

Acknowledgments

Editing a book is harder than one thought and more rewarding than one could have ever imagined. None of these would have been possible without the recognition of these key persons worthy of thanks who are behind the publication of this book. A special thanks to Rev. Fr Dr Innocent M. Osuagwu and Rev. Fr. Dr. Stephen Egwim for their inspiration and advice towards the publication of this enormous project as well as Rev. Fr Samuel Uzoukwu for his brilliant and useful suggestions and guidance. I would also extend my gratitude to all the contributors for their ernest collaborations and responses. The promptness and rich varieties of your contributions from your diverse areas of speciality add to the intellectual repertoire in celebratining Archbishop Obinna.

My appreciation also goes out to my esteemed colleagues Rev. Fr Dr William Owire, Fr Maurice Emelu and Rev. Fr Paschal Okpaleke, who have been helpful in their critical remarks in certain parts of this book. A warm gratitude also goes to Fr. Ikenna Okagbue for his financial contribution for this project.

Importantly, I am grateful to the Catholic archdiocese of Owerri and the Katholieke Universiteit Leuven, Belgium, for proving the platform and creating the academic atmosphere to venture into this project. Special thanks to Professor Dr Annemarie Mayer and Professor Stephan Van Erp for their accompaniment in realizing this project.

Kenneth Ameke

Introduction

Situating a Theological Biography and Content

Kenneth Ameke

When His Grace Most Rev. Anthony John Valentine (Chiedozie) Obinna was approaching twenty-five years of his episcopacy in the Catholic Archdiocese of Owerri, he thought of assembling together his theological thoughts and reflections into an articulate document. Consequently, this desire led to the idea of publishing a Festschrift in his honour with the challenge of identifying a theme that would capture Obinna's wide range of concerns in theological, philosophical, management, biblical, political, moral, and pastoral perspectives. The follow-up to his theological thought gave rise to the responses to his ideas from diverse scholarly approaches. Indeed, Archbishop Obinna's theological thinking resonates with the hope and expectation of John Paul II's postsynodal apostolic exhortation *Ecclesia in Africa* §. 63, which maintains that 'it is to be hoped that theologians in Africa will work out the theology of the Church as family with all the riches contained in this concept, [showing] its complementarity with other images of the Church drawn from the Scripture'. This statement indicates an empowerment of a theological concept(s) that express(es) an understanding of the church emanating from the African perspective.

Archbishop Anthony J. V. C. Obinna was born on the twenty-sixth of June 1946 into the family of Mr Michael and Mrs Grace Obinna in Emekuku, Imo State, Nigeria. We will access the personality of Archbishop Obinna here through the lens of the theology in the names he is called. The 'Anthony' in Archbishop Obinna's names calls to attention the nearest saint celebrated in the month of June around the time of his birth—that is, St. Anthony of Padua. The connection to this patron saint tells us something about Archbishop Obinna's pastoral zeal. In his autobiographical statements, it appears that before his birth, it was expected that he would have been given a name closer to the saint celebrated, but it turned out that he was born later. As one of his patron saints, Anthony in the personality of Archbishop Obinna shows his love and predilection for the poor and the oppressed. The Eu-Care Outreach is a programme he sets up in this regard, which becomes, till the present day, the arena where he encounters and shows concern to the marginalized people of different walks of life. He is compassionate to the plight of the voiceless in society. Again, from the perspective of St. Anthony of Padua, who was recognized as an evangelical doctor (*doctor evangelicus*), Archbishop Obinna manifests the character of a thirst for excellence, learning, and teaching. His study of moral theology shaped his pastoral demeanour and his personal life. His theofiliation has become a springboard that serves as the unbreakable commitment to evangelization.

Moreover, Archbishop Obinna equally goes by the name John, especially John the Baptist, whose celebration of his sainthood is connected to the days of his birth. John, which means 'God is gracious' or 'Yahweh has been gracious', brings to limelight the missionary framework Archbishop John is known for. It is William Ward who once said that 'every great person has first learned how to obey, whom to obey and when to obey'. Archbishop Obinna owes his obedience to his Master Jesus Christ, who called him to His service. After the manner of Christ's obedience (cf. Hebrews 5:8, 'Though Son He was, He learned obedience from what He suffered'), the key to Archbishop Obinna's pastoral enthusiasm is built on obedience to Christ. Based on this foundation, his episcopal motto becomes the explicit expression of this obedience. His episcopal coat of arms reads, 'To serve God and His people.' Thus, the attitude of service becomes the driving mindset in discharging his pastoral duty. This coat of arm eloquently describes or provides the road map to his mission. His call to priesthood on April 6, 1972, and by extension his episcopal consecration on September 4, 1993, and the elevation of Owerri Ecclesiastical Province into a metropolitan see on March 26, 1994, by His Holiness Pope John Paul II are all embedded in this motto. The force of obedience implied in his coat of arms describes the manner he intends to discharge his priestly/episcopal ministry by facilitating the bond that unites Christians to Christ and especially the poor, the evangelizing of the culture, and positively penetrating the political space.

However, from the point of view of demeanour, Archbishop Obinna is a man of simplicity in fashion and even in his diet just as John the Baptist. His simplicity does not affect the forcefulness of his proclamation of the message of salvation to his flock. Evidently, the prominence to catechesis speaks volumes about Archbishop Obinna in a similar way John the Baptist made strong impact upon his hearers in proclaiming the message of repentance. Archbishop John addresses his audience in strong and forthright language. This is comparable to the way the religious leaders and some civil authorities approached John the Baptist in order to listen to him. In fact, Archbishop John Obinna, without any political office, exercises influence in challenging the political system and injustices in the State where he resides. John the Baptist confronted King Herod and political elites in his time, so also the weight of the message of authority of Archbishop John Obinna towards the legal, civil, and religious authorities.

Moreover, the aspect that John the Baptist is known as the only voice prophetically crying out in the wilderness re-echoes in Archbishop John's voice to the situations affecting the well-being of the people. This voice is not a voice of anguish nor is it full of lamentations; it is rather a voice that acknowledges the dignity of the human person and that he is not the centre of attraction. He does not desire to feel great, but he can be the channel of the greatness of the goodness of God to the people entrusted to his care as the chief shepherd. Archbishop John considers his voice on mission to preach the message of love, justice, and equity to all. It is a voice that cannot be intimidated by any human prestige, fame, or class. In addition, his message is equally directed to the unjust and oppressive traditional systems/customs against human dignity. His personality deriving from John goes a long way to show his pastoral strength, especially his fidelity and commitment to his ministry and the unwavering focus that he is dedicated to do. This sense of mission does not claim to distinguish him exclusively; rather, it tells us about the uniqueness he brings to his pastoral ministry.

Furthermore, the archbishop is also addressed as Valentine. Valentine, which literally means 'strong, vigorous, and to be in good health', is associated with St. Valentine. One might immediately see him as a bishop of love or a bishop who likes the celebration of love. On the other hand, Archbishop Valentine's 'love' is anchored in 1 John 4:8, 16, 'God is love', as well as the celebration of the abundance of love enshrined in John 10:10b, which reads, 'I have come that they may have life and have it to the full.' These two grounds of love tell us the perspectives of love that Archbishop Obinna shows by taking this name. Archbishop Valentine shows this love in two ways; for instance, celebration of pure love among couples and peoples and love for life towards the helpless (especially the babies). As Valentine, he manifests himself as an arch-prolifer. In fact, his theofiliation is also his story of love for the human person without divide. This is seen in his relentless campaign against the discrimination evolving in the *osu-ume-diala* caste system. As a pastor of soul, he manifests this love by always giving himself personally and being actively committed.

Finally, the episcopal jubilarian is scarcely addressed as Chiedozie, which means 'God's plans are the best'. This Igbo name, even though not common with him, indicates the intensity of his propensity for culture and inculturation. It appears that it was not given to him immediately after his birth or Christian baptism; rather, it came as a response from his mother, Mrs Grace Obinna, at the time of his studies in America. Suffice it to underline that the prefix *Chi* in this name later evokes his consciousness of the significance of the concept to his identity as an Igbo person. The complement to *Chi* is *Chi-Ukwu*, meaning 'the Great God, Spirit energy is perceived as generically active in the whole creation as the Creator'. In the anthropological realm, *Chi* becomes the personal reflex of the Creator *Chi-Ukwu* in creation. He later developed his thought around this concept as a dynamic force and being that keeps the Igbos connected with the rest of humanity as humans and later as Christians. This leads to the perceivable ecclesiological aspect of *Chi*, which underpins that there is a certain continuity between the significance of *Chi* for the Igbo Christians and the universal mission of Christ. This leads Archbishop Chiedozie into the theological inquiry of understanding the correlation between the goal of the Trinitarian communion and the mission of Christ who engrafts humanity into a family.[1] Evidently, there are variations of names associated with *Chi* because it is the creative, saving, healing, and fructifying fulcrum of all life for the Igbo Africans.[2]

It is in honour of the silver jubilee of his episcopacy that these conversations are put together in this first volume titled *Emerging Conversations on Theofiliation: Essays in Honour of Archbishop Anthony J. V. Obinna*. This volume discusses and enlarges insights inherent in Archbishop Obinna's theological thinking on theofiliation. Therefore, the contributors to this volume critically examine his idea of theofiliation from their areas of speciality as a further exploration of this theological term. The willingness of the contributors has resulted in a collection that envisage the eclectic and heterogeneous scholarly vision of its honouree. Besides, the contributors to this maiden edition encompass both illustrious theologians and promising researchers in theology, philosophy, psychology, and management. The themes discussed by the contributors are grouped into biblical/comparative study, systematic/ pastoral, ethical/management, philosophical/political and anthropological issues. The enriching and diverse collections of this volume have five thematic sections that theofiliation brings together.

The first section focuses on the biblical theology and comparative biblical study. Stephen Egwim analyses the content of Archbishop Obinna's concept of refiliation and reconfiliation. This analysis also explores on the conditions and additional insights implied in the divine filiation. For Egwim, the concepts of reconfiliation and refiliation offer us insight into the place of the human person in the original *filiation*, the *new filiation*, and the *ongoing filiation*. He identifies ways the human persons are refiliated, namely filiation by creation by blessing, by election and by covenant, and ultimately, by adoption in Christ. Thus, he underlines the human response as key to our refiliation in God after sin defiliated the human person. In another heading, 'Colonial Beauty and Harmony of Creation: Anthony J. V. Obinna's Poetic on New Epiphany of Creation,' Egwim critically analyses the structure of the poem in which Obinna recounts his Incarnational re-experience. Egwim unravels the latent meanings in Obinna's Incarnational

---

1   Anthony J. V. Obinna, "Roots, Branches, Graftings and Fruits: The Reconfiliatory Challenge to African-Americans and Humanity at Large' (lecture delivered in Charleston, South Carolina, June 21, 2003), 5.

2   Obinna, "Roots, Branches, Graftings and Fruits', 5.

poem by building a theological structure of the theology of experience implicit in our daily encounters (encounters that sometimes are not reflected upon). By systematically analysing the unreflected structure of the poem, Egwim, thus, assigns importance to the lived experience of a Christian. He then offers a coordinated interpretation of the images and actions in Obinna's poem, putting them in context through a biblical framework.

From a comparative biblical analysis, Vincent Onwukwe examines Obinna's idea of reinGodment as a paradigm for reconstructing the segmented priestly mission in an extreme secularized materialistic world. In his argument, the concept of reinGodment enables us to recapture and prioritize Christian values that can lead Christians to flourish in holiness of life and close relationship with God. He challenges the clergy and other religious leaders to prioritize the *ụkọChukwu* metaphor over *ụkọChukwu* parallel in the lives of the spiritual/religious leaders. From a feminist perspective reading, Alexander Abasili reflects on the contextual reading of Genesis 38 through the prism of confiliation and its application to the African context. This suggests an informed African reaction to the problem of childlessness in marriage. Through the perspective of Igbo culture as a case study, he opted for African contextual hermeneutics, especially its feminist component that has similarity with the Hebrew biblical story of Tamar. Therefore, he proposes positive implications of this reading of Genesis 38 for the contemporary African audience.

The second section contains the fundamental and systematic theological engagements with Obinna's theofiliation as well as the inculturation/interculturality and ecumenical interpretations. In the first venture, John Egbulefu offers an educative, logico-linguistic, and systematic theological study of Archbishop Obinna's theofiliation. Egbulefu identifies theofiliation as a theological novelty in light of the renewal theology that accompanies the Second Vatican Council. He brings theofiliation into the dialogue with another theological novelty from an African thinker, which is theology in a technoscientific age, thus demostrating that renewal theology is getting its expansion from African theologians. In a joint paper, Innocent Osuagwu and Bede Ukwuije focus on the fundamental theological thrust of Obinna's divine filiation and the pastoral theology of God's divine filiation. In this joint reflection, Osuagwu and Ukwuije concentrate on the theological explication of the content and intent of Obinna's filiation as the soul of evangelization and the church's and Christians' life of faith.

Furthermore, Michael Konye mines out the theological anthropology inherent in Obinna's theofiliation. For Konye, the theology of the human person in theofiliation highlights the human reinGodment as the lens to the reconstruction of the cultural divide, prejudice, and enslavement in the *diala-osu-ume* caste system in Igboland and other contexts where similar enslavement system operates. Therefore, a reinGoded anthropology underlines the core of our common humanity in Christ. Again, anthropology through the lens of theofiliation inspires a return to and intensification of faith in God over faith in technology prevalent in our time.

Moreover, skewed by Obinna's Chukwu-Kristic celebration of the Archdiocesan Odenigbo series as a religio-cultural project, Patrick Mbarah' investigates into the Odenigbo project as a cultural approach for grassroot evangelization and platform for interreligious actions in African context from the Igboland perspective. He reappraised the Odenigbo programme as projecting the rich African values in accordance with the good news of salvation. Hence, Odenigbo Religio-Cultural Project could be seen as an indigenous 'gift to Christianity'. With ecumenical interest, Kenneth Ameke and Emmanuel Obi engage Obinna's Chifiliation theology by investigating his concepts of reconfiliation and reinGodment as relational frameworks for restoring the spiritual and moral trust of the evangelized people. They argue that through Obinna's concepts, the indigenous people are led to the illumination and proper perception of Christianity as a bearer of the message of salvation rather than as a tool of invasion. Hence, the wounds of the colonial invasion and missionary despise of the indigenous traditional beliefs and cultures are reconciled by identifying Christ as present in all cultures and contexts.

The third section is concerned with the pastoral, anthropology, and management. Bede Ukwuije focuses on a critical pastoral relevance of the theology of theofiliation in its holistic sense and reconfiliation in its particular pastoral significance in the African sociocultural and anthropological context. For Ukwuije, theofiliance possesses the theological ingredients that respond to the contemporary anthropological crisis identified in the loss of the sense of the sacredness of the human person and sense of God manifest in our society and context. Therefore, through the reconfiliatory dynamics, humanity can rediscover their divine filiation and relate in love and peace. In a similar vein, Andrew Nkwocha drew insight from Obinna's reconfiliation theology to argue for a pastoral undertone in the realization of the human connection as brothers and sisters in Christ. For Nkwocha, this realization through reconfiliation will enable us to return to the fundamental human dignity and restore the beauty of creation at various level of human existence.

Samuel Uzoukwu explores the dynamics of leadership theory and engagement in Obinna's life that is manifest in the tripartite aspects of leadership: the leader, the follower, and the culture. While exploring Obinna's theological model of confiliation, he highlights insights and practical approaches to issues related to politics, culture, education, religion, family, human life, and community. Thus, looking at leadership through the perspective of confiliation will lead to the discovery of the human resource model of the transformational and servant leadership structure for any organization. This servant leadership structure reveals the quality of belongingness of all, which transcends family skirmishes and social clashes, and most importantly, it proposes a leadership model that rectifies human dignity. From an administrative perspective, Boniface Anusiem, being inspired by Obinna's theofiliation, re-examines how interpersonal communication can be seen in the pastoral context. He compares and contrasts the modes of interpersonal communication of the non-ecclesiastical organization with the ecclesiastical setting. He underlines that Christ is the communicator par excellence, which theofiliation illustrates as an essential characteristic of God. Hence, interpersonal communication in light of theofiliation not only provides us with the basis for the horizontal communication but also brings the vertical dimension into view. The horizontal aspect of communication through the lens of theofiliation can govern the interpersonal pastoral communication skill and structure in the parish ministry between the priest and the pastoral collaborators.

The fourth section consists of a political philosophy, postcolonial and psychological reading of theofiliation. In this discussion, Donald Ude explores Obinna's filiation from a politico-social philosophy and critical theory as providing inspiration for sociopolitical attitudes and critique to the apolitical society in Igbo context. For Ude, this filiation framework can provide a paradigm for social critique of our society bedevilled by 'filiation deficiency', which requires recti-filiation from social divides in the *osu-diala* saga. In this chapter, too, Moses Chikwe offers a postcolonial reading of Obinna's thought in light of understanding reconfiliation as healing the African past encounter with the colonizers and missionaries. Thus, reconfiliation expresses the ingredient that heals mental/spiritual wounds enslavement inflicted upon the African mindset. Therefore, reconfiliation serves as a new prism through which Africans can understand and regain the common humanity in Christ in order to have a positive attitude towards everybody. Also, from a psychological perspective, Edmund Aku brings Obinna's theofiliation into dialogue with Erik Erikson's theory of generativity in order to evaluate the success associated with the pastoral work of a priest. In Aku's critical study of generativity, he underlines that success of a 'theofiliated minister' is not evaluated based on political or economic standard of success. He rather underscores that priestly ministry in itself is a path to generation after the manner of Christ who spiritually nourishes and cares for the family of God's people.

In the final section, the legacies of Obinna is examined in the realms of human morality, care for the human life, and entertainment. From a Catholic social magisterium that is a response to the social and ecological challenges of our time, Ndubueze explores the dynamics of theofiliation, which brings into perspective the importance of human care to the non-human creatures in our environment. Also, looking at the impact of Obinna's Odenigbo lecture series, he emphasizes the importance of the integration of the environmental and cultural heritage that are inherent in our African identity and Igboland in particular. Therefore, through Odenigbo, we can proactively engage our culture and environment in this era of ecological crisis. Ikenna P. Okpaleke, in his reflection, brings the debate between the proponents of 'the right to life' and the advocates of the 'gift of life' established in Genesis 1 account into contention. He argues that the claim of the right to life (which allows, among other things, the claim that one could take or spare one's life) is secondary, while the position on the gift of life is primary. Therefore, he underlines human responsibility as basically stewardship and care. Hence, he cautions that the 'gift of life' perspective should not be politically interpreted but should be viewed from a theofiliated dimension as a divine creativity. The final discussion in this chapter reflects on music as one of Archbishop Obinna's pastoral outreach and inculcation of spirituality into the hearts of the people of God entrusted to his care. Nze shows that through music, there is a connection between the spiritual content of the song and our daily experiences. In other words, there is the echo of music in Obinna's theology of confiliation.

The issues discussed by the contributors in this volume show the pedagogical significance of Obinna's theofiliation as well as highlighting the catechetical prominence implied in his thought. While there are various interpretations and views of Obinna's work, this volume has no grand ambition to settle any of these issues, nor does it assume to exhaust everything his theological idea insinuates. However, it is a beginning for a theological and philosophical engagement with his theofiliation. Accordingly, Obinna's theological ambition is coming at a time when the indigenous people of Africa are grounded and already settled with the traditional or Western theological methods and approaches. Rather, his theology and practice of theofiliation will go a long way to offer the indigenous people theological categories of reflection and understanding of the church and our society in relation to the church. That is to say that his theological ideas will usher us into the new possibilities and the challenges of the changing contexts. It is a pleasure to constructively engage his thought as well as welcome further exploration, diversification, and systematization. This should spark and provoke scholars of interest and critics to expound this theological thinking. This Festschrift contributes to the expansion and reconstruction of his theofiliation. I wish you a happy reading.

Section One

Biblical and Comparative Study

Chapter One

The Filiation Dynamic: When God Does Something on Condition

Stephen C. Egwim

Introduction

Filiation of human beings to God and to one another has been the major thrust of Most Rev. Anthony J. V. Obinna's recent theological reflection. He has approached it from different perspectives using varied cognate concepts such as Christofilance and theofiliance[1] on the one hand and filiation, infiliation, refiliation, confiliation, and reconfiliation[2] on the other. He has discussed it in his public talks and lectures both local and international.[3]

---

1   Anthony J. V. Obinna, 'Culture and Development: A Provocative-Fertile Terrain', pp. 11–15. See also 'African Cultures and Development: The Rectifying Challenge' (delivered at the First Colloquium on Culture and Development in African Theology held in Abidjan, Ivory Coast, September 27—October 1, 2010), pp. 11–16; 'Culture, Human Development and the New Creation Dynamic', p. 5.

2   Confer 'Confiliatory Collaboration between the Church in Africa and Europe: A Theo-Filio-Logical Background', especially p. 2; 'Culture, Human Development and the New Creation Dynamic' (a keynote address delivered at The Fourth Annual Convention of the Catholic Biblical Association of Nigeria held at the Seat of Wisdom Seminary, Owerri, October 20, 2011), pp. 4–5.

3   See notes 1 and 2 above.

He made it a choice topic and a core message of the provincial centenary jubilee of the establishment of the Catholic church in Owerri Ecclesiastical Province celebrated in 2012. At the international seminar organized to mark the centenary, one of the papers titled *Evangelization Locally and Globally: The Filiation Dynamic* and jointly delivered by I. M. Osuagwu and Bede Okwuije, CSSp, focused on fundamental theological remarks on divine filiation and pastoral theology of divine filiation.

Reading through the papers written by A. J. V. Obinna on the issue as well as those presented at the international seminar, one finds no reference to or discussion of the conditions implicated in the filiation dynamic.[4] The present discourse intends to fill that gap while adding content to A. J. V. Obinna's concept of refiliation and reconfiliation. It offers a discussion of some textual bases for filiation in the Bible and shows how repentance, forgiveness, and reconciliation are the necessary conditions for both human and divine refiliation. An explanation of the term *filiation* will lead us first to its bases in Scripture; to a distinction between original filiation, new filiation, and subsequent ongoing refiliation; to *reconciliation* as the biblical term for filiation; and to repentance, forgiveness, and reconciliation as conditions for refiliation as well as our agency in reconciliation and refiliation.

Explaining the Term *Filiation*

The word *filiation* is not found in the Bible, neither in the Hebrew or in the Greek. It is a theological term used to describe the relationship between Jesus Christ as Son and God as Father, on the one hand, and our relationship with God and with one another in and through Christ on the other. In secular usage, *filiation* is a legal term that recognizes or refers to the legal status of the relationship between family members, or more specifically, the legal relationship between parent and child. It underscores the fact of being descended or derived from something or someone as well as the relationship it accords. Its theological usage is derived from the dogma of divine filiation of Jesus Christ to God the Father as Son in His being of the same substance with the Father. In the view of the

---

4   Even when they mention or discuss repentance, forgiveness, or reconciliation, they are not treated explicitly as conditions for refiliation.

present discourse, the fact of being descended, derived, or being of the same substance with someone is important; but the most essential factor in filiation is functional or active relationship: one must be aware of one's descendedness or derivedness, acknowledge it, and respond positively to it. Where one considers one's descendedness or derivedness as mere accident and responds negatively to it, the sense of filiation or filiatedness is lost.

Biblical Bases for Filiation

The dogma of divine filiation is based on God's revelation of Jesus in the New Testament as 'My Son' (*ho huios muo* [Matt. 3:17]) and Jesus's references to himself as 'the Son of God' (*tes phones tou huiou tou theou* [John 5:25]; *huios tou theou eimi* [John 10:36]; *ho huios tou theou* [John 11:4]; *ton huion mou* [Mark 12:6]) and to God as 'my Father' (*to thelema tou patros mou* [Matt. 7:21]; [Luke 10:22]; [John 15:15]; [Rev. 3:5, 21]). As God the Son, Jesus Christ shared our human nature by becoming man; and through being man, he lifted our human nature into sharing in his divine nature and divine sonship. In and through Christ, we become born of God and addressed as 'children of God' (John 1:12). Jesus caps his many references to our sonship with references to God's parental role of provision for us as His children (cf. the admonition not to worry about tomorrow [Matt. 6:25–33]), as well as our role of honouring and obeying God while depending on Him for our every need (cf. the 'Our Father' prayer [Matt. 6:9–13]). By teaching us how to come to God in prayer through the Our Father, Jesus lets us discover our special participation in divine filiation, which St. John speaks of in the prologue to his gospel: 'But to all who received him, who believed in his name, he gave power to become children of God' in the sense of being born of God (John 1:12). In that same sense in which to do the will of the Father is to be mother, brother, and sister of Jesus (Luke 8:19–21).

While elevating us to the status of sons and daughters, Jesus distinguishes His own Sonship from ours. He uses the terms 'My Father' and 'your Father' (John 20:17) but does not use 'our Father' except in the 'Our Father' sample prayer He gave His disciples as a way of teaching them how to pray. Since Jesus would not use the phrase 'our father' except in the context of teaching His disciples how to pray, it may be taken to mean that His use of *our* in the 'Our Father' prayer does not include him. If this is correct, it implies that we are sons and daughters of God not in the same way Jesus is Son of God (we do not share equal sonship with Him), and God is our Father not in the same way He is the Father of our Lord Jesus Christ. By 'my Father', Jesus refers to His unique, natural, divine filiation as different from 'your Father', which refers to our supernatural (divine, common) filiation by adoption. St. Paul's doctrine on adoption (Rom. 8:14–17; Gal. 4:45; Eph. 1:3–6) makes the distinction more vivid: Jesus is the only begotten Son of God by nature; He is the Son of God, while we humans who have been redeemed by Jesus's blood are God's children by supernatural adoption. The 'our' at the beginning of the Lord's Prayer, like the 'us' of the last four petitions, refers to all who have been redeemed and adopted. It excludes no one,[5] neither Jew nor Gentile, freeborn or slave, *diala, osu ma obu ume* (Gal. 3:28). We are all God's children by creation, and as such, 'there is only one race in the world: the race of the children of God.'[6] What Jesus did in 'Our Father', as an example of an articulated prayer, is not to give us the exact words we ourselves should use in addressing God but to teach how to relate with God in prayer, what to ask for in prayer, and what the demand our relationship with God and our prayer petitions make on us. He did not say 'our Father' in a way that includes Him. As individuals, we may address God in prayer as 'my God' or 'my Father', but the message of 'our Father' is that we belong together; and 'give us … our daily bread' means that we should share God's provision in common. That is, what I have or receive should be seen as God's provision through me for others and myself.

A. J. V. Obinna's theological reflection on filiation is anchored on the Incarnation—the taking of the flesh of the Son of God in the womb of the Virgin Mary and being born of her. He considers Jesus's divine conception and birth as God's filiation of Himself to humanity through Mary (Jesus as Son of Mary and as Son of man) and His filiation of humanity to Himself (Jesus in the human flesh as Son of God). Jesus in His human flesh and human nature as Son of God elevates our human nature to divine adoptiveness, which is fully realized when we are baptized with the Trinitarian formula (Father, Son, and Holy Spirit) into Jesus's divine nature as the true and only begotten Son of God. Then we become, like Him, sons

---

5   *Catechism of the Catholic Church*, revised edition (London: Chapman, 1999), §. 2792: 593.

6   St. Josemaria, *Homilies: Christ is Passing By* (New York, NY: Sceptre, 2002), 13.

and daughters of God. For Obinna, this is the new creation matrix,[7] which the present discourse would call a refiliation or new filiation. Our filiation to God and confiliation to one another as brothers and sisters has their beginning in the Old Testament. At creation, we were made of the same stock, in the same image and of the same breath (Gen. 1:26–27; 2:7). With Abraham, we were filiated by means of blessing (Gen. 12:2–3). In Exodus 4:22, God refers to the people of Israel in Egypt as 'my firstborn son', and in Hosea 1:10, they are referred to as the 'children of the living God'. At Sinai, the covenant was a bonding, a filiation of Israel to God. These give us four types of filiation: filiation by creation, by blessing, by choice or election, and by treaty (covenant). The fifth type is the New Testament's new filiation by adoption.

Our Original Filiation to God and to One Another

Genesis 1:26–27 and 2:21–23 creation accounts are overviews of our original filiation to God and to one another. This is filiation through creation, or creation filiation. The understanding of filiation as the fact of being descended or derived from someone helps us see how our being created in the image and likeness of God constitute our original filiation with God. We are filiated to Him through His image and likeness that we bear. This is the original theofiliance. It is also the original Christofiliance since Christ pre-exists with God and is eternally of the same image and likeness with God. We are also originally filiated and confiliated to one another through the same semblance as well as through being made of the same material stuff: the earth and the rib— 'the bone of my bone and the flesh of my flesh' (Gen. 2:23). The first sin of mankind in Genesis 3 was a disconnection that defiliated us from the original filiation. It teaches us how wrongdoing separates us from God and from one another. It was a disconnection, a de-filiation that required a reconnection or a refiliation to God (retheofiliation) through Christ (re-Christofiliation) and to one another (reconfiliation). Subsequent individual, collective, and/or generational wrongdoings typical of covenant breaking and covenant renewal make the work of refiliation to be ongoing.

---

7   Obinna, 'Culture, Human Development and the New Dynamics,' 4.

The New Filiation

The New Testament is, like the Old Testament, a testament; but unlike the Old Testament, it is new in terms of being a development as well as a departure from the old. The original filiation—creation filiation—is a verbal act of primordial creation in God's image, likeness, and breath of life. The New Testament talks of a new creation to which the creation accounts in the Old Testament are termed old (2 Cor. 5:17). It is new as opposed to the old, but like the old and in tandem with the meaning of filiation given above, the new creation is also in God's image, likeness, and life. Being in Christ who is 'the image of the invisible God' and in whom 'all the fullness of God' dwells (Col. 1:15, 19) is being a new creation. This new creation of being in Christ, of being crafted into Christ, and of being in the likeness of Christ is the new filiation. It is in the light of this that the present discourse considers 2 Corinthians 5:17–20 and Colossians 1:15–23 to be the *textus classicus* of filiation in the Bible in its two prongs of relatedness (descendedness and derivedness) and relationalness (functional or reciprocal relationship). Reproducing the two passages here will be helpful.

2 Corinthians 5:17–20 and Colossians 1:15–23

As the *textus classicus* of filiation in the Bible, 2 Corinthians 5:17–20 states:

> So, if anyone is in Christ, there is a new creation: everything old has passed away; see, everything has become new! All this is from God, who reconciled us to himself through Christ, and has given us the ministry of reconciliation; that is, in Christ God was reconciling the world to himself, ... and entrusting the message of reconciliation to us. So, we are ambassadors for Christ, since God is making his appeal through us; we entreat you on behalf of Christ, be reconciled to God.
>
> He is the image of the invisible God, the firstborn of all creation; for in heaven and on earth were created, things visible and invisible, ... all things have been created through him and for him. He himself is before all things, and in him all things hold together. He is the head of the body, the church; he is the

beginning, the first born from the dead, so that he might come to have first place in everything. For in him all the fullness of God was pleased to dwell, and through him God was pleased to reconcile to himself all things, whether on earth or in heaven, by making peace through the blood of his cross. And you who were once estranged and hostile in mind, doing evil deeds, he has now reconciled in his fleshly body through death, so as to present you holy and blameless and irreproachable before him—provided that you continue securely established and steadfast in the faith, without shifting from the hope promised by the gospel that you heard. (Col. 1:15–23)

These two texts contain the doctrine or teaching on the reconciliation of humanity to God. While dealing with this doctrine, they capture the two aspects of filiation: relatedness (descendedness or derivedness) and relationalness on the basis of which they are here proposed as the classical texts on filiation in the Bible. The texts go further to highlight three points: that God is the one who takes the initiative, that He chooses to accomplish it through human agency, and on condition that those He wants to reconcile to Himself choose to be reconciled and remain reconciled.

Filiation's Aspect of Relatedness

The texts underscore the Incarnation principle (the union of the divine and the human)—our sharing in the divine nature of Christ who humbled Himself to share in our human nature as the basis of our being truly made in the image, likeness, and life of God. The creation accounts in Genesis, which are here considered our original filiation, do not match the spoken word (And God said, Let us make man in our own image and likeness [Gen. 1:26–27]) with the actual work of creating man (Gen. 2:7, 22), nor do they literally and descriptively capture our being made in the image and likeness of God in the actual act of making man. The NT's taking of the flesh of the Son of God, which brings us to sharing in God's divine nature, the new birth of baptism into His life, and our being crafted into Christ the vine as his branches (John 15:1–11) literally and descriptively capture our new creation in the image, likeness, and life of God in Christ and being born again from above (John 3:3); that which comes down from heaven gives life to the world (John 6:33).

The texts bring together the original filiation and the new filiation. Christ, as the image of God right from the beginning of creation and who is before all things, embodies that image in which humanity was originally created and filiated. In His human existence, He brings that same image into His new creation and new filiation of humanity. In Him all things hold together filiated into one body, the Church, with Him as the head.

Filiation's Aspect of Relationalness: Reconciliation as the Biblical Term for the New Filiation and the On-going Refiliation Dynamic

In the Greek texts of 2 Corinthians 5:17–20 and Colossians 1:15–23, the Greek noun translated into English as *reconciliation* is καταλλασγη (*katallage*).[8] It means 'being put into relationship with God' and 'leading others to be put into relationship with God'. The two shades of meaning show that the term has both passive and active senses. Its verbal form is καταλλασσω (*katallaso*), meaning 'to change', 'to exchange', 'to reconcile', 'to reconcile oneself'. These shades of meaning are within the domain of the relationship between humans ('to relate/reconcile with someone', 'reconcile ['of man and wife']' and between God and humans ('put [someone] into relationship with God'). While denoting change, the verbal form connotes transformation or renewal of the state of the relationship between God and man, and therewith of man's own state of well-being. In 2 Corinthians 5:18, this change is presented as 'the basis of the most comprehensive renewal possible for man, namely, that he has become a new creature, that old

---

8 'NT passages in which the term *katallage* occurs are: Matt. 5:24; Rom. 5; 2 Cor. 5:18-20; Eph. 2:16; Col. 1:20-22. In these passages, reconciliation (*katallage*) is presented either in the noun or verb forms as a doctrine, except in Matthew 5:24. In the OT, we have two Hebrew terms associated with the meaning of *katallage*: *kaphar* (2 Chr. 29:24) and *ratsah* (1 Sam. 29:4), a Hebrew word that means 'to make benevolent or well-disposed', 'to placate', 'to reconcile oneself', 'to be reconciled or appeased'. In the Septuagint (LXX), the Greek translation of the OT, the Greek word used to translate *ratsah* in I Samuel 29:4 is *diallaso*, which is also the Greek word in 1 Corinthians 7:11 translated as reconcile and which noun form is *diallage*. In the book of Maccabees, which was written in Greek, we have the noun form—*katallage*—in 2 Maccabees 5:20 and the verb forms in 2 Maccabees 1:5, 7:33, and 8:29.

things have passed away and that all things have become new ... There is a change, not merely in the disposition of man or his legal relationship to God, but in the total state of his life. On the other hand, it cannot be maintained that there has been any change of mind on the part of God, since His gracious will had been revealed long before in the OT.'[9]

The 'putting into relationship with God' may mean the establishment of a new relationship in line with the new life in Christ offered by the New Testament, but it is not totally new as though there has never been any former relationship. It is rather new in the sense that it renews or re-establishes on new terms and bases the severed old relationship given in the OT. It is in this sense of renewal or re-establishment that almost in all English Bibles, *katallage* is translated as *reconciliation*—the re-establishment of functional or reciprocal relationship. *Reconciliation* itself, as an English word, presupposes a previous bond, solidarity, intimacy, cooperation, or relationship that has been lessened, broken, left dormant, or degenerated into mistrust, opposition, or enmity due to hurt, guilt, violence, rejection, misunderstanding, indifference, wrongdoing, or infidelity. So *katallage* as *reconciliation* is the reactivation, restoration, and refiliation of estranged parties to their former relationship.

We, as humans, have existing relationships with God. First is the bond of our creation in the image, likeness, and breath of God, which established the relationship of creature and creator or make and maker between us and God. Every person is born with this bond as an inherited natural bond intrinsic in our humanness. Second is the bond of our new birth in baptism into Christ as adopted children of God. This is a supernatural bond that establishes the parent-child relationship between the baptized and God. It is not natural, and we are not born with it. It is a bond and a relationship entered into individually and freely and never collectively or by compulsion. It is neither transferable nor inheritable. To enter into this new bond of baptism in Christ, each individual has to first admit that the old bond has been damaged by human sin then renounce sin and the devil and confess faith and belief in God and his Christ. We can now see how the thrust of the two passages on reconciliation makes reconciliation the biblical term for the new filiation and refiliation to God (retheofiliance)

---

9   Friedrich Buchsel, '*allasso, antallagma, ap-, di-, katallasso, katallge, apokat-, metallasso*', in *Theological Dictionary of the New Testament*, ed. Gerhard Kittel, trans. by Geoffrey W. Bromiley, vol. 1 (Grand Rapids, MI: Eerdmans, 1964), 255.

through or in Christ (re-Christofiliance) and to one another (reconfiliation). Reconciliation is made possible by the acknowledgment of an existing bond that has been broken through wrongdoing; the wrongdoing is regretted and confessed followed by request for forgiveness and restoration to the former bond (refiliation) or the establishment of a new bond (new filiation).

God's Interest in Human Agency

God is all-powerful in the sense of being able to bring about His purposes, but He chooses to accomplish His purposes through human agency. Right from the beginning, right after creating, God engages humans in the furtherance of his work of creation (Gen. 1:28): He uses Noah to repopulate the earth after destroying it with flood because of human wickedness (Gen. 6–10), He begins a progressive revelation of Himself and opens up new contact and relationship with humanity with Abraham (Gen. 12ff), He brings about His liberation of Israel and bonded them to Himself through Moses (Exodus), and He defends the people of Israel in the land of Canaan through the judges and speaks to them through the prophets. In the New Testament, He perfects His revelation of Himself through and in His Son whom He made man for that purpose, calling mankind to repentance, redeeming and reconciling humanity to Himself (2 Cor. 5:18; Col. 1:20–22). It pleases Him also to appoint, commission, and entrust to us the continued divine project of reconciling individuals and peoples to Himself (2 Cor. 5:18–20). Having filiated creation to Himself as creation's source, God's project is to continually connect and reconnect creation to Himself in a functional relationship. He does this in the OT through the prophets and definitively in the NT through His Son made man. He continues that today through us.

The Dynamic of On-going Refiliation

The new reality of our reconciliation/refiliation to God is basically and continually brought about by God's action towards man because man himself never ceases to be a sinner. The death and resurrection of Jesus, which accomplished our reconciliation to God, is done and completed and can never be repeated, except its commemoration in the Eucharist. But the ministry or work of realizing in each individual, and indeed all humanity, the reconciledness so achieved or accomplished is ongoing. If Paul believed that reconciliation was concluded in the death and resurrection of Jesus in such a way that what followed no longer formed any part of it, he would not have considered his own work as 'the ministry of reconciliation', nor the content of his message as 'Be (you) reconciled to God'. Since the ministry of reconciliation has not yet come to an end and the world has not yet heard in all its members 'the word/gospel of reconciliation', reconciliation itself must not be thought of as concluded.

In the general sense, all the works of God as recorded in the Bible from Genesis to Revelation may be said to be works of filiation and refiliation. The God who created and filiated man unconditionally to Himself at creation takes the initiative to refiliate mankind to Himself after the fall through Abraham (refiliation by blessing) and his descendants (refiliation by choice or election and covenant). In the NT, Jesus, through the new creation matric (2 Cor. 5:17), accomplishes a new filiation of humanity to God. We may then say that God is filiation in the same way we say that God is love. Love itself is that which defines the filiated relationship between father and son/children.

The Bible contains not only the record of God's unconditional original filiation initiative but also his conditional refiliation initiative and man's response to that initiative. If filiation and refiliation are God's initiative running through the Bible as explicated above, what does the Bible present as man's response to God's refiliation initiative? In the Old Testament, humanity was first and originally filiated to God at creation. But the fall terminated that filiation. God took the initiative to reconcile as to refiliate humanity to himself through Abraham, thanks to Abraham's obedience and docility. If Abraham did not respond positively, it would not have taken place, at least not with him, unless by compulsion as in the case of Jonah. The family of Lot was saved from immoral life and destruction in Sodom and Gomorrah, but his wife preferred it and got destroyed with it.

What makes the refiliation of the people of Israel to God possible is not only God's choice or election but also Israel's positive response to God's election, which made the Sinai covenant of filiation possible. If they said no to it, no filiation would have taken place. Having been filiated, they remained filiated to the extent that they remained faithful to the terms of the covenant and its obligations. We know of Israel's many cases of infidelity, which caused them many hardship, defeat, and exile, and against which the prophets continually called them to be loyal to the covenant. Israel's many cases of infidelity and her realization of same are the things that made Joshua refiliate his family to God and invited all Israel to do the same (Josh. 24:1–28); it made Josiah refiliate Israel to God by a covenant renewal ceremony in 2 Kings 23 (cf. 2 Chr. 34:29–33); it also occasioned the national confession ceremony and refiliation under Nehemiah (Neh. 9–10).

The earliest stories in the Bible contain tales of almost unimaginable betrayal and barbarism. 'The essential features of man's state prior to reconciliation are his entanglement in a self-seeking which cannot fulfil the divine command of love … and his consequent standing under the divine displeasure … wrath and judgment.'[10] After the first sin by Adam and Eve (Gen. 3), we have Cain murder his brother Abel (Gen. 4); Jacob swindles Esau of his birthright and blessing (Gen. 25:29–34; and Gen. 27); Shechem rapes Dinah and gets killed together with Hamor, his father, and all his kinsmen (Gen. 34); Joseph is sold by his brothers (Gen. 37:12–36); Potiphar's wife gets Joseph imprisoned for not acquiescing to her lustful desires (Gen. 39); the Egyptians maltreat the Israelites as foreigners and as slaves (Exod. 1:8–22); Moses kills an Egyptian in defense of his fellow Israelite (Exod. 2:11–12); Miriam and Aaron revolt against Moses (Num. 12); Aaron leads in the molding and worship of the golden calf (Exod. 32:4); the people complain and protest severally against Moses and God in the wilderness (Num. 11); Delilah betrays Samson (Judg. 16); Saul envies David and seeks to kill him (1 Sam. 18:10ff); David plans the death of Uriah and coverts his wife (2 Sam. 11); Amon violets Tamar and is killed by Absalom (2 Sam. 13); Absalom revolts against his father David; Shimei curses David (2 Sam. 16:5–8); Sheba rebels against David (2 Sam. 20); Jeroboam rebels against Solomon (1 Kings 11:26ff); Jezebel plots to kill Elijah (1 Kings 19); Ahab gets Naboth killed and takes over his vineyard (1 Kings 21); Jonah feels sad over the repentance and forgiveness of the Ninevites (Jon. 4); Herod coverts his brother's wife and beheads John the Baptist (Matt. 14:1–12); etc. These are instances of what A. J. V. Obinna calls 'humanity's hate-prone cleavages and civilization fault-lines'.[11] And

10   Buchsel, 'allasso, antallagma, ap-, di-, katallasso, katallge, apokat-, metallasso', p. 257. 10
11   Obinna, Confiliatory Collaboration between the Church in Africa and Europe: A Theo-Filio-Logical Background, pp. 3-4.

it is these hate-prone cleavages and fault lines that God seeks to heal us of through his ongoing reconciliation/refiliation project.

Explicating the Conditions for Refiliation

God's conditionality for His refiliation initiative is that man responds positively to it. That response involves conscious acknowledgment of acts that undid and continually undo existing filiation, regret of such acts, and desire for refiliation. In most of the above biblical accounts, the wrongdoing is followed by divine reprimand, repentance, forgiveness, and/or punishment. After the sin of Adam and Eve, God confronted them with their sin, but both shifted the blame to someone else and failed to own up, then God punished them. Cain killed Abel; he was confronted by God but failed to own up and was punished. After Miriam and Aaron claimed equality with Moses, God confronted them and punished them. David got Uriah killed and coveted his wife, Bathsheba. He was confronted by God through Prophet Nathan; he owned up and got forgiven but had to lose the child born to him by Bathsheba. More remarkable is the case of Ahab, who got Naboth killed through the plotting skills of his wife, Jezebel, and coveted his vineyard. He was confronted by Elijah, owned up, repented, and was forgiven. The Ninevites were facing divine wrath, but when God's Word was preached to them by Jonah, they repented and received divine forgiveness. The sin that cut Judas Iscariot off and defiliated him to Christ, to God, and to the eternal life of the filiated may not be graver than that of Peter, who publicly denied his master and his filiatedness to him. The difference is that when God spoke to Peter through his conscience, Peter regretted and repented of his sin and was refiliated and restored to his prime position. The same is true of Mary Magdalene, Zacchaeus, and the repentant thief crucified with Jesus. God refiliates us on the condition that we repent (Luke 13:1–5) and remain filiated on the condition that we do not deviate, 'provided that you continue securely established and steadfast in the faith, without shifting from the hope promised by the gospel that you heard' (Col. 1:23).

Between humans, reconciliation may be reciprocal. We decide to forgive one another's failings: I forgive you, you forgive me, and we reconcile with one another. But with God, this is not the case. Between God and humans, reconciliation is not reciprocal. God does not need reconciliation or to be reconciled; rather, He offers reconciliation to humans and reconciles us to Himself just for the asking. We humans do not and cannot offer reconciliation to God; rather, we stand always in need of His reconciliation and to be reconciled to Him. In 2 Corinthians 5:18ff, God takes the initiative to reconcile us to Himself because He has both the power and the will to forgive and forgo. He is not reconciled, nor does He reconcile Himself to us because He does not offend us. We are the ones that offend God in one another, which is why 2 Corinthians 5:20 enjoins us to respond to God's initiative by reconciling ourselves to (asking for forgiveness from) him as a conditionality for being reconciled.

Our discourse so far is best illustrated with the Ahab/Naboth narrative in 1 Kings 21. The narrative helps us understand how individuals or group of individuals are caught up in the web of moral wrongdoing against God and their neighbour, which brings about de-filiation. It also helps us understand that God is the one who takes the initiative to reconcile and refiliate us to Himself, that He does that through human agency, and on condition that we repent of our defiliating wrongdoings. The narrative also helps us understand anger in context, as well as our role as God's agents of reconciliation.

The Contriving of Humanity's Hate-Prone Cleavages and Civilization Fault Lines

The thought, desire, and act of doing something good or bad occur within the dynamism of human existential situation. They are implicated in a number of concrete circumstances, beginning with a recognized presence of a reality, which may be a person, a thing, or a goal. The present reality that was the object of the original sin in Genesis was the tree of good and evil. In the case of the sin of Cain, it was the good deed of Abel. In the case of Esau and Jacob, it was ambition or desire for greatness. In the case of the brothers of Joseph, it was envy against the perceived bright future of Joseph. In the case of Ahab against Naboth, it was covetousness. In some cases, it was lustful desire for the opposite sex: Potiphar's wife desired Joseph, Amon desired Tamar, David desired Bathsheba, and Herod coveted his brother's wife.

The instruments involved in the processes leading to good or bad actions are the instruments of sight (sense perception), thought, desire, and the strive via the processes of seeing or sensing, thinking, desiring, and striving. When a thing is seen or sensed, it is sent to the mind, which, through the process of thought, perceives it either as good or as bad. When it is perceived as good, desire sets in either as desire to have, possess, rule or desire for honour, recognition, etc. Desire is then followed by striving, which consists of planning and execution of what is desired. The four processes or faculties of sight (sense perception), thought, desire, and strive are the four components of the will to power. The desire to have and possess breads avarice and envy and leads to various forms of violence and evil. The desire to rule breads ruthlessness and leads to lust for power. The desire for honour and recognition breads sycophancy, blackmail, backbiting, etc. and leads to selfish ambition. The desire to possess, to rule, and to prevail forms the context within which evil begins to brew and develop. That is, it is the connection between will and desire that makes possible 'evil-desiring-and-doing'. Evil-desiring-and-doing springs from our human condition, situation, context, and circumstance. This is eloquently evident in the narrative on Ahab and Naboth's vineyard in 1 Kings 21.

Reading through 1 Kings 21, we notice first that the vineyard of Naboth is situated beside the palace of King Ahab. This is a coincidence. The text holds neither Naboth nor Ahab responsible for this coincident near location of the vineyard and the palace; and they cannot physically and practically relocate them. However, it is precisely this near location that causes something to go on inside Ahab.

Ahab's sight of the vineyard and its nearness to his palace puts ideas into his head. He considers it good and begins to desire adding Naboth's vineyard to his palace as something that will add more value to his palace and give him more power and prestige. He approaches Naboth with a proposal to purchase his vineyard. It is like removing the boundary between what is his and what is Naboth's so that both that which is his and that which is Naboth's will all be his. He makes his proposal even more enticing by promising Naboth a better vineyard in its place (v. 2). This is like a reallocation, change, or exchange of ownership so that what is Naboth's becomes Ahab's, and vice versa. At this stage everything is happening like normal everyday economic transaction, based on mutually well-understood self-interest, without any thought yet of injustice, violence, or murder. To this point, Ahab's desire has no evil intent even where it points to covetousness.

Naboth's response to Ahab's desire is one of refusal to sell or exchange his vineyard. Ahab takes the refusal so seriously to heart that he allowed it to affect the moral quality of his desire: he nurses his desire to the point where lapse into evil takes place. Why does he do this? Is it that Naboth has no right to refuse? Is it that, as king, Ahab's desires, requests, and proposals are never to be turned down? On the side of Naboth, why does Naboth refuse to sell or exchange even for a better one? Can't he be charitable and consider his neighbour's interest or desire? Can't he sense the danger of his refusal, knowing that the proposal is coming from a person in a very high position of authority and power? Is it not reasonable for him to have avoided the danger?

The idea to sell or exchange does not originate from Naboth. It could be that Naboth has never thought of selling or exchanging the vineyard or it is not sellable or exchangeable. Information from the text shows that the vineyard is not just some property Naboth bought on pure economic grounds as an investment intended to be engaged in further business of making profit. The vineyard is indeed more than a property. It has a deeper identity-giving significance. Namely, it is the inheritance of his family (vv. 3–4), which he possesses and preserves out of 'ancestral piety'. By it he acquires his place, power, and prestige in the community, and as an inheritance, he is obliged to hand it on to the next generation out of ancestral piety and religiosity.

Naboth's refusal frustrates Ahab's desire. Only an avaricious desire can be thus frustrated. Frustrated desire is a kind of injury on one's personal ego, which lapses into 'evil-contriving and evil-doing'. Here is the connection between desire and vices such as jealousy, envy, blackmail, skimming, injustice, bloodletting, etc.

The Network of Evil

The planning and the execution of evil are in most cases not a one-man event. That is, it is not always what one does alone all by oneself. They take place in a relational and social context wherein all forms of seduction, guile, lies, bribery, implication, and complicity play conniving roles. The next stage in the Ahab-Naboth narrative highlights this.

When Ahab returns home frustrated (v. 4), there is still no mention of devising evil against Naboth. This idea develops only when his wife, Jezebel, comes to him and asks why he is moody and refusing to eat (v. 5). Ahab then sets the stage for Jezebel's role by giving her half-truth: stating Naboth's refusal without stating Naboth's reason for the refusal. When Ahab explains to her why he is moody and unwilling to eat, she plays on his desire and links together the three components of desire, viz. 'to possess', 'to rule', and 'to prevail'. She charges up his frustration by referring to his power position: 'Do you now govern Israel?' (v. 7). Jezebel injects into Ahab's frustration the position of humiliation due to his apparent lack of executive guts. Jezebel not only introduces the seed of evil into Ahab but she also becomes an accomplice. She identifies with and takes the lead in contriving and executing evil. She assures Ahab, saying, 'Get up, eat some food and be cheerful, I will give you the vineyard of Naboth the Jezreelite' (v. 7). In the sin of Adam and Eve, the evil is contrived by the serpent, while in the Amon's rape of Tamar, the evil is contrived by Amon's crafty friend Jonadab (2 Sam. 13). We propose that Ahab should know what his wife is capable of (she is known to act wickedly and device evil plans) and so should not have told her about the Naboth issue if he did not desire to elicit his wife's evil schemes to his advantage.

Jezebel thus prepares to resort to corruption and murder just to achieve the goal of Ahab. To this, she employs all her creative and inventive ingenuity in a manner typical of her as 'Mrs Fix It'. Her ingenuity leads her to seek the services of other accomplices, which she easily gets through the use of Ahab's royal authority. As Roger Burggraeve puts it, 'A social, economic, financial or political power position makes it easy to secure accomplices, since many "inferiors" are dependent on this support power for their own existence and income, their power position and social prestige.'[12]

The complicity involves both nobles and elders as well as scoundrels who are to bring false charges against Naboth. Complicity, thus, takes

---

12   Roger Burgraeve, 'To Love Other-Wise: Essays of Biblical Thinking on Sameness and Difference, Responsibility for the Earth, for the Other and for Future Generations, on Evil, Retribution and Forgiveness, Faith, Biblical Thought and Ethics' (Belgium: K. U. Leuven, Faculty of Theology, Unpublished Lecture Note, First Semester 2002–2003), p. 90.

place as an expanded network. Although one tries to involve as few people as possible due to the risk of leaks, turncoats, and traits, a crime can often indeed not be executed by one individual. Just as in the narrative of Naboth, collaborators or accomplices are needed with whom one further enters into a sort of pact based on an oath of secrecy and solidarity in the evil scheme. Jezebel needs trustworthy collaborators who, blindly and in attachment to the power holders, execute her villainous plans.[13]

Evil Always Seeks to Justify Itself

Apart from human accomplices, the network of evil takes on also human institutions such as the judiciary and other judicial bodies. In verses 9–10, we see that the evil is sanctioned as justified at a town assembly in a legal and judicial way thus: 'Proclaim a fast, and seat Naboth at the head of the assembly. Then take him out, and stone him to death.' The setting is to make the crime not appear felonious. This is precisely why a trial is set up, with false charges or accusations, witnesses, and compromised judges as in Psalm 109:6–20.

The use of a public legal arraignment is part of the grand plan set up for the purposes of presenting Naboth in a bad light. The true reason is kept hidden, and at the same time, the city assembly is deceived. Thus, evil is not only disguised but also presented as something good; something justified and therefore something not evil.[14] So evil is usually embellished and touched up to take on an air of fairness and decency via increminalization. By means of false accusation, Naboth is made to appear bad precisely in order to have him condemned and eliminated. He has to be made into an enemy, a symbol of evil, so that people will denounce him. Crime gets at its victim by manipulating the clear demarcation lines between good and bad, with the victim clearly marked bad. The more the victim is just and the more he gets in the way of the wicked, the more is he marked bad.

The legal justification of evil spills over into religious justification. Once one is legally convicted, he becomes religiously ostracized. The

---

13 Burgraeve, 'To Love Other-Wise', p. 90.
14 Didier Pollefeyt, 'Ethics, Forgiveness and the Unforgivable After Auschwitz,' in *Incredible Forgiveness: Christian Ethics between Fanaticism and Reconciliation* (Leuven: Peeters, 2004), 121–159, 137–140.

ostracization gives the evil a religious coverage and justification. Thus, the religious sphere can also be deceived and misled.

Expressed Anger as an Invitation to Forgiveness

Anger when expressed is good and has its value. It is different from an unexpected anger that is sustained over a period which does harm to the self and keeps the other in the dark. The values of expressed anger are the following: (a) it is a sign of honesty to self and (b) it has the possibility of creating in the other a kind of awareness that lets him or her see his or her action from the objective point of view of the victim. When an action is perceived to be hurting or has hurt the victim, the possibility further exists that the other might become contrite, confess, ask for forgiveness, and be forgiven. This is the next stage presented in the Ahab-Naboth narrative. The evil plan is completed and execute. Verses 17 to 29 conclude the narrative with an encounter between Elijah and Ahab, which presents God's anger as a function of His mercy. God sends the prophet Elijah to Ahab with detailed knowledge of where Ahab is and what he has done. God had such knowledge about Adam and Eve when they sinned and hid in the garden. He had such knowledge about Cain when he killed Abel; He also had such knowledge about David when he killed Uriah.

Elijah is to give Ahab a clear and precise message from God: 'Have you killed, and also taken possession?' What can be so arresting than a short sentence that summarizes in precise terms the deed that has been done? The first reaction is to challenge the speaker to ascertain his certainty of what he said. Elijah is not an official of the king; he is rather the king's adversary or archenemy simply because the king has sold himself to do what is evil in the sight of God. When Elijah meets Ahab after the crime is committed, the bitter reaction of Ahab is clear: 'Have you found me, O my enemy?' to which Elijah replies frankly: 'I have found you' (v. 2). Elijah is Ahab's enemy in the very same way good is enemy to evil, light to darkness, God to the devil. Elijah proves the certainty of his statement by pronouncing more severe punishment on Ahab, which brings him to submission in verse 27.

In the encounter herein narrated between Ahab and Elijah, Elijah does not speak out of the established social and political order, symbolized in the royal power of Ahab, neither does he speak out of himself nor out of the deceived and misled religious order. He speaks out of God, out of justice, out of truth. This is also the case with Prophet Nathan when he confronts David with his sin against Uriah in 2 Samuel 12:1–15. The truth, the justice out of which Prophet Elijah speaks is God's anger and indignation over evil that has been committed.

The refiliatory work of God accommodates and employs anger as a positive tool. As such, it is neither correct nor complete to present God as a kind, loving, and sympathetic God who shows sympathy to those who suffer but manifests no disapproval and condemnation of the evil that people inflict on one another. It is the same incorrectness we find in the understanding of the image of God in the OT as that of a vindictive God and in the NT as that of a loving God. Love and justice as attributes of the one God are present in both testaments. The love and mercy of God manifested in the OT in his dealings with Israel, David, Ahab, the Ninevites, etc. are no less loving and merciful than those manifested in the NT to Mary Magdalene, Zacchaeus, Peter, the repentant thief, etc. And the anger and justice of God pronounced on Ananias and Sapphira (Acts 5:1–11) are no less severe than that pronounced on Miriam, Moses, or King Saul in the OT. So '(t)he image of a God who is angered by inflicted evil is an essential part of the biblical revelation of the ever-loving God ... A good God who commits himself to the victims of evil is also a God who becomes angry at those who have made the victims what they are.'[15]

If God would only show compassion and commiseration for Naboth as a victim, then His love would be imperfect and incomplete. It would be cheap and sentimental in the way our commiseration is when we hear stories about victims of kidnapping, armed robbery, accidents, etc. Involvement is only authentic when it bears within itself the outrage over evil that is committed. The prophet precisely interprets God's sympathy and compassion with Naboth by accusing the perpetrators and demanding that they take account of their wrongdoing. Thus, the commandment to love includes not only the demand to forgive but also the demand to protect the victim as well as the demand to confront the offender with his wrongdoing.[16]

---

15 Burgraeve, 'To Love Other-Wise', p. 96.
16 Richard Bauckham, *The Bible in Politics: How to Read the Bible Politically* (London: SPCK, 1989), 10.

Through reproach and accusation, the prophet not only gives a voice to the voiceless (the dead Naboth) but he also shows inadvertently the liberating and healing value of expressed anger. According to the narrative, this expression of anger has its significance in the fact that the prophet speaks up precisely on account of the passion of God. That such an outburst of outrage is allowed or even is obliged according to the Bible in the name of God can have a therapeutic value. The feeling of anger is quite human and legitimate. Anger as an emotion is a healthy psychological reality. It manifests our sensitivity and our tangibility; it is our nonindifference towards forms of evil, insult, injustice, humiliation, impolite treatment, abuse of trust, etc. Some think that in order to be able to forgive, one must first repress the negative feeling of anger. It is precisely the opposite. Just as it is impossible to grant forgiveness when one is not first made aware of one's wrongdoing and has accepted this, thus it is likewise so when one does not permit and recognize one's anger. To blur the feeling of anger is a form of self-deceit. Only when forgiveness flows from the heart that has come to terms with its own injury and the ensuring anger can it be authentic and deeply felt and appreciated.

Many Christians think, from a kind of one-sided, sugary-sweet image of a loving God, that the expression of anger against those who have done injustice to themselves, to their neighbour, or to their fellow human beings is utterly wrong. The prophet Elijah shows that the contrary is true—that anger is not always a vice but can also be a virtue. Quite a number of people who have been deeply hurt or injured by others can be helped by these prophetic and other biblical expressions of anger, as we find in the so-called lament psalms for instance, in coming clean with their emotive feelings and reactions.

If anger is correctly channeled, it can contribute to the good functioning of human relations. This is because those who justifiably and correctly express their anger make it known that they desire to restore the contact and refiliate. Anger is a sign of involvement[17] that reaches farther than anger itself and thus desires to break down any obstacle to communication and interrelationship. Anger rouses in us the moral energy to expose evil and injustice and bring about their renunciation. By means of being threatened with a similar punishment (life for a life), Ahab and Jezebel

---

17 Abraham J. Heschel, *The Prophets* (New York, NY: Perennial Classic, 2001), 364–365.

are able to account for what they have done to Naboth. The confrontation of the criminal with his crime is important for the awareness of one's own guilt and the renunciation of evil.

A remarkable character of the nonviolent anger expressed by the prophet is that it is not directed towards the death and eternal damnation of Ahab and Jezebel. It is rather aimed at their self-examination by means of which healing and forgiveness are possible. The wrath of God proclaimed by the prophet aims at causing the sinner to come to terms with the evil he or she has done.[18] By means of its passion, divine anger wants to strike a chord in the heart of Ahab so that he becomes aware of the terrible evil he has done to Naboth. By means of this awareness, repentance and confession are then made possible, which in its turn creates space for forgiveness, reconciliation, and refiliation.

The Ahab-Naboth narrative helps us see how God is subject to the reconciling action of men in prayer, penance, sacrifice, etc. as we find in 2 Chronicles 7:14, which reads: 'If my people who are called by my name humble themselves, pray, seek my face, and turn from their wicked ways, then I will hear from heaven, and will forgive their sin and heal their land.' Through the conversion, confession, and prayers of humans, God renounces His wrath and is gracious again. This is found throughout the books and pages of the Bible in both OT and NT. God's anger aims at the conditions for bringing about divine mercy. God, who is loving mercy, absolutely wants to forgive and so liberate the perpetrator from his guilt. But in order to be forgiven, the perpetrator must also come to self-examination, which is precisely the intention of God's anger and indictment. The wrath of God thus directly stems from His love for both the victim and the perpetrator of evil. This is why the expression of anger and the pronouncement of judgment do not end the Ahab-Naboth narrative. In verses 27–29, we have the penitent confession of Ahab and the forgiving mercy of God.

---

18 Roger Burggraeve, 'Christian Ethical Radicalism without Fanaticism', in *Incredible Forgiveness: Christian Ethics between Fanaticism and Reconciliation* (Leuven: Peeters, 2004), 53–83; 58–59.

Our Work as God's Agents of Reconciliation, New Filiation, and Refiliation

Who are God's agents of reconciliation, new filiation, and refiliation? It is the 'us' in 2 Corinthians 5:17–20 to whom the message of reconciliation is entrusted and the ministry of reconciliation given. The 'us' is not just the religious ministers alone but all Christians. The process of forgiveness and reconciliation may be initiated by the offender, the victim, or by a third part. Because forgiveness ought normally to begin with the offender acknowledging his or her offense, we would expect the offender to initiate the process like the son in the parable of the Prodigal Son (Luke 15:20). But this is less often the case. In most cases, the offender needs to be confronted with his or her offense by either the victim or a third part. The confrontation of the offender by the victim often results in both parts claiming right. The role of a third part is the surest bet in establishing the existence of an offense as well as who the offender is. The role of all Christians, and religious ministers in particular in the manner of Elijah, Nathan, etc., is to be God's agents playing the third-party role in leading offenders to penitence and confession, which make the granting of forgiveness and reconciliation with one another, the community, and God possible.

In carrying this role out, we often miss the focus when we focus only on the victim preaching the gospel of forgiveness as if the offender has no need to repent of his or her wrongdoing, confess, and be forgiven or as if the work of the offender is to keep offending, while the work of the victim is to keep forgiving[19] without the offender coming to terms with his or her wrongdoing. In the event of wrongdoing, forgiveness presupposes confession as we see in the Ahab-Naboth narrative where Ahab comes to self-examination and confession precisely in response to the third-party

---

19   This is what some scholars refer to as 'facile forgiveness'. Cf. Didier Pollefeyt, "Introduction: Incredible Forgiveness', in *Incredible Forgiveness: Christian Ethics Between Fanaticism and Reconciliation*, Didier Pollefeyt ed., (Leuven: Peeters, 2004), 1–6:1. However, in the event of the offender not owning up his or her wrongdoing and not asking for forgiveness, it is important to focus on the victim and admonish him or her to forgive as a Christian injunction and as a psychological self-relief, healing, and wholeness. See Pollefeyt, 'Introduction,' 5. Neither the denial of one's debt as a perpetrator nor the burying of oneself in one's right as a victim does good to the process of forgiveness and reconciliation. Someone has to break the circle of wrongdoing, hurt, and resentment.

role of the prophet. That response merits him God's mercy as a healing grace. In the example of prophets Elijah and Nathan, the focus should be on the offender; he or she is the problem, not the victim or the offended. Even where no third part is involved, the primary focus is on the offender as Matthew 18:15–17 makes clear:

> If another member of the church sins against you, go and point out the fault when the two of you are alone. If the member listens to you, you have regained that one. But if you are not listened to, take one or two others along with you, so that every word may be confirmed by the evidence of two or three witnesses. If the member refuses to listen to them, tell it to the church; and if the offender refuses to listen to the church, let such a one be to you as a Gentile and a tax collector.

And Luke 17:3–4 says:

> If another disciple sins against, you must rebuke the offender, and if there is repentance, you must forgive. And if the same person sins against you seven times a day, and turns back to you seven times and says, 'I repent,' you must forgive.

This means that even the demand in Matthew 18:21–22 to forgive 'seventy-seven times' presumes the repentance and confession of the offender. When we focus primarily on the offender as the above passages require, we make the right move that already begins the process of healing the hurt being suffered by the victim such that when success is attained in bringing the offender to penitence and confession, the victim will most likely be easily persuaded to grant forgiveness. Whatever has happened only becomes conscious and acknowledged when it is spoken before someone who listens to it. By means of telling what has occurred, the evil that one has committed to someone else, one not only helps to realize and understand this evil but also understands it from the standpoint of the other, the victim or the guilty.

Evil that is not acknowledged and for which the perpetrator does not take responsibility does not call for forgiveness because strictly speaking, there is nothing to be forgiven: the perpetrator supposes that there is actually no evil or that he or she has done no evil, but something good on the contrary. According to Gaines, repentance and confession do not concern 'people who do not believe they need forgiveness or do not care whether they receive it'.[20] Such attitude ridicules every intention to forgive. All this implies that forgiveness is never concerned with evil in itself but only with the perpetrator. Evil in itself is unforgivable; only perpetrators can be forgiven. This is why forgiveness is always a relational event, on condition that the guilty one confesses. It involves the two principal parties: the one confessing and the other forgiving facilitated by the mediating role of a third party.

An important aspect of forgiveness and reconciliation as relational events is that the redemption/refiliation they offer is revealed as grace freely given. That is, forgiveness must be given to me by someone else. I cannot offer it to myself.[21] Because I cannot heal myself of my guilt; I ask it from someone else. That is, in order to be forgiven, I should not only confess my guilt but also ask for forgiveness. In other words, confession takes place as an entreaty, as a prayer of petition, expressed at times in ritual and symbolic forms as Ahab does. Thus, the deep awareness arises that I have no power over forgiveness but that it is given to me by another person as a gratuitous grace or gift.

Forgiveness is often taken to be the same thing as reconciliation. This is a misunderstanding. Forgiveness is not the same thing as reconciliation. The difference between the two is that forgiveness comes first before reconciliation. There can be forgiveness without reconciliation, but there can be no reconciliation without forgiveness. Reconciliation is the desirable goal of forgiveness that is not always achieved in all cases between humans.

The Bible does not offer any definition or explanation of forgiveness. In the field of psychology, *forgiveness* is defined as 'a voluntary foreswearing of negative affect and judgment by an injured party directed at someone who has inflicted a significant, deep, and unjust hurt; this process also involves viewing the wrongdoer with love and compassion.'[22] Forgiveness

---

20   Janet Howe Gaines, *Forgiveness in a Wounded World: Jonah's Dilemma* (Atlanta, GA: Society of Biblical Literature, 2003), 155–156.

21   In counselling, there are times self-forgiveness is admonished, especially on people who exhibit signs of scrupulous conscience, who doubt that they have been truly forgiven, and who therefore keep on nursing their guilt and become victims to it. At other times, references to self-forgiveness is nothing but attempts to silence our consciences, deny wrongdoing, or see them as things already done after all that should be consigned to history and forgotten as not deserving any feeling of guilt.

22   Elizabeth A. Gassin and Robert D. Enright, 'The Will to Meaning in the Process of

is the willful expression of good will for the offender, whether the offender asks for it or not. Jacob Loewen identified four kinds of forgiveness: divine, religious, social, and self.[23] He believes all four types are necessary for one to feel fully forgiven. This is because each is strongly connected to the other. The self is an entity socially connected to other selves and religiously connected to the divine.

The achievement of reconciliation depends on how sincerely and truly penitent the offender is and how willing and honest the victim is in granting forgiveness. To achieve reconciliation, one must be prepared to examine in all honesty the causes and the escalating processes of the breach and openly talk about it with each other, possibly in the presence of a third party—an objective witness. On the one hand, the acknowledgment of wrong done and the show of remorse or repentance on the part of the offender does justice to the victim and heals him/her of the hurt he/she suffers. On the other hand, forgiveness as mercy on the part of the victim or the offended frees the offender from the burden of guilt. In this regard, reconciliation is the completion of forgiveness. It takes two persons or parties to achieve reconciliation, but it takes one person or party to offer forgiveness. Forgiveness brings about inner peace and freedom. After having been forgiven, reconciliation is about finding each other once again, accepting and opening up once more to relating, interacting, and encountering each other.[24] In order to bring about reconciliation, therefore, repentance and forgiveness must play their two important roles of justice and mercy respectively.

When reconciliation does not follow forgiveness, two things may be responsible: it could be that the offender has not acknowledged his fault and has not asked for forgiveness and so has nothing to reconcile with the one who forgives. It could also be that the one who forgives is afraid that if he reconciles with the offender, the offender is likely going to hurt him/her again. This is why we should not insist that reconciliation must necessarily follow forgiveness. Such insistence can make some people to refuse even to forgive. We should do our best to work towards reconciliation, but

Forgiveness', *Journal of Psychology and Christianity* 14 (Spring 1995): 38–39.

23   Jacob A. Loewen, 'Four Kinds of Forgiveness', *Practical Anthropology* 17 (July–August 1970): 153.

24   Pollefeyt, 'Ethics, Forgiveness and the Unforgivable After Auschwitz', 158.

when there are insurmountable obstacles to reconciliation, we should work towards forgiveness with hope that with time reconciliation will be achieved.

Conclusion

The Hebrew Scriptures unambiguously require human beings to confess and repent of past misdeeds before forgiveness occurs. Most Bible passages involving God's forgiveness also show people doing their own part by humbling themselves, admitting guilt, and asking for forgiveness. Though God embodies forgiveness, sincere human participation is usually required in the process. Forgiveness is not a one-sided, unilateral undertaking in which God alone participates; usually this necessitates a kind of human and divine partnership in mutual responsibilities in which man turns toward God in penitence and God relents and forgives. While wrongdoing against others alienates us from our true selves, from others, and from God, confession of known misconduct links the offender to God's forgiveness and the promise of community filiatedness.

Filiation is an unconditional work God did when He created humans in His own image and likeness. Human work in the form of wrongdoing—the evil one inflicts on another or humanity's hate-prone cleavages and civilization fault lines—undid that filiation as we find on the pages of the Bible and in our world today. God's initiative to refiliate humanity to Himself necessitates that humans come to terms with their wrongdoing. While wrongdoing separates us from God and from one another, our coming to terms with our wrongdoing and being forgiven of them brings us back together reconciled and refiliated. To come to terms with his or her wrongdoing, the offender may need to be confronted with his or her wrongdoing by the offended or by a third party. The role of a third party means involvement. We cannot successfully preach the message of reconciliation entrusted to us and exercise the ministry of reconciliation given to us by distancing and non-involvement. God got Himself involved in the wrong done to Naboth. In our third-party role, we must not only take a side, we must take side rightly. God rightly took sides with the poor-but-wronged

Naboth rather than with the rich, powerful, but wicked King Ahab. Only an honest confrontation of the offender with his or her wrongdoing can reveal the wonder of forgiveness and reconciliation as well as the inner peace and joy of refiliation.

Chapter Two

Ụ̀kọ̀Chukwu na Ụ̀kọ́Chukwu (1 Sam. 2:11–4, 1–22; 7:3–17): Continuing the ReinGodment Theology of A. J. V. Obinna in a DisinGoded Christianity

Vincent Chukwuma Onwukwe

Abstract

Today's Christianity (especially in Nigeria) has been deeply infected by what A. J. V. Obinna refers to as the 'the religio-materialist strain', which has to do with extreme material understanding of Christianity and 'the secular-materialist force', which suggests a secularization of human mind, which negatively affects one's prioritization of Christian values. These two factors have led to the abandonment of the values of holiness of life and close relationship with God. The contributions of the clergy and other religious leaders in sustaining this deceptive trend are enormous. This situation calls for a search for models for priestly life and Christian religious leadership. While a lot of articles has been written to challenge the priests and religious leaders to be genuine in carrying out their responsibilities, not much has been written about models for religious leaders in our cultural heritage. Hence, I want to explore this area by analysing some Igbo concepts used to capture the idea of priesthood and religious leadership—ụkọChukwu, ụkọChukwu, and eze-mmuo. By discussing the meanings of the above Igbo terms and relating them to the reinGodment theology of A. J. V. Obinna and the biblical narratives of Samuel and the sons of Eli, this article demonstrates how the lives of religious leaders can lead to the loss of genuine Christian relationship with God and how this lost life can be regained. By a critical analysis of the above terms and the biblical narratives of 1 Samuel 2:11–4, 1–22; 7:3–17, my aim is to propose models for genuine Christian life, especially in the Nigerian Christianity.

Key terms: A. J. V. Obinna, *ụkọChukwu*, *ụkọChukwu*, *eze-mmuo*, ReinGodment, and DisinGodment

1. Introduction

'ReinGodment' is a brainchild of A. J. V Obinna, which is in line with his filiation theology.[1] He is also one of the ardent propagators of inculturation, which among other things has to do with situating the Christian faith within the African cultural context in order to bring about 'a marriage between the Gospel and culture'.[2] In his article, 'Inculturation as ReinGodment and Resplendouring: the Great Jubilee Illumination', he proposes that 'inculturation should become "reinGodment" and "resplendouring" effort in favour of all peoples and cultures'.[3] The idea of reinGodment, as he uses

---

1   Anthony J. V. Obinna, *Confiliating Americans: Recti-valuing One Another.* This is a pamphlet containing a lecture delivered at Beeson Divinity School, Campus of Samford University, Birmingham, Alabama. It was published by Assumpta Press, Owerri.

2   Teresa Okure, 'Feminist Interpretations in Africa', in *Searching the Scriptures: A Feminist Introduction*, ed. Elisabeth Schüssler Fiorenza (New York: SCM, 1993), 79.

3   Anthony J. V. Obinna, 'Inculturation as ReinGodment and Resplendouring: The Great Jubilee Illumination', in *Inculturation in the Third Millenium*, a book published in honour of the 10th CIWA Theology Week, ed. Patrick Chibuko and Simeon Eboh (Port Harcourt: CIWA, 1999), 10.

it (and as expressed by the prefix *re*), presupposes a share in the life of God
after it has been lost. More so, the concept of and the need for reinGodment
indicates that there was a 'disinGodment'[4] (loss or lack of divine life). In
other words, reinGodment can be understood in the light of the doctrines
of original sin and Incarnation (and indeed the paschal mystery), a sharing
of God's life with humanity in the person of Christ, which was necessitated
by the loss of divine life in the garden of Eden (cf. Gen. 3; CCC 50–64;
386–412). Hence, the paschal mystery can be seen as a whole process
of reinGodment in the sense that it was/is geared towards making human
beings share in the life of God. Obinna also opines that 'evangelization
should be essentially seen as the communication ... of God's life in Christ
into every person ... [and every culture] so that they may return to God
to give Him due honour and glory'.[5] The idea of returning to God again
implies that there was a straying from God, which I choose to refer to as
disinGodment.

According to Obinna, there are two major challenges to genuine
Christian and cultural life in Nigerian Christianity: first, 'the religio-
materialist strain,' which has to do with extreme material understanding
of Christianity, and 'the secular-materialist force,' which suggests a
secularization of human mind, which negatively affects one's prioritization
of Christian values.[6] These two factors have led to the gross abandonment of
our cultural and Christian values. The loss or lack of genuine Christianity
is based on the fact that many Christians, including religious leaders,
have failed to give God His rightful place in Christian worship and have
abandoned the values of holiness and close relationship with God. On
the contrary, the quest for wealth, prosperity, position, and authority has
preoccupied Christians and Christian leaders. Material prosperity and well-
being have replaced genuine relationship with God. This situation calls
for great emphasis on going back to the roots and adopting the Christian
and cultural values that we have abandoned. The situation of materialised
and secularised Christianity, which I see as a situation of disinGodment,
calls for a reinGodment in our worship of God. Just like the original sin

---

4   I use the term 'disinGodment' as a cognate for Obinna's reinGodment. In this sense, it refers
      to a loss of divine connection; it is also related to the Igbo term *ụ̀kọ́Chukwu*, which expresses
      a lack or insufficiency of the divine life.

5   Obinna, 'Inculturation as ReinGodment and Resplendouring', 16.

6   Obinna, 'Inculturation as ReinGodment and Resplendouring', 12–13.

necessitated the Incarnation (and indeed the whole paschal mystery), the above situation of disinGodment points to the need for reinGodment.

Against the above background, a search for models for a genuine Christian relationship with God is expedient. Since I am writing this article in honour of the episcopal silver jubilee of A. J. V. Obinna, I will concentrate more on how we can restore and maintain genuine Christian worship, especially in the lives of Catholic priests and other religious leaders. If the members of the clergy (and other religious leaders) are genuine in their Christian lives and inculcate this genuineness into the members of their congregations, there is no doubt that they will guide the flock of Christ towards a genuine Christian life. The model for genuine Christian life and priestly life can be found in the life of the biblical Samuel.[7] Hence, the need to explore some biblical narratives about the priestly and prophetic life of Samuel. Meanwhile, A. J. V. Obinna's conviction that inculturation should be a reinGodment inspires me to search for some Igbo cultural and religious value(s) that can help us to 'regain God (be reinGoded)' in our Nigerian Christianity. I find (the meaning of) the Igbo concepts of *ụ̀kọ̀Chukwu* and *eze-mmuo* (both used to indicate the life of a priest or religious leader) as great models for genuine priestly and Christian life.

This article therefore demonstrates how the life of the biblical Samuel, whom I regard as a genuine *ụ̀kọ̀Chukwu* and the concept of *eze-mmuo* in the Igbo Traditional Religion, can be compared with genuine priestly life and help to regain genuine priestly (Christian) values. It also exposes through the analysis of 1 Samuel 2–4 and 7 how the lives of religious leaders can lead to the spiritual death of Christians and how this lost life can be regained. I will begin by explaining the Igbo terms *ụ̀kọ̀Chukwu*, *ụ̀kọ́Chukwu*, and *eze-mmuo*. This will include an etymological

---

7   One may raise the question on why Jesus Christ is not presented in this article as a model for priesthood. Nevertheless, I have written about the need for religious leaders to see the life of Jesus as a model in another article. See Vincent Chukwuma Onwukwe, "The Unmerited Glory: Reading Psalm 8 in the Context of Catholic Priestly Ministry; Embracing the Model of Servant-Leadership in the Nigerian Church', in *In Defence of Excellence: A Festschrift in Honour of Rev. Fr. Dr. Uzochukwu Jude Njoku*, ed. Emmanuel Madu et al. (Owerri: Wounded Messiah, 2017), 11–21. I have chosen the biblical narratives of Samuel and the sons of Eli specifically to demonstrate how a religious leader can either lead people to God or away from Him. While Samuel represents the religious leaders that behave in a way that can bring people closer to God, the sons of Eli stand for the religious leaders whose ways of life lead people away from God or lead people astray. This will be done by a constant reference to the terms *ụ̀kọ̀Chukwu* and *ụ̀kọ́Chukwu*.

interpretation of these terms. By so doing, I shall show the relationship
between *ụ́kọ̀Chukwu* and *ụ̀kọ́Chukwu* and also compare the qualities
of *eze-mmuo* with that of biblical prophets and priests, bringing out his
lifestyle that can be emulated in the priestly and Christian life. Second,
I will analyse the biblical narratives of 1 Samuel 2–4 and 7 (the story of
Eli and his sons and Samuel). This will enable me to illustrate further the
meanings of the terms *ụ́kọ̀Chukwu* (priest) and *ụ̀kọ́Chukwu* (lack of God
or disinGodment) and demonstrate how the life of *ụ́kọ̀Chukwu* (priest or
servant of God) can either lead people to genuine relationship with God or to
the situation of *ụ̀kọ́Chukwu* (lack or absence of God). Third, I will discuss
the aspects of worship in Nigerian Christianity that calls for reinGodment,
pointing out how the situation of materialism and secularised mindset
have affected our Christianity and how religious leaders have contributed
to this situation. Finally, I will suggest that genuine, sincere, and constant
communication and interaction with God and sincere pursuit of the life of
holiness should be the greatest priority of every priest (religious leader)
and every Christian.

2. Ụ̀kọ̀Chukwu and Ụ̀kọ́Chukwu

The two Igbo terms *ụ́kọ̀Chukwu* and *ụ̀kọ́Chukwu*[8] have the same
alphabetical spelling but are different in phonetics and meaning. The
difference in their meaning is on the basis of the accent of the word *uko*,
which has been combined with *Chukwu* (God). The term *ụ́kọ̀* means
'servant' or 'slave', while *ụ̀kọ́* indicates a lack or absence. On the basis of
this explanation, therefore, *ụ́kọ̀Chukwu* and *ụ̀kọ́Chukwu* respectively
means 'servant of God' and 'lack or absence of God (the divine life)'. This
lack may not be entire but suggests some level of insufficiency.

The word *ụ́kọ̀* ('servant') is, to an extent, connected to the infinitive
ikọ (to till, to cultivate to farm, to make [ridges or mounds], etc.). The
latter indicates the work of a farmer. Tilling the earth presupposes a kind
of 'service' to the land in the sense of dependence on what it offers. The
farmer also provides the nutrients that the land needs in order to make

---

8   From a grammatical perspective, the word *Chukwu*, when it does not take the first position
     in its combination with another word, is not capitalized. It is capitalized when it stands alone
     as a word. I have capitalized it here for the sake of emphasis. The God we are referring to is
     the Christian God.

it yield fruit. In this sense, one can say that the farmer is at the service of the land. This connotation of service is in line with the meaning of the Hebrew word *avad*, used to capture the activity of Adam (tilling the earth) in the Garden of Eden. Ludwig Koehler and Walter Baumgartner opine that 'to till' is the basic meaning of this word.[9] Note, however, that the verb is related to the noun *ebed*, meaning 'servant', in which case it would correspond to the verb 'to serve',[10] which is a work of a servant (*úkọ̀*). In the same vein, as a result of his tilling the earth and planting in it, the farmer becomes a servant to the earth that he/she is tilling. This service to the earth is to a great extent as a result of some level of lack (*ùkọ́*) of food, which the farmer wants to prevent or eradicate. One of the basic responsibilities of the farmer is therefore to work in order to prevent a lack of food in his/ her own life, the lives of his/ her family members and indeed the lives of other people's families (*Onye oru ugbo na-ako ugbo ka o were kwusi ùkọ́ nri*).

In relating the agricultural implication of the term *iko* and its relationship to *úkọ̀* to the meanings of *úkọ̀Chukwu* and *ùkọ́Chukwu*, one sees clearly the relationship between the two terms *úkọ̀Chukwu* and *ùkọ́Chukwu*. Just as the farmer works basically to avoid *úkọ̀ nri* (lack of food), the *úkọ̀Chukwu* (the servant of God) should also serve God to the best of his ability in order to avoid *ùkọ́Chukwu* (lack of God, insufficiency of the divine life) either in his own life or in the lives of others. *Onye úkọ̀Chukwu na-akonye ndi mmadu Chukwu iji kwusi ùkọ́Chukwu.* A great example of this relationship between the above two terms is the celebration of the Sacraments of Baptism and Reconciliation. Through the celebration of Baptism, the priest initiates the baptised into a divine life that was hitherto lacking. In the same vein, through the Sacrament of Reconciliation, the penitent regains the life of grace that was lost through the life of sin. The regaining of divine life through the celebration of the Sacraments is in line with Obinna's reinGodment terminology, which we have referred to in the introduction. At any rate, it is noteworthy to mention that the responsibility of preventing the situation of *ùkọ́Chukwu* in the lives of Christians is not limited to the sacramental and individual lives

---

9   See Ludwig Koehler and Walter Baumgartner, eds., *The Hebrew and Aramaic Lexicon of the Old Testament* (Leiden: E. J. Brill, 1995), 773.

10   The Hebrew verb *avad* is translated as 'to dress' in KJV and 'to till' in the NRSV. Some lexica add other meanings like 'to serve', 'to honour', 'to worship', 'to subjugate'.

of Christians. It extends to the social structure that affects the mental disposition of people in different societies and their interpretation of Christian values. In other words, the priests and religious leaders have some sociopolitical roles to play. The Christian society in Nigeria has been seriously infected with materialistic and secularistic values. This situation has been captured by Jeff Mirus as 'the secularization of the message of Christ'.[11] This situation is deceptive because it makes people feel they are worshipping God when in actual fact, they are not.

Furthermore, the *ụ̀kọ̀Chukwu* will be more effective in his fight against *ụ̀kọ́Chukwu* if he himself is not in the camp of the enemy (*ụ̀kọ́Chukwu*) he is fighting. The divine life should not be lacking in him. He must therefore be filled with the divine life and God's glory through his constant and sincere communication with God. Of course, one can only offer what he or she has. Another key Igbo concept used to capture the idea of priesthood and religious leadership is *eze-mmuo*. In what follows, we shall analyse the meaning of the term.

3. Eze-Mmuo

The term *eze-mmuo* comprises two different words: *eze* (king) and *mmuo* (spirit). *Eze-mmuo* is therefore a king in matters relating to the spiritual lives of a particular community; he is literally a 'king of the spirits'. What *ndi* Igbo refer to as *eze-mmuo* is known as chief priest or simply priest among non-Igbo writers in African Traditional Religion.[12] As has been revealed by scholarship in Igbo religion, the *eze-mmuo* ensures that the members of the community live in accordance with the direction of the deity that he and the community are serving.[13] He does this by mediating between the deities and the people. But for him to be able

---

11   Jeff Marius, 'The Secularization of Christ: A Case Study', https://www.catholicculture.org/ Commentary/ authors.cfm?authorid=17 [accessed November 1, 2018].

12   Bolaji Idowu, *African Traditional Religion: A Definition* (London: SCM, 1973). See also, John S. Mbiti, *African Religions and Philosophies* (Garden City, NY: Anchor Books, 1970); *Introduction to African Religion* (London: Heinemann, 1975).

13   See F. A. Arinze, *Sacrifice in Igbo Religion* (Ibadan: Ibadan University Press, 1970). See also Emeka Onwurah, 'Priesthood in the Traditional Religion of the Igbos of Nigeria'. *Journal of Dharma: Dharmaram Journal of Religions and Philosophies* 15, no. 1 (1990): 45–54. Prudentius Emeka Aroh, *Priestly Celibacy: A Gift and Commitment (can. 277 & 1): Adaptation to Igbo Culture* (Gregorian Biblical Bookshop, 2014), 228.

to do this, he must be in constant communication with the deities. This mediating role of the chief priest (*eze-mmuo*) has also been captured by John Mbiti: 'The priest is the chief intermediary: he stands between God, or divinity, and men [and women] ... [he] is the religious symbol of God among His people.'[14] This point has been reiterated by Emeka Onwurah as follows: 'He [the *eze-mmuo*] knows the divinity, hears him and speaks to him for himself and other worshippers. He is the embodiment of the presence of the deity among the people.'[15] The idea of 'knowing,' 'hearing', and 'speaking', which was used by Onwurah to portray the communication between the deity and *eze-mmuo*, shows great level of intimacy between the *eze-mmuo* and the deity he is serving. Communication with the deity appears to be an important aspect of the life of *eze-mmuo*. As a result of this communication, he knows the deity intimately; he understands him and knows what he wants at any given time. He hears the language that the deity speaks, and the deity in turn hears and understands him. More so, the description given by Mbiti and Onwurah about the embodiment of the presence of God by the *eze-mmuo* presupposes that the members of the community should feel some divine aura when they see the *eze-mmuo*.

As mentioned above, the *eze-mmuo* plays a mediatory role between the deity and the members of the community. This mediatory role also implies some sociopolitical commitments. For instance, he warns the people about the ways of life that could annoy the deities and bring about their anger to the community. Sometimes, he is sent by the deity he is serving to warn the people about an impending danger. This may include challenging political leaders who make life unbearable for the people (cf. Exod. 4–14; 1 Sam. 8–31; 2 Sam. 11–12; 1 Kings 16–22; 2 Kings 1–9). In carrying out this sociopolitical and prophetic role, the *eze-mmuo* should only say what the deity tells him to say, not adding his own words because he is only a servant of the deity. This is in line with the role played by the biblical prophets who use the customary 'thus says the Lord'. In other words, *eze-mmuo* can be said to be a prophet.

There are other details about the person and character of *eze-mmuo* in Igbo Traditional Religion, but we have mentioned three major points about him that I consider very useful to the members of the clergy and other Christian religious leaders. First, in order to play his mediatory role

---

14   . Mbiti, *African Religions and Philosophies*, 246.
15   Prudentius, *Priestly Celibacy*, 49.

effectively, the *eze-mmuo* must constantly communicate with the deity
he serves. Second, he embodies the presence of the said deity. Finally,
he plays a sociopolitical role, which includes cautioning the members
of the community and their political leaders when they go astray. In the
same vein, constant communication with God and consistent presence
in the presence of God will help a religious leader enter into a deeper
relationship with God and become conscious of his role as a servant of God.
This constant communication with God inculcates in the religious leader
a divine aura that is both attractive and scary. It is attractive because the
people can rely on the religious leader as one who can communicate to
them what God wants and directs them to Him. It is scary in the sense that
the people placed under his or her care are afraid to do the wrong things in
the presence of this spiritual leader. To understand further what it means to
be a genuine or nongenuine priest or religious leader, we shall analyse the
biblical narratives about Samuel and the sons of Eli in 1 Samuel 2:11–4,
1–22; 7:3–17).

4. Samuel, Eli, and His Sons (1 Sam 2:11–4, 1–22; 7:3–17)

The two Igbo terms *ụ̀kọ̀Chukwu* and *ụ̀kọ́Chukwu* can be used to
capture the characters of Samuel and the sons of Eli respectively in 1
Samuel 2–4; 7. One observes a careful and skilful comparative analysis by
the narrator of the lives of, on the one hand, Samuel, who was presented in
the positive terms, staying always in the presence of Yahweh and serving
Him, and on the other hand, the sons of Eli, who were supposed to minister
to Yahweh as successors of Eli, the priest, but who instead brought the
anger of Yahweh upon themselves and upon the entire people of Israel
by their godless, greedy, and immoral lifestyle. In order to analyse these
narratives, it is necessary that we break the narratives into structural units.
This will enable us to identify the clear-cut distinctions that the author
makes between the two major parties in the narratives. I shall analyse
the lives of the major characters in the narratives—Samuel, Hophni and
Phinehas, Eli, the Man of God and the People of Israel—and bring to the
fore the types of relationships they had with God. In line with the above

criterion, I have decided to utter to some extent the structural sequence in the narratives. Six major units can be identified therein:

1. Samuel and His Presence in the Temple (2:11; 18–21; 26; 3:1; 19–21)
2. Hophni and Phinehas: Sons of Belial (2:12–17; 22–25)
3. The Man of God and the Boy of God (2:27–3:11b–14; 17–18)
4. The Blind Old Priest and the Visionary Young Servant (3:2–11a; 15–17)
5. The Departed Glory (4:1–22)
6. The ReinGodment of Israel: Bringing Back the Departed Glory (7:3–17)

4.1. Samuel and His Presence in the Temple

Samuel whose name means 'name of God' or 'His name is God',[16] is presented in our narratives as one who spent most part of his time in the presence of Yahweh. As his parents returned to their home in Ramah, he commenced a kind of service in the temple that can be compared to that of a priest. However, an important question to be addressed here is whether Samuel was called to be a priest or a prophet. This question is necessitated by the comparative analysis that the narrator makes between the boy and the sons of Eli, who were supposed to be priests but failed to perform the duties of the priests. Moreover, Samuel was not from a priestly family and would only be seen in the future performing majorly the prophetic and not the priestly function—anointing kings and informing them about the message of Yahweh (cf. 1 Sam. 15–17). Finally, he was known by the people as a trustworthy prophet and not a priest (2:20).

At any rate, Samuel performed all the three functions mentioned by the man of God as the functions of the priest (cf. 2:11; 18; 3:1; 7:8–10), which Eli and his sons were not reported to have done in the narratives (2:27–36): to go up to the Lord's altar, to offer incense, and 'to wear an ephod before me' (2:28). Samuel's service to Yahweh is mentioned in 2:11, 18, 3:1; and the Hebrew term *shārat*, which was used to capture this act of service, is also used in Exodus and Numbers to denote the

---

16 S. Szikzai, 'Samuel', in *The Interpreter's Dictionary of the Bible*, ed. George Arthur Buttrick et al. (New York: Abingdon, 1962), 201–202.

priestly activities of Aaron, the high priest and his sons (cf. Exod. 28:35, 43, 29:30; Num. 1:50).[17] Moreover, scholars like Kyle McCarter and Ralph Klein both present Samuel as a priest. Commenting on the priestly role of Samuel, McCarter states: 'By a deliberate selection of terminology, Samuel is implicitly characterised as a priest, ministering to Yahweh and clad in sacerdotal garments.'[18] The careful selection of terminology that McCarter talks about has to do with the constant presence of Samuel in the presence of the Lord and the wearing of the ephod. And as we have already mentioned, the word *shārat* used to designate the activity of Samuel in the temple is also used to refer to the functions of priests at the altar.

From the foregoing, one can rightly say that even though Samuel grew to be a great prophet and not explicitly a priest, his life and activities in our narratives were more priestly than those of Eli and his sons. He is presented as a great model for the priestly life in contrast to the immoral sons of Eli, who, though priests, had no priestly qualities. Samuel's service to Yahweh is in line with the meaning of the Igbo concept of *ụkọ̀Chukwu* (servant or slave of God), a word used to refer to priests. Whether as priest or prophet, he was qualified to be referred to as *ụkọ̀Chukwu* at least on the basis of his activities and dispositions. The concept of *ụkọ̀Chukwu* also indicates a divine presence since the one who is *ụkọ̀Chukwu* should spend most of his time in the presence of Yahweh. He is therefore filled with the Spirit of Yahweh (*Mmuo Chukwu*) and the glory of God (*ebube Chukwu*) and can only direct the people to Yahweh and not away from Him.

The sincere and genuine service that Samuel rendered to Yahweh did not go unnoticed or unrewarded. In 2:26 and 3:19–21, we are presented with the effects of the continuous presence of Samuel in the temple and in the presence of Yahweh. 'The boy Samuel continued to grow both in stature and in favour with the Lord and with the people' (NRSV 2:26). This translation does not capture entirely the impression that the Hebrew Bible presents to us about Samuel. There are three important Hebrew verbs used to capture the character of Samuel in this verse: *hālak* ('to walk, to go'); *gādal* ('to be great, to grow'); and *tuv* ('to be pleasing'). The word *hālak* seems not to have been accounted for in the above translation. The first two verbs, *hālak* and *gādal*, were used in a *qal* participle form, which indicates a continuous and consistent action. In other words, Samuel was consistent in walking

---

17   Ralph W. Klein, *1 Samuel*, Word Biblical Commentary (Waco, TX: Word Books, 1983), 24.

18   Kyle McCarter, *1 Samuel*, The Anchor Bible (Garden City, NY: Doubleday, 1980), 82, 85.

(*hālak*) with[19] the Lord, and he continued to grow in Him so that what he did pleased both Yahweh and the people of Israel. Because of this consistency and sincerity of Samuel, God was with him and made his words powerful; and he won the respect, admiration, and trust of the people (cf. 3:19–21). The people saw God's glory (*ebube Chukwu*) in him. The situation is different in connection to the lives of Hophni and Phinehas, whose actions displeased Yahweh and brought calamity upon the people of Israel. In what follows, we shall analyse the worthless activities of the sons of Eli.

4.2. Hophni and Phinehas: Sons of Worthlessness

Unlike the name Samuel and its meaning, 'His name is God', the names of Hophni and Phinehas have nothing godly attached to their meanings. The meaning of the name Hophni is not certain. Tony Cartledge suggests that it may have been derived from the Egyptian word meaning 'toad.' According to him, in its Hebrew meaning, it is similar to the term describing the empty hollow of a hand.[20] In other words, the name Hophni suggests a form of emptiness. In the same vein, Phinehas means 'brass lips', 'an uninspiring name for one who is called to speak for God'.[21] The brass is a musical instrument that makes a lot of sounds but is empty inside. So the idea of emptiness is suggested by the meaning of the names of Hophni and Phinehas. On the basis of the meaning of their names, it is not surprising that they displayed a divine emptiness, a 'lack of God' (*ùkọChukwu*).

It is interesting to observe how the narrator introduces the sons of Eli in 2:12. The first part of the verse describes them as 'sons of [Belial] worthlessness', while the second part tells us the basis for their worthlessness: 'they did not know the Lord'. The Hebrew expression *yādu*, which is in the *qal qatal* plural form, expresses a variety of implications that are not unrelated to one another. Its root *yāda* can mean the following: 'to know, observe, realise, recognize, perceive, care about, become acquainted with,' et cetera.[22] The root *yāda* is also used to denote sexual relations:

---

19 Here, 'walking with' means living according to God's direction; another way of saying that Samuel did what was pleasing to Yahweh.

20 Toni W. Cartledge, *1 & 2 Samuel*, Smyth & Helwys Bible Commentary (Macon, GA: Smyth & Helwys, 2001), 51.

21 Cartledge, *1 & 2 Samuel*, 51.

22 Terence E. Fretheim, 'yāda', in *New International Dictionary of Old Testament Theology and Exegesis* 2 (1997), 409–414.

'Adam knew Eve his wife, and she conceived and bore Cain' (Gen. 4:1).
One can therefore argue that *yāda* connotes a level of intimacy that can
be compared with that between a husband and wife. This intimacy (with
Yahweh) was lacking in the lives of Hophni and Phinehas but evident in
the life of Samuel. They did not care about their relationship with Yahweh
and their duties as priests (v. 13); they did not acknowledge Him and had
no reverence for Him. They were concerned with what they would gain
from the sacrificial animal to the extent that they demanded that they get
their share before Yahweh's portion was offered. This is why their sin was
directly against the Lord and very great in His sight. They treated the
offering of Yahweh with contempt (2:17).

The legislation concerning the share of the priest from the sacrifices
presented in the temple is found in Leviticus 7:31–36, where the members
of the clergy were to take the breast and thigh of the sacrificial animals, and
in Deuteronomy 18:3, in which they were supposed to take the shoulder,
the two jowls, and the stomach. What was obtainable at Shiloh was different
from the above priestly legislations. At Shiloh, the priests were supposed to
take all the three-pronged fork brought from the boiling sacrifice. (2:14).
But Hophni and Phinehas deviated from this and wanted a bigger share
from the sacrifice to the point of taking it by force. And apart from their
greed, they were also immoral to the point of sleeping with the women who
served at the entrance of the tent of meeting (2:22). They also disobeyed
their father, not listening to him when he admonished them to resist from
their evil ways (2:25).

From the foregoing, one can observe that the lives of the sons of Eli
capture the idea of *ụkọChukwu*. Unlike Samuel, in whom there was a
manifestation of God's power through the words he spoke (3:19–21), the
sons of Eli were empty of God's glory and power. This is clearly expressed
in 1 Samuel 4, where they carried the ark of the covenant of Yahweh
during the Israelites' war against the Philistines and yet a great number
of the Israelites were killed. The ark was captured, and they themselves
were killed. The carrying of the ark by them can be said to be a case
of possessing the symbol of God's presence without being possessed by
God. And indeed, they made themselves gods (by failing to honour and
acknowledge Yahweh) and had blocked any form of relationship with
God. On the contrary, Samuel was presented as ministering to the Lord
and being in His presence. But it was not reported that the sons of Eli

did the same. The only moments the narrator recounts with regard to their presence in the temple were with reference to collecting their share of the sacrifice. This portrays a form of gross materialism and a lack of connection to the divine (ùkóChukwu) in their religious life.

The situation of the sons of Eli was irredeemable, and no one could intercede for them. Their heart had been hardened by God, whose will it was to kill them (2:25). The admonition of their father fell on deaf ears. They could have repented and become reinGoded, being genuine in their priestly ministry (ùkòChukwu). But they were far from doing this. It was too late, and the only option that was left was a proclamation of God's judgment and punishment on them and the entire family of Eli. This decision of Yahweh was proclaimed by an unnamed man of God and revealed to Samuel, 'the boy of God.'

4.3. The Man of God and the Boy of God (2:27–3, 11b–14; 17–18)

The expression **ish elohim**, translated as 'a man of God', was used to refer to an unnamed messenger from God who announced God's judgment on the family of Eli. Many authors suggest that the term 'man of God' was used to refer to holy men or prophets. For instance, McCarter opines that it was 'a generalised designation used often of an oracle giver or prophet.'[23] The expression was used six times in the Hebrew Bible, and out of these six occurrences, three referred directly to the prophet Elijah (cf. 1 Sam. 2:27; 1 Kings 13:1, 17:24; 2 Kings 1:10, 4:9). It is most likely that the man of God who came to Eli was also a prophet since his message began with the customary 'Thus says the Lord'. The summary of the oracle presented by the man of God is presented in verse 30:

> Therefore, the LORD the God of Israel declares: 'I promised that your family and the family of your ancestor should go in and out before me forever'; but now the LORD declares: 'Far be it from me; for those who honor me I will honor, and those who despise me shall be treated with contempt.

---

23 McCarter, *1 Samuel*, 89.

The implication is that Eli and his sons had shown a great disrespect
and disregard to Yahweh and therefore would not escape His punishment.

To show the seriousness and the certainty of the punishment pronounced
on the family of Eli, it was also revealed to Samuel, even though he lacked
experience and it was rare for people to receive such messages from God.
Hence the same prophetic role that was played by the man of God was also
carried out by Samuel, 'the boy of God,' in spite of his inexperience. At the
insistence of Eli, 'Samuel told him everything and hid nothing from him.'
Samuel therefore acted like a genuine prophet, telling Eli all that Yahweh
had said without hiding or adding anything to it. The identity of Samuel
as a great prophet was re-iterated in verses 19 and 20. 'The Lord was with
him and let none of his words fall to the ground. And all Israel from Dan
to Beer-sheba knew that Samuel was a trustworthy prophet of the Lord'
(NRSV). While in chapter 2 the narrator brings to the fore the priestly
identity of Samuel, chapter 3 portrays him as a prophet. The privilege of
receiving a prophetic oracle from God also distinguishes him from Eli, who
was his blind master, and indeed his two sons.

4.4. The Blind Old Priest and the Visionary Young Servant (3:2–11a; 15–17)

'What was the crime of Eli?' one may rightly ask. Why should his
whole family and lineage be punished on account of the transgressions
of his wantonly stubborn sons? From the perspective of the narrator, the
whole blame was on Hophni and Phinehas, who were very persistent in
their evil ways and failed to listen to their father. Eli is presented as an old
man who was not so active because he lacked physical strength and had
a very bad sight (cf. 2:22; 3:2). The expression 'Now Eli was very old' in
verse 22 shows that Eli admonished his sons when he was very old. All he
could do as an old blind man was to advise his sons about the danger of the
path they were treading. The narrator does not inform us about his attitude
towards the worthlessness of his sons when he was younger. Furthermore,
Eli played an important role in the life of Samuel, directing him to Yahweh
and telling him how to respond to his call (3:4–10). However, from the man
of God's perspective, Eli tolerated the godlessness of his sons, honouring
them more than Yahweh (2:29). The expression 'fattening yourselves on
the choicest parts of every offering' seems to suggest that Eli partook from

the meat that his sons forcefully and fraudulently appropriated from the sacrificial animals in the temple. Perhaps the notion of his blindness can be metaphorically explained as his lack of moral courage to reject the actions of his sons since he took part in the eating of the meat; and lack of care towards the lifestyle of his sons. In this direction, one may wonder why none of the sons of Eli had the name of God, '*el*,' attached to their names. One may conclude on this basis that Eli cared less with reference to his sons' relationship with *el*. The case is different in the situation of Samuel, whose mother gave him a 'godly name' and offered him to God for His service.

Though Eli had a lot of experiences in the priestly ministry, he was metaphorically short-sighted, not sensitive to the doom that was coming upon his family. He knew about the Lord and all the details involved in offering sacrifices but seemed not to have known the Lord. He lacked the intimacy with God that could have led to a direction from God. Samuel, on the other hand, was an inexperienced boy who had not known the Lord but who came to know the Lord the very night that God revealed Himself to him. While Eli did not know about the doom that was about to befall him, this was revealed to Samuel. The narrator had prepared his readers for this divine revelation. Samuel had spent most of his time in the presence of Yahweh. It is not surprising that God, in whose presence he had been, would speak to him. But Eli and his sons received no revelation from God. They rather contributed to the departure of God's glory from Israel.

4.5. The Departed Glory (4:1–22)

The fourth chapter of the book of 1 Samuel narrates the humiliation and the double defeat of the Israelites in their war against their neighbors and perennial foes, the Philistines. In spite of the involvement of the ark of the covenant—which, among other things, represented God's presence— the Israelites were disgracefully defeated. First, four thousand Israelite troops were killed (v. 2). Not satisfied with this situation, the elders of the Israelites had to look for a solution to their problem. 'Why has the Lord put us to rout today before the Philistines?' they asked (v. 3). As rightly noted by Carteledge, 'Yahweh was thought of as a 'warrior-god' who fought and won victory for His people (cf. Exod. 15:3; 1 Sam 17:45; Isa. 42:13).[24]

---

24   Carteledge, *1 & 2 Samuel*, 73.

But why is the situation different here? They thought that this situation had arisen because they had not involved the ark of the covenant. So they brought the ark from Shiloh into their camp (v. 4). When the ark arrived the camp, there were contrary reactions from the camp of the Israelites and the camp of the Philistines respectively. The Israelites, thinking that they had found a solution to their initial nightmare (the humiliation of Israel by the Philistines) and assured of victory this time, because of the presence of the ark, 'gave a mighty shout so that the earth resounded' (v. 5). But the Philistines were afraid, for they had heard how the ark had helped the Israelites to become victorious in their numerous wars. But guess who were carrying the ark? The same people who had attracted the rage of Yahweh, Hophni and Phinehas. For 'only priests and Levites were allowed to touch the ark.'[25] But the ark did not solve their problem. On the contrary, the situation became worse; forty thousand people from the camp of the Israelites were massacred, making the total number of the people killed forty-four thousand; and the ark was also captured.

What then was the problem? Why were the Israelites shamefully defeated to the point of capturing the ark? I concur with McCarter, who answered the above questions thus: 'The ark was captured because Yahweh had chosen to abandon Israel on account of the wickedness of the Elides.'[26] The sons of Eli had brought the anger of the Lord upon themselves, their family, and upon the whole people of Israel. The problem became more complicated. Not only were the Israelites defeated in war, the ark had been captured and Eli gave up the ghost on hearing this disheartening news (v. 18).

The capture of the ark was a great expression of the loss of *ebube Chukwu* (the glory of Yahweh), a situation that was caused by the wickedness of the sons of worthlessness, Hophni and Phinehas. What an irony! The people who were supposed to bring down the glory of Yahweh (*ebube Chukwu*) expelled the glory of Yahweh and brought about a situation of darkness and absence of the glory of God (*ụkọChukwu*) in the lives of the people. This situation was captured by the name given to the son of Phinehas, *Ichabod*, meaning 'no glory' (v. 21); the glory had departed, and the divine presence expressed by the presence of the ark had been lost (*ụkọChukwu*). *Ichabod* here becomes a metaphoric term

---

25 Carteledge, *1 & 2 Samuel*, 73.

26 McCarter, *1 Samuel*, 109.

denoting the effect of the wickedness and worthlessness of the sons of Eli. Just as Ichabod was given birth to, Hophni and Phinehas, the priests (*ùkọ̀Chukwu*) of Shiloh had given birth to *ùkọ́Chukwu* in the land of Israel. They could only offer what they had, namely, divine emptiness. They were suffering from lack of God's glory (*ùkọ́Chukwu*) and transmitted this spiritual disease to the people of Israel. But their major role as priests should be to end the situation of *ùkọ́Chukwu* by bringing about *ebubeChukwu* (*ikọnye ndi mmadụ Chukwu*). This role was later played by Samuel in 1 Samuel 7.

4.6. The ReinGodment of Israel: Bringing Back the Departed Glory (1 Samuel 7:3–17)

The situation that the people of Israel found themselves in after they had lost the glory of God was a miserable one. Since nature abhors vacuum, they gave in to the worship of Baal and Astarte[27] (vv. 3–4). But Samuel had to play a role of a priest (*ùkọ̀Chukwu*), mediating between the people and God and thus bringing back the glory of God. He called for Israel's return to the Lord without reservation: 'If you are returning to the Lord with all your heart, then put away the foreign gods ... from among you. Direct your heart to the Lord, and serve him only, and he will deliver you out of the hands of the Philistines' (v. 3). This statement of Samuel presumes a longing in the heart of the Israelites to return to the Lord. Samuel made it known to them that a return to Yahweh, which strongly requires a change of direction, must be done 'with all your heart'. This involves that they must stop the worship of the foreign gods and direct their entire heart to the Lord. The key terms in this verse are *qol* (all), which depicts entirety and wholeness, and *lēvāv* (heart), which among other things, indicates an

---

27 Baal was the fertility god who was chiefly worshipped by the Canaanites. The term also signified 'ownership', an indication that the Israelites had rejected Yahweh as the one who owns their lives but submitted to the ownership of Baal. Astarte was the 'ancestral consort of Baal'. Both of them were worshipped together by their worshippers through feasts, offerings, and cultic prostitution. The term 'Astarte' (sometimes called Asherah) is 'the Greek form of the name of the goddess called Ashtoreth in Hebrew'. The fact that the Israelites joined their Canaanite neighbours in worshipping Baal and Astarte indicates that they have lost their identity as a nation that was deeply connected to Yahweh and had taken up the identity that did not belong to them. For further readings, see Carteledge, *1 & 2 Samuel*, 73.99; S. Cohen, 'Baal', in *The Interpreter's Dictionary of the Bible* (1962), 328–330. See also E. R. Achtmeier, 'Astarte', in *The Interpreter's Dictionary of the Bible* (1962), 304.

inwardness and internalness. Only by the wholehearted return to the Lord can the Israelites be liberated from the hands of the Philistines, who had become their nightmares.

The Israelites responded positively to the requirements presented to them by Samuel. They were gathered for a special prayer at Mizpah.[28] They drew and poured out water before the Lord, fasted, and renounced their sins. McCarter thinks that the ritual of pouring water has its origin in the ceremony designed to ensure the autumn rainfall. He however suggests that in the context of 1 Samuel 7, it is a sign of purification; in other words, a washing away of guilt and cleansing of the land.[29] In line with McCarter, David Tsumura opines that the pouring out of water is for penitential purposes, connected with fasting and confession of sins.[30] The Israelites, by their acts of sincere repentance, had fulfiled the requirements that Samuel proposed to them for returning to the Lord.

The Philistines heard that the Israelites had camped at Mizpah and decided to attack them. The attitude of the Israelites is different compared to the context of chapter 4. This time, there were no shouts of joy and confidence. They were frightened and asked Samuel to pray for them to Yahweh. Here the text points out the priestly and prophetic role of Samuel as an intercessor who prays for God's salvation upon Israel. This is a role that the sons of Eli could not play. Their attempt to save Israel from the hands of the Philistines by carrying the ark compounded the problem of Israel. Samuel also offered a burnt offering to the Lord, again a priestly responsibility. And as he was doing this, the Philistines drew near. This time, the Lord was with the Israelites and was not silent as in the case of the humiliation of Israel (cf. ch. 4). On the contrary, 'the Lord thundered loudly against the Philistines on that day and confused them and they were struck before Israel' (v. 10b). While the Israelites gave a mighty shout in 4:5; the Lord produced the sound here in a thunderous way.

---

28 Mizpah seems to be a very special place in the ministry of Samuel. He judged all Israel there (1 Sam. 7:6); he is 'said to have gone on a circuit from Bethel to Gilgal to Mizpah to judge Israel' and also anointed Saul king there. (cf. 1 Sam. 10:17–27). Other references to Mizpah include Judges 20:21 and I Kings 15:16–22. For further reading see, David Toshio Tsumura, *The First Book of Samuel*, The New International Commentary on the Old Testament (Grand Rapids, MI: William B. Eerdmans, 2007), 234.

29 McCarter, *1 Samuel*, 144.

30 Tsumura, *The First Book of Samuel*, 234.

Biblical scholars have preoccupied themselves with what the thundering of Yahweh could mean here. As noted by Tsumura, some scholars see expressions like this as indicating the non-historical implication of the story. He however argues against this position as follows: 'Assyrian records also mention divine interventions in battles and no non one claims that those are unhistorical.'[31] In any case, what is clear about the Lord's thundering is that it reveals God's intervention in the plight of Israel who had reconciled with Him. In the Hebrew Bible, Yahweh's intervention in human affairs is often mediated through natural elements[32] of storm, thunder, lightning, fire, et cetera (see Josh. 10:14, 24:7; 2 Sam. 22:14–15; 1 Kings 18:38; Ps. 18:13, 29, 81:7; Isa. 29:6; Job 37:4–5, 40:9). What is more important to us here is that Yahweh's intervention shows that His glory, which had been hitherto lost because of the worthlessness and divine emptiness of Hophni and Phinehas, had returned to Israel through the instrumentality of Samuel, the priest and prophet.

Having explored our chosen biblical narratives, we shall proceed to x-ray, on the basis of how, Obinna's views on the religio-materialist strain and secular-materialist force how material values and secular values have led to the loss of our Christian values. We shall also make suggestions on how to regain these values.

5. Materialism and the Secularization of Christianity: The Nigerian Experience

Here we discuss the areas that call for reinGodment in Nigerian Christianity. As we have noted in the introductory part of this article, A. J. V. Obinna points out two major factors, which are related to each other, that have immensely affected the Christianity in Nigeria. These two factors include religio-materialist strain and secular-materialist force.

---

31   Tsumura, *The First Book of Samuel*, 234.
32   Carteledge, *1 & 2 Samuel*, 101.

5.1. The Religio-Materialist Strain

Obinna opined that there is a rising trend of gross materialism among
Nigerian Christians that has continued to increase until today. According
to him:

> The colonial arm which had seemingly been withdrawn with
> the political independence of many African nations has
> returned more aggressively with the multiple arms of sectarian
> religious ideology and commercial technology, both of which
> are combining to inject into Africa's economically distressed
> peoples a materialistic ideology that is coated colorfully
> and religiously. The militarization of the world by western
> competitive technology which express itself in Nigeria…in the
> form of military dictatorships and in ruthless expropriation
> of the commonwealth has created in our Nigerian Christian
> environment a religio-materialist aggressiveness that draws
> courage from the prevailing militarism.[33]

From the above quotation, we observe that Obinna sees a connection
between what he refers to as 'the western militarization of the world'
(which is a new form of colonialism and brought about by competitive
technology) and the materialism that we experience in our Christianity. This
militarization is upheld by most African leaders who dance to the tones of
the Western economic powers to the detriment of the African citizens who
are exposed to the danger of economic crisis. The issue of militarization
referred to by Obinna is attested to by the cruel dictatorships and fraud, on
the part of political leaders, experienced in most African countries. These
materialistic, deceitful, and militarization tendencies often play out in the
Nigerian Christianity. From the perspective of religious leaders, so much
emphasis is placed on issues like sowing of seeds, payment of tithes, and
other forms of fund-raising in the church as conditions for knowing who
is genuine in his or her Christian life. Most of the time, these payments
and fundraisings are forcefully demanded for. These deceitful activities
have been masqueraded as forms of genuine Christianity and have misled
so many Christians. On the part of the other members of believers, the
tendency is to place (financial) prosperity, material well-being, long life,

---

33   Obinna, 'Inculturation as ReinGodment and Resplendouring,' 12.

absence of sickness, marriage, childbearing, and other economic and social needs over genuine relationship with God and the values of holiness. Hence a political leader who has embezzled the common fund can become a *saint* and a man or woman after the pastor's heart because he or she builds churches and makes great donations in the church. In the same vein, a Christian businessman or woman may not worry about doing his business according to Christian principles as far as he or she makes gains and pays his or her tithes and sows seeds in the church.

While we appreciate Obinna's position that one of the major factors that has brought about the materialist trend in the Nigerian Christianity is the Western militarization of the world, we must also keep in mind that African Traditional Religion, to an extent, has a theology that may support this materialistic trend. As has been noted by Benno van den Toren, African Traditional Religion is anthropocentric in the sense that 'all religious practices are used to serve the harmony and flourishing of human being, or better of the human community ...'[34] Based on the above conviction, van den Toren maintains that most African people have adopted the materialistic trend of Christianity because it suits the goals they would want to achieve in the traditional African religion. We must, however, note that what is different from the materialistic trend of today's Christianity and the anthropocentric nature of African religion is that there is a lot of deception in the former. As we have noted in our discussion on *eze-mmuo*, the religious leader in Igbo Traditional Religion can only communicate what the deity he serves had told him to say, without deceiving the members of the community.

Whatever be the case, in the midst of the faulty Christianity marked with gross materialism, Jesus becomes an economic messiah, ensuring that our needs are provided and not a person to enter into relationship marked with holiness with. In the words of Obinna, in the religio-materialist ideology of Igboland and Nigeria, 'in Jesus name has become a banner for covering and covering up a multiplicity of religious and irreligious business and projects'.[35] This situation is a form disinGodment; it makes many Christians serve so many gods in the name of Christianity while its basic aspects (genuine relationship with God and holiness of life) are giving little

---

34   Benno van den Toren, 'Secularization in Africa: A Challenge for the Churches' *Africa Journal of Evangelical Theology* 22, no. 1 (2003): 11.

35   Obinna, 'Inculturation as ReinGodment and Resplendouring,' 13.

or no attention. Related to this materialistic trend is the secularization of Christianity. In what follows, therefore, we discuss what Obinna refers to as the 'secular materialist force'.

5.2. *The Secularization of Christ and Christianity*

Secularization is a major theme in the study of theology and the social sciences. The necessity of the study of secularization in theology today is on the basis of its impact in the lives of individual Christians and on Christianity as an institution.[36] In two essays written by Jeff Mirus, 'Measuring the Synod of Youths' and 'Secularization of Christ', in honor of the synod of youths concluded in October 2018, he consistently argues that the major problem facing the church today is the secularization of Christianity. He regrets that 'the institutional apparatus of the church is so deeply infected by secular values'.[37] The implication is that it is difficult for many Christians to differentiate between their Christian values and other values. Another striking point observed by Mirus is that 'so many churchmen find their moral high ground in the purification of the environment rather than in the purification of our bodies. Or in blaming sinful institutions rather than correcting sinful persons.'[38] In other words, the personal Christian life of relationship with God and the values of individual holiness of life are not adequately stressed. One major factor that has fueled this secularist tendency is the quest for individual freedom or emancipation. Christianity is seen by those who champion this mission of individual emancipation as an institution that prevents human freedom with its dogmas and principles. To attain this freedom, therefore, the impact of Christianity in the public sphere has to be

---

36 The term *secularization* is a very broad term, with a variety of meanings, which has been explained from various perspectives by both theologians and social scientists. Jose Casanova, for instance, makes a distinction between its historical sense, in which it means a transfer of things, persons, or ideas from ecclesiastical or religious use to non-religious use and the broadest sense, in which it implies the decline of religious beliefs. Cf. Jose Casanova, 'Secularization', in *International Encyclopedia of the Social & Behavioural Sciences*, 2nd edition, Volume 21 (2001), 382–387. See also Jürgen Habermas and Joseph Ratzinger, *The Dialectics of Secularization: On Reason and Religion* (San Francisco: Ignatius Press, 2006) and Charles Taylor, *A Secular Age* (Cambridge, MA: Belknap Press of Harvard University Press, 2007).

37 Jeff Mirus, 'Measuring the Synod on Youth: Whose Seismograph', an essay written in honour of the Synod of Youths, 9 October 2018, https://www.catholicculture.org/news/headlines/index.cfm?Storyid=38935 [accessed November 17, 2018].

38 Mirus, 'Measuring the Synod on Youth'

challenged and her values forced to serve the secular values. The secularist Christian does not want to be confronted about his or her personal sinful and immoral life, but he or she wants to identify himself or herself as a Christian.

There is a temptation to think that secularization is a Western factor and has not affected the African society. On the contrary, scholarship on African theology and social sciences reveals that the issue of secularization has affected the African Christianity. In affirmation to the above fact, Obinna writes:

> The intensified exposure of Nigerian-Africans to western secular education, sometimes in Nigeria and sometimes in Europe and America, and the twenty-four-hour media/television of the commercial and entertainment world of Euro-America into Nigerian villages, towns and cities have combined to create among Nigerian-Africans an increasing trend towards secular-materialistic acquisitions, life-style and interpretation which threaten many of our religio-cultural values. While the external outlook of many of us may still exude of devoted religiosity, the inner spirituality may have been totally evacuated.[39]

Migration to the Western countries, through which secularist mentality is inculcated in African migrants, Western secular education, and the media are three major factors that can be identified from the above view of Obinna as some of the causes of secularization of Christianity in Nigeria. While we may find so many young and old people in the western world who do not want to have anything to do with Christianity, the Nigerian situation is different and more deceptive. There are so many Christians who may participate in religious activities even when they are empty in their inner Christian spiritual lives. This situation has also been observed by Abel Ngarsouledé. According to him, 'many [Nigerian] African societies are characterized by religious indifference and unbelief, though in their depths they have a natural sense of the presence of the supreme God'.[40] The issue of religious indifference and unbelief and the lack of inner spirituality are pointers to the insufficiency of the divine life (*ùkọ́Chukwu*) in most

---

39 Obinna, 'Inculturation as ReinGodment and Resplendouring', 13.
40 Abel Ngarsouledé, 'Social and Theological Perspectives of Secularization in Africa', *Cairo Journal of Theology* 2 (2015): 96.

Christians. For such Christians, while they may physically participate in religious activities, such activities make little or no impact on them.

To a great extent, the materialist and secularist attitude to Christianity have been sustained in Nigeria because of the enormous role played by religious leaders in proclaiming the gospel of prosperity and physical well-being with little or no emphasis on the values of holiness and genuine interaction with God. There is therefore an urgent need for reinGodment in the life of both religious leaders and lay persons.

6. Conclusion

Through our analysis of the key terms—*eze-mmuo*, *ụ̀kọ̀Chukwu*, reinGodment, and disinGodment—and our exegetical study of the biblical narratives of Samuel and the sons of Eli, we have, among other things, pinpointed the following: first, constant presence in the presence of God and constant communication with Him is a very essential aspect of the life of a priest and other Christian religious leaders. This will help the religious leader to have a genuine and intimate relationship with God, hearing from Him and understanding what he or she is expected to communicate to the Christian community. The importance of this genuine communication with God should also be inculcated into the lives of laypersons. Second, the religious leaders should embody the presence of God so that when people see them, they feel some divine aura. Third, the life of a religious leader can either lead people to God or away from Him. In our analysis of the narratives of Samuel and the sons of Eli, we demonstrated how the sons of Eli brought about the departure of God's glory and how Samuel brought back this departed glory. Finally, the Nigerian Christianity has been infected by secularization and materialist mindset, a situation that concentrates on secular and material values without giving God His rightful place in our hearts and without adequately stressing the need for genuine Christian relationship with God through the life of holiness. This is a form of disinGodment. The implication is that there is an urgent need for reinGodment.

What then should be done to bring about a more genuine Christianity in Nigeria? Just like Samuel called for a wholehearted and inward return to Yahweh after the Israelites had lost the glory of God and plunged into the worship of other gods, there is a need to 'bring back our God' in the Nigerian Church. For material and secular values have become gods that so many people worship. Bringing back our God involves a wholeheartedness and sincerity in worshipping God. It is necessary that we rethink our misguided understanding of Christianity. In order to live a genuine Christian life, we must take note of the following: first, Christianity is a theocentric[41] relationship with God. God is the centre and object of worship. He ought to be worshipped regardless of our human challenges. Christianity is a relationship in which we surrender our whole being to God. Second, union with Christ is the goal of this relationship. This union is not determined by our material gains. Third, holiness of life is a major factor in this relationship. Finally, our material values should be at the service of our relationship with God.

Bibliography

Arinze, Francis A. *Sacrifice in Igbo Religion.* Ibadan: Ibadan University Press, 1970.

Aroh, Prudentius Emeka. *Priestly Celibacy: A Gift and Commitment (can. 277 & 1): Adaptation to Igbo Culture.* Rome: Gregorian Biblical Bookshop, 2014.

Achtmeier, E. R. 'Astarte'. In *The Interpreter's Dictionary of the Bible.* 1962, 304.

Cartledge, Toni W. *1 & 2 Samuel.* Smyth & Helwys Bible Commentary. Macon, GA: Smyth & Helwys, 2001.

Casanova, Jose. 'Secularization'. In *International Encyclopedia of the Social & Behavioural Sciences,* 2nd edition, Volume 21. 2001, 382–387.

Cohen, S. 'Baal'. In *The Interpreter's Dictionary of the Bible.* 1962, 328–330.

Fretheim, Terence E. 'yāda'. In *New International Dictionary of Old Testament Theology and Exegesis* 2. 1997, 409–414.

---

41 See Herman Paul, 'Secularization in Africa: A Research Desideratum', *Cairo Journal of Theology* 2 (2015): 67–75.

Habermas, Jürgen and Joseph Ratzinger. *The Dialectics of Secularization: On Reason and Religion*. San Francisco: Ignatius Press, 2006.

Idowu, Bolaji. *African Traditional Religion: A Definition*. London: SCM, 1973.

Klein, Ralph W. *1 Samuel*. Word Biblical Commentary. Waco, TX: Word Books, 1983.

Koehler, Ludwig and Walter Baumgartner, eds. *The Hebrew and Aramaic Lexicon of the Old Testament*. Leiden: E. J. Brill, 1995.

Mbiti, John S. *African Religions and Philosophies*. Garden City, NY: Anchor Books, 1970.

_____. *Introduction to African Religion*. London: Heinemann, 1975.

McCarter, Kyle. *1 Samuel*. The Anchor Bible. Garden City, NY: 1980.

Mirus, Jeff. 'Measuring the Synod on Youth: Whose Seismograph'. An essay written in honour of the Synod of Youths. Accessed on November 17, 2018. https://www.catholicculture.org/news/headlines/index.cfm?Storyid=38935.

_____. 'The Secularization of Christ: A Case Study'. An essay written in honour of the Synod of Youths. Accessed on November 17, 2018. https://www.catholicculture.org/Commentary/authors.cfm?authorid=17.

Ngarsouledé, Abel. 'Social and Theological Perspectives of Secularization in Africa'. *Cairo Journal of Theology* 2 (2015): 88–102.

Obinna, A. J. V. *Confiliating Americans: Recti-valuing One Another*. Owerri: Assumpta Press. (This is a pamphlet containing a lecture delivered at Beeson Divinity School, Campus of Samford University, Brimingham, Alabama.)

_____. 'Inculturation as ReinGodment and Resplendouring: The Great Jubilee Illumination'. In *Inculturation in the Third Millenium*. Port Harcourt: Ciwa, 1999.

Okure, Teresa. 'Feminist Interpretations in Africa'. In *Searching the Scriptures: A Feminist Introduction*, edited by Elisabeth Schüssler Fiorenza. New York: SCM, 1993.

Onwukwe, Vincent Chukwuma. 'The Unmerited Glory: Reading Psalm 8 in the Context of Catholic Priestly Ministry; Embracing the Model of Servant-Leadership in the Nigerian Church'. In *In Defence of Excellence: A Festschrift in Honour of Rev. Fr.*

Dr. Uzochukwu Jude Njoku, edited by Emmanuel Madu et al. Owerri: Wounded Messiah, 2017, 11–21.

Onwurah, Emeka. 'Priesthood in the Traditional Religion of the Igbos of Nigeria'. *Journal of Dharma: Dharmaram Journal of Religions and Philosophies* 15, no. 1 (1990): 45–54.

Paul, Herman 'Secularization in Africa: A Research Desideratum'. *Cairo Journal of Theology* 2 (2015): 67–75.

Szikzai, S. 'Samuel'. In *The Interpreter's Dictionary of the Bible,* edited by George Arthur Buttrick et al. New York: Abingdon.

Taylor, Charles. *A Secular Age.* Cambridge, MA: Belknap Press of Harvard University Press, 2007.

Tsumura, David Toshio. *The First Book of Samuel.* The New International Commentary on the Old Testament. Grand Rapids, MI: William B. Eerdmans, 2007.

Van den Toren, Benno. 'Secularization in Africa: A Challenge for the Churches'. *Africa Journal of Evangelical Theology* 22, no. 1 (2003): 3–30.

Chapter Three

Seeing Tamar through the Prism of an African Woman: A Contextual Reading of Genesis 38[1]

Alexander Izuchukwu Abasili

Abstract

It is a truism that marriage is deeply appreciated in Africa. This, among others, is rooted in Africans' love of children. In most African societies, the begetting of children is a social and religious duty attached to marriage and is vital to it. Bearing of children is, in a sense, an end of marriage upon which the well-being of the spouse depends. A successful marriage should be 'fruitful'. As a result, marriage becomes a big challenge when it is 'childless'. Due to the patriarchal nature of most African societies, it is the women that often bear

---

1   This paper was first presented at the Contextual Interpretation of the Bible session of the *Society of Biblical Literature*'s international conference, held at King's College London, UK (July 3–7, 2011). Based on the good suggestions of the participants, few modifications have been made to the original paper. It was first published in the International Old Testament Journal—*Old Testament Essays*—in 2011. See Alexander Izuchukwu Abasili, 'Seeing Tamar through the Prism of an African Woman: A Contextual Reading of Genesis 38'. *Old Testament Essays* 24, no. 3 (2011): 555–573.

the brunt of childlessness in marriage. By embarking on a contextual reading of Genesis 38 and applying its implications to an African context, this article joins many concerned individuals in suggesting more informed reactions and solutions to the so-called grave problem of childlessness in marriage.

A. Introduction

In many Africa societies, marriage and procreation are intertwined and inseparable. It is almost always presumed that readiness for marriage is readiness for procreation; to get married is an opportunity to contribute freely, through procreation, to the survival of the lineage and society at large. During marriage (both traditional and Christian), one of the most appreciated and common gestures of goodwill shown to the newly married couple is praying for the fruit of the womb: 'may God grant you many children', 'you shall give birth to male and female', 'in nine months we shall gather to celebrate the birth of your baby'. In these wishes, both the societal perception of marriage and the use of sexuality in marriage as primarily geared towards the begetting of progeny are encapsulated. The problem arises when a marriage fails to lead to procreation. In a cultural context that emphasizes procreation and blames a woman for any failure in this regard, what is the way out for a 'fruitless' marriage? Reading Genesis 38 (Judah/Tamar narrative) against this backdrop reveals a resonance with the African cultural emphasis on progeny and heir. As such, the plight of Tamar represents, in particular, the ordeal of a married childless African woman searching for a child and in general, the injustice suffered by women in a patriarchal society. The overriding target of my interpretation of Genesis 38 is the application of the theological meaning of this text to the African sociocultural context so as to engender a more informed and just reaction to the so-called grave problem of childlessness or the search for a male child in today's Africa. To avoid being too general in referring to the African context, I will use the Igbo culture of Nigeria as my case study.[2]

Methodologically, this article has opted for African contextual hermeneutics, especially its feminist strand. According to Justin S. Ukpong, it is an approach in which

> the African context forms the subject of interpretation of the bible. This means that the conceptual framework of interpretation is informed by African socio-cultural perspectives ... In this way, the people's context becomes the subject of interpretation of the biblical text.[3]

Using African feminist hermeneutics, I will seek to interpret Genesis 38 from the perspective of the experience of an Igbo (African) woman.[4] An Igbo woman's experience of subjugation, intimidation, and injustice will be related to similar experience(s) in the Hebrew Bible. However, the similarity between the two will be non-essential but only existential (based on similar life experiences). The great separation in time, space, and context between the Hebrew Bible and Igbo society does not allow for essential similarity between them. This approach in combination with narrative analysis will reveal the relevance of Genesis 38 for today's Igbo (African) sociocultural context and society, especially in the face of childlessness and the search for a male child. This article is divided into four parts: (1) the Judah/Tamar pericope vis-à-vis the African emphasis on procreation—Genesis 38:1–5; (2) Tamar's childlessness vis-à-vis the childless married African

---

2   Geographically, the Igbo people (*Ndi Igbo*) are the indigenes of Southeastern Nigeria, West Africa. Approximately, they occupy an area of 15,800 square miles (see Victor Uchendu, *The Igbo of Southeast Nigeria* [Chicago: Holt, Rinehart and Winston, 1965], 3.) Following the division of Nigeria into thirty-six states, Igbo people occupy Anambra, Imo, Enugu, Abia, Ebonyi, part of Delta, Cross River, Rivers, and Akwa Ibom states. The 2006 Nigerian census places the population of Igbo people at about 21 million. The majority of the Igbo people are Christians (about 80 percent), while pockets of traditional religious practitioners spread throughout Igbo land (see Toyin Falola, ed., *Igbo History and Society: The Essays of Adiele Afigbo* [Trenton, NJ: African World Press, 2005], 141).

3   Justin S. Ukpong, 'Developments in Biblical Interpretation in Africa: Historical and Hermeneutical Directions', in *The Bible in Africa: Transactions, Trajectories and Trends*, eds. Gerald West and Musa W. Dube (Leiden: Brill, 2000), 24. See also Joseph Enuwosa, 'African Cultural Hermeneutics: Interpreting the New Testament in a Cultural Context', *Black Theology* 3/1 (2005): 88.

4   Ukpong, 'Developments in Biblical Interpretation in Africa: Historical and Hermeneutical Directions', 21–22.

woman—Genesis 38:6–10; (3) Tamar's desperate search for offspring as a mirror of the desperation of the childless African woman—Genesis 38:12–26; (4) conclusion, i.e., the implications of the Judah/Tamar story for today's African audience.

B. The Judah/Tamar Pericope vis-à-vis African Emphasis on Procreation—Genesis 38:1–5

The story of Gen 38:1–30 began with Judah's 'going-down' (ירד) from his siblings and father and settling in Canaan with a Canaanite friend named Hirah. There Judah *took* (ויקחה) a Canaanite woman, the daughter of Shua (v. 2). Although the Hebrew root לקח has a rich semantic field, its usage here unambiguously denotes marriage.[5] In other words, Judah *married* a Canaanite woman. By the quick succession with which Judah's children were born, the narrator highlights the establishment of a family and the having of progeny as the goals of his marriage. Hence, within three verses (vv. 3, 4, 5) the birth of three sons (Er, Onan, and Shelah) of Judah is described. In addition, each sexual intercourse of Judah with his wife in the narrative constitutes procreation, suggesting that the end of sexual relations is not only the bearing of children but also the ultimate purpose of Judah's marriage. It is fair to conclude that in these five verses (vv. 1–5) the narrator makes overt the pivotal role procreation plays in the Judah/Tamar narrative.[6] Moreover, Er's inability to beget offspring with Tamar will pose a big challenge to Judah's aspiration for progeny.

---

5   The root ל÷ק can denote 'to take, grasp, be carried away, to select/choose, to marry, to capture/seize', etc. See P. J. J. S. Els, *New International Dictionary of the Old Testament Theology and Exegesis* (NIDDOTTE), vol. 2, (Carlisle: Paternoster, 1996), 812–817. Obviously, the usage of ל÷ק here points to marriage. See Francis Brown *et al.*, *The Brown-Driver-Briggs Hebrew and English Lexicon of the Old Testament* (Oxford: Clarendon, 1952), 544. BDB, 544.

6   Unlike some authors like Steven Mathewson who see these first five verses as playing a subordinate and peripheral role in the pericope, the current reading agrees with someone like Esther Menn, who sees it as announcing the theme of the pericope and preparing the reader for what follows. See Steven D. Mathewson, 'An Exegetical Study of Genesis 38', *Bibliotheca Sacra* (1989): 376 and Esther Marie Menn, *Judah and Tamar (Genesis 38) in Ancient Jewish Exegesis: Studies in Literary Forms and Hermeneutics* (Leiden: Brill, 1997), 17 and Alexander Izuchukwu Abasili, 'Genesis 38: The Search for Progeny and Heir', *SJOT* 25, no. 2 (2011): 278.

The understanding of Judah's marriage to Shua's daughter as rooted in 'bearing of his heirs' resonates with an African emphasis on progeny. Just as the narrator depicts Judah's marriage to Shua's daughter and every sexual relationship in this narrative as primarily geared towards procreation, so are most marriages in several African contexts primarily geared towards begetting an heir for the family. In Igbo society of West Africa, for example, the begetting and training of children are the primary ends of marriage.[7] The social worth of the spouses flows from and depends on the idea of procreation. The perpetuation of the lineage is vital to the Igbo people, and marriage is the natural and cultural way of guaranteeing the survival of the lineage. For the Igbo people, according to Emmanuel Obunna, 'children are the uniting link in the rhythm of life guaranteeing the continuation of the family from one generation to the next'.[8] Begetting children, therefore, is a social and religious duty attached to marriage and is central to it. It is this centrality that informs the strong religious and social opinion against the use of contraceptives and the practice of abortion in Igbo society.[9] As Lucy Mair explains, the basis of this emphasis on procreation 'is that the religious values associated with sex are concentrated on procreation and not on sexual activity as such'.[10] Thus, sex between married couples is seen primarily as an act of procreation and not mere gratification.[11] With sex as an act of procreation par excellence, the idea of voluntary childlessness (often described as living *child-free* in marriage), seen in some parts of the world in which married couples for various reasons wittingly abstain from having children, may seem strange.[12] Among the Igbo people, for instance, every case of childlessness is not only involuntary but also a staggering problem to the couple in question, especially for the woman. In this type of cultural context, one wonders what would have become of a childless woman like Tamar.

7   Anthony Mary, *The Fifty Steps to Happy Marriage* (Owerri: Assumpta, 1999), 21.

8   Emmanuel Obuna, *African Priests and Celibacy* (Ibadan: Ambassador Books, 1986), 29.

9   Adiele Afigbo, 'Religion and Economic Enterprise in Traditional Igbo Society', in *Igbo History and Society: The Essays of Adiele Afigbo*, ed. Toyin Falola (Trenton, NJ: African World Press, 2005), 298.

10   Lucy Mair, *African Marriage and Social Change* (London: Frank Cass, 1969), 3.

11   Jomo Kenyatta, *Facing Mount Kenya: The Tribal Life of the Gikuyu* (London: Secker and Warburg, 1953), 163.

12   Diana Payette-Bucci, 'Voluntary Childlessness', *Direction* 17, no. 2 (1988): 37.

C. Tamar's Childlessness vis-à-vis the Childless Married African Woman—Genesis 38:6–10

Just as childlessness ignites tension in those African contexts where procreation is of utmost importance, so does it also initiate the first tension in the Judah/Tamar narrative (Gen. 38:6–10). In Genesis 38:6–10, the narrator tells us that Judah gets a wife for his first son Er: 'And Judah took a wife for Er his first-born and her name was Tamar' (v. 6). Of course, the transition from the birth of Judah's children (vv. 1–5) to the marriage of his first son (Er [vv. 6–10]) must have taken a reasonable number of years.[13] Perhaps the narrator skipped the intervening period because of his focus on procreation of Judah's progeny. Judah's finding a wife for Er to marry once more underlines his strong intent on guaranteeing his future generation. Judah's action fuels the expectation that Er's marriage to Tamar will lead to children.[14] However, the expectation of children remained unfulfiled because Er did 'what was evil in the eyes of YHWH and YHWH killed him'. Er's untimely death without an heir introduces narrative tension into the story. Judah's intent on having a progeny now hangs by a thin thread. At this stage of the narrative, Tamar has mourned her husband and is going into a second marriage, with the reader still hearing no word from her at this stage.

The narrator says nothing about the nature of Er's evil deed and his family mourning his death but goes straight to announce Judah's next move towards getting a progeny. As Robert Alter observes, 'Here, as at other points in the episode, nothing is allowed to detract our focused attention from the primary, problematic subject of the proper channel for the seed.'[15] Judah says to his second son, Onan (v. 8): 'Go into the wife of your brother and perform the duty of a brother-in-law to her; raise up offspring for your brother.'

By presenting Judah's words as an imperative and direct speech, the narrator underlines the importance of the continuity of progeny to Judah. Without wasting time, Judah orders Onan to step in and rescue the situation by begetting an offspring for Er, his brother.

---

13   Mathewson, 'An Exegetical Study of Genesis 38', 373.

14   Esther Marie Menn, *Judah and Tamar (Genesis 38) in Ancient Jewish Exegesis: Studies in Literary Form and Hermeneutics* (Leiden: Brill, 1997), 20.

15   Robert Alter, *The Art of Biblical Narrative* (New York: Basic Books, 1981), 6.

There are indications that Judah's command to Onan hinges on the law of Levirate, which makes it a duty of a widow's brother-in-law to raise a child for the deceased brother (Deut. 25:5–10). If Onan refuses to fulfil this duty, he will expose himself to a harmful public ridicule specifically reserved for a man 'who will not build up his brother's family line' (Deut. 25:7–8). Onan, without openly rejecting his father's command to beget a child for his deceased brother (maybe for fear of public ridicule), has intercourse with Tamar. But his obedience is only a facade. The narrator tells us that whenever (אם־בא)[16] Onan has intercourse with Tamar, he spills his semen on the ground because 'he knew that the child will not be his' (v. 9).

Since Onan consciously denies Tamar the possibility of procreation, it can be interpreted that he merely uses Tamar as an object of sexual gratification. The unjust implication of such action becomes more significant when interpreted against the background of the role of married women in patriarchal Israel society. In this regard, Susan Niditch notes that the primary duty of a married woman in ancient Israel is to bear children.

> Those who have trouble in producing offspring, like Sarah, Rebecca, and Rachel, are objects of scorn to the fruitful women in the clan (Gen 16:4). Moreover, they believe themselves cursed, the most unfortunate of women. Rachel's emotional outcry to Jacob, 'Give me children or I will die' (Gen 30:1), must be understood in this context (see also 1 Sam 1:6, 7).[17]

Against this backdrop, it is fair to assume that Onan's refusal to provide Tamar a means of conception is a grave injustice that exposes her to ridicule. Furthermore, unlike Sarah, Rebecca, and Rachel whose initial childlessness is natural, that of Tamar is caused by Onan's sexual injustice. But how does Tamar react? For her own part, Tamar says nothing. Perhaps her silence signals her powerlessness to correct Onan. As a woman in a patriarchal society, she can only wish and hope that Onan stops his sexual injustice and does what is right.

---

16 Following Driver's explanation, Mathewson holds that 'the constructionàíîáä should be understood as a frequentative use of the perfect and translated 'whenever he went in' instead of 'when he went in'. Mathewson, 'An Exegetical Study of Genesis 38', 377.

17 Susan Niditch, 'The Wronged Woman Righted: An Analysis of Genesis 38', *Harvard Theological Review* 72/1 (1979): 143–149.

The narrator tells us that 'what Onan did was evil in the sight of the YHWH and he also killed him' (v. 9). We note that this is the second time YHWH is appearing in this narrative, and in each occasion, he has killed one son of Judah. As Johanna Bos notes, this is surprising 'especially in the Genesis context where God is always portrayed as actively involved in the procreation of male offspring not its elimination'.[18] One wonders, What exactly is the crux of the matter? Is it Onan's monumental injustice to Tamar? Is it his act of spilling of the semen on the ground (coitus interruptus)? Is it his disobedience to his father by refusing to raise a child for his deceased brother Er? Even though coitus interruptus may not be approved in the Hebrew Bible, there are indications that Onan's refusal to provide progeny for his deceased brother Er is the crux of the matter.[19] There is some consensus among scholars on the reason for Onan's death.[20] Thus, it is not the **means** but the **end** of his action that is the bone of contention. Since Onan, by refusing to provide progeny for his brother, disobeyed his father and used Tamar unjustly as a mere object of sexual satisfaction, both transgressions are also (indirectly) implied in his death penalty. As Wenham notes, Onan's action thwarts the realization of YHWH's promise to the patriarchs of giving them numerous offspring (Gen. 17:6, 28:3, 35:11, 15:5, 22:17, 26:4, 32:13).[21] In addition, Onan's action goes against YHWH's command in the Decalogue to respect and honour one's parents (Exodus 20:12). Perhaps such transgression of YHWH's promise and law justifies Onan's death sentence.

Having lost two sons (Er and Onan) both of whom were married to Tamar, Judah is now left with Shelah, his last son. Naturally, he does not want to lose him and run the risk of having no progeny. Since Judah is ignorant of Onan's coitus interruptus and YHWH's action thereof, he perceives Tamar as his sons' agent of death (v. 11cd). From his point of view, marriage with Tamar leads to death.[22] As a result, he does not want to give Shelah to Tamar as prescribed by the customary (levirate) obligation.

---

18 Johanna W. H. Bos, 'An Eye Opener at the Gate: George Coats and Genesis 38', *Lexington Theological Quaterly* 27/4 (1992): 122.

19 Alexander Izuchukwu Abasili, 'Genesis 38: The Search for Progeny and Heir', *SJOT* 25/2 (2011): 280.

20 Gordon Wenham, *Genesis 16-50*, Word Biblical Commentary, vol. 2 (Dallas, TX: Word Book, 1994), 376. Thomas L. Brodie, *Genesis as Dialogue* (Oxford: Oxford University Press, 2001), 363.

21 Wenham, *Genesis 16-50*, 367.

22 Bos, 'An Eye Opener at the Gate: George Coats and Genesis 38', 119.

Instead, he sends Tamar home with this instruction:[23] 'Live as a widow in
your father's house until Shelah my son grows up.' In other words, he uses
Shelah's young age as an excuse. But the dilemma of Tamar's position is
that being a betrothed widow, she is not free to marry because the right
over the use of her sexuality belongs to her in-laws.[24] In other words,
she is neither in her in-law's house nor is she 'free' to use her sexuality.
Tamar, who until now has said nothing in the narrative, responds to Judah's
instruction with action. Hence, 'she went and dwelt in her father's house'.[25]
Her action depicts a childless widow who has no other legal option than to
obey her father-in-law's command.[26]

Tamar's plight of wallowing childless in a society that places emphasis
on procreation and where offspring (especially male) guarantees a woman's
security parallels the dilemma of the childless married African woman.[27]
In Igbo society, it is the dream of every woman not only to get married
but also to become a mother. Her inability to have children as a means
of acquiring mother status is detrimental both to her personality and her
social status. As Ikenga Metuh notes:

> Motherhood is a much sought-after status in most African
> societies. It is the dream and self-fulfilment of every African
> young woman. A woman who cannot or has not given birth is a
> social misfit. If she has never conceived, she is openly ridiculed
> and told that she is not a woman.[28]

It is only by becoming mothers that African wives in this kind of
context feel that their womanhood really being vindicated, authenticated,
and satisfied. In such African patrilineal societies, an almost similar fate
awaits a woman who has 'only' girls without boy(s). For instance, in Igbo
society, property inheritance (especially assets) is the exclusive right of the

---

23 Brodie, *Genesis as Dialogue*, 363.

24 Madipoane Masenya, 'Killed by Aids and Buried by Religion: African Female Bodies in
Crisis', *OTE* 19/2 (2006): 493.

25 Abasili, 'Genesis 38: The Search for Progeny and Heir', 281.

26 See Alter, *The Art of Biblical Narrative*, 7.

27 Dvora Weisberg has observed a contrast between men's reaction to levirate marriage and that
of women. Men reject it while women in search of lineage continuity and security are very
eager to embrace it (See Deut. 25:5–10; Ruth 4). See Dvora E. Weisberg, 'The Widow of Our
Discontent: Levirate Marriage in the Bible and Ancient Israel', *JSOT* 28/4 (2004): 406.

28 Emefie Ikenga Metuh, *Comparative Studies of African Religions* (Enugu: Snaap,
1999), 188.

male child.[29] Thus, a woman with female children but without a male child suffers, to a large extent, the plight of a childless woman. The extended family and cultural pressure make life unbearable for such a woman, and she runs the risk of losing her husband to a 'fruitful' woman. The 'lucky' ones are obliged to accept sharing their husbands with another woman in a polygamous family setup 'caused' by barrenness.[30] Against this unfair background, no woman wants to be childless or to have only female children. Those finding themselves in such a 'predicament' are ready to go the extra mile. From this perspective, Tamar's desperation in search of progeny is understandable to an African woman in this context (Gen. 38:12–26).

C. Tamar's Desperate Search for Offspring as a Mirror of the Desperation of Childless African Women—vv. 12–26

By introducing a time indicator—וירבו הימים ('many days later')—the narrator indicates the lapse of a reasonably lengthy period of time after Tamar was sent home.[31] The evident injustice of allowing her, a childless widow, to stay at her father's house without attention for such a long time is implied here.[32] But how desperate is Tamar to resolve her childlessness?

At this point of the narrative, the narrator tells us that Judah's wife died and he mourned her (Gen. 38:12). By revealing Judah's intention to go up and shear his sheep at Timnar, the narrator signals Judah's readiness to recommence with his normal activities. We may assume that Tamar sees Judah publicly assuming normal duties and responsibilities after mourning his wife as a veritable opportunity to take her destiny into her own hands and resolve her childlessness.[33] Tamar, one might argue, presumed that the death of her father-in-law's wife leaves him sexually starved and in search

---

29 See Ben Okwu Eboh, 'Feminism and African Cultural Heritage', *Journal of Inculturation Theology* 5/2 (2003): 134.

30 Emmanuel C. Uwalaka, *Towards Sustainable Happy Marriage: A Functional Approach* (Owerri: Danstaring 2008), 47.

31 Wenham, *Genesis 16–50*, 367.

32 Alter, *The Art of Biblical Narrative*, 7. See also Abasili, 'Genesis 38: The Search for Progeny and Heir', 281.

33 Abasili, 'Genesis 38: The Search for Progeny and Heir', 281.

of sexual gratification.[34] So she decided to try her luck with a trick.[35] On getting the news of Judah's intended movement, Tamar embarked on a plot (v. 14):

> Then Tamar removed her widow's clothing, and she covered herself with a veil and wrapped herself, and she sat in an open place, which is on the road to Timnar.

That Tamar made a concerted effort to conceal her real identity and disguise herself is evident in the combination of two verbs of concealment, הסכ ('to cover')[36] and ץלע (*hitp.*, 'to enwrap oneself'):[37] ותעלתו סכתו ויעצב ('and she covered herself with a wrap and enwrapped herself'). As I argued elsewhere, it is significant the measure Tamar took to conceal herself.[38] The narrator's parenthetic note ('because she saw that Shelah had grown up, but she was not given to him in marriage' v. 14f–h) reveals the reason and justification behind Tamar's action. She is motivated by Judah's failure to fulfil his promise of giving her to Shelah. She wants to resolve her dilemma and reinstate herself in a society that has no *real* place for a married but childless woman. In ancient Israel, as Niditch notes,

> The young woman is allowed only two proper roles. She is either an unmarried virgin in her father's home or she is a faithful, child-producing wife in her husband's or husband's family's home.[39]

It is clear that Tamar as a childless widow was in an awkward and very disadvantaged position.

The narrator tells us that 'when Judah saw Tamar, he thought her to be a harlot (זנה), for she had covered her face' (v. 15). Presuming Tamar to be a harlot, Judah immediately reveals his intention to have sexual intercourse with her. Tamar acting like a harlot requests for a price for her service. 'What will you give me to come into me?' (v. 16h). Judah without

---

34 Phyllis Bird, 'The Harlot as Heroine: Narrative Art and Social Presupposition in Three Old Testament Texts', *Semeia* 46 (1989): 123.

35 Bird, 'The Harlot as Heroine', 123.

36 BDB, 492.

37 BDB, 763.

38 Abasili, 'Genesis 38: The Search for Progeny and Heir', 281.

39 Niditch, 'The Wronged Woman Righted: An Analysis of Genesis 38', 145.

hesitation promises her a young goat. 'I will send you a young female goat from my flock' (v. 17). At this point, Tamar exploits her advantaged position and requests for Judah's signet ring, his cord, and his staff as a pledge till he brings the goat (vv. 17–18).[40] Judah's dire need for sexual gratification makes him hand over, without restraint, his signet ring, cord, and staff to the harlot (Tamar) as collateral. In the Ancient Near East, these personal items have immense value because they legally identify the owner.[41]

The narrator informs the reader that Judah, having fulfiled Tamar's demand, 'went into her and she conceived by him'. Without doubt, Tamar has succeeded in her ploy; she obtained her most sought-after means of survival: conceiving a child. At the same time, Judah satisfied his thirst for sexual gratification. Hence both (actor and actress) left the scene satisfied.[42]

Given the protracted discussion that transpired between Tamar and Judah, it is puzzling that he failed to recognize Tamar. Madipoane Masenya remarks the following:

> What makes one curious as one reads this part of the episode is whether since his proposition to Tamar as well as throughout their entire sexual encounter, Judah had no clue whatever that he was sharing his body with his daughter-in-law. Is this plausible?[43]

She wonders whether it is not 'a deliberate strategy used by the narrator to keep the language of this part of the story ambiguous?'[44] Alternatively, one may ask whether the narrator's consistent presentation of Judah's ignorance of Tamar's real identity is a strategy to force the reader to see the story in a particular way. Or perhaps it is indeed Judah's 'blindness' to Tamar's real identity that allows him to sleep with her and provide Tamar with a legitimate means of conception. Obviously, Judah's presumed ignorance of the 'harlot's' identity helped the progression of the narrative and may explain why the narrator opted for that angle of vision.

---

40   Abasili, 'Genesis 38: The Search for Progeny and Heir', 282.
41   Alter, *The Art of Biblical Narrative*, 9.
42   Abasili, 'Genesis 38: The Search for Progeny and Heir', 282.
43   Masenya, 'Killed by Aids and Buried by Religion: African Female Bodies in Crisis', 494.
44   Masenya, 'Killed by Aids and Buried by Religion: African Female Bodies in Crisis', 494.

The narrator tells us that Tamar, having successfully played the 'harlot', returns to her garments and status as a widow: 'She removed her veil from her and put on her widow's garments' (v. 19). Meanwhile, in fulfilment of his promise, Judah sends a young goat to the 'harlot' through his friend the Adullamite. Surprisingly, the temple prostitute (קדשה [v.20]) is nowhere to be found, and even questioning the townsfolk about her whereabouts yields nothing. Judah's inability to find the harlot (or temple prostitute as the Adullamite calls her) left him with only one option: to keep his goat and forgo his personal items. 'Let her keep it for herself' (v. 23b). With this statement, Judah laid to rest the story of his sexual intercourse with the 'harlot'.

The narrator begins the new episode (Gen 38:24–30) with a time indicator:ויהי כמשלש חדשים ('after three months'). In this way, he informs the reader that Tamar's conception has now become a visible pregnancy. The visibility of her pregnancy is confirmed by the accusatory report given to Judah: 'Tamar your daughter-in-law has committed sexual infidelity. And even, she is pregnant with a child through her sexual unfaithfulness' (v. 24). Without doubt, the report is judgmental and will have severe repercussions not only for Tamar but definitely also for Judah.[45] Since Tamar is a betrothed widow, only her in-laws have a right over her sexuality. Thus it is understandable that they would regard her pregnancy presumably as a result of marital infidelity.[46] As I noted elsewhere, 'with Tamar's pregnancy as a legal exhibit, obtaining the two or three witnesses required for condemning a person to death is very simple' (Deut. 17:6).[47] Obviously Tamar is in a serious predicament, ultimately facing the death penalty for adultery (Lev. 20:10; Deut. 22:21).

How does Judah react to the report? He picks up on the suggestion of adultery and condemns her to death: 'Then Judah said, 'Bring her out to be burned!' (ירשתו והאיצוה [v. 24]). Without hesitation, Judah pronounces a death sentence over Tamar.[48] The imperative nature of Judah's statement suggests that it is an authoritative command upon which people will react. The narrator tells the reader that Judah's command was eventually carried out by a willing anonymous (male) crowd. Once 'Tamar was brought out' (v. 25a), presumably,

---

45   Abasili, 'Genesis 38: The Search for Progeny and Heir', 283.
46   Wenham, *Genesis 16–50*, 368-369.
47   Abasili, 'Genesis 38: The Search for Progeny and Heir', 283.
48   Abasili, 'Genesis 38: The Search for Progeny and Heir', 284.

at the city gate (Deut. 22:21–24),[49] all that was left was the execution of the second and deadly part of Judah's order: 'to burn her to death'.[50] Tamar, now at the brink of death and up to now in the narrative since her encounter with Judah, very quite suddenly and quite openly offers a self-defense (v. 25).[51]

> Tamar sent to her father-in-law saying, 'by the man to whom these belong I am pregnant.' And she said, 'Take note please, whose signet ring, cord and staff are these?'

Her defense is a startling revelation. Tamar vindicates herself from the accusation of marital infidelity and succeeds in overturning the death sentence. Her defense constitutes a rather weighty statement, revealing to Judah that Tamar was indeed the harlot he 'went into'.[52] At this moment it dawns on Judah that by pronouncing death sentence on Tamar, he has in fact condemned himself.[53] Thus, it is Judah who is now in trouble. Unquestionably, 'his insignia have implicated him beyond reasonable doubt. Like a man fallen on his own sword, Judah says: "She is more righteous than me because I did not give her in marriage to Shelah my son (v.26).'"[54] Without mincing words, Judah pleads guilty and declares Tamar innocent. The narrator's explanatory statement, 'and he did not again sleep with her (*know her* [ידעתה])' once more underlines the unintentional nature of the first intercourse and assures the audience that Judah never had sexual intercourse again with Tamar. 'In this way, the narrator explains why Judah was not accused of incest (Lev. 18:15); he took Tamar for a harlot.'[55] Remarkably, Tamar's dubious means of obtaining legitimate means of conception is not condemned. One can argue that the gravity of the injustice she suffered vindicated her action.

At the end of the pericope, the narrator informs the reader that Tamar has twins (Perez and Zerah). Notably, the twins, being fathered by Judah, can now legitimately be regarded as the sons of her late husband, Er. So the hitherto childless woman is now blessed with twins; the once-abandoned

---

49   Claus Westermann, *Genesis: A Practical Commentary, Text and Interpretation*, trans. David E. Green (Grand Rapids, MI: Eerdmans, 1987), 269.

50   Abasili, 'Genesis 38: The Search for Progeny and Heir', 284.

51   Abasili, 'Genesis 38: The Search for Progeny and Heir', 284.

52   Niditch, 'The Wronged Woman Righted: An Analysis of Genesis 38', 148.

53   Abasili, 'Genesis 38: The Search for Progeny and Heir', 284.

54   Abasili, 'Genesis 38: The Search for Progeny and Heir', 284.

55   Abasili, 'Genesis 38: The Search for Progeny and Heir', 285.

widow is now a mother and reinstated in her husband's family. Hence, the story ends on a positive note for Tamar. She is not only a mother but she also provided a male progeny that ensures the survival of her husband's lineage.

There can be little doubt that married African childless women in a similar situation would dream to have the happy ending of Tamar. She is doubly blessed in having twins, and moreover, they are male! From a childless woman's perspective in a similar African context, Tamar's worries were entirely eradicated, and her joy fully restored. Nevertheless, since the means of conception for which Tamar finally opted (deceiving her father-in-law into sleeping with her) is not readily available to a childless Igbo woman. She has to look for a solution elsewhere. For instance, if a childless Igbo woman is a Christian, she may resort to praying for divine intervention. Praying as an instrument to heal barrenness leads to the search for a miracle in what is called prayer houses and 'miracle centers' that are littered throughout Igboland and Nigeria.

In the past, if the childless woman is a traditionalist, she might visit traditional healers and fulfil all the ritual prescriptions and sacrifices suggested by them. Nowadays, a good number of women in this predicament seek the help of orthodox medical practitioners. Meanwhile, as long as there is hope of acquiring a child, the husband will (or pretend to) be willing to participate in the search for a solution; but his resilience is not as enduring as his wife's perseverance. The husband's apparent lack of enthusiasm should not be mistaken for his manly acceptance of the situation. Indeed, for an Igbo man to die childless or without a male child is a calamity. In Igbo society, 'to die childless is tantamount to a descent into oblivion, to be forgotten by both the living and the dead. This is because such a person has left no heir to pour libation for him.'[56] As a result, faced with this terrible predicament in the famous Igbo novel, *Things Fall Apart,*

> Okonkwo felt a cold shudder run through him at the terrible prospect, like the prospect of annihilation. He saw himself and his father crowding round their ancestral shrine waiting in vain for worship and sacrifice and finding nothing but ashes of bygone days.[57]

---

56   Alexander I. Abasili, *Resolving the Dilemmas of Life: Way out When There Seems to be no Help and Hope* (Enugu: Snaap, 2004), 54.

57   Chinua Achebe, *Things Fall Apart* (Ibadan: Heinemann Educational Books, 1985), 108.

In addition, a man without progeny is not admitted into the prestigious status of an 'Igbo ancestor' after his death. Becoming an ancestor requires having children. African names like *Ahamefuna* ('my name shall not be lost' [an Igbo name]), *Kewan* ('marriage and everything parents do are for the child' [a name from Nso tribe of Cameroon]), *Nyamekye* ('a child is the highest gift to parents from God' [a name from Akans tribe of Ghana]) reveal the strong yearning for heir and progeny rooted in the desire for the continuance of the lineage.

To avert the calamity of dying childless or heirless, some men normally look for solution by either divorcing their wife and marrying a 'fruitful' one or in starting polygamy. The implication is that the husband is tacitly laying the blame of childlessness or the inability to provide a male heir on the wife; a presumption that is both unjust and sometimes unfounded. Indeed, not every case of childlessness can be ascribed to the woman, and only medical examination can identify the reasons for the failure to conceive. Medical science has revealed that some cases of childlessness and infertility are caused by sexually transmitted diseases (STD), poor ejaculation, low sperm count and/or poor ovulation.[58] When discovered early enough these can be cured medically. Regrettably, not all married African couples finding themselves in a context where progeny is regarded as the be all and end all of marriage seek the help of orthodox medical practitioners. Often it is women who bear the brunt of this neglect when orthodox medicine could have helped.

In addition, medical science has shown that the gender of a baby is a natural biological process for which women should not be blamed.[59] Research into preconception sex selection shows how difficult it is to manipulate this process.[60] Nonetheless, child adoption, which is a genuine solution to involuntary childlessness, is seldom seen, especially by men, as a viable solution. In some instances, child adoption is not appreciated because it

---

58 Sylvanus Okechukwu, *Christian Marriage and Genetic Engineering: A Dialogue* (Owerri: St John, 2001), 61.

59 As the analysis of gender-determination reveals, it is a chance process, and if anybody is to be 'blamed' for the gender of the baby, it is the man. Women have only two XX chromosomes, while men have XY. 'As a result, among the millions of sperms a man discharges during coitus, some have XY others XX, of which he will contribute X or Y to determine the sex of the fetus.' So in this 'chance process' of sex selection, it is the man that determines the sex of the baby, though unconsciously. See Uwalaka, *Towards Sustainable Happy Marriage: A Functional Approach*, 47.

60 Uwalaka, *Towards Sustainable Happy Marriage: A Functional Approach*, 47.

is regarded as a way to import a 'foreigner' into the lineage. It is always a reluctant last resort, which normally exposes the adopted child to ridicule later in life. Subsequently, parents who want to adopt do so secretly and paint a picture of bearing the child in question biologically. To this end, some mothers go as far as feigning pregnancy for nine months before adoption, and others take a long leave of absence from their family members.

Conclusion: The Contextual Implications of Judah/Tamar's Story for Today's Africans

Studying the Judah/Tamar narrative through the perspective of African women in a similar predicament indicates some positive contextual implications for addressing concrete unjust treatment of women in an African patriarchal society. Indeed, the parallel between the ordeal of Tamar (in Gen. 38) and the unjust treatment of childless (and maleless) African woman is in itself a critique of the status quo in Africa. Here are some of the contextual implications.

1. Marriage as Search for Progeny and Procreation is Minimalistic

The pericope of Genesis 38 began with procreation (v. 2) and ended with the birth of twins (vv. 27–30).[61] In all, five children were born within the scope of the narrative, and the narrator carefully underlined each of these births. Given the scope of the narrative, one can conclude that the overriding theme of Genesis 38 is the search for offspring or progeny.[62] This theme resonates with the emphasis on progeny in some African contexts. As a result, begetting children defines the success of marriage. Thus, a childless marriage is regarded as a bad omen, and societies, when being mainly patriarchal, often lay the blame on women (wives).

However, in the present global context, this approach to marriage is no longer satisfying. Based on the well-being of the couple and on today's economic exigencies, such an approach to marriage and sex is questionable. Marital sexual intercourse should not merely be reduced

---

61   Menn, *Judah and Tamar*, 15.
62   Abasili, "Genesis 38: The Search for Progeny and Heir', 285.

to its procreative function. It constitutes a minimalistic view of the use of human sexuality. Companionship and mutual assistance between married partners are a vital purpose of marriage that also deserves attention. Even without children (resulting from causes beyond a couple's control), the companionship of married couples rooted in love constitutes enough grounds for happy married life. In addition, defining marriage solely on the basis of its procreative function strips marriage of some of its vital aspects and meaning. It reduces married women to child-producing machines. Hence, just as a machine is discarded when it stops fulfiling its designated function, so women are discarded when they cannot bear children, especially, male ones. Married women are valuable for who they are, not merely for their procreative function. However, the realization that a childless marriage remains a good marriage and retains its core and happiness remains in stark contrast with the status quo in many patriarchal societies.

2. Patriarchalism Should Be Replaced with Marital Justice and Sexual Fairness

In spite of the vital role played by Tamar in this pericope (Gen. 38), her voice is never heard. Without fear of contradiction, Tamar emotionally suffered more than any other character in Genesis 38: she lost Er, her first husband; she was unjustly denied a means of procreation by Onan (her second husband); she suffered the death of her second husband, Onan; she was unjustly sent back to her father's house by Judah to wallow childless for a long time; and later, she was innocently condemned to death. But the narrator, apart from her self-defense, never allowed her to express her feelings. The treatment of Tamar in this narrative parallels the ordeal of many married childless women especially in patriarchal society.

The patriarchal inclination that makes women speechless and powerless in matters that affect them is rejected by article 1 of Universal Declaration of Human Rights: 'All human beings are born free and equal in dignity and rights.' Hence, the gender difference in expectations, rights, rewards, duties and obligations of married couples in Africa which tilts in favor of men is no longer acceptable. YHWH's punishment of Onan with death for his sexual injustice against Tamar for denying her a means of conception signals his condemnation of sexual injustice against women and his support for fairness in the treatment of (childless and maleless) married women. The implication is that sexual intimidation, exploitation, and coercion perpetrated against women in marriage is unacceptable.

3. The Unjust Punishment of Women in a Patriarchal Society

Judah's first declaration of Tamar as guilty of adultery ('Bring her out to be burned!' [v. 24]), his later withdrawal of the sentence (based on Tamar's indisputable proof), and his acceptance of complicity ('she is more righteous than me' [v. 26]) suggest that men in patriarchal society sometimes blame women for their mistakes (Gen. 38:24–26). Men sometimes use their advantaged position in the patriarchal society unjustly against women.[63] For example, in Igbo society, some men tacitly blame women for childlessness and bearing of only female children—an action tantamount to holding them responsible for the biological process of gender selection, as if it is in their power to choose their children's gender. Such action is against the UN Convention on the Elimination of All Forms of Discrimination against Women of December 1979 (article 1 [CEDAW]).[64] Against this backdrop, unjust accusations of women and the appreciation of male over female children need to be seriously questioned. In children's value, there is neither male nor female.

4. Asymmetry in Sexual Freedom in Favour of Men is Questionable

There are indications that Judah, as a male in patriarchal society, enjoys more sexual freedom and rights than Tamar. For the satisfaction of his sexual desires, he freely meddles with a 'harlot', even in the presence of his friend, the Adullamite. All he needs to do is to satisfy the emolument demand by the harlot for her sexual services. The narrator's refusal to

---

63   Adrian Thatcher, *Marriage after Modernity: Christian Marriage in Postmodern Times* (New York: New York University Press, 1999), 45.

64   The constitution of most African countries prohibits discriminations against women. For instance, Nigerian constitution (section 15.2) rejects any discrimination in treatment of persons based on their sex.

condemn Judah's action tacitly signals the acceptance of such behaviour from men in patriarchal biblical Israelite society. In other words, Judah can have intercourse with a harlot to satisfy his sexual desires and she can conceive, but he has no obligation towards her and the children.

Conversely, Tamar lacks such sexual freedom. As a betrothed widow, Tamar's sexuality is under the control of her husband's family. She has no right and power over her sexuality. Since her husband is dead, it is Judah (the *pater familias*) who is in charge of her sexuality and decides her sexual partner. Even while dwelling in her father's house at the order of Judah, she is neither free to marry nor 'free' to exercise her sexuality (Gen. 38:10). No wonder her 'unauthorized' sexual intercourse is tantamount to adultery warranting the death sentence (Gen. 38:24). Certainly, from a contemporary perspective such a lopsided treatment of sexuality is unjust.

Unfortunately, such sexual inequality in the treatment of men and women is still existent today. For instance, although constitutionally adultery is banned for male and female,[65] in praxis some men treat it almost as only a married woman's sin in Igboland (and some other patriarchal societies). The sexual injustice inherent in asymmetrical treatment of sexuality (in marriage) in favour of men is grave and unacceptable. In the use of sexuality, both married men and women have equal right and power over each other's sexuality and have equal claim to damages in the event of marital infidelity. The threat posed by sexually transmitted diseases (STD), especially HIV/AIDS, in Africa calls for responsible use of sexuality and sexual fairness among married people. No married person has the right to endanger a partner's life through sexual promiscuity.

5. **Tamar's Fight for Justice as Model for Subjugated Women**

Melisa Jackson brands Tamar a trickster,[66] but I perceive her as a brave and courageous woman who stops at nothing in her fight for justice. She suffered injustice in a world dominated by men, but she was resilient to injustice and courageous in fighting against it. This is evident in her

---

65 In the Nigerian law, adultery refers to the voluntary extramarital sexual relationship between a married man or woman with any other man or woman not his wife or her husband. Hence, it is gender symmetrical. See 'Matrimonial Causes Act' in *Laws of the Federation of Nigeria 1990, Chapter 220*, section 15, 2 (b).

66 See Melissa Jackson, 'Lot's Daughters and Tamar as Trickstars and the Patriarchal Narratives as Feminist Theology', *JSOT* 98 (2002): 30–32.

decision to conceal her noble identity as a wife and assume the despicable identity of a harlot (זנה) for the sole purpose of obtaining justice from Judah, her father-in-law. Even though deception is not a virtue, the narrator's parenthetic note ('because she saw that Shelah had grown up but she was not given to him in marriage' v. 14f–h) justifies Tamar's actions and leaves us without any doubt about her options for obtaining justice.[67] Tamar's success in deceiving Judah and obtaining means of conception is a triumph of justice over injustice for women in a patriarchal society.

To African women in particular and women living in patriarchal society in general, Tamar is a model for courageous fight against injustice and male subjugation in such a society. Tamar's success against all odds suggests that if they keep up the fight for justice and their right, they will succeed not only in obtaining justice but also in changing the unjust status quo.

6. The Dream of Bearing Biological Children Needs the Support of Adoption

By tricking Judah into sleeping with her, Tamar eventually resolves and solves her ordeal of searching for a male heir for Er (Gen. 38:11–23). From the African perspective, one wonders, What would have happened if her twins had both been girls? Luckily, she bore two baby boys, and her joy at their birth is infectious and completely wipes away her sorrows. Such is the dream of every married African woman: to be able to bear not only their own children but also a male child (children). However, it is paradoxical that African society (for instance Igbo society), where barrenness and a woman's inability to bear a baby boy are treated as a calamity, does not see child adoption as a viable solution to barrenness. Nonetheless, research has shown that, apart from biologically *bearing* one's children, adoption is the second viable alternative to becoming parents.[68] This option assumes a higher value in a society like Igboland where having (at least) a child is a sine qua non in every marriage. In such a society, it is very reasonable for childless parents to adopt a child. It is better and easier solution than divorce and polygamy. Surely nurturing a child who calls one father or

---

67   Westermann, *Genesis: A Practical Commentary*, 269.

68   Brent Waters, *Ethics and Technology: Towards a Theology of Procreative Stewardship* (Wiltshire: Longman, 2001), 70.

mother from very early childhood to adulthood constitutes in a real sense 'parenting' and makes a couple a real father and mother.

Bibliography

Abasili, Alexander I. 'Genesis 38: The Search for Progeny and Heir.' *SJOT* 25/2 (2011): 275–287.

———. *Resolving the Dilemmas of Life: Way out When There Seems to be no Help and Hope.* Enugu: Snaap, 2004.

Achebe, Chinua. *Things Fall Apart.* Ibadan: Heinemann Educational Books, 1985.

Afigbo, Adiele. 'Religion and Economic Enterprise in Traditional Igbo Society'. in *Igbo History and Society: The Essays of Adiele Afigbo.* Edited by Toyin Falola. Trenton, NJ: African World Press, 2005.

Alter, Robert. *The Art of Biblical Narrative.* New York: Basic Books, 1981.

Bird, Phyllis. 'The Harlot as Heroine: Narrative Art and Social Presupposition in Three Old Testament Texts'. *Semeia* 46 (1989): 119–139.

Bos, Johanna W. H. 'An Eye Opener at the Gate: George Coats and Genesis 38'. *Lexington Theological Quaterly* 27/4 (1992): 119–123.

Brown, Francis, Charles A. Briggs, and S. R. Driver. *The Brown-Driver-Briggs Hebrew and English Lexicon of the Old Testament.* Oxford: Clarendon, 1952.

Brodie, Thomas L. *Genesis as Dialogue.* Oxford: Oxford University Press, 2001.

Els, P. J. J. S. *New International Dictionary of the Old Testament Theology and Exegesis* (NIDDOTTE), vol. 2, Carlisle: Paternoster, 1996.

Eboh, Ben O. 'Feminism and African Cultural Heritage'. *Journal of Inculturation Theology* 5/2 (2003): 123–140.

Enuwosa, Joseph. 'African Cultural Hermeneutics: Interpreting the New Testament in a Cultural Context'. *Black Theology* 3/1 (2005): 88–98.

Falola, Toyin, ed. *Igbo History and Society: The Essays of Adiele Afigbo.* Trenton, NJ: African World Press, 2005.

Jackson, Melissa. 'Lot's Daughters and Tamar as Trickstars and the Patriarchal Narratives as Feminist Theology.' *JSOT* 98 (2002): 29–46.

Kenyatta, Jomo. *Facing Mount Kenya: The Tribal Life of the Gikuyu*. London: Secker and Warburg, 1953.

Mair, Lucy. *African Marriage and Social Change*. London: Frank Cass, 1969.

Mary, Anthony. *The Fifty Steps to Happy Marriage*. Owerri: Assumpta, 1999.

Masenya, Madipoane. 'Killed by Aids and Buried by Religion: African Female Bodies in Crisis'. *OTE* 19/2 (2006): 486–499.

Mathewson, Steven D. 'An Exegetical Study of Genesis 38'. *Bibliotheca Sacra* (1989): 373–392.

Menn, Esther M. *Judah and Tamar (Genesis 38) in Ancient Jewish Exegesis: Studies in Literary Form and Hermeneutics*. Leiden: Brill, 1997.

Metuh, Emefie I. *Comparative Studies of African Religions*. Enugu: Snaap, 1999.

Niditch, Susan. 'The Wronged Woman Righted: An Analysis of Genesis 38'. *Harvard Theological Review* 72/1 (1979): 143–149.

Obuna, Emmanuel. *African Priests and Celibacy*. Ibadan: Ambassador Books, 1986.

Okechukwu, Sylvanus. *Christian Marriage and Genetic Engineering: A Dialogue*. Owerri: St John, 2001.

Payette-Bucci, Diana. 'Voluntary Childlessness'. *Direction* 17/2 (1988): 26–41.

Polzin, Robert. 'The Actress of Israel in Danger'. *Semeia* 3 (1975): 81–98.

Richter, Wolfgang. *Biblia Hebraica Transcripta: Genesis*. Vol. 33.1. St Ottilien: Erzabetei, 1991.

Robinson, Robert B. 'Wife and Sister through the Ages: Textual Determinacy and the History of Interpretation'. *Semeia* 62 (1993): 103–128.

Sharon, Diana M. 'Some Results of Structural Semiotic Analysis of the Story of Judah and Tamar'. *JSOT* 29/3 (2005): 289–318.

Uchendu, Victor. *The Igbo of Southeast Nigeria*. Chicago: Holt, Rinehart and Winston, 1965.

Ukpong, Justin S. 'Developments in Biblical Interpretation in Africa: Historical and Hermeneutical Directions'. In *The Bible in*

Africa: Transactions, Trajectories and Trends. Edited by Gerald West and Musa W. Dube. Leiden: Brill, 2000, 11–28.

Uwalaka, Emmanuel C. *Towards Sustainable Happy Marriage: A Functional Approach.* Owerri: Danstaring, 2008.

Waite, Linda J., and Maggie Gallagher. *The Case for Marriage: Why Married People as Happier, Healthier, and Better Off Financially.* New York, NY: Doubleday, 2000.

Weisberg, Dvora E. 'The Widow of Our Discontent: Levirate Marriage in the Bible and Ancient Israel'. *JSOT* 28/4 (2004): 403–429.

Wenham, Gordon. *Genesis 16–50.* Vol. 2 of Word Biblical Commentary. Dallas, TX: Word Book, 1994.

Westermann, Claus. 'Structure and Intention of the Book of Ruth.' *W&W* 19/3 (1999): 285–302.

Chapter Four

Coloured Beauty and Harmony of Creation: A. J. V. Obinna's Poetics on New Epiphany of Creation

Stephen C. Egwim

Introduction

As a poet and an academic, A. J. V. Obinna's theological reflections have for some years now been driven by two experiences he recounts he had: (1) within two hours of celebrating Mass on March 25, 1988, being the feast of the Annunciation of the conception of Jesus, the Son of God to the Blessed Virgin Mary and (2) a few months after the first experience. He articulated the experiences in two poems reproduced here below as poem A and poem B respectively. These experiences have so driven and inspired his recent theological reflections that one may not fully understand him without first understanding the said experiences and what they meant for him. The understanding helps one to grasp and appreciate the message he has been bringing to the public discourse through his theological themes drawn from and linked to his pet concept—theofiliation.

This write-up presents a study of Obinna's poetic articulation of the two experiences. The study will try to identify what type of experiences they are and relate them to other documented experiences similar to them so as to identify and highlight anything that might be unique to them. The study will also try to find out what the experiences meant for him and their connection to his recent theological reflections as a way of helping to understand and appreciate his message.

Theoretical Considerations

The analysis of literary texts, in general, involves the study of their context/setting, structure, literary devices or elements, discourse patterns, unity, coherence, etc. The things are perceived and comprehended in terms of their shape (head, body, and foot) or in terms of their structure (introduction/ beginning, main body, and conclusion/end). A text, like a speech, is a communication with a beginning (introduction) and an end (conclusion). In between the beginning and the end is the communication proper, which presents main issues, message(s), or viewpoints being put forward. A text or speech does not go on and on without end. It has an end, and its end is neither impulsive nor arbitrary and is not brought about by an interruption of a new flow of words from another text or speaker. It ends deliberately and purposefully at that point when the intended message or viewpoint being put forward is believed to have been completed.

A theoretical approach to text analysis, whether poetic or prose text, helps to see how it has been structured and how its structures function.[1] Structure defines and gives meaning to a thing. Different structures give different meanings. So an author or writer develops and presents his views and ideas in a pattern or in a structure that gives his text his intended meaning. The making of a text, therefore, is constructural and architectural: it has tools and building materials and is built according to plan. Ferdinand de Saussure, the father of modern linguistics, maintained that every language is a unique structure or system and that the units— sounds, words, or meanings—derive their essence and existence purely from their relationship to other units in the same language system.[2] It is a

---

1 Julian Wolfreys, "Introduction: Border Crossings, Or Close Encounters of the Textual Kind,' in *Literary Theories: A Reader and Guide*, Julian Wolfreys, ed., New York, NY: New York University Press, 1999, 1-14, 2-3. Wolfreys discourses the views of Terry Eagleton on literary theory. See Terry Eagleton, Literary Theory: An Introduction, Oxford, 1983.

2 Ferdinand de Saussure, *Cours de Linguistique Generale* (Paris, 1916). English translation: *Course in General Linguistics* (New York, NY: Philosophical Library, 1959); (London:

system in which words and phrases are structural or building elements at the sentence level, while sentences are structural elements at the text or discourse level.

Structure is the mutual relation of the constituent parts or elements of a thing in its wholeness or completeness. The structure of a literary text may, therefore, be said to be the manner of arrangement or organization of its dependent parts and the logic of the links between them as a whole. The analysis of any literary text requires the study of its structure to discover its artistic elements and its artistic qualities and the openings they bring to the overall understanding of the text. The understanding of a text from the point of view of its structure is known as the structural approach, where emphasis is placed on describing linguistic features in terms of structure and systems as the study of mutual relation of the constituents, parts, or elements of the whole in a field of study so as to determine its nature, character, or features. The area of structural approach that is relevant to us here is the study of the mutual relations that are inherent in the discourse structures and pragmatic features that characterize Obinna's poetics on a new epiphany of creation.

According to Peter Cotterall and Max Turner, a speaker or writer communicates his or her meaning through the fine texturing of the verbal structure of his or her material. For them, the considerations of the different ways smaller units like individual prepositions cluster together to make larger ones, how these larger units relate in turn to one another to make up whole discourse, and the issue of personal style are relevant to the understanding of a text. The texturing of the verbal structure depends on the kind of language employed by the speaker or writer. The language could be literal, metaphorical, affective, etc. It is part of the task of interpretation to discover the kind of language employed. Where the language is metaphorical, decision is to be taken to determine what correspondence with reality is intended. Where the language is affective, effort is made to gauge its significance. The speaker's or writer's texturing of his or her verbal structure involves his choice of words. In view of this, the task of interpretation will have to deal with questions such as, Why has he chosen this particular word here rather than another with closely related meaning? In what ways might such and such a proposition relate to those

Owen, 1960).

around it, and what signals are there in the text to suggest one possibility is more probable than another?[3]

Discourse analysis attempts to study the organization and actual mechanism by which communication, understanding, and interaction are maintained by the speaker-hearer above the clausal and sentential levels.[4] The theories of Grimes[5] and that of Beaugrande and Dressler[6] are relevant here. The one focuses on elements of event and non-event acts, while the other focuses on cohesion and coherence in text or discourse.

Grimes' theory of events and non-events divides a text into its constituent parts and discusses what could be called events or happenings and non-events consisting of setting, background, evaluative, and collateral features in a text. Three important components at the heart of Grimes' study of discourse are content, cohesion, and staging with emphasis on the interplay between them. Content refers to the semantic structure of the text, cohesion refers to how a new piece of information is related to the given, while setting or staging is the viewpoint used by the poet or narrator in his presentation of information.

Beaugrande and Dressler's theory of cohesion and coherence prominentizes elements that combine in making a text unified and meaningful. Relevant to our work here are three important concepts in discourse analysis covered in the theory. They are informativity (the way we balance old against new information), situationality (the relevance of a text to its situational setting), and intertextuality (the relevance of a text to other texts).

Context is the sociological and historical setting of the text. No string of words can be contextless because every string of words is produced by someone, somewhere, and somehow. According to Cotterell and Tuner, contextualization was central to the semantic theories of J. R. Firth, and it consisted in the identification of the total context of any utterance. For Firth, the correct identification of context is important in the determination of author's/speaker's intended meaning.[7]

---

3   Peter Cotterell and Max Turner, *Linguistics and Biblical Interpretation* (Downers Grove: IL: InterVarsity Press, 1989), 32.

4   B. Okolo, Topic 'Shading in an Unplanned Igbo Discourse', *Studies in African Linguistics* vol. 18, no. 2 (1987): 212.

5   Joseph E. Grimes, *The Thread of Discourse, Mouton: The Hague*, 1967.

6   Robert-Alain de Beaugrande and Wolfang U. Dressler, *Introduction to Text Linguistics* (United Kingdom, UK: Longmans, 1981).

7   Cotterell and Turner, *Linguistic and Biblical Interpretation*, 41.

According to Cotterell and Turner, the synchronic and diachronic studies of language guide us against 'the error of thoughtlessly explaining one writer's use of a word, by reference to another person's use of the "same" word, and the error of explaining one person's use of a word by reference to how it was used by someone else and at a different time.'[8] In fact 'the speech of the individual is a complex blend of the idiosyncratic and the commonplace, a mixture of words pronounced and employed as no one else does, and words pronounced and employed more or less as most other people do'.[9] There are individual idiotics, common/collective dialect, and language as there are idiotics of same dialect, dialects of same language, and commonalities of languages.[10]

The meaning, cohesion, and coherence in Obinna's use of commonalities and individual idiotics in the textual structuring of his poems will be seen in the synchronic and diachronic analysis that will come after the contextual background and foreground of his poems.

Obinna's Poetics on New Epiphany of Creation
Poem A

1. Out of my *nightly shed*
   I *stepped* out
2. ***Gazed*** heaven-ward
   And *stood arrested*
   By <u>sky-blue beauty</u>
3. I *lowered* my ***gaze***
   It *was* <u>green-beauty</u> all-over
4. I *tuned* to the trees
   It *was* <u>chirping-melody</u>
   From <u>colour-spiced</u> birds
5. I ***glanced*** earth-ward
   And *smiled* to discover
   My own <u>colour – earth colour</u>
6. I *shook* my head
   In believing <u>awe</u>

---

8   Cotterell and Turner, *Linguistic and Biblical Interpretation*, 25–26.
9   Cotterell and Turner, *Linguistic and Biblical Interpretation*, 19.
10 Cotterell and Turner, *Linguistic and Biblical Interpretation*, 20.

7. I had *caught* that moment
   When God *took* a ***look***
   At everything He *made* –
   It *was* so <u>beautiful</u>.

A few months later, a familiar tree appeared differently to him and he added:

Poem B

1. There it *stands*
   Majestic
   In all its green freshness
2. *Reaching* out this way and that
   Inviting all to its shade
3. Instantly a line egret *alights*
   Responding as I *am*
   To the invitation.[11]

Background to the Poems and the Experiences That Gave Rise to Them

Things do not happen in isolation. More often than not, something leads to another or something is the reason why another is or occurs. In this case, what was the causal background or reason why Obinna experienced his 'new epiphany of creation'? What was the historical or life context, the *Sitz im Leben* ('the setting in life') of this epiphany in the lived life of Obinna? These questions do not call for reflective postulation but for data and facts.

Poems, like psalms, are verbal articulations of individuals expressive of their inward disposition, which might be their inner mood, their feelings, or their perceptions. Moods, feelings, and deceptions, as inward realities domicile in the individual, are merely subjective realities. They are not external events, data or facts that can be objectively verified. As subjective realities, only the individual that experience them can give expression

---

11 Versification of the two poems and all emphases are mine and are added to direct our study.

to them. When they are expressed in poems, they form the immediate background that give rise to the poems. The poems they give rise to also reflect and give expression to them. The subjective data and facts that form the life setting to Obinna's poems are to be sieved from Obinna's narratives of his subjective experience of a 'new epiphany of creation'.

In one of his many unpublished public lectures, Obinna writes: 'In 1988, six years after the ruin of creation in my lived-reflective experience, I was beside myself in joy as the whole of creation re-appeared visibly around me ... in riveting splendour. I burst out into celebration.'[12] This highlights the six years of 'lived-reflective experience of the ruin of creation in the life of Obinna' as the background, the life setting, or the existential context of his experience of a new epiphany of creation. We are dealing here with someone who is good in coining words and constructing concepts and phrases. We need to pay further attention to what he calls lived-reflective experience. This is a three-word clause construction, and the key word or term there is *reflective*. The term *reflective* places or locates the whole thing at the mental level as a mental state of intellection, reflection, and research. This is brought out clearer in his informal unwritten speech to the Owerri Provincial Catholic graduates at an informal evening interaction during their 2013 annual reunion precisely on Saturday, the tenth of August 2013 where he said: 'On the 25th of March, 1988 when I thought and had all things fallen apart, I was going down delusion because I tried to understand God and the Universe via research and radical questioning; I fell into an abyss.' The key word again here is *thought*— 'when I thought'. It was a thought, a mental intellectual effort to do what? 'To understand God and the Universe via research and radical questioning.' The result of the effort was failure.

In the secular world, ideas matter because ideas rule the world. Ideas are fruits of thought, intellection, intellectual investigation, or research. Why did these fail to produce in the above case ideas of the understanding of God and the universe? The answer to this question is found in another unpublished public lecture given by Obinna where he writes: 'Shaken up at some stage in my own life by the imperiousness of science, philosophy and egoism while smarting under the wounds of colonialism, racism and contempt for Africa, my faith in Christ was subjected to severe test, as

---

12   A.J.V. Obinna, *Confiliatory Collaboration between the Church in Africa and Europe: A Theo-Filio-Logical Background*, 6.

I was tempted towards a world of meaninglessness, nothingness and bitterness.'[13] The effort failed because it was not backed by strong faith due to the negative influence of science, philosophy, and egoism as well as colonialism, racism, and contempt for Africa. The effort did not just fail; it caused 'things to fall apart' and the things kept falling 'down delusion' because there was no more cohesion until the 'abyss' was reached—the 'world of meaninglessness, nothingness and bitterness'. It was six years of experience lived and reflected up on.

Foreground to the Experience and the Poems

Obinna's state of mind after the experience of a 'new epiphany of creation' was one of rescue and reaffirmation of faith. Referring to the effect the experience had on him, Obinna writes, 'By God's grace a rescue and a re-affirmation of my faith in Christ has occurred.'[14] It was an experience that led to a change in Obinna's state of life—a deliverance from bitterness to joy, from the bitterness of nothingness to the joy of riveting splendour. As he puts it, 'I was beside myself with joy as the whole of creation re-appeared visibly around me ... in riveting splendour.'[15] As an interiorized experience or state of mind, 'the radiation of God's filiation to humanity with the Annunciation event so glowed in me that my whole being became ecstatic: I had caught that moment when God took a look at everything he made it was so beautiful.'[16] This was the source of his joy.

Poem B is a reflection of that joy. In it, Obinna gave a joyful expression to his realization that the new insight he received was not meant for him alone but for all. The invitation to see things as they are, as God made them and as God intended is an invitation to one and to all. That which arrested him is meant to arrest everyone.

---

13 A. J. V. Obinna, *Culture, Human Development and the New Creation Dynamic*. A keynote address presented at the Fourth Annual Convention of the Catholic Biblical Association of Nigeria (CABAN) held at the Seat of Wisdom Seminary, Owerri, on October 20, 2011, 5.

14 Obinna, *Culture, Human Development and the New Creation Dynamic*, 5.

15 Obinna, *Confiliatory Collaboration between the Church in Africa and Europe*, 6.

16 Obinna, *Culture, Human Development and the New Creation Dynamic*, 5.

Content of the Poems

The text of poem A as given above is composed of nineteen lines or cola divided unevenly into seven verses or stanzas.

v.1. <u>Out</u> of my ***nightly shed***

I stepped <u>out</u>

Out, the first word of poem A is a locational deixis. As a locational deixis, it indicates where Obinna is: he is out of his nightly shed; he is not in it. The second ***out*** at the end of the second line reiterates the first ***out*** and adds emphasis on the location. What Obinna presents himself in verses 2–5 to have done from the stated location agrees with that location. That is, they are things that can be done only from that location. The ***nightly*** in nightly ***shed*** is an attributive descriptive adjective describing shed and attributing night or darkness to it. A nightly shed as implying darkness can mean the darkness or lack of sight, of insight, of knowledge or the presence of ignorance. Only from a location out of nightly shed, out of darkness, of an enclosure, of a house, or of anything that obstructs or blurs physical vision and sight is one able to look up and see the sky-blue beauty of heaven or the firmament (v. 2), look down and see the greenishness of vegetation (v. 3), look straight and see the trees and the birds (v. 4), and look at the soil and realize that the earth has one's skin colour (v. 5). These graphic presentation of physical objects of sight can as well be Obinna's verbal expressions of an inward insight, which he gained through intellectual inquiry, reflection, mental search, or research, which cleared his bush or darkness of ignorance and opened him up to knowledge, insight, or inward realization.

Nightly shed may be read as a metonymy as well as a temporal deixis (of time). As a metonymy, it substitutes for night or darkness ***out*** of which is day or light in which one can see things in their different shapes, sizes, and colours. As a temporal deixis, 'Out of my nightly shade' implies morning or daytime. Its temporal sense is complemented by the temporal particle—***when*** in verse 7, line 2—that, as a chronological conjunction[17], linked a present event to a past event: the present event of Obinna's sight of goodness (beauty) in creation and God's past sight of goodness in his

---

17　Gary A. Long, *Grammatical Concepts 101 for Biblical Hebrew: Learning Biblical Hebrew Grammatical Concepts through English Grammar* (MA: Peabody, Hendrickson, 2002), 33.

creation. The last three lines likened Obinna's present moment of visual experience or insight to the Genesis account of the moment God looked at each thing he created and saw that they are good.

On getting out of his nightly shed, Obinna is arrested not just by the things he saw but by their colour: sky blue, green, colour-spiced birds, and earth colour, which constitutes their beauty. Colour is a principle of differentiation in physical visible material things, especially when and where things are differently coloured. Each colour has its own beauty in its finest form. They also radiate another beauty when the colours blend together in their difference in any ecstatic form in different things or parts of a thing such as the colour-spiced birds. The green colour is said to signify life, the blue colour signifies peace, while the earth colour— chocolate colour—signifies neutrality.

The poems are written in free verse like most African poems. They may be considered to be lyrics, haiku, or ode poems. As lyrics, they express the observations and feelings of a single speaker—the author. They concentrate on describing particular moments or experiences of the speaker. As haiku poems, they make nature their subject and use simple but powerful imagery to show the all in the small, the world in a grain of sand. And as Ode poems, they address a particular subject-matter— nature—in a praise manner.[18]

Poetic Devices

As a free verse, the poems do not have regular metrical pattern, rhythm, or end-rhyme. In poem A, there is repetition of *out* in lines 1 and 2; *gazed/gaze* in lines 3 and 6; *beauty* in lines 5, 7, and 19; and *colour* in lines 10 and 13. And there is metaphor—nightly shed—in line 1. In poem B, the object of vision, the tree, is personification all through. *There* in line 1 is adverbial accusative of place/location[19]; *majestic* (honorific) in line 2; *green freshness* and in line 3; *line egret* (metaphor).

The poems extol the wonder and beauty of creation as is evident in the expression of awe, wonder, delight, and response. Their mood is hilariously

---

18   Obasi Kelechi Nkwocha, *Understanding Poetry: Analyses of Selected Poems Based on WASSCE/NECO Syllabus* (Port Harcourt: M & J Grand Orbit, n.d.), 3–7.

19   Long, *Grammatical Concepts*, 129.

full of excitement and delight with a tone that is exclamatory, entertaining, and inviting, expressing pleasant satisfaction with the rediscovery of the wonder of creation in its original or prime time beauty.

Poem B is figurative. The implied tree is given human characteristics. 'Reaching out this way and that' and invitations are activities typical of humans. It is a reaching out to people/things near and people/things far. 'A line egret' is metaphoric. Egret is of the bird family. Though singular as used, the clause 'a line egret' makes it plural, implying more than one as one or alone egret cannot form or make a line. The reference to line is metaphoric, signifying that the flight formation of the egret is straight characteristic of a line.

Poetic Structure

Poem A presents five main incidences: (1) change of location from a sight-impaired location to a sight-enabled location, (2) consequence of the change in location, (3) cause of the consequence, (4) further consequence, and (5) benefit of the change in location. The poetic structure may thus be given as the following:

> v. 1ab Moment of sight
> > v. 2b Arrestedness by what appears in sight
> > > v. 2c Sky-blue beauty seen heavenward
> > > v. 3ab Green beauty
> > > v. 4abc Colour-spiced birds
> > > v. 5abc My own colour—earth colour
> > v. 6ab Believing awe as a result of what is seen
> > v. 7abcd Moment of awareness of heaven seen as God saw

The resultant chiastic structure of the poem is the following:

> **A** v. 1ab Moment of sight
> > **B** v. 2b Arrestedness as a result of what appears in sight
> > > **C** vv. 2c, 3ab, 4abc, and 5abc Colour beauty of creation
> > **B¹** v. 6ab Believing awe as a result of what is seen
> **A¹** 7abcd Moment of <u>awareness</u>

Or better still is the following:

> **A** v. 1ab Sight
>> **B** v. 2b Arrestedness
>>> **C** vv. 2, 3, 4, and 5 Colour beauty
>> **B**^{1} v. 6 Belief
> **A**^{1} v. 7 Awareness

Poem B has three incidences: (1) present reality, (2) invitation, and (3) response.

> **A** v. 1abc Present/presented reality
>> **B** v. 2ab Invitation by the present/presented reality
> **A**^{1} v. 3abc Response to the present/presented reality

The seven verses of poem A have an overall **ABCB**^{1}**A**^{1} chiastic structure based on the envelop structure provided by v. 1ab (**A**) and v. 7abcd (**A**^{1}) and strengthened by v. 2b (**B**) and v. 6ab (**B**^{1}). It is a structure in which **C** is the ground for **B** and **B**^{1}, a ground made possible by **A** leading to **A**^{1}. The structure prominentizes the colour beauty of the objects seen as causes of Obinna's arrestedness and his awe-inspiring belief made possible by his movement to a sight-enabled location, which led to an awareness-enabled moment. The verses of poem B also have a chiastic structure of **ABA**^{1} where **A**^{1} responds to **A** on the basis of **B**.

Poem A has only one main active subject—the 'I' of the poet. He is the active subject in six out of the seven verses of the poem, taking the initial position in each verse except the first verse where it begins the second line. The birds are active only in the melody they produce. God is mentioned by way of recollection of what he saw in the past, which the poet likens to what he himself has seen.

The poem has a total of sixteen main verbs: twelve active verbs, three verbs of being, and one passive verb. Out of the twelve active verbs, ten have the poet as their subject, while two have God as their subject in retrospect. The passive verb—arrested—has the poet as its object; he is the one arrested. With the exclusion of two actions of God recalled in the last three lines of the last verse, Obinna is the sole actor as well as the one acted upon. He stepped out, gazed, got arrested, lowered his gaze, tuned to, glanced, smiled, and shook his head, believing he had caught or seen the beauty or the good God saw in his creation at the beginning.

The primary actions of Obinna are those of looking and seeing (vv. 2, 3, and 5) on the one hand and listening and hearing (v. 4) on the other hand. The dominant sense in the two poems is the sense of sight. The poems are full of: (1) the directions of the sight ('heaven-ward', 'to the trees', 'earth-ward', 'there') and (2) the description of the things seen ('sky-blue beauty', 'green beauty', 'chirping-melody', 'colour-spiced', 'earth-colour', 'believing awe', 'green freshness', 'line egret'). Direction and description are the domains of sight and vision. One looks towards a direction and describes what one sees. What Obinna saw is the colour beauty of created things. As he looked and saw, something was happening or taking place in him. The colour beauty of the created things he saw brought him to his most important actions of affirmation of faith (poem A) and response (poem B), which are consequent on the results of the primary actions of sight. Who is responsible for what happened to Obinna? Who used the colour beauty of creation to bring Obinna to an affirmation of faith? The next section will help answer these questions.

Poetic Centre

The poetic centre is the theological high point or peak of a poem. It may or may not be located at the middle point of the poem in the form of the chiastic structuration of the poems. The poetic centre of poem A may be located in verse 6 (structure **B¹**). Obinna's elicitation of faith is the theological high point of his poetic articulation. Elicitation of faith is the desired or intended goal and result of what happened to him—the visual experience and mental insight. There is another high point, peak or centre—the dramatic centre—in structure **C** (v. 5). The drama of looking and of getting arrested by the colour of the sky, the trees, the birds, and the vegetation in general reaches its peak with Obinna looking at himself and realizing his own colour is the same as the colour of the earth. The dramatic centre sealed the experience and brought Obinna to faith. The poetic centre and the theological high point of poem B is the all-embracing spatial and elemental divine invitation in structure **B** (v. 2), while the attendant response of all in structure $\mathbf{A}^1$ (v. 3) is the dramatic centre or high point.

Interpretation

Obinna's intellectual quest, the six years of his 'lived-reflective experience of the ruin of creation' due to the negative influence of science, philosophy, egoism, colonialism, racism, and contempt for Africa—which put him in a world of meaninglessness, nothingness, and bitterness—and his 'new epiphany of creation' that brought about his deliverance from bitterness to joy, from the bitterness of nothingness to the joy of riveting splendour, which culminated in the experience he expressed in the two poems, reflect the situation painted by Jesus in Matthew 13:13–17 while explaining to his disciples why he spoke to the crowd in parables.

> The reason I speak to them in parables is that 'seeing they do not perceive, and hearing they do not listen, nor do they understand'. With them indeed is fulfilled the prophecy of Isaiah that says: 'You will indeed listen, but never understand, and you will indeed look, but never perceive. For this people's heart has grown dull, and their ears are hard of hearing, and they have shut their eyes; so that they might not look with their eyes, and listen with their ears, and understand with their heart and turn—and I would heal them'. But blessed are your eyes, for they see, and your ears, for they hear. Truly I tell you, many prophets and righteous people longed to see what you see, but did not see it, and to hear what you hear, but did not hear it (Matt. 13:13–17).[20]

We make good to say, therefore, that what happened to Obinna as he articulated in the poem was a spiritual insight, a revelation. He looked, saw, and perceived. Previously, his heart was dull, and his eyes were closed as a result of his meaninglessness, nothingness, and bitterness caused by the negative influence of science, philosophy, egoism, colonialism, racism, and contempt for Africa. Perhaps the Mass he celebrated prior to the

---

20   All biblical texts are taken from the *New Revised Standard Version* (NRSV), Cross Reference Edition (London: HarperCollins, 1989).

experience rescued him and predisposed him for the visual experience. It opened his eyes to see and his heart to perceive. In religious parlance, spiritual insights and/or revelations are gifts from the divine. That is what 'blessed' in the above biblical passage means. Jesus confirmed this in His response to Peter's confession: 'Blessed are you, Simon son of Jonah! For flesh and blood has not revealed this to you, but my Father in Heaven' (Matt. 16:17). In Luke 10:21–24, Jesus thanks the Father for the insight He grants those whose minds and heart are open to Him as against those who trust only in their intellect and rationality.

> At that same hour Jesus rejoiced in the Holy Spirit and said, 'I thank you, Father, Lord of heaven and earth, because you have hidden these things from the wise and the intelligent and have revealed them to infants; yes, Father, for such was your gracious will. All things have been handed over to me by my Father; and no one knows who the Son is except the Father, or who the Father is except the Son and anyone to whom the Son chooses to reveal him'. Then turning to the disciples, Jesus said to them privately, 'Blessed are the eyes that see what you see! For I tell you that many prophets and kings desired to see what you see, but did not see it, and to hear what you hear, but did not hear it' (Luke 10:21–24).

The 'wise and the intelligent' are the 'experts' whose personal accomplishments, capabilities, and competencies make them feel no need for God as for a wisdom higher and outside of themselves. In the lived experience of Obinna, 'the wise and the intelligent' are those under the influence of science, philosophy, egoism, colonialism, racism, and contempt for Africa. That was why, as a person of faith, he experienced ruin, meaninglessness, nothingness, and bitterness when he was under that influence. Conversely, 'infants' are those who do not trust solely in themselves as the be all and end all but who open their heart, mind, and intellect to God, a wisdom higher and outside of themselves. It is this openness that Obinna gave expression to in the poem. Perhaps, he was able to elicit this openness by the grace of the Mass he celebrated prior to the visual experience. The feast of the Annunciation is a feast that commemorates a particular communication of God's message to someone through somebody else. The celebration of the feast and what it commemorates must have opened Obinna up to the visual insight communicated to him through the colour and beauty of the natural things he saw.

For Luke, 'these things' and 'All things' hidden from the wise and intelligent but revealed to the infants are 'the nature of God's kingdom, the union of Jesus' disciples with him in mission and Jesus' relationship to God'[21]. For Obinna in his poems, they are the (coloured) beauty and harmony in created things and beings.

The 'invitation' the imagined tree gives and the 'reaching out this way and that' are ways of drawing and attracting not just one, some, or many but all to itself. This evokes the imagery and significance of the tree on which a serpent was hung (Num. 21:8–9) and the tree of the cross on which Christ hung (John 19:17–19). The tree on which a serpent was hung 'invited' people bitten by snake to look at it and receive healing. The tree of the cross on which Christ hung took away the wounds of sin of all who confess faith in him who hung on the cross. Jesus said of himself, 'And I, when I am lifted up from the earth, will draw all people [or all things] to myself'[22] (John 12:32; see also 3:14, 6:44, 7:37, 8:28; and Matt. 11:28). For Obinna, being drawn to Christ means being filiated to him.[23]

Theology

The theological trust of the two poems is the God-given human possibility of seeing, perceiving, and/or receiving God's revelation. By the means of sight, Obinna saw as God saw and was thus able to perceive coloured beauty and harmony as revealed in and through created things and beings. The perception opens him up to the reality of the Creator. The poems thus give expression to human theistic behaviour and religiosity. After observing nature in its colourful beauty and harmony, Obinna confesses himself to have seen things in nature the same way the divine saw them. The observation of the beauty and order in creation moved him to confess his faith and belief in God, who made and saw that what he made

21 Robert J. Karris, *The Gospel According to Luke*, in *The New Jerome Biblical Commentary*, eds. Raymond E. Brown, Joseph A. Fitzmyer, and Roland E. Murphy (India: Bangalore, 1994), 675–721: 702. Other biblical passages that refer to things hidden and things not understood or perceived include Luke 8:10, 9:45, and 18:34.

22 Bracket mine.

23 See Obinna, *Culture, Human Development and the New Creation Dynamic*, 5.

was good. The beauty and order in creation elated him as he discovered his own colour, earth colour.

The poems' most direct theological impact, on the one hand, is the expression it gives to man's mental and intellectual disposition of docility and openness as grounds for divine insight, perception, or revelation. On the other hand, it presents the senses, in this case the sense of sight, as mediums of divine insight, perception, or revelation through the impression they make in the mind or in the intellect.[24] Secondarily, it presents the negative influence of science, philosophy, egoism, colonialism, racism, and contempt for Africa as what distort, blur, and block the divine gift of insight. Those who are caught up in that influence are not able to perceive the order, harmony, and beauty of creation and are therefore not able to acknowledge God.

Revelation, whether brought about solely by God or in conjunction with the conscious action of the human person or agent, is personal. That is, it is experienced as a personal encounter by the individual. But then, though it is personal, it is not to be privatised. It is for the community of faith. That is, it is to be made public so that the whole of creation may come to the knowledge of its creator. This is taken up in the second poem. Obinna's belief in the universal thrust of divine revelation and salvation moves him to invite us to see what he had seen. He does this with the use of an adverbial accusative of place or location indicated by the initial word *there.* He points out the object of his vision to us so that we may respond to the divine invitation to faith as he and others—the line of egret—have done. Our response filiates us to God who first filiated himself to us in the Incarnation.[25]

The Poem's Biblical Corollaries

The use of the sense of sight to bring about revelation is well-documented in many places in the Bible. The verb of seeing (*ra'ah*) in the creation account in Genesis 1 describes God as looking at and seeing the various creatures he created and appreciating them as good. The eyes, through

---

24 See my unpublished lecture note on the exegesis of Psalm 8, which I titled 'Revelation as a Product of the Contemplation of the Human Mind Fed with Impressions from the Senses (Especially the Sense of Sight)'.

25 Obinna, *Culture, Human Development and the New Creation Dynamic,* 5.

the act of looking and seeing, make the appreciation possible. When the eyes see, the mind and the entire person is drawn to that which is seen. This is the case of Moses and the burning but unconsumed bush in Exodus 3:2–3. Other instances of the sense of sight as vehicle of divine revelation abound. We have a good example in Jeremiah 1:11–19, where God uses solely the sense of sight to reveal his message to Jeremiah. Even the case of the Potter and the Clay in Jeremiah 18:1–11, where we encounter no verb of seeing, the attendant revelation is brought about through the sense of sight or of insight. All cases of vision are cases of revelation via the sense of sight as we have in Revelation. 1:9–20. Nonetheless, all these cases of revelation via the sense of sight imply the absence of spiritual blindness. When there is spiritual blindness, one may look and look but will neither see, contemplate, nor comprehend, as is the case of the blind man and the Pharisees in John 9:35–41.

The biblical text most directly evoked by the two poems is the text of Psalm 8. The theological trust of the psalm is God's majesty as revealed in creation. It shows that the things perceived through the sense of sight and contemplated upon by the intellect or will lead to the awareness and praise-worship of God's majesty. God is revealed in nature. When humans observe and contemplate on nature and on natural phenomena, they are able to come to some knowledge of God or some aspects of God.

The psalm gives expression to mankind's theistic behaviour and religiosity. After observing the mystery and wonder of the created universe, mankind turns her mind in adoration to the Creator and confesses the greatness of God. The observation of the beauty and order in creation moves mankind to contemplate and behold how artful, masterful, and wonderful God is. He established the order, maintains it, and cares for it. The beauty and order in creation humbles mankind to acknowledge that her exulted position in the created universe, which she had no hand in, has been accorded her by God himself. The psalm adds expression to the fundamental distinction between God and humans: humans are not God; they are but created beings like other creatures. Whatever they are is what God made them to be. Their insignificance before God is well brought out by the diminutive question, What is man? as compared to God, whose glory and greatness are known and praised above the heavens and in all the earth even by little infants.

The psalm's most direct theological impact, on the one hand, is the expression it gives to the masterful work of God and his lordship over creation. He not only brought creation into being, he remembers (is mindful of) it and cares for it. On the other hand, it teaches that the duty of creation, especially humans, the crown of creation, is to praise and worship God. Those who fail in this duty are foes and rebels who will regret their failure. Apart from failure to praise and worship God, those who distort the order, harmony, and beauty of creation rebel against God. The exulted position God gave mankind is for the purpose of maintaining the order harmony and beauty God has established in creation.

Contemplation as demonstrated in the psalm underscores the church's teaching that God speaks to us not only in verbal sounds (words) but also in silence. It is in silence that we hear him clearer. Consequently, silence is a big sermon of God. The necessity of what we see as leading us to God is highlighted in the psalm. But then, what we see and the way we see can also lead us away from God.[26]

The Theology of Obinna's Poems vis-à-vis Other Theologies and Philosophies

The implication of the two poems is that they agree with the church's teaching on natural revelation. By this teaching, mankind comes to a certain knowledge of God through insights obtained from created things. In this sense, the poems recall Thomas Aquinas's proof of the existence of God in the *Quinque Viae*.

Furthermore, the poems demonstrate the teaching of the church on sacramentality. By this teaching, creation is seen as a shadow of the divine. Everything created bears an imprint of the divine—the imprint of beauty, order, and harmony. Besides, the psalm's presentation of eyes as medium of sense impression and mind as medium of contemplation shows the unity between the physical and the spiritual and at the same time presents man not just as physical being but also a spiritual being. The human body is therefore presented as a sacrament, a vestibule of God's revelation.

---

26 See my unpublished lecture note on Psalm 8 titled 'Revelation as a Product of the Contemplation of the Human Mind Fed with Impressions from the Senses (Especially the Sense of Sight)'.

Conclusion

Poems with an *inclusio* usually have a general point they wish to reveal. The title given to this paper is justified by the overall structure we established for each of the two poems. Poem A has a structure in which **C** is the ground for **B** and **B¹**, a ground made possible by **A** leading to **A¹**. The structure prominentizes the colour beauty of the objects seen as causes of Obinna's arrestedness and his awe-inspiring belief made possible by his movement to a sight-enabled location, which led to an awareness-enabled moment. Poem B also has a chiastic structure of **ABA¹** where **A¹** responds to **A** on the basis of **B**—the invitation to see, perceive, and believe. God is revealed in nature. When humans observe and contemplate on nature and on natural phenomena, they are able to come to some knowledge of God or some aspects of God.

God in Genesis 1 looked at his creation and saw that it was good. The psalmist in Psalm 8 looked at creation and saw that it was good. Obinna in his two poems looked at creation and also saw that everything is beautiful. When man looks as God looks, man sees as God sees. God's interaction and communication with humanity in Genesis 1 is still ongoing. God still interacts and communicates with us in the ordinary, everyday natural phenomena and existential experiences. If our connection with God is on and running, when we look, we will be able to see what God is showing, our mind will be stayed on it, and we will certainly comprehend the divine communication, message, or revelation. Objects of sight/vision do thus turn out to be objects or channels of divine revelation. Obinna's poems are the fruits of revelation anchored on the Incarnation. It the revelation of God drawing and foliating all persons, peoples and things to himself in and through Christ.

Section Two

Fundamental, Systematic Theology, Interculturality, and Ecumenism

Chapter Five

Filiation Theology And New Vision And Practice Of Theology

A systematic-theological reflection in honour of Archbishop Anthony J.V. Obinna as the theologian of Deus-filiation, on the occasion of his twenty-fifth anniversary (Silver Jubilee) as Catholic bishop.

John O. Egbulefu

Introduction

@1 The fame of the theologian-bishop Archbishop AJV Obinna of the Catholic Archdiocese of Owerri, Nigeria, is already spread; and rightly so for his many and diverse outstanding performances towards the advancement of culture and the quality of the human life among his people and beyond.

@2 In the spectrum of this fame, the image of him that passes across the mind is that of a pyramid of a person that has at its base a pentagon of interests comprising education, knowledge, languages, theology, and the sacraments of Christ, while having at its apex the courage to educate, to know, to speak, to theologize, and to celebrate. Obinna's interest in languages is closely linked with his interest in the Word of God and hence intellectually in theology, morally in education, and spiritually in the sacraments. The following reflection in honour of him at his twenty-fifth anniversary as a bishop intend, in the spirit of his interests, to be educative and of logico-linguistic and systematic-theological interest to the reader and a gift to the jubilarian to increase his joy and delight with some novelties going on in one of the areas of interests that he shares in common with the author.

@3 I am making the reflection from my proper field, systematic theology, with the intent also to promote interest in the African contributions to the realization of that renewal of theology on which the church has embarked since the Second Vatican Council. I begin the reflection with discussing a certain novelty introduced in theological terminology by the Nigerian Archbishop A. J. V. Obinna. I make the reflection in such a way that the results of the discussion introduce logically into the presentation of two other novelties in theology that come from another African theologian in dialogue with Obinna; the two concern the vision and practice of theology in the technoscientific age and heighten the African contribution to that renewal of theology that can only pass through innovations as the introduction of novelties into the tradition.

@4 My paper is thus divided into three parts. The first part justifies theofiliation as a novelty in theological terminology coming from Obinna and highlights the idea of divine filiation encapsulated in the term. The second part presents the new vision of theology as a coordinate system of scientific, practical, mystical, and technical theologies, as a novelty. The third part itemizes the new practice of theology as technoscience beyond theology as merely science, as another novelty.

Part I:
Theofiliation, a Novelty in Theological Terminology, and the Idea of Divine Filiation Encapsulated in the Term

@1 The term *theofiliation* was coined by His Grace Archbishop Anthony John Valentine Obinna out of two words: *theos*, the Greek word for 'God', and *filius*, the Latin word for 'Son'.

@2 But this coinage, not the idea wrapped in it, has long been disputed among linguistic scholars because of its etymological derivation from two different languages that are therefore fraught with two different traditional thinking patterns, since there is inherent and adherent relation between language and thought, thought inhering in language, and language adhering to thought. The fear that the derivation of a single term from any two languages that are contrary to one another can lead to ideas that are contradictory to one another made some critical observers of Obinna's development of his theology of theofiliation remain sceptical for long about his novelty.

@3 But these sceptics have so far watched out in vain for such contradiction—in vain not only in so far as Obinna's theological ideas are orthodox but also because the sceptics themselves have not taken much into consideration that contrary premises must not lead to contradictory conclusions but rather to compatible fruits that should, however, remain in fraternal relationship and not enter into spousal relationship, as can be clearly illustrated and exemplified with a recent linguistic theory. The theory has been developed within the two precise coordinates of the system of the proper relationship between the man and the woman as the primary contraries—opposites that are but not opposed to one another in every human family. The theory states that there is a certain family of languages in which Greek is the husband as the first man in the family and Latin is his wife as the first woman in the family. And both are the father and the mother respectively of six children, whereby the two children that are male issues as the sons of the family are German and English, while the rest four children who are female issues as the daughters of the family are Italian, French, Spanish, and Portuguese, with the consequence that those two and these four are related to one another as brothers and sisters in the family of altogether eight languages, in which Greek and Latin as the father and the mother respectively of their six children are not of the same blood and, therefore, on this basis of nonconsanguinity, can marry one another without contravening the natural law, whereas their children who are all of the same blood with one another cannot marry one another without going against nature and incurring damages; and likewise it is against the natural law for any of the parents and any of the children to marry one another.

@4 Therefore, within the family of the named eight languages, it is against the law for a thinker to create or coin a term out of more than one of those six that are the children of the linguistic family or a term out of two, one of which is one of the two parents while the other is one of the six children; but it is not illicit to coin or create out of the two parents of that linguistic family one single term as Obinna has done in the case of his coined terminology *theofiliation*.

@5 Besides, the same type of coinage as Obinna had done in the term *theofiliation* is found in the history of thought to have been done several centuries before Obinna in the construction of the term *theodicy* out of two words taken from the two parents of the named linguistic family, namely the Greek noun *theos*, meaning 'God', and the Latin verb *dico, dicere, dixi, dictum*, meaning 'to speak', 'to say a word', whereby the two words are united to form the synthetic word *theodicy* as the name for the science about that 'eternal speaking act' as that 'eternal act of saying an eternal word', through which God created all beings.

@6 However it has many more advantages, like freer flow of thought, more univocal, and less equivocal expression of ideas, etc., to coin one term from two words taken not from two languages but rather from one and same language. And such is exemplified in the case of the coinage of the terms *theology* from only the Greek language and *sacrament* from only the Latin language.

@6a For the term *theology* has been coined from two words taken from the one and same Greek language. The first word being the noun *theos*, meaning 'God', while the second is the noun is *Logos, Logos tou Theou*, meaning 'Word, the Word of God', and the two are unified (through joining the *Logos tou Theou*, the Word of God as the primary means of knowing the God of the Word as the proper object of theological knowledge, into the one term *theology*—from joining *Logos* to *theos*, hence from *theoslogos*, and suppressing one or two letters therein as in *theo[s]log[os]* and then adding *ia* to *theolog* to form *theologia*. Or like one forms the term *trinus* from joining *unus* to *tria*, hence from *triaunus*, and suppressing one or two letters therein as in *tri[au]nus* but without adding any further letter to form *trinus*) to 'designate' that branch of science in which the truth-containing Word of God is taught, researched upon, and studied methodically, i.e., with a system of methods, by the human spirit to lead humans to the knowledge of the perceived self-revealing God of the Word and hence to more love of Him and hence to better service of Him.

Science is the aggregate of 'teaching about', 'researching on the taught' and 'studying of the searched for' reality as structured and, only so, the intelligible existing being in order to make the reality understood and hence known and hence more loved and hence better served (better worked for). In science, to study means to learn from a master as an authoritative and exemplary teacher some theoretical goods, like good ideas, to be put into practice in emulation of him, while in technics, to study means learning from a master of work, *magister operis*, the technique, the craft, the skill, and the technical know-how of producing material goods in the form of objects by imitating him and his models of creativity, reproducing the works he has produced and producing so with material goods similar to those that he has produced.

In the theological science, to research means searching (*quaerere*) more and more to make really understood (*intellectum*) the Word (*verbum*) of God as long as it is a word spoken by a person (spirit capable of producing words that are intelligible and understandable to his fellow spirits as to intelligent living beings), is virtually intelligible and understandable (*verbum intelligible*) to spirits in fellowship with God. The process of understanding passes through reading between the lines—*inter lineas legere, interlineaslegere, inte(r)l(ineas)legere, hence intellegere*—of the structure of the reality of God, whose Word is required to be understood (*Verbum intellegendum*). The understanding is arrived at when the human spirit, through reading between the lines of the structure (as the principle of intelligibility) of the researched reality, arrives at the truth (as at that one being, *ens,* that underlies and sustains the trueness and truthfulness of the reality required to be understood and without which the reality were untrue, false, inauthentic, counterfeit, and untruthful, dishonest, deceitful, unreliable); and only through the understanding[1] of the Word of God can the human spirit arrive at the knowledge[2] of the God of the Word as at the ultimate goal of the scientific-theological activities of teaching and researching on and studying the Word of God towards the knowledge (and hence more love and hence better service) of the God of the Word.

@6b Likewise, the term *sacrament,* in Latin written *sacramentum,* has been coined from two Latin words—the one being the noun *juramentum,* meaning 'oath, solemn promise', while the other is the noun *sacralitas,* meaning 'sacredness'. And the two are unified through uniting the prefix *sacra* of the word *sacralitas* with the suffix *mentum* of the word *juramentum* into the one term *sacramentum,* which 'de-sign-ates' that instrumental expression of the Christian religion in which the mysteries of the Christian faith are celebrated in symbols of some hidden reality of salvation. The Christian religion is that aggregate of the faith, cult, and morals based on Christ, which is the object of traditional Christian doctrines, devotions, and disciplines and is practiced under the centre of gravity of the threefold task of teaching, sanctifying, and governing the people of God,[3] whereby the execution of this threefold task is informed by the underlying and sustaining, vitalizing and propelling, directing and regulating, three theological virtues of faith, hope, and charity (which contrast with the three elements that constitute science, namely teaching, research, and studies) infused at baptism into the soul of the believer in Christ.

The doctrines mean the taught revealed supernatural truths of faith as of the truths that are already believed and are required to be believed more and more, deeper and deeper, for one to understand more and more,

---

1 cf. Hermeneutics.

2 cf. Epistemology.

3 *munus docendi, munus sanctificandi, and munus gubernandi.*

deeper and deeper the Word of God (*credo ut intelligam, credo semper amplius ut intelligam amplius*) in that activity of the human spirit that is called theology as the activity of the human spirit in searching more and more into the intelligible Word of God in order to understand the Word (through reading between the lines, *inter lineas leggere*, of the structured Word till the arrival at the truth—as at the ultimate being that is underlying and sustaining the trueness and truthfulness—of the Word) to make it understood (*quaerens intellectum facere verbum intelligibile*) to others and, with the help of the attained understanding, to search further for the knowable in the believed Word till the arrival at knowing the loved God of the Word (*scibile in credito quaerens amplius amo quod nosco ut congnoscam quod amo*).

The *devotions* mean the prayers and celebrations based on and regulated by the doctrines according to the rule that what and how to pray and to celebrate depends on what and why one believes such that the latter determines the former (*lex credendi lex orandi et celebrandi*). The *disciplines* mean the rules and regulations as the laws that regulate the doing of the duties and the conserving and promotion of the rights among the people of God and thus that regulate the comportment of the Christ-faithful humans in the church into making each of them an abundantly fruit-bearing adherent of Christ as the true disciple of Him. *Symbols* are the syntheses of natural and conventional signs in the form of objects or actions. A symbol is the symphonic synthesis as unity resulting from the synchronic union of a natural sign with a conventional sign. A *natural sign* is that perceptible—visible, audible, sensible—present sign, the significance of which is fixed in nature by God and (i) can be a certain past reality that is the cause of a present sign (like the present footprints on the sand are the sign of a certain passer-by who has made a passage in the past or is making one in the present and through such passage has caused the present footprints), (ii) can be a certain present reality that is the cause of the present sign (like the present fire burning underneath a smoke is the cause of the present smoke), or (iii) can be a certain future reality that is the cause of the present sign (like the present thick dark clouds in the sky are going to cause an imminent rainfall).

A *conventional sign* is that sign that the significance of which is fixed by humans on the basis of their agreement (convention) among themselves about such significance. The agreement (convention) consists in that common consent of humans that is based on the human common sense and on the common experiences of a certain human collectiveness (be it family, community, clan, tribe, people, society, nation, race). An example of conventional sign in the secular human society is the red traffic light seen on the road that signifies among humans in the society that there is danger, whereby the drivers of vehicles should stop and let the pedestrians cross the road as long as the light is green for the pedestrians and red for the drivers or that the pedestrians should stop and let the drivers drive past the road as long as the light is green for the drivers and red for the pedestrians. An example of a conventional sign in the sacred human community is the red light seen in the sanctuary of a Catholic church signifies among Catholic believers that there is the Blessed Sacrament in the Church and hence that Christ is really, substantially, and truly present in that church. 'Really present' means present with His humanity as with the aggregate of His human body, human soul, and human spirit; 'substantially present' means present with His divinity as with the aggregate of the divine Word, divine life lived by the Word, and divine will done by the living Word; and 'truly present' means present with the unity resulting from the union of His divinity and His humanity.

The symbols in which the Christian mysteries are celebrated are symbols that are religious (i.e., rebinding man to God) by nature, as different from scientific (e.g., mathematical, symbols) and are thus called sacraments. A sacramental celebration is a union of administration and reception of the grace contained in the sacrament. The administration of the grace consists in the actions performed by the minister of the sacrament, and such actions are of two types, namely the ceremonials as the actions not accompanied with words and the rituals as the actions accompanied with words spoken by the agent as the minister to a believing addressee as to the proper receiver not only of the words of instruction but also of the graces contained in the words spoken and in the action performed by the agent. The reception of the grace, on the other hand, consists in the union of the inward sincere acceptance by the human addressees of the divine gift made gratuitously to them and the outward utterance of words that contain a serious promise made by the same humans to observe the instructions and collaborate with the accepted salvation-bringing grace, whereby they, the speakers, take their promise as a sacred thing—something sacrosanct or untouchable—to the observation of which they are ready and willing to remain faithful for life, or till death, with the divine assistance ever remaining with them.

Mystery is by essence that supernatural (metahistorical, hence transcendental) reality worthy of belief and required to be believed that, by nature, addresses itself to the whole of man (body-soul-spirit) whereby it, (a) addressing itself to the human body, transcends (goes beyond) the power of the sensory organs to perceive[4]; (b) addressing itself to the human spirit, enchants the mind (*mysterium est fascinosum*); and (c) addressing itself to the human soul, subordinates the natural human reason to its own supernatural laws.[5] The mysteries of the Christian faith celebrated in those sacred symbols in the form of actions that the Sacraments are involve the mysteries of God, of the Godman Christ, of Mary, of the church, of the sacraments, and of the Holy Spirit as that Spirit of the Father and of the Son that operates in Christ as well as in Mary and, together with Christ, operates in the church and in the sacraments of Christ.

@7 The main idea that is encapsulated in the disputed term *theofiliation* is the idea of 'the divine filiation'.

@7a *Divine filiation* is an idea that descends as an answer to a complex question that has been asked as follows: If filiation is an act—namely first and foremost the act of begetting or getting children as sons (*filii*) and daughters (*filiae*); secondly the act of making a son or a daughter out of a person, as in the case of adoption, or out of a thing, like out of a substance, as in the case of generating a substantial image of the parent; or thirdly the act of making a son or daughter with another person, as in the case of procreation—what can one call God's act of begetting a son, generating a son, making a son out of a thing, out of His own substance, and making sons and daughters out of persons, etc.?

@7b Divine filiation is an act of God that puts the children of God resulting from it into a state, the state in which (status in quo) the sons

---

4   Cf. *Mysterium est imperscrutabile.*

5   Cf. *"Mysterium est tremendum'*. See also, John Egbulefu, "The Trinity, the Incarnate Word and Mary,' in *De Trinitatis Mysterio et Maria: Sectio Africana et Asiatica*, Vol. II, Jean-Pierre Sieme Lasoul and Milanros Gregorio, eds., 185-311 (Vatican City: Pontificia Academia Mariana Internationalis, 2006), 185-186. See also, Clement IV, *Quanto Sincerius*: A Letter to Archbishop Maurinus of Narbon, 28/10/1267, in DH 849.

and daughters of God in heaven and on earth have found themselves as humans possessing a new and integral sense of kinship with God ever since they got into a relationship with the only one begotten, eternal Son of God whose Sonship is a triad—the three constitutive elements of which are 'His being the substantial image of God', 'His being the Wisdom and power of God', and 'His being the eternal creative Word of God', and who, being eternal, is truly God but has become Man, the Son of Man, through the Incarnation of the eternal Word, but without ceasing to be the Son of God, hence without stopping to be God, and who thus, ever since the Word was made flesh in the immaculate womb of the Blessed Virgin Daughter of God called Mary, is at once true God and true man in one single divine person and is thus called the Godman (***Theandros***) in whom humans are made sons and daughters of God through doing the will of the Father of the only begotten Son of God by the grace and power of the Holy Spirit as the Spirit of the Father and of the Son, the Spirit leading and teaching and reminding the sons and daughters of God as the brothers and sisters of the Son of Man as the Son of God made man for them and for the sake of their salvation.

@7c Out of divine filiation results, first and foremost, the family of God is the aggregate of 'God the Father', 'the Son of God', 'the sons and daughters of God as the brothers and sisters of the incarnate Son of God as the Godman', 'the Mother of the incarnate Son of God as Mother of the Godman, and hence the Mother of God and Mother of the sons and daughters of God as of the brothers and sisters of the Son of Man, hence Mother of the Church', 'the Holy Spirit by the grace and power of whom the doers of the Will of the heavenly and eternal Father of the eternal Son of God have become the brothers and sisters of the Son of Man.

Thus the journey to the formation of the family of God passes through five successive stages: (1) the intradivine originations of the Son of God from only the Father and of the Holy Spirit from the Father and the Son together; (2) the act and state of becoming sons and daughters and mother of God by humans through their becoming the brothers and sisters and mother of the Son of Man as of the Son of God made Man; (3) the act and state of becoming brothers and sisters and mother of the Son of Man as of the Son of God made Man by humans through their doing the will of the eternal and Heavenly Father of the Son of God; (4) the doing of the will of the eternal and Heavenly Father of the Son of God by humans only with the divine assistance ever remaining with them, namely through the grace and power of the Holy Spirit as the Spirit of the Father and of the Son without whom humans can do nothing; (5) the reception of the grace and power of the Holy Spirit by humans under the condition that before and during and after the reception, they exercise or practice their natural (not artificial and not forced), inborn (innate) asking (requesting and questioning) to be given the requested, searching (and researching) to find (invent) the sought, and knocking to get the gate and door opened to them for entrance and exit because divine grace presupposes and perfects nature and practice makes perfect.

@7d One would have expected that on the basis of the unity—numerical oneness—of the one and indivisible common Father of the diverse children of the family of God, there would be goodness (i.e., suitability, usefulness, and desirability), trueness and truth and truthfulness, beauty and beautifulness in the family of God among its members, since unity as a transcendental value is interchangeable with goodness (i.e., suitability, usefulness, and desirability), trueness and truth and truthfulness, beauty and beautifulness. But that is not the case; rather, in the family of God, there are found not only goodness but also evil (privation and deprivation of goodness as of suitability, of usefulness, and of desirability); not only trueness or authenticity and truth and truthfulness or honesty but also inauthenticity, lies, dishonesty in all its ramifications like deceitfulness and insincerity, tricks, giving and taking bribes, and the resulting corruption of the soul and spirit; and not only beauty and beautifulness but also ugliness in all its ramifications like lawlessness and disorder.

@7e The question arises as to what to do and how to do to prevent or to eliminate from the family of God the evil, inauthenticity, lies, dishonesty in all its ramifications like deceitfulness and insincerity, tricks, giving and taking bribes, and the resulting corruption of the soul and spirit, as well as ugliness in all its ramifications like lawlessness, disorder, etc., in and among the diverse children of the one and indivisible common Father of the family of God.

@7ea Some thinkers and researchers, like Archbishop Anthony Obinna, see the solution of this problem in the conscientization of all men and women that they are children—sons and daughters as fruits of God's act of filiation in the family—of a common Creator God as their primary and ultimate common Father.

@7eb But we mean that beyond the strategy of conscientization, there should be, and we have consequently meanwhile, developed out of the unity—numerical singularity—and indivisibility of a common supernatural Father and the diversity of interhuman natural and extrahuman conventional filiations, the globalized theory of inseparably united and yet inevitably diverse fatherlands. According to such a theory, each of us humans, as long as we are created persons, has a supernatural Father, the Creator God, from whom primarily we as offspring originate and therefore have a supernatural fatherland from where we have come; and as long as such a Father is in heaven and is God from whom and all good created persons and things come and each of us humans came to be born good into our natural family (and hence into our village, nation, continent, into the earthly planet, the entire universe as the whole world, and into the entire humanity) as our native home, and to whom every good created person is going back, it follows that each one of us is passing from our common heavenly fatherland, through our respective native fatherlands (which comprise one's village, one's country, one's continent, one's planet, the earth, and the entire universe as the whole world, and the entire humanity), and our fatherlands by adoption (which comprise our diverse religious families and diverse intellectual families, our diverse political families and diverse cultural—literary, linguistic, musical, artistic—families), to our common celestial fatherland (as the supernatural world where God our Father is living as the only one Father of the only one family of God).

And the belonging not only of each member of the human collectiveness to only one natural father and native fatherland but also of the diverse members to diverse religious and cultural and to diverse intellectual and political fathers and fatherlands by adoption on the one hand and the belonging of all the members to a single and indivisible common celestial Father and fatherland on the other hand constitute together a basic font and foundation of the permanent contrariety, but not contradictoriness, of unity and diversity that characterizes our—His children's, namely His sons' and daughters'—ways of seeing and judging things, our values and priorities, our interior and exterior worlds of behaviour and of action, but which not seldom produce tensions, generate conflicts and divisions, inside us and in our midst, when and where the moral—affective and performative—bonds or ties to the various fatherlands to which we belong are not organically synchronized and harmonized.

Such a new theory of dynamic system of fatherlands also corrects and overtakes the old vision of factual and cultural fatherlands (in the figure of static concentric circles) as proposed by Erasmus of Rotterdam and according to which the fatherland is first and foremost the country where one is born, then the fatherland of adoption, then finally and above all, the Christian world, Europe, the republic of letters, and the entire humanity, in expectation of the heavenly fatherland. For while the old sees the factual and cultural fatherlands in the figure of static concentric circles, the new sees the dynamic system—unity resulting from the union—of the three diverse, namely the native and the adoptive and the heavenly fatherlands rather in the figure of only one standing sphere formed out of two mutually contrary, i.e., opposite but not opposed concave and convex, curves through their fusion with one another at their two ends, with the upper end representing the heavenly fatherland as the one fatherland up there in heaven above, as the point both of the departure of the convex curve and of the arrival of the concave curve, and with the lower end representing the togetherness of the diverse religious and cultural fathers and fatherlands of adoption and the diverse intellectual and political fathers and fatherlands of adoption as the two fatherlands down here on earth below, as the point both of the arrival of the convex curve and of the departure of the concave curve).

For the reduction of the frequent tensions that are produced, and of the conflicts and divisions that are generated inside and in the midst of, the children of the common Creator God as common Father of the creatures (by the diversity that characterizes our—God's children's, namely His sons' and daughters'—ways of seeing and judging things, our values and priorities, our interior and exterior worlds of behaviour and of action) when and where the moral—affective and performative—bonds or ties to the various fatherlands to which we belong are not organically synchronized and harmonized, we mean that there should be, and we have consequently meanwhile, developed a system, an organic whole of diverse parts, out of the common human flesh, common human nature, and common human personhood that all humans have and the three of which are made out of the diverse unions of the three components of the human being, namely the body, soul, and spirit, among themselves (whereby the human flesh is that single unit the unity of which results from the mediated dissoluble union of the human body as a material and directly or indirectly visible and mortal creature with the human soul as an immaterial and invisible and immortal creature through the human spirit as equally immaterial and invisible and immortal creature that is contained in the body and contains the soul and therefore unites the body and the soul, while the human nature is that single unit the unity of which results from the immediate and dissoluble union of the human spirit with the human body, whereas the human personhood is that single unit the unity of which results from the immediate and indissoluble union of the human spirit with the human soul).

And it is the system of the movement (yet to be known and made by many humans) from the created body, through the created soul and created spirit, to God the Creator, and hence a movement from the natural father and native fatherland that corresponds to the created human body, through the diverse religious and cultural fathers and fatherlands of adoption that correspond to the created human soul and the diverse intellectual and political fathers and fatherlands of adoption that correspond to the created human spirit, to the one and indivisible heavenly Father and fatherland that corresponds to God the Creator, hence a movement from the object of the empirical sciences (dealing with the natural world of material, directly or indirectly visible, and mortal creatures—embracing person and things, things as objects and events, events as actions of persons and occurrences of things), through the meta-empirical sciences (dealing partly with the preternatural world of immaterial, invisible, and immortal creatures like human soul and spirit and the angels—cf. metaphysical sciences, namely general metaphysics and ontology as special metaphysics—and partly with the world of numerical and structural symbols as of abstract creativities of man, the world of symbolic objects abstracted by man from visible creatures of God, cf. the exact sciences, namely logic and mathematics, the latter comprising geometry as the exact science occupied with the form of the container-component of realities, arithmetic as the exact science occupied with the quantum as that numerical strength of the content-component of realities that can be increased by addition and multiplication or decreased or reduced by division and subtraction, and algebra as the science occupied with a station, the condition for the container to contain the content adequately and which is thus the science of equations as formulae symbolizing equalities and equivalences, required for equilibrium or balance of forces, and for equity or distributive justice, as conditions for a good government), to the sacred sciences (dealing with the supernatural world of invisible and eternal, noncreated realities as persons—namely God as collective person as Creator and King and Saviour of all creation—and as things, namely heaven, paradise, as where God lives) that comprise theology (as the science about the Logos as of the eternal creative Word of God through whom in His preincarnate state all beings are called into existence by God and through whom in His incarnate state all men are saved as God has wanted it for them), theodicy (as the science about the very unending speaking act through which God created all beings), and the science of religion (as the science of the self-binding of the spiritual creature man to the absolute Spirit God as to his Creator and King and Saviour).

Part II
The New Vision of Theology as a Coordinate System of Scientific, Practical, Mystical, and Technical Theologies

2.1 Sketch of the Sequence of Thoughts Leading to the New Vision of Theology

@1 Our theological thinking in a technoscientific epoch is updatedly a technoscientific theological thinking, in which our reasoning (*ratiocinatio*) begins with our belief (*fides*) that God created man so that man may, in this world, *know the sensed God, love the known God, and serve the loved known God* in order that man may, in the next world, *having lived wisely* on earth, *live in communion with God in heaven in the community of the three persons in the numerically one God*, namely the Father and the Son and the Holy Spirit, who have created man in their own image and resemblance in view of this dynamic communion that stretches from 'Man's arrival in front of God and seeing and contemplating the joy-giving face of God', through 'God's admitting of Man into Himself and uniting Man to Himself and communicating His life to Man', to 'Man's sharing or participating in *the eternal life of God as life of eternal love for one another, eternal joy at one another, eternal glorification of one another and eternal peace with one another, going on among the three persons in one God*'.

@2 Our thoughts are so then sharpened by the logical reasoning (*ratiocinatio logica*) that in order to merit living in communion with God in the hereafter in heaven, we humans have to carry out our task of knowing the sensed God, loving the known God, and serving the loved known God here on earth *with wisdom*, but with wisdom both as a person and as a thing.

@2a. On the one hand, the wisdom as a thing with which we humans have to carry out the task of knowing the sensed God, loving the known God, and serving the loved known God here on earth is that virtue that, since the beginning of wisdom as a thing, is the virtue of the fear of offending the Lord and that is one of the seven gifts of the Holy Spirit (cf. Prov. 2:10–20—wisdom and knowledge in verse 10, counsel or prudence and understanding or discernment in verse 11, fear of offending the Lord or keeping away from evil and from men of deceitful speech in verse 12, piety as bending to God as the way of good men and fortitude as persisting in the paths of the virtuous in verse 20) as the Spirit that rests on wisdom (Isa. 11:1–2—the Spirit of the Lord in verse 2a; a spirit of wisdom and insight in verse 2b; that does not judge by appearances, gives no verdict on hearsay, judges the wretched with integrity, and with equity gives a verdict for the poor of the mind in verse 3; a spirit of counsel and power or fortitude in verse 2c; one whose word is a rod that strikes the ruthless and whose sentences bring death to the wicked and whose loincloth around the waist is integrity and whose belt about his hips is faithfulness in verse 4; the spirit of knowledge and of the fear of the Lord in verse 2d; whereby because of being filled with the knowledge of the Lord things or persons that otherwise would not stay or go together rather stay and go together in peace in verses 6–9). It would be intelligent of us to do in a wise manner our existential duty of knowing God, loving God, and serving God in this world. To do it in a wise manner and to do it wisely is to do it with wisdom. To do it basically with that virtue is the beginning of wisdom. To do it with the fear of offending the Lord, wherefore to be doing this duty without wisdom as a thing would mean to be doing it without the beginning of wisdom, thus without the fear of offending the Lord; but not to be doing it with the virtue of the fear of offending the Lord is to be doing it without the fear of offending the Lord. It means to be doing it in a way that can offend the Lord, thus it means to be doing it unwisely. But to do it unwisely would not lead us to attaining in the next world the communion with God that is the ultimate goal of our doing such a duty. In other words, to be doing this duty unwisely in this world would be like running the race but outside the track, *praeter viam*. It would thus mean to be doing the duty in a foolish and ridiculous manner.

But as long as this indispensable virtue of fear of offending the Lord in which consists the beginning of Wisdom as a thing can only be received as a gift from the Holy Spirit that is inside Wisdom as a person, we need Wisdom as a person for us to do the duty wisely. Thus, it would be intelligent to seek the face of Wisdom as a person, to ask her and request her for the Holy Spirit in her who alone can give the necessary virtue of doing the duty wisely.

@2b. Wisdom as a person with whom humans have to carry out the task of knowing the sensed God, loving the known God, and serving the loved and known God here on earth, is that person who, being generated before all ages from the innermost Self of God as from the substance of God and born from the womb of the generating God, is a supernatural being and the image of the substance of God and is consubstantial with God and, hence, has the divine nature and, hence, the divine essence and is, therefore, called the Son of God. And since no one knows the Father if not the Son and he to whom the Son wants to reveal Him (cf. Matt. 11:27), for the Father loves the Son and shows to the Son what He the Father does (cf. John 5:20), the Son is the only access, the only way, to the Father (cf. John 14:6).

The essence of God consists in God's being (*esse*) the first and the last Being (*Ens*). The nature of God consists in the union of all those divine attributes that derive from the divine essence, namely the divine eternity, absoluteness, catholicity, i.e., all-embracing character, hence omnipresence, omniscience, omnipotence, holiness, perfection, etc. The substance of God consists in that all-embracing power underlying and sustaining the infallible efficacy of the words and actions—and hence of the infallible efficiency—of the three persons in one God that is constituted by the unity existing out of the nature of God and specifically embraces all the three most powerful powers that can exist, namely the power to do all things that are good (i.e., suitable, useful, and desirable) and to do each well at the absolutely superlative level of its being well done; the power to do nothing that is bad (i.e., privy of goodness) *and to* make no mistake; and the power to overpower and overthrow, overcome and overtake, everything that is bad and to eliminate every evil.

Wisdom is particularly *omnipresent* in the sense that she pervades and penetrates everything (cf. Wisd. 7:24) and is more mobile than every movement (cf. Wisd. 7:24). And Wisdom is particularly *omnipotent* in the sense that she can do everything (cf. Wisd. 7:27), whereby (1) she can produce everything (cf. Wisd. 8:5) and is thus the designer of everything (cf. Wisd. 7:21b); she is the one that puts things into rightful order (cf. Prov. 8:30); she puts each created thing and each created person at the proper place where the thing or the person belongs, namely where God in His love wants the thing or the person to be: the one here, the other there, the one on earth, the other in heaven, such that every person has his or her mission, and consequently not all are prophets, not all are apostles (*non omnes prophetae, non omnes apostoli*); she is the architect that carries out God's design, putting all beings created by God at their proper places, such that man, contemplating creation, may discover this design and encounter God in it (cf. Wisd. 13:3–5; Rom 1:19–20) and (2) she renews all things (cf. Wisd. 7:27).

And above all, Wisdom is particularly *omniscient* in the sense that she knows all beings that exist and understands all beings that exist (cf. Wisd. 9:11).

(1) She knows the Creator as the Shepherd that knows and loves and serves His Creatures as His flock of sheep and lambs.
(2) She knows the creatures at the same time.
    (2a) She knows them because for all eternity, the Wisdom of God was in God and God has made her come out of His womb

before He created the universe (cf. Proverb 8:22–30), such that Wisdom was present when God was creating the world (cf. Wisd. 9:9); and each time that God wants to create, it is always Wisdom that chooses out the works to be realized (cf. Wisd. 8:4b); among the infinite possibilities of the divine omnipotence, Wisdom chooses out the one to be called into existence; already from there results that.

(2b) Wisdom knows every work of God (cf. Wisd. 9:9), for since she was present when God was creating each creature and it was herself that chose each out for realization, she knows every creature till the marrows of the bone; she knows every creature from head to toe, from part to part, till the depth of the soul; and she knows why God created all creatures differently and why the diverse creatures are so as they are: the one so, the other so (*unum sic, alium autem sic*).

(2c) She knows also what God had in mind for creating each creature, thereby she knows the creatures that are created to know, love, and serve their Creator as their Lord and Shepherd; and she knows how to know God, love God, and serve God adequately and therefore how Man can reach the ultimate goal of his struggle to know God, love God, and serve God.

(3) Therefore, she can teach how to know God, love God, and serve God adequately; for 'Wisdom can teach the things that are most useful to humans in life' (Wisd. 8:5). And there is nothing more useful to humans in life than the things that can lead them to reach hereafter in heaven the ultimate goal of their struggle here on earth, and such things are to know, love, and serve God as the proper purpose for which God has called the human being into existence here on earth. Alone from there, it would be intelligent of us to allow Wisdom as a person to do with us our existential duty of knowing God, loving God, and serving God.

But we can allow Wisdom as a person to do such a duty with us only after our leaving her to make her home in us and our making our home in her (cf. John 15:4) by remaining in her in order that, with her in us, we may bear fruit in plenty since being cut off from her, we can do nothing (cf. John 15:5) and since if we remain in her and her words remain in us, we shall get all for which we ask or request or supplicate (cf. John 15:7).

But such Wisdom in person that is needed and is to be allowed to do the work with us *is* that Christ the Emmanuel, the God-with-us (cf. Matt. 1:23; Isa. 7:14) as the God-united-with-us-humans, God-in-solidarity-with-us, who is the incarnate Son of the living God (cf. Matt. 16:16) and whose Father is God, by name the Lord (Yahweh, *Dominus*, Exod. 3:15). Christ is that 'Wisdom and power of God' (cf. 1 Cor. 1:24) that is powerful, particularly because there is in Him a Spirit—i.e., intelligent living being—that is unique, manifold, subtle, active, incisive, unsullied, lucid, invulnerable, benevolent, sharp, irresistible, beneficent, man-loving, steadfast, dependable, unperturbed, almighty, all-surveying, all-intelligent-and-pure-and-most-subtle-spirits-penetrating Spirit (cf. Wisd. 7:22–23).

But such a unique and yet manifold Holy Spirit that is inside Wisdom is a God-knowing, God-loving, and God-serving Spirit. He is God-knowing Spirit as long as this intelligent, almighty, all-surveying, lucid, unsullied, subtle, sharp, incisive, irresistible Spirit is the all-intelligent-and-pure-and-most-subtle-spirits-penetrating Spirit. But the most pure and most subtle spirits that exist are God the Father and God the Son, wherefore this Holy Spirit is said to know the profundity of God. And He is a God-loving Spirit as long as this benevolent and beneficent Spirit is a man-loving Spirit, and such a loved man is the one created by God in the image and resemblance of God. And He is a God-serving Spirit as long as this active and yet unperturbed Spirit is a dependable and steadfast Spirit.

And as long as this Spirit that is inside Wisdom is God-knowing, God-loving and God-serving, it would be intelligent of us to do our existential duty of knowing God, loving God, and serving God with such a Spirit together.

Thus, we generally need Wisdom to help us do our duty of knowing God, loving God, and serving God and particularly need the Spirit that is in her. We need Him as our helper, namely as our reminder of what Wisdom has said to us *in the past* and as our teacher of everything *in the present* and as our teller of the things to come *in the future* as things that the Spirit himself has learnt and that belong to Wisdom and to the Father of Wisdom together, and hence as our Leader to the *complete* truth. But first of all, we need the Father to send such a Spirit in Wisdom's name to us. And meanwhile, Wisdom has promised to tell the Father to send such a Spirit in His name to us to be our helper in the midst of our need of Him, to remind us of all that Wisdom has said to us, and to teach us everything (cf. John 14:26), as well as to lead us to the complete truth and tell us of the things to come, which are only what He Himself has learnt and has taken from what belongs to Wisdom and to the Father of Wisdom, who are two persons that have everything in common (cf. John 16:13–15). But for the Father of Wisdom to send the Holy Spirit that is inside Wisdom in Wisdom's name to us, the Father of Wisdom must be loving us. But for the Father of Wisdom to love us, we must be loving Wisdom ('the Father Himself loves you for loving me' [John 16:27]; 'Anybody who loves me will be loved by my Father, and I shall love him and show myself to him' [John 14:21b]; 'If anyone loves me he will keep my word, and my Father will love him, and we shall come to him and make our home with him' [John 14:23]).

But our love for Wisdom is a manifold act that presupposes our knowing Wisdom, accomplishes itself in an affective and effective (i.e., performative) love of Wisdom, and leads to the service of Wisdom. Our knowledge of Wisdom, presupposed by our love for Wisdom, comprises a chain of complex actions and activities:

(1) waking up (from the sleep of indolence and laziness of mind) for the desirable Wisdom (cf. Wisd. 6:15b, waking up), getting up for her early in the morning (cf. Wisd. 6:14) and thinking about her (cf. Wisd. 6:15), desiring her (cf. Wisd. 6:20) as longing and requesting for her, asking and praying to receive her or supplicating that she be given to the praying one (*petite et accipietis* or *petite et vobis dabitur* [Mt 7:7], prayerful Desire and supplicatory Prayer)

(2) going in search of her (cf. Wisd. 6:12) and following thereby her footprints (cf. Wisd. 6:22b, research, *quaerite et invenietis* [Matt. 7:7]), for 'Wisdom is bright, and does not grow dim. She is readily seen by those who love her and found by those who look for her. Quick to anticipate those who desire her, she makes herself known to them' (Wisd. 6:12–14a)

(3) after having found her or met her,

    (3a) desiring to be instructed by her and leaving oneself be taught by her as by a master, an authoritative and exemplary teacher (cf. Wisd. 6: 11–17, teaching and grasping)

(3b) listening to her words (cf. Wisd. 6:1–2, audition)

(3c) striving for how to be able to comprehend the words of Wisdom, i.e., to take with oneself all of them together (cf. Wisd. 8:18) as one's companion of life (cf. Wisd. 8:9) for the whole of one's life or as one's bride (cf. Wisd. 8:2)

(3d) grasping the laws of Wisdom and bringing through them to light the knowledge of her (cf. Wisd. 6: 22f, science)

Our affective and effective (i.e., performative) love of Wisdom in which our love for Wisdom accomplishes itself comprises a chain of complex actions and activities:

(1) those that express affective love of Wisdom embrace

(1a) seeking to see the face of the Origin of Wisdom (*vultum Dei quaerere* [knocking for an opening], *'pulsate et aperietur vobis'* [Matt. 7:7]) as of the proper Speaker of the words of Wisdom ('My word is not my own: it is the word of the one who sent me' [John 14:24]) and upon seeing the face of the speaking Origin of Wisdom,

(1b) looking at the paradoxical, i.e., at once fascinating and yet tremendous and inscrutable, hence mysterious face of the prigin of Wisdom as of her Father (contemplative Mysticism), and

(1c) adoring—i.e., admiring with devotion and with praises—the Origin of Wisdom whose face is being contemplated, while

(2) those that express effective love of Wisdom embrace

(2a) observing the laws of Wisdom by putting them into practice (cf. Wisd. 6:9a, 10, 18b, discipline),

(2b) respecting the laws of Wisdom by cultivating the education received from them (cf. Wisd. 6:18a, culture), with the ever remaining divine assistance of the Holy Spirit (cf. Wisd. 6:9a, Spirit-filled pactice. 'Anybody who receives my commandments and keeps them will be the one who loves me' [Jn 14: 21a]; 'If you love me you will keep my commandments. I shall ask the Father, and he will give you another Advocate to be with you forever, that Spirit of truth whom the world can never receive since she neither sees nor knows Him, but you know Him because He is with you, He is in you' [John 14:15–17]).

Our service of Wisdom to which leads our love for Wisdom embraces (1) our admiring and imitating Wisdom herself (cf. Wisd. 6:9b), her skill and technical know-how of producing works, and her models of creativity in creation, and thus (2) our producing, inventing or fabricating, works similar to Wisdom's created works by reproducing them (technics), (3) our honouring Wisdom (cf. Wisd. 6:21b) with the new products, inventions, fabrications that have been technically made by applying such invented material goods to defend and promote the human life and to propel the progress or advancement of the development of the seven basic capacities in the living human being, as the seven characteristics of every living being, towards their perfection (technology).

And it is precisely through honouring Wisdom, that one is able, at the end, to reign with God in eternity, because 'doing honour to Wisdom leads one to reign eternally' (Wisd. 6:21) in that Kingdom to which one's initial desire for Wisdom leads ('The desire for Wisdom leads to the Kingdom' [Sap. 6, 20]).

And the Trinitarian structure of the aggregate of these components of man's manifold act of love for Wisdom is in similarity, parallelism, and correspondence to the Trinitarian structure of the purpose of God's creation of man as the purpose of man's existence and life here on earth and in the hereafter in heaven.

For on the one hand are the three distinct correspondences here on earth, whereby to the fact that (A_1) God created man so that man in this world may know God corresponds to the fact that (A_2) the knowledge of Wisdom, presupposed by the love for Wisdom, comprises a chain of complex actions and activities:

(1) waking up (from the sleep of indolence and laziness of mind) for the desirable Wisdom (waking up), getting up for her early in the morning and thinking about her, desiring her as longing and requesting for her, asking and praying to receive her or supplicating that she be given to the praying one (prayerful desire and supplicatory prayer);

(2) going in search of her and following thereby her footprints (research, for Wisdom is readily seen by those who love her and found by those who look for her. Quick to anticipate those who desire her, she makes herself known to them); and

(3) after having found her or met her,

(**3a**) desiring to be instructed by her and leaving oneself be taught by her as by a master, an authoritative and exemplary teacher (teaching and grasping),

(**3b**) listening to her words (audition),

(**3c**) striving for how to be able to comprehend the words of Wisdom, i.e., to take with oneself all of them together as one's companion of life for the whole of one's life or as one's bride,

(**3d**) grasping the laws of Wisdom and bringing, through them, to light the knowledge of her (science).

And to the fact that (**B$_1$**) God created man so that man may in this world love the known God corresponds the fact that (**B$_2$**) the affective and effective (i.e., performative) love of Wisdom in which the love for Wisdom accomplishes itself comprises a chain of complex actions and activities, whereby

(1) those that express affective love of Wisdom embrace

(**1a**) seeking to see the face of the origin of Wisdom (***vultum Dei quaerere***, cf. knocking for opening) as of the proper speaker of the words of Wisdom ('My word is not my own: it is the word of the one who sent me') and, upon seeing the face of the speaking Origin of Wisdom,

(**1b**) looking at the paradoxical, i.e., at once fascinating and yet tremendous and inscrutable, hence mysterious, face of the origin of Wisdom as of her Father (contemplative Mysticism), and

(**1c**) adoring—i.e., admiring with devotion and with praises—the Origin of Wisdom whose face is being contemplated, while

(2) those that express effective love of Wisdom embrace

(**2a**) observing the laws of Wisdom by putting them into practice (discipline),

(**2b**) respecting the laws of Wisdom by cultivating the education received from them (culture), with the ever remaining divine assistance of the Holy Spirit (Spirit-filled practice. 'Anybody who receives my commandments and keeps them will be the one who loves me'; 'If you love me you will keep my commandments. I shall ask the Father, and he will give you another Advocate to be with you forever, that Spirit of truth whom the world can never receive since she neither sees nor knows him, but you know Him because He is with you, He is in you').

And to the fact that (**C₁**) God created man so that man may in this world serve the loved, known God corresponds the fact that (**C₂**) the service to Wisdom to which leads the love for Wisdom embraces (**1**) admiring and imitating Wisdom herself, her skill and technical know-how of producing works, and her models of creativity in creation (admiration and imitation); and thus (**2**) producing, inventing, or fabricating works similar to Wisdom's created works by reproducing them (***technics***); and (**3**) honouring Wisdom with the new products, inventions, fabrications that have been technically made by applying such invented material goods to defend and promote the human life and to propel the progress or advancement of the development of the seven basic capacities in the living human being, as the seven characteristics of every living being, towards their perfection (***technology***).

On the other hand stands the only one correspondence in the hereafter, whereby to the fact that (**D₁**) man has to know, love, and serve God in this world, here on earth, to be able in the world to come, in the hereafter in heaven, live in communion with God in the community of the three divine persons the eternal life of God as their life of eternal love for one another, eternal joy at one another, eternal glorification of one another, and eternal peace with one another corresponds the fact that (**D₂**) it is precisely through honouring Wisdom that one is able, at the end, to reign with God in eternity because 'doing honour to Wisdom leads one to reign eternally' (Wisd. 6:21) in that Kingdom to which one's initial desire for Wisdom leads ('The desire for Wisdom leads to the Kingdom' [Sap 6:20]).

Therefore, our human love for Wisdom here on earth—without which the Father of Wisdom would not love us and therefore would not send that Holy Spirit in the name of Wisdom to help us and without whose being our helper, namely our reminder of what Wisdom has said to us *in the past,* our teacher of everything *in the present,* our teller of the things to come *in the future* as things that the Spirit himself has learnt and that belong to Wisdom and to the Father of Wisdom together, and hence our leader to the *complete* truth—we *cannot* know God, love the known God, and serve the loved, known God with Wisdom and therefore *cannot,* in the hereafter, live with God in communion in the community of the Father and of the Son and of the Holy Spirit. This involves three groups of actions and activities: (1) waking up, prayerful desire and supplicatory prayer, research and teaching and grasping, audition, and science; (2) *vultum Dei quaerere,* knocking for an opening, contemplative mysticism, discipline, culture, Spirit-filled practice; (3) admiration and imitation, technics, and technology.

Science is that human love for Wisdom by bringing the knowledge of Wisdom to light, which presupposes grasping the laws of Wisdom and comprehending the words of Wisdom as taking with oneself the whole of them as one's companion of life for the whole of one's life or as one's bride. Culture is that love for Wisdom by cultivating the education received from the words of Wisdom, which presupposes respecting the laws of Wisdom and comprehending the words of Wisdom as taking with oneself the whole of them as one's companion of life for the whole of one's life or as one's bride. Discipline is that love for Wisdom by becoming a disciple of Wisdom through bearing much fruit to the glory of the Origin of Wisdom, which presupposes observing the laws of Wisdom, putting them into practice ('It is to the glory of my Father that you should bear much fruit, and then you will be my disciples. As the Father has loved me, so I have loved you. Remain in my love. If you keep my commandments you will remain in my love, just as I have kept my Father's commandments and remain in his love' [John 15:8–10]). Technics is that human love for Wisdom by admiring and imitating Wisdom and reproducing her creativity, which leads, with its products, to technology and has science as her immediate requisite. Technology is that human love for Wisdom by honouring Wisdom through the application of technically invented material goods to propel the progress of the development of the seven capacities of every living being found in the living human being towards their perfection, which has technics as its immediate requisite and leads to reigning in eternity.

In correspondence to the structure of God as of the First and the Last (cf. Isa. 44:6) in whom the Primary and the Ultimate are united into the numerically one God, it is generally the uniting of the knowledge of Wisdom, presupposed by the love for Wisdom, with the service of Wisdom to which the love for Wisdom leads, but particularly the uniting of science (as the last element of the knowledge of Wisdom, presupposed by the love for Wisdom) with technology (as the last element of the service of Wisdom to which the love for Wisdom leads and which presupposes admiration, imitation, and technics) to give rise to technoscience. In other words, technoscience is the unification of science and technology or the unity resulting from the mediated union of science and technology through admiration, imitation, and technics.

Now, as long as (i) science is that human love for Wisdom by bringing the knowledge of Wisdom to light, which presupposes grasping the laws of Wisdom and comprehending the words of Wisdom as taking with oneself the whole of them as one's companion of life for the whole of one's life or as one's bride, but (ii) Wisdom as person contains the Holy Spirit from whom comes that fear of offending the Lord God, which is the beginning of Wisdom as a thing (being a virtue), but (iii) religion consists in man's binding of himself to God, as the opposite of separating himself from God, whereby such self-separation of man from God is a sin, an offence against God, and therefore contrary to the virtue of the fear of offending the Lord, (iv) it follows that science and religion are united through science's need for the virtue of fear of offending the Lord so necessary in the practice of religion and hence through science's need for Wisdom as a thing, the beginning of which such a virtue that the fear of offending the Lord is, and hence through science's need for the Holy Spirit from whom such a virtue comes, and hence through science's reinforced need for Wisdom as person inside whom such an almighty Spirit is, and through science's need to bring the knowledge of Wisdom as person to light for her to be a lover of Wisdom, and hence to be herself.

This union is deepened by the natural mutual beneficence of the two to one another. Generally, religion inspires science, while sciences are used to justify religious tenets (which belongs to the task of theology as science); and particularly, sciences are used to fecundate the believed supernatural truths of the Christian religion (which belongs to the task of theology as technoscience) by first getting such truths as religious symbols translated into mathematical, particularly into geometrical figures as scientific symbols of the translated religious truths—regarding the structure of the originations in God and of the intertwining relationships that arise from the order of such originations and of the Trinitarian structure of such perichoresis among the persons in God—as of the tenets or creeds as symbols of Christian religious faith in order then to deduce laws of stability and of dynamism from such geometrical figures and apply them to the field of the natural sciences and of the human sciences to produce through such application abundant material good for the defence of promotion of the human life to perfection.

@3 One would have expected that science and religion should remain united through the fivefold need of science for the virtue of fear of offending the Lord, need for Wisdom as a thing with which Wisdom as a thing begins, need for the Holy Spirit from whom comes such a virtue, reinforced need for Wisdom as a person in whom such an almighty Spirit is, and need to bring the knowledge of Wisdom as a person to light for her (i.e., for science) to be a lover of Wisdom and hence to be herself.[6]

But that is not the case today, for rather since the age of secularisation as of the dichotomization between the secular and the sacred in which the secular separates itself from the sacred, autonomizes itself, and absolutizes itself (like once in history, man separated himself from God, autonomized himself, and absolutized himself), which has since continued to manifest itself among men in different ramifications, particularly in the dichotomization between reason and faith in which reason separates itself from faith, autonomizes itself (cf. rationalism) and absolutizes itself (cf. *cogito ergo sum*), there is today on board a scandalous, humanly introduced, manipulated, and engineered artificial dichotomization between science and religion in which science separates itself from religion, autonomizes itself, and absolutizes itself (scientism).

The question arises as to what the church can do in her Christ-given mission in the world to undo this dichotomization between faith and reason in which reason has separated itself from faith, autonomized itself (cf. rationalism) and absolutized itself (cf. *cogito ergo sum*).

6   John Egbulefu, 'Mutual Inclusion or Exclusion of "Prayer" and "Medicine" in the Search for Health as Wholeness? A Theological Answer in the Light of Soteriology,' in *Law and Ethics of Healthcare*, eds. Maurice Okechukwu Izunwa and Dozie Remigius Izunwa (Onitsha: Great-M Prints and Ideas, 2016), 323–350.

The answer that most of us thinking believers in the incarnate Wisdom of God, Jesus Christ the Emmanuel, have meanwhile given to this question is that the church has to do something similar to what Christ as mediator between God and the humankind has done—and do it the way Christ did it—to undo the dichotomization between God and man in which man separated himself from God and sought to autonomize and absolutize himself.

But what Christ as the incarnate Wisdom of God has done to undo the dichotomization between God and Man is an external manifestation of what the Holy Spirit as the Spirit inside Wisdom as a person has done in the incarnate Wisdom of God, the incarnate Word of God, Jesus Christ, as Godman, namely the Spirit's uniting of the divine in the Godman Christ with the human in Christ; and the way Christ has done His undoing of the dichotomization between God and man is an external manifestation of the way the Holy Spirit has united the divine in the Godman Christ with the human in Christ.

But the way the Holy Spirit has united the divine in Christ with the human in Christ at that Incarnation of the Word from which has resulted the incarnate Word is by uniting the Word of divine nature with the flesh of human nature (cf. John 1:14) and uniting also the divine nature of the Word with the human nature of the flesh[7] in such a manner that the union as the proper relation between the divine and the human in the Godman is characterized by coherence between the divine and the human components of the Godman, with the consequence that every saying and doing of the incarnate Logos is characterized by logicality and therefore by credibility and therefore by reliability.

Therefore what the church can do in her Christ-given mission in the world to undo the dichotomization between faith and reason in which reason has separated itself from faith, autonomized itself (cf. rationalism), and absolutized itself (cf. *cogito ergo sum*) is to (re)unite faith and reason to give rise to a synthesis called Christian theology (as that God-believing and God-loving activity of the human spirit that is carried out within a system the two precise coordinates of which are 'faith and reason' [*fides*

---

7   Heinrich Denzinger, *Enchiridion Symbolorum Definitionum et Declarationum de Rebus Fidei et Morum, Compendium of Creeds, Definitions and Declarations on Matters of Faith and Morals*, Latin-English, 43rd Edition, Peter Huenermann ed., §.301-302 (San Francisco, SA: Ignatius Press, 2012), 109.

et ratio]) and do it in such a manner that this union as the proper relation between the Christian faith and the human reason is characterized by coherence between the divine and the human components of Christian theology, with the consequence that every self-expression of Christian theology is characterized by logicality and therefore by credibility and therefore by reliability.

But we mean that such coherence, logicality, credibility, and reliability can only be given when, on the one hand, the human component of the Christian theology, namely reason, stands for those human questions about God's reasons or intentions or purpose or aim for creating man, for calling the human being into existence in this world, which humans have raised out of their experience with life here on earth and have directed at God as at the Giver of the life, while on the other hand, the divine component of the Christian theology, namely faith, stands for God's answer to the questions asked by humans at Him about the human life and hence about the human existence, hence about why God created the human being, an answer that has been revealed by God to humans and is contained in the God-revealing Word of God (*Logos tou Theou*, from which the word *theology* has meanwhile been created) that humans ought to believe and either have already believed and have to believe it ever more or have not yet believed, though they should not fail to believe it, or do not believe any longer, though they should not stop to believe it.

But as long as theology is that God-believing activity of the human spirit that is carried out within a system the two precise coordinates of which are faith and reason (*fides et ratio*) but faith can mean diversely and reason can mean diversely, it follows that theology can mean diversely.

On the one hand, there is formal theology there where faith (*fides*) stands for the act of believing with which—through that theological virtue of faith as capacity to believe supernatural things and in supernatural persons, which is divinely infused into the human spirit together with the other two theological virtues, namely love for God and hope in Him—a supernatural reality gets believed by man (*fides qua otentia*), while reason (*ratio*) stands for the act of reasoning (*ratiocinatio*) in two ways, be it analogically by comparing between two similar things whose similarity goes back either to a certain genetic relationship between the two (like between a parent and the child or between two children of the same parents) or to a certain parallelism between the two (like between a type and its prototype or archetype, whereby the type is forerunner or precursor of the prototype, prefigures the prototype, anticipates the arrival of the prototype as its antitype, or between an imagery and its significance within a metaphor or metaphorical language as a word, or within a proverb or proverbial saying as a statement, or within a parable or parabolic expression as mythos, i.e., descriptive or narrative story), be it syllogistically by arguing deductively from universals as premises to particulars as conclusion, or be it inductively from particulars as premises to a universal as conclusion.

On the other hand, there is material theology present, where faith (*fides*) stands for each doctrine of the Christian faith—i.e., that taught, revealed divine truth—which is believed wholly and entirely by every Christian (cf. *fides quae otentia*), while reason (*ratio*) as a basic component of the soul stands for that particular faculty of the soul in man by which man accomplishes the act of reasoning (ratiocination, *ratiocinatio*, 'ratio-cinatio'), of praying as imploration (*oratio ut otentialn*, 'o-ratio ut impl-o-ratio'), and of adoration as admiration with devotion (*adoratio devote*, 'ad-o-ratio devote').

But these diversities between formal theology and material theology notwithstanding, there is this new perception, vision, and insight gained that theology is systematically (i.e., in the sense of being a system, organic unity resulting from the union of two diverse parts of a whole) the result (product) of the act of theologizing as of that believing and thinking (a thinking underlain and sustained by faith, hence a synthesis of faith and reason) on the Word of God (*Logos tou Theou*) within a coordinate system that has as its two general coordinates faith (*fides*) and reason (*ratio*), which is done within the space between, on the one hand, the horizontal axis called the reasons for the existence of man on earth as the proper object of the questions that men have raised at God regarding His reason, intention, purpose, and aim for making the living human being (*rationes existendi hominis in terra*), i.e., for creating man, calling the human being into existence on earth through His eternal creative Word, and on the other hand, the vertical axis called the believed Word of God (*verbum Dei creditum*) as the proper source of the answer God has given to the human questions about the human life and, hence, about the human existence on earth.

2.2 Christian Theology as a Coordinate System of Scientific, Practical, Mystical, and Technical Theologies

@1. There is a theology there where and when (1) on the one hand, faith (*fides*) stands for the humanly believed Word of God, which is linguistically structured and composed by the quartet 'the Semantic of the humanly believed divine Word', 'the Grammar of the humanly believed divine Word', 'the Syntax of the humanly believed divine Word', and 'the Pragmatics of the humanly believed divine Word', whereby this quartet is the intrarelational quartet that has the structure of a vertical line to which belong the four points that represent the four named characteristic features of the Word of God as a lingual reality; while (2) on the other hand, reason (*ratio*) stands for the divine reasons (*rationes*) for the human existence in this world, i.e., when and where reason stands for the reasons why man is existing, why God created man, why God called the human being into existence in this world, whereby (2a) the answer is that such reasons are numerically four, a quartet, (2aa) be it the extrarelational quartet as an ensemble that has the trinitarian structure of God, insofar as the system of the aggregate of the four constitutive elements of the quartet consists in the organic unity resulting from the union of those three divine reasons for man's existence here on earth.

Namely that man may know God, love God, and serve God, the accomplishment of which here on earth is the requisite for man's living with God in the hereafter, with the one and indivisible divine reason for man's existence hereafter in heaven, namely to live in communion with God in the community of the three divine persons that have jointly created man in their own image and likeness and in such a way that man, similar to them already in the sense that like there are three persons in one God and among these three persons only one, namely the Father as the first person, has no origin, while the rest two, namely the Son as the second person and the Holy Spirit as the third person, have origin though each originates in a diverse way and manner from the Father, the Son originating from only the Father and in a passive way by being generated and born from the substance of the Father, while the Holy Spirit originates from the Father and the Son together, and this in an active manner by proceeding from both at the same time.

So also, there are three things that constitute every living human being: the human body, the human soul, and the human spirit contained in the human body and containing the human soul and therefore uniting the human body and the human soul to one another; and among these three things, only one, namely the human body, is material and visible and mortal, while the rest, namely the human soul and the human spirit, are immaterial and invisible and immortal, whereby the spirit, which contains the soul and not vice versa, has something in common with them on which the three build this communion with man to which they have invited him and which consists in the triad communication and union and sharing, namely their truly uniting man to themselves, their graciously communicating their life to him, and man's spirit-filled sharing and participating in their eternal life as in that unique life of eternal love for one another, eternal joy at one another, eternal glorification of one another, and eternal peace with one another, which is eternally going on inside God among these exclusively three divine persons in the numerically one God, (2ab) be it the intrarelational quartet that has the structure of a horizontal line to which belong four points.

Thus, points that are aligned, i.e., four points that belong to one and same line, the four points that represent those four divine reasons that result from a differentiated understanding of man's love for God as of the second of the originally called three divine reasons for Man's existence here on earth and such resulting four divine reasons for man's earthly existence as the reasons why God created Man, i.e., why God, through His eternal creative Word, the divine Logos, called man into existence, are namely that man may know God; love God affectively (giving Him an affectionate love) by adoring Him (admiring Him devotedly, i.e., with the whole soul and whole heart and whole mind) as worshipping Him in Spirit and truth, both in the spirit as a thing that the soul and heart and mind and strength are and in the Spirit as a person that the Holy Spirit is, and both in the truth as a thing that the wholeness (i.e., the entirety and totality of the soul and of the heart and of the mind and of strength is and in the truth as person that the incarnate Word as incarnate Son of God, Jesus Christ) is; love God effectively (giving Him a performative love) by keeping His commandments; and serve God by working for Him the way He likes, through imitating the way Himself. This has worked for Man, namely it has created the human being in general and created the woman in particular and caters for every human holistically and devotedly.

(2b) The structure of the theology done here on earth precedes the one done hereafter in heaven and bears the staurologico-theandric structure of the earthly church of Christ in which such earthly theology is done. As long as the earthly church is a people that is moving at once horizontally on mission towards fellow men, to all the peoples, to all the nations, down here on earth, and vertically on pilgrimage towards God, to God the Father and His ascended incarnate Son, Christ, up there in heaven, and the structure of whose movement is at once outwardly in the form of the cross (*stauros*) and inwardly in the form of the Godman (***Theandros***).

@2. The four points that are aligned to form (i.e., through a conjunction of them successively to one another constitute) the horizontal line as the second axis are man's knowing God; man's loving God affectively or in an affectionate manner by adoring (i.e., devotedly admiring and praising) God for which God created him; man's loving God effectively (i.e., in a performative way) by observing God's commands to him, putting God's words into practice, hence doing the will of God for which God created him; and man's serving God as working for God in the way that pleases God, i.e., the way God Himself works for man, hence, by man's adopting, and adapting to, God's method, skill, technique, and technical know-how of working and creating and producing, thus by man's imitating how God created the living human being and created the woman too—for which God created Man.

@3. The four points that are aligned to form (i.e., through a conjunction of them successively to one another constitute) the vertical line as the first axes are the semantics of the Word of God, the syntax of the Word of God, the grammar of the Word of God, and the pragmatics of the Word of God. The semantics of the Word of God consists in the system of the meanings of the Word of God, be it the meaning of the Word of God in person, both in His preincarnate state as the Word through whom all things were created, and in His incarnate state as the incarnate Word, the Godman, in the person of Jesus Christ, through whom God has saved the created humanity. Be it the words of God as things, i.e., the aggregate of the (assertive, imperative—invitatory and mandatory—and admonitory, promissory, and interrogatory) words spoken by God and deposited partly in the old-testamentary and new-testamentary Holy Scriptures and partly in the doctrinal, devotional, and disciplinary tradition of the church. The syntax of the Word of God consists in the laws regulating the harmony of the parts of speech of this Word—the verbs in harmony among themselves with regard to their past or present or future tenses and in harmony with the nouns with regard to their singular or plural number and the nouns and pronouns in harmony among themselves with regard to their genders, to their adjectives, and to their singular or plural numbers.

The grammar of the Word of God consists in the laws regulating both the subjects and predicates of the sentences (as questions or statements) and regulating the proper positioning of the words within a sentence, the proper place and role of the prepositions, the verbs, the adverbs, the nouns, the adjectives, the conjunctions, the articles, etc., to build up a sentence that makes sense. The pragmatics of the Word of God consists in the technical use of the words and phrases—metaphorical, metaphysical, mathematical language—to achieve the desired effect, e.g., the linguistic use of elocution, elegant style of intonation or of pronunciation of the words, or the use of oratory to whip up sentiments of annoyance and anger or of sadness or of sympathy of joy or to demoralize or to instil courage or whip up consent in the listener or the addressee by the speaker or writer of the word.

@4. The four species of theology that arise from the coordination of every one of the four constitutive points of the vertical axis with its corresponding or homologous point among the four constitutive points of the horizontal axis as the point with which it coincides to form a subsystem of coordinates within the main system (the two coordinates of which are the two axes standing for faith and reason respectively) are (in their systematic, not historical, order): scientific theology (as was emphasized in the practice of theology in the Middle Ages in medieval scholastic theology), mystical theology (as was emphasized in the practice of theology by the church fathers before the Middle Ages in premedieval patristic theology), practical theology (as was emphasized in the practice of theology in the period of Modernism after the Middle Ages in postmedieval modern theology), and technical theology (as it is today beginning to be emphasized after the age of Modernism in the postmodern technoscientific theology of the incipient Third Millennium).

@4a. That specie of theology is called scientific theology. This results from the coordination of the first point on the horizontal axis, i.e., the first of the reasons for the existence of man on earth, the first of the reasons why God has made the living human being (*rationes existendi hominis in terra*), why God created man, i.e., has called man into existence on earth through His eternal creative Word, namely 'Man's knowing God', and the first point on the vertical axis, i.e., the first of the four characteristic features of the believed Word of God (*verbum Dei creditum*), namely the semantics of the Word of God. Such a specie of theology is named scientific, seeing that the word *scientific* is the adjective taken from the Latin verb '*scio, scire, scivi, scitum*', meaning 'to know'. Therefore scientific theology can be defined as that theology that is done within the space between, on the one hand, 'Man's search for the knowledge of God' (as of the first point on the horizontal axis, namely the first of the reasons for the existence of Man on earth—the reasons why God has made the living human being, i.e., created man and has called man into existence on earth through His Word [*rationes existendi hominis in terra*]).

On the other hand, the semantics of the Word of God (as of the first point on the vertical axis, namely the first characteristic features of 'the believed Word of God'), with the aim to bring out, from latency to evidence, that proper meaning of this divine Word, which consists in the divine answer, contained in the divine Word, to the human questions concerning the reason why God created man, a reason that presupposes man's knowledge of the God from whom the answer contained in the Word has come. In fact, what is being most urgently expected of Christian theologians in the society of today is the uniting of the human questions (*quaestiones*) about the divine purpose for the creation of humans as about the source of the proper reason (*ratio*) for the life, and hence for the existence, of humans on earth with the believed and intelligible biblical and traditional Word of God as the source of the ever valid, and never expired, divine answer to the human questions. But the uniting of the human questions (*quaestiones*) about the divine purpose for the creation of humans as about the source of the proper reason (*ratio*) for the life, and hence for the existence, of humans on earth with the believed and intelligible biblical and traditional Word of God as with the source of the ever valid, and never expired, divine answer to the human questions into a truly scientific theology passes through thinking.

@4b. That specie of theology is called mystical theology, which results from the coordination of the second point on the horizontal axis, i.e., the second of the reasons for the existence of man on earth, the second of the reasons why God made the living human beings (*rationes existendi hominis in terra*), why God created man, i.e., has called man into existence on earth through His eternal creative Word, namely Man's loving God affectively or in an affectionate manner—by adoring (i.e., devotedly admiring and praising) God—for which God created him, and the second point on the vertical axis, i.e., the second of the four characteristic features of the believed Word of God (*verbum Dei creditum*), namely the syntax of the Word of God (consisting in the system of the laws regulating the harmony among the symbolic parts of speech in the sentence, embracing the symbolic verbs in harmony among themselves with regard to their past or present or future tenses, or in harmony with the symbolic nouns with regard to their singular or plural number and the symbolic nouns and pronouns in harmony among themselves with regard to their genders, to their adjectives, and to their singular or plural numbers).

Such a specie of theology is named mystical, seeing that the word *mystical* is the synthesis of the prefix *myst-* of the word *mysterious* as of the adjective of the noun *mystery* on the one hand and the suffix *-ical* of the word *paradoxical* as of the adjective from the noun *paradox* on the other hand. Therefore mystical theology can be defined as that theology that is done within the space between, on the one hand, man's loving God affectionately by adoring, i.e., devotedly admiring and praising God (as the second point on the horizontal axis, namely, the second of the reasons for the existence of man on earth—the reasons why God created man, i.e., as through His Word, He called man into existence on earth) as its horizontal axis and, on the other hand, the syntax of the Word of God (as the second point on the vertical axis, namely, as the second of the characteristic features of the believed Word of God) as its vertical axis. The otent-theological engagement is done with the aim to express in symbols that proper harmony of the symbolic parts of speech of the Word of the mysterious—fascinating and yet tremendous and inscrutable—God, perceived by us humans who are made by Him in His image, thereby making the human being into a paradoxical being out of mutually contrary elements, i.e., such that are opposite but not opposed to one another, namely out of the one visible material and mortal element called the human body and the two invisible immaterial and immortal, inseparably united elements called the human soul and the human spirit.

And the syntax as the system of the laws regulating the harmony of the symbolic parts of speech in the Word of God is that which derives (1) from the powerfully synthetic and synthesizing character of the Word of God as of Him who is characterized by oneness or unity (as epitomized in the Trinity of the triune God who merits to be loved affectively or affectionately, namely to be adored, i.e., admired with devotion and to be honoured and praised and glorified for His Goodness, His Trueness and Truth and Truthfulness, and His Beauty and Beautifulness, by all His creatures each in their own way); (2) from the admirable symphonic character of the diverse—imperative, invitatory, mandatory, admonitory, promissory—tones of the one and same Word of God as of Him who is characterized by goodness (as epitomized in the special action of God the Father towards humans); (3) from the admirable synchronized and synchronizing character of the Word of God as of Him who is characterized by trueness and truth and truthfulness (as epitomized in the special action of God the Son towards humans); and (4) from the admirable symmetrical character of the Word of God as of Him, who is characterized by beauty and beautifulness (as epitomized in the special action of God the Holy Spirit towards humans).

The otent-theological activity of the human spirit consists in the contemporaneous (1) listening (cf. audition) to the triune God that has, through His eternal Word, called the human being into existence and meditating on His words (*verba*) as on that truth of the Word of the living God, which is deposited inside the togetherness of scripture and tradition and the presence of which therein is sustained by the Holy Spirit proceeding from, and sent by, the Father and the Son and (2) looking (cf. vision) directly at Him and contemplating, in admiration, His divine Trinity as His otherwise dazzling constant face (*facies*) and variable countenance (*vultum*) and praising Him for the greatness and wonders, the magnificence and wonderfulness, of His excellent works (opera) as at that light that His Word is, a light that, with its bundles of rays, not only illumines men, their life, and their paths but also upon striking them, engenders in them warmth, heat, and fire to render them warm, hot, and fiery for the supernatural, the eternal, the divine.

The act of meditating on that truth of the Word of the living God, which is deposited inside the togetherness of scripture and tradition and the presence of which therein is sustained by the Holy Spirit proceeding from and sent by the Father and the Son, is (done) like meditating on that image of the face of the shining sun that has sunken into the limpid and sparkling, crystal-clear and mirror-like water mass, and the presence of which therein is sustained by the same bundle of rays emitted by the sun and emanating from the face of the sun. The act of looking directly at Him and contemplating, in admiration, His divine Trinity as His otherwise dazzling constant face (*facies*) and variable countenance (*vultum*) *and* praising Him for the greatness and wonders, the magnificence and wonderfulness, of His excellent works (opera) as at that eternal light that His Word is, which, with His radiant splendour that His brilliant rays release, not only illumines men, their life, and their paths but also, upon striking them, engenders in them warmth, heat, and fire to render them warm, hot, and fiery for the supernatural, the eternal, the divine, is (done) like looking directly at the otherwise dazzling face of God with the mind and heart (*mens et cor*) as with the two natural spiritual eyes through the two lenses of that supernatural (hence spiritual) pair of spectacles constituted by the system of the seven gifts of the Holy Spirit that (as the unity resulting from the union of a pair of lenses with a frame) is constituted by **(i)** the two gifts of intelligence and wisdom as the two diverse—telescopic and microscopic—lenses through which the mind and the heart respectively look at God and **(ii)** the five gifts that jointly constitute the frame of the spectacles, comprising the two gifts of knowledge and counsel as the two sockets into which the two lenses—intelligence and wisdom—are respectively sunken, the two gifts of piety and fear of offending the Lord as the two hangers that connect the two sockets (knowledge and counsel) and, hence, also the therein contained lenses (intelligence and wisdom) for seeing the face and countenance (i.e., for the vision) of the speaking God with the two ears ('the Conscience as the voice of God' and 'the innate capacity in Man to obey the Word of God, the *otential oboedientialis*') for hearing the voice and word (i.e., for the audition) of the speaking God, and the one and unique gift of fortitude as the bridge that unites the two sockets and sustains the unity of the entire pair of spectacles. It is like looking directly through the antireflex lenses of a pair of spectacles at (the contours—the aggregate of lines and curves of) the stable face and variable countenance of the shining sun and at the wide horizon of the beautiful blue sky and heavenly bodies that surround the sun and go together with it.

@4c. That specie of theology is called practical theology, which results from the coordination of the third point on the horizontal axis, i.e., the third of the reasons for the existence of man on earth (***rationes existendi hominis in terra***), the third of the reasons why God has made the living human being and why God created Man, i.e., has called man into existence on earth through His eternal creative Word, namely man's loving God effectively or in a performative way by observing God's commands to him, putting God's words into practice, hence doing the will of God, and the third point on the vertical axis, i.e., the third of the four characteristic features of the believed Word of God (***verbum Dei creditum***), namely the grammar of the Word of God (consisting in the system of the laws regulating both the subjects and predicates of the sentences—questions or statements—and regulating the proper positioning of the words within a sentence, the proper place and role of the prepositions, the verbs, the adverbs, the nouns, the adjectives, the conjunctions, the articles, etc., to build up a sentence that makes sense). Such a specie of theology is named practical, seeing that the word ***practical*** is the adjective taken from the Greek noun ***praxis***, translated into the English noun ***practice***, meaning the application of principles or of theories or the translation of words into action, into facts, into deeds. Hence, practical theology is theology that is developed within the two precise coordinates of, on the one hand, man's loving God effectively or in a performative way (by observing God's commands to him, putting God's words into practice, hence doing the will of God—for which God created him) as its horizontal axis and, on the other hand, the grammar of the Word of God (consisting in the laws regulating both the subjects and the predicates of the sentences—questions or statements—and regulating the proper positioning of the words within each sentence, the proper place and role of the prepositions, the verbs, the adverbs, the nouns, the adjectives, the conjunctions, the articles, etc., to build up a sentence that makes sense) as its vertical axis.

@4d. That specie of theology is called technical theology, which results from the coordination of the fourth point on the horizontal axis, i.e., the fourth of the reasons for the existence of man on earth (*rationes existendi hominis in terra*), the fourth of the reasons why God has made the living human being, why God created Man, i.e., has called man into existence on earth through His eternal creative Word, namely to serve God (by putting oneself always at the disposal of God and working for Him in a way that pleases Him, namely adopting the same method, skill, technique, technical know-how of doing, with which God works for humans to work for God) with the fourth of the four characteristic features of the Word of God, the pragmatics of the Word of God (consisting in the technical use of the words and phrases and metaphorical, metaphysical, mathematical language to achieve the desired effect, hence the use of elocution, elegant style of intonation or of pronunciation of the words, or the use of oratory to whip up sentiments of annoyance and anger or of sadness or of sympathy or of joy or to demoralize or to instil courage or whip up consent in the listener or the addressee by the speaker or writer of the word) as the fourth point on the vertical axis called the believed Word of God (*verbum Dei creditum, ex auditu, non ex visu, non ex tactu*). Hence technical theology is that theology that is developed within the two precise coordinates of serving God (by putting oneself always at the disposal of God and working for Him in a way that pleases Him, namely adopting the same method, skill, technique, technical know-how of doing with which God works for humans to work for God) and the pragmatics of the Word of God heard and believed by humans. The word *technical* is the adjective from the Greek substantive *techne*, which means craftsmanship, skill, technical know-how, inventiveness, la capability—capacity and ability—to invent, fabricate, produce, create a material object as a good that can serve for the well-being of humans. Technical theology is 'technical' as far as it is concerned with inventing, fabricating, producing, creating material goods in the form of objects (like medicine, food and drinks, means of mobility or of transport, means of perception and of reacting to the perceived reality, means of movement and of communication) or in the form of ideas (like laws or theories on how to make, do, equal distribution, and hence arrive at distributive justice and hence at governing well, justly, and adequately).

@5. In sum, these four species of theology done in the earthly church of Christ and each of which is a coordinate system (namely scientific theology, practical theology, mystical theology, and technical theology) are aligned, i.e., they lie on a single line; and that line is precisely the oblique line that stretches **(A)** from the point where the vertical line (constituted by the four divine reasons for the human existence on earth) that symbolizes the faith-axis of the system of coordinates the two proper coordinates of which are faith and reason in general crosses the horizontal line (constituted by the four characteristic features of the divine Word as a lingual reality) that symbolizes the reason-axis of the same system of coordinates the two proper coordinates of which are faith and reason; **(B)** through **(Ba)** the point where the semantics of the believed divine Word meets and coincides with the God-willed human knowledge of God, **(Bb)** the point where the grammar of the believed divine Word meets and coincides with the God-willed human effective (performative) love for God, and **(Bc)** the point where the syntax of the believed Word of God meets and coincides with the God-willed human affective (or affectionate) love for God; to **(C)** the point where the pragmatics of the believed divine Word meets and coincides with the God-willed human services to God.

In the various (patristic, medieval, modern, and contemporary) epochs of the history of theology, theologians have put varied accentuations on the various (scientific, practical, mystical, and technical) species of theology: in the patristic epoch, they put the accent more on mystical theology, while in the Middle Ages, they put the accent rather more on scientific theology. Whereas in the modern period, they put the accent rather more on practical theology, while in the contemporary epoch, they have begun to put the accent rather more on technical theology, having seen the signs of the times, particularly the shift from science to technoscience, which has made the shift from theology as science to theology as technoscience an imperative, and the option for globalization not only of the spiritual but also of the material means of effecting and defending and promoting the human life and its progress or advancement to its full stature, to full life, to the fullness of life, and of Man to fulfiled life through the perfection of each of the seven capacities that characterize the living being in the human being—the capacity to perceive and react to the perceived reality, to make movement, to respire, to nurture oneself, to grow, to reproduce oneself, and to throw out from oneself and far away from one's environment life-endangering waste products.

@6. Methodology is the theory of the methodics. **Methodics** means the system of methods. **Method** means that act or action of a person (e.g., running) or process of a thing (e.g., flying) by which a subject (cf. a runner) or an object (e.g., a bird) operates the means (i.e., instruments, e.g., the legs of the runner, the wings of the bird) of arriving at the set goal (e.g., a place like a city or a country). The theological methodology is the system (unity resulting from the union) of diverse theological methods of the four species of theology: the method of scientific theology, the method of mystical theology, the method of practical theology, and the method of technical theology.

@6a. The method of scientific theology consists in man's act or action of seeking to know God through the human spirit's act or action of (i) researching on the semantics of the Word of God and interpreting—i.e., reading between the lines (*inter lineas legere, intellegere*)—the divine Word; (ii) searching thereby to find (cf. *quaerite ut invenietis,* Matt. 7:7) the meaning both of the Word of God (*Logos tou Theou*) as a person sent to humans by God and of the words of God (*logoi tou Theou*) as the words spoken to humans by God; and (iii) following thereby the guideline like how the Son of God was made man through that act by which the Word is made flesh, i.e., through the Incarnation of the Word so man can know God through that act by which the human spirit searches and finds the meaning of the Word of God. And since such a meaning—both of the Word of God as a person and the words of God as things—consists in the fact that the Word of God (contains the divine truth) is God's answer to the (worries and) questions (arising from the experiences) of humans in life concerning the origin and the goal, the reason, and the sense of purpose, the length, and the hereafter, the irrepetability, irreversibility, irrevocability, of the human life after the life on earth.

It follows that the goal of scientific theology is (the human spirit's interpreting task) to show that the Word of God (contains the divine truth) is God's answer to the (worries and) questions (arising from the experiences) of humans in life concerning the origin and the goal, the reason and the sense of purpose, the length and the hereafter, the irrepetability, irreversibility, irrevocability, of the human life after the life on earth. And since the method through which man can know God must be like the act through which the Son of God was made man, but the act through which the Son of God was made man is the act by which the Word was made flesh, i.e., the Incarnation of the Word, but the act of the Incarnation consists in the union of the Word of divine nature with the flesh of human nature and the union of the divine nature of the Word with the human nature of the flesh, it follows that the method through which man can know God, hence the method of scientific theology, must be like the twofold union of the Word of divine nature with the flesh of human nature *and of* the divine nature of the Word with the human nature of the flesh.

@6b. The method of mystical theology consists in man's actor-action of seeking to love God affectionately through the human soul's act or action of (i) willing, thus asking, questing and requesting, longing, and supplicating for the syntax of the Word of God; (ii) asking, questing, and requesting to be given the harmony of the verbs among themselves with regard to their past or present or future tenses, the harmony of the verbs with the symbolic nouns with regard to their singular or plural number, and the harmony of the symbolic nouns and pronouns among themselves with regard to their genders, to their adjectives, and to their singular or plural numbers; and (iii) following thereby the guideline that like the Son of God was made mystery through that act by which the substantial image of God is made the primordial or prototypical (i.e., archetypal) sacrament (*Mysterion*), so can man love God with affect or affectionately through the act by which the human soul wills, thus asks, desires, quests and requests, longs and supplicates to be given the harmony of the parts of speech of the Word of God. And as long as the soul is willing, thus asking, questing and requesting, longing, and supplicating for this threefold harmony of the symbolic parts of speech of the Word of God, this threefold harmony derives fourfold.

(1) From the powerfully synthetic and synthesizing character of the Word of God as of Him who is characterized by oneness or unity (as epitomized in the Trinity of the triune God who merits to be loved with affect or affectionately, namely to be adored, i.e., admired with devotion and with praise, and to be honoured and glorified, for His Goodness, His trueness and truth and truthfulness, and His beauty and beautifulness).

(2) From the admirable symphonic character of the Word of God as of Him who is characterized by goodness (as epitomized in the action of God the Father towards all His creatures).

(3) From the admirable synchronized and synchronizing character of the Word of God as of Him who is characterized by trueness and truth and truthfulness (as epitomized in the action of God the Son towards humans in particular) and from the admirable symmetrical character of the Word of God as of Him who is characterized by Beauty and Beautifulness (as epitomized in the action of God the Holy Spirit towards humans in particular).

(4) It follows that the ultimate goal of mystical theology is the human soul's willing possession of the God of the Word as the God who is characterized (i) by oneness or unity as epitomized in the Trinity of the triune God who merits to be loved with affect or affectionately—namely to be adored, i.e., admired with devotion—and to be honoured and praised and glorified for His goodness, His trueness and truth and truthfulness, and His beauty and beautifulness; (ii) by goodness as epitomized in the action of God the Father towards us; (iii) by trueness and truth and truthfulness as epitomized in the action of God the Son towards us creatures; and (iv) by beauty and beautifulness as epitomized in the action of God the Holy Spirit towards us creatures.

@6c. The method of Practical Theology consists in man's act or action of seeking to love God effectively or in a performative way through the human soul's act or action of **(1)** willing, thus asking, questing and requesting, longing, and supplicating for the grammar of the Word of God; **(2)** asking, questing, and requesting to be given the laws regulating both the subjects and predicates of the sentences—questions or statements—and regulating the proper positioning of the words within a sentence, the proper place and role of the prepositions, the verbs, the adverbs, the nouns, the adjectives, the conjunctions, the articles, etc., to build up sentences that make sense; and **(3)** following thereby the guideline that like how the Son of God was made the norm (the standard, the criterion of judgment) through that act by which the substantial image of God is made the law, the commandment, itself in person, so can man love God effectively or in a performative way through that act by which the human soul wills, thus asks, desires, quests and requests, longs, and supplicates to be given the laws of the Word of God. And as long as the human soul is willing, thus asking, questing and requesting, longing, and supplicating for these laws regulating both the subjects and predicates of the sentences—questions or statements—and regulating the proper positioning of the words within a sentence, the proper place and role of the prepositions, the verbs, the adverbs, the nouns, the adjectives, the conjunctions, the articles, etc., to build up sentences that make sense, it follows that the ultimate goal of practical theology is to observe and teach fellow men to observe all the commandments of God to humans.

@6d. The method of technical theology consists in man's act or action of seeking to serve God, work for Him with both hands, and the way that pleases Him as the way that He Himself works for man through the living human body's hands' or fingers' act or action of

(1) Knocking at the Word of God (***pulsate et aperietur vobis*** [Matt. 7:7]) to expose (lay bare) its pragmatic relevance to the material human life—in other words, knocking
   (i) to have it opened to the knocking living human body so that
   (ii) the latter may see the therein contained values (laws of stability and of dynamism and the theandric unions) which are to be applied to creatures (chemical and physical as existing but not living beings, the biological comprising botanical and zoological as living but not intelligent beings, the intelligent human as rational beings with a fascinating nervous system worthy of emulation) in order, through such application
   (iii) to fabricate, invent, create, material goods for the defence and promotion of the progress of the human life towards its perfection;

(2) adapting to or adopting or imitating, the same method or skill or technique, hence technical know-how, that God exercises at work; and

(3) following thereby the guideline that like how the Son of God was made miracle through that act by which the power and Wisdom of God was made the Resurrection, the Light of the world, the living Bread from heaven, the Good Shepherd, the Door of the sheep, the Way and the Truth and the Life, the true Vine, so can man serve God, i.e., work for Him, through the living body's hands' or fingers' act of knocking at the Word of God to expose (lay bare) its pragmatic relevance to the material human life. And as long as the body's hand or finger is knocking at the pragmatics of the Word of God to get it opened to the knocking living body or hand or finger or

(i) to see the therein contained values, laws of stability and dynamism and the theandric unions, which are

(ii) to be applied to creatures (chemical and physical as existing but not living beings, the biological comprising botanical and zoological as living but not intelligent beings, the intelligent human as rational beings with a nervous system) in order through such application

(iii) to fabricate, invent, create, material goods for the defence and promotion of the progress of the human life towards its perfection, it follows that the ultimate goal of technical theology is to fabricate, invent, create, material goods for the defence and promotion of the progress of the human life towards its perfection

Chapter Six

Evangelization Locally and Globally: The Filiation Dynamic

Innocent Maduakolam Osuagwu and Bede Ukwuije

Structure

The structure of this joint reflection is portioned out into two parts (a) Part One makes vital Fundamental Theological Remarks (b) Part Two dwells on The Pastoral Theology of Divine filiation. It expands and deepens entries made in part one, drawing out for praxis the implications and challenges.

Part One: Fundamental Theological Remarks

Introducing the Topic

"Evangelization Locally and Globally: The Filiation Dynamic" is the choice topic of this reflection. It identifies two cardinal pillars of our Christian faith and life and declares a fundamental doctrinal position that filiation is, in content and intent, the soul of evangelization. The one is so much about the other that it is right to state that to evangelize is to filiate and to filiate to evangelize. As source and summit of evangelization, filiation rereads Christ's mandate: go into the whole world and make sons and daughters for God, in the name of the Father and of the Son and of the Holy Spirit. In the final analysis, Christianity is a filiation religion; my Christian faith like yours, a filiation faith.

The Task of this Paper

The task of our paper is to demonstrate the significance of filiation for the mission of evangelization and life of faith of the Church and Christians. In a special way, the Ecclesiastical Province of Owerri is concerned as, progressively, we mature as an indigenous Church that has taken over from expatriates the prophetic mantle and pastoral staff of being missionaries to ourselves locally and to foreign lands globally. In this new status and role of living the life of faith, of witnessing and missioning, there is need to get engaged in the theological discourse, and to do so creatively yet faithfully without prejudice to orthodoxy. Given the new time or context, there is need to identify and develop our theological foundations, our fundamental options, and the formation guidelines and catechetical framework of our spirituality and socio-pastoral actions.

Topic Impetus and Relevance: Option for the Gospel of Divine Filiation

Three major sources of our paper's impetus and relevance include:

1. The pastoral insight and solicitude of the Chief Shepherd of our Province: Archbishop Obinna is an ardent proponent of divine filiation, from various dimensions called "Theofiliation", "Christofiliation" with their other cognates. These form part of his new conceptual repertoire and theological language. Since his episcopacy, he has dedicated sustained attention to it.[1] For him, divine filiation is, for humans in general and

---

1 See Anthony J. V. Obinna, "Roots, Branches ... Graftings and Fruits: The Reconfiliatory Challenge to African- Americans and Humanity at Large," lecture, Charleston, USA, 2003. See also, Id., "Confiliatory Collaboration between the Church in Africa and Europe: A Theo-Filio-Logical Background," symposium paper, Owerri, (2004). Id., "African Cultures and Development: The Rectifying Challenge," vol. XVIII, no. 4 (2010): 321-331, given at the First

for Christians especially, individually and collectively, the dynamic, the driving force or the soul of our mission of evangelization and life of faith.

Thinking like the Archbishop, divine filiation ever remains the canon for measuring and defining every aspect of our being Church, Christian and human.[2] It is the grand norm for directing our conduct and actions as Christians in particular and as humans in general. Its ethical and spiritual imperatives regulate our relationships. As the second part of this reflection demonstrates, the practical relevance of divine filiation is, for the Archbishop, in its application as a sublime effective tool for responding[3] to burning existential-pastoral issues within our Province as well as around the world.

Our chief pastor has carried the divine filiation doctrine far and wide.[4] He gives it fundamental primacy, systematic articulation and catechetical prominence.[5] And in this way, he adds a special note to leading voices in contemporary African theology, Christology, ecclesiology, anthropology and missiology. In doing this theological discourse, we call to mind the Archbishop's clarion call that divine filiation, as

---

Colloquium — Culture and Development in African Theology organized by the Pontifical Council for Culture, Vatican, in Abidjan, Ivory Coast, 27 September — 1 October 2010. Id., "Culture, Human Development and the New Creation Dynamic," keynote address at the fourth annual convention of the Catholic Biblical Association of Nigeria, Seat of Wisdom Seminary, Owerri, 2011; see below footnote 3.

2   The filiation theology of Archbishop Obinna joins in the African response to the Post-Synodal Exhortation, Ecclesia in Africa, 1995, no. 63 of Blessed Pope John Paul II to theologians in Africa to work out the theology of Church as family. We decipher in the Archbishop's thoughts echoes of filiation theology, filiation pneumatology, filiation ecclesiology, filiation sacramentology, filiation Mariology, filiation spirituality, filiation diaconal ministry, filiation anthropology, filiation psychology, filiation ecology, etc. Cf. Real Tremblay, "Filial anthropology," in Chapter VII of his *L'homme qui Divinise. Pour une Interpretation Christocentrique de Vexistence* (Montreal: Paulines & Paris, Mediaspaul, 1993).

3   See his Interview: "The Pastoral Approach to the Challenges of Caste Systems" in Beyond Frontiers to the End of the Earth: 2011/2012 Edition: "The Challenges of Caste Systems, Stereotypes and Social Inequalities", a Nigerian Spiritan Publication, p. 14-18.

4   See footnote 1 above.

5   So much is evident in his prayers, homilies, catechesis, lectures, pastoral caritative works, exchanges, etc. He sees the *Odenigbo* Igbo lecture series, the Eu-Care charity and social ministries he founded as "Theo-Christo-filial" events. "Theofiliance", "Christofiliance", "Christo-Theo-filiance", "co-filiation", "con-filiation", "reconfiliation" are all his neologisms in developing his theology of divine filiation.

the new integral kinship of creation in Christ ... be critically examined and welcomed as a rectifying and fructifying dynamic...[6]

2. The Light and Spirit of our Provincial Centenary offer us another special impetus and favourable occasion for the topic. Our special insight into the centenary considers it a memorial of foreign missionary evangelization among us seen in the light of the doctrine of filiation. Our Centenary prayer, anthem and actions are strongly anchored on filiation. We begin the centenary prayer by calling "God our Father"; we go on to acknowledge his fatherliness because he created us in his image and likeness; he made us one human family, and sent Jesus Christ his only begotten Son to reunite us with him and with one another. So much filiation runs through the Centenary Anthem "The Light of Faith": it is the Light of faith that has come among us spreading the Good News of salvation with focus on "making us sons and daughters of Christ" and "building the Church Family in Owerri Province", and so in a manner and to a degree no other traditional or foreign value system has or could possibly do.

To a great extent, what we are celebrating is a hundred years of filiation event: the filiation presence and residence of Jesus Christ, the Word-Incarnate Son of God the Father and of His Church-Family of God, among our people. We are jubilating because of Christ's fraternal sonship relationship with us these hundred years. For our people, the language of God being Father of a Church-family, of Jesus being the Son, the firstborn son,[7] and we the member children, is a most homely and endearing one.[8] Father, mother, children, sons and daughters, brothers and sisters and family: concepts which are nearest, dearest and sweetest to our people's

---

6   Obinna, A. J. V., African Cultures and Development: The Rectifying Challenge, op p. ae See
     Bede Ukwuije, Theofiliance: Our Kinship in God through Jesus Christ as one Response; in
     Beyond Frontiers, to the Ends of the Earth, op. cit., p. 11-13.

7   See Lk 2:7; Rom 8:29; Col 1:15,18; Rev 1:5.

8   On our African admiration for this paradigm of family ecclesiology, see the First ee aie =
     Africa of the Synod of Bishops, Instrumentum Laboris, no. 26; John P aul Ul, te ae : 'of God
     tn synodal exhortation, Vatican 1995, nos. 37, 41; Peter Cardinal Turkson, The C eee oe
     Africa, 2009; Lineamenta (Nov. 2012) to Nigeria's 24 National Pasion. ie et erie —— through
     Reconciliation, Justice and Peace, Chapter Five: "The Church as = y A 7 es Pins Communion
     and Dialogue", p.83ff.; Osuagwu, I. M., The Church is the Family of God in Ekei, J. Church
     and Family in Africa, 2009, p. 98-119.

heart have come to acquire their full and superior spiritual import, their complete existential-pastoral dynamic.[9]

Through evangelization filiation we have, according to the will of the Father, become a new creation in Christ and through the Holy Spirit. In this, our people become transformed into the sublime filiation status of the children of the true God, of the family members of his true Church. This means a radical and resolute exit, a passage and a transformation from our old Igboness. A majority of our people have been largely converted away from our traditional Igbo superstitious lifestyles, false value systems and mythical institutions. Even though the old residues may still be tugging, we have largely changed from our customary and religious affiliations to our ancestral deities and worship. So much has changed that it is no longer the same as it used to be under the old order.

For our Provincial Church and Christians, the centenary is a graceful occasion to rediscover, renew and develop our divine filiation roots and branches. Furthermore, it becomes for us, in the new era and project of evangelization, a favourable sensitivity, a veritable catechetical method or pedagogical tool—for enriching, enhancing our Christian faith and works.

3. The Spirit of the New Era of Evangelization and the Year of Faith.

The importance of divine filiation stands out prominently in the agenda of the Universal Church for the New Evangelization (2012) by the 13th Ordinary General Assembly of the Synod of Bishops just concluded as it is for the Year of Faith (2013) just inaugurated in the same month of October by the Pope Benedict XVI.[10] The deliberations enable us as African Church and people, to rediscover, refocus and re-invigorate the Good News of our intimate and inestimable filiation with God in Christ and through the Holy Spirit. The aim is to help us renewand deepen our faith, to make us become more authentic vocation of being, like Christ and in imitation of Christ, true Christian sons and daughters of God the Father in his Church-family, and true and effective evangelizers locally and globally.[11]

---

9   A filiation psychology, filiation psychedelics and filiation sociology can be developed around this.

10 See Proposition 4 of the Final List of Propositions submitted to the Holy Father by the Synod Bishops at the General Assembly.

11 In Vatican II spirit of *Ecclesia Semper Reformanda* and *Aggiornamento*. See also, Pope Paul VI, "Encyclical Letter, *Ecclesiam Suam* on the Church, August 6, 1964,"

On the Basic Doctrinal Meanings and Dimension of Filiation

Filiation takes the center stage of this reflection because it is *de fide*, the centrepiece of Christianity. So much is evident when one turns to our Christian sources, to the Old Testament, and especially to the New Testament, the Gospels and the other writings, to the Magisterium, the Saints, the Fathers and theologians of the Church.[12]

What does filiation mean? In everyday parlance, it means the intimate relationship between a child and the parent, between a son or daughter and the father or mother. As can be seen, it is an all-gender inclusive concept. It concerns not only human beings but also nonhuman beings, all creation. Filiation is about roping, threading, stringing, tying, linking up, bonding, uniting, connecting... In Igbo, we will be talking the rope or cord language: "*nliko, nlikota, njiko, njikota, nkeko, nkekodo* or *nkekota*' that ties, threads, strings, links up a child and the parent.

The Christian concept of divine filiation, like that of divine fatherhood, differs greatly from our natural, biological, physiological, psychological, ethnic and cultural filiation. It is defined not on the inferior terms of our being the children of our parents through carnal conception, pregnancy, procreation and nurturing, neither is it measured in terms of our blood or genetic ancestry of *nwanne* (mother's child) or *nneji* (mother-filiated), of *nwannaa* (father's child) or *nnaji* (father-filiated); it is not calculated by our problematic, discrimintory, divisive, narrow- minded or petty-minded *nwa afo* (child of the same womb), *nwa ala, diala* (son of the soil and daughter of the soil) stratification still upheld and practiced among many of us Christians and in our Church circles. Our natural, biological parental filiation must be seen in reference and completion to divine filiation which is its origin, source or foundation; because being parent by pro-creation is only a participation in the original and full parentage that belongs to God who is ultimately the real Creator of human beings.

The filiation we are discussing is essentially divine and Christian. It refers, first and foremost, to the sonship nature and status of Jesus Christ, who is God the Son and -the Son of God in his relationship with

---

12   See Eph 3:14, Catechism of the Catholic Church, nos. 2214; nos. 1-3, 1655-1658, 1303, 222-267, 2779-2793; Benedict XVI; John Paul II; St. Cyril of Jerusalem; Athanasius of Alexandria; St. John Chrysostom (on St. Mathew's Gospel); St. Irenaeus (against heretics); St. Ambrose; St. Anselm; St. Augustine of Hypo (on St. John's Gospel); St. Peter Chrysologus (on the Our Father); Blessed Columba Marmion; St. Thomas Aquinas; St. Charles Borromeo, etc.

God the Father, his Father. As we shall later explain, this is filiation in the Godhead. Historically at the first creation of God and later with the Incarnation of Christ, humans became filiated as sons and daughters or children like Christ to God who is Father, the Father of Jesus Christ and their Father.

As already noted, our Christian concept of filiation applies not only to humans but also to nonhumans, to the entire creation. As Archbishop Obinna expresses it, divine filiation is "the new integral kinship of creation in Christ". In this, he connects with what could be called St. Paul's filiation hymn: that God the Father set forth a purpose in Christ as a plan for the fullness of time, to unite all things in him, things in heaven and things on earth (Eph 1:1).

In the rest of this presentation, we shall dwell on major dimensions (forms) of divine filiation: Pro-filiation, Trinitarian Filiation, Creation as Filiation, and Incarnation as Filiation. Their various sub-types will be outlined below.

Pro-Filiation in God's Mind Since Eternity

Pro-filiation is filiation in God's mind and providential plan since eternity, long before any occurrence in history or at the end of history. God chose humans and destined them for adoption in Christ before creation (cf. Eph 1:4f.).

Trinitarian (Transcendental) Filiation 'in Deo'

This is divine filiation par excellence, the transcendental Trinitarian archetype at its most meta-mystical dimension.[13] According to New Testament revelation and as the Church believes and teaches, the fundamental theological meaning of divine filiation refers principally to the mysterious relationship in and within the Godhead, between the three consubstantial Persons in the one God: God the Father and God the Son and God the Holy Spirit. A sublime intimate relationship reigns between the Second Person of the Blessed Trinity, Jesus Christ who is God the Son

---

13 With God the Father and God the Holy Spirit, God the Son is de fide a dogmatic matter of the Trinity in the New Testament teachings, sacramental formulas, prayer greetings, sign of the Cross and creeds.

and the Son of God and the First Person who is God the Father and both in the community of the Third Person who is God the Holy Spirit who proceeds from both the Father and the Son (the Creed).

Creation a Filiation '*in Imago Dei*'

In the Old Testament, the language of filiation, as of fatherhood, may not be that directly evident as is the case in the New Testament. But the truth remains that God's creation covenant is all about filiation between him and his people, between him and his creation. Archbishop Obinna calls this "Theofiliation" for, on creating them, God, by that very act, filiates humans to himself, bonds them to himself.

In creation, God fathered humankind as his children. He created them in his image and likeness, male (sons) and female (daughter). He is the one absolutely responsible for letting humans come to be, by liberating them (*ex nihilo*), from no-thingness (nonentity) into some- thingness (some-entity) or existence (*cum fundamentum in re*). God plays the father by communicating the spirit, by breathing into them the power of life that. originates from him.[14] In this way, they are accordingly and proportionately connected, bonded Hed to God, to others and to one another. God is the metaphysical source, the primary, efficient and sufficient cause of their being (their origin, source, originator, author, giver and owner). He is also father in providing them with the vital resources to sustain and secure them. In this way, he is the guarantor, assurer, provider and redeemer of the life of all he begets at creation. He is the archetype from whom all fatherhood or family, in heaven and on earth, takes its title[15] - the way Christ is the archetype of all filiation, of all sonship and daughtership.

Alas, and as the Old Testament tells us, humankind breached the relationship and so failed to be good children to their Father. With the fall of our first human parents, all humankind lost the pristine filiality. However, that was not to be the end of the story. Imperfect, sinful, evil, bad, unfaithful or disobedient as humans are, God was not yet done with these

---

14   As we profess in Igbo: *Chi na-eku, Chi na-eke; Eke kere uwa; Chi enye ndu, Chi ji ndy Chi nwe ndu.*

15   God is the grand designer of all family filiality. He enjoys pre-eminent creative fatherhood as his proper divine predicate. Humans only share from him a delegated procreative fatherhood. The parental role they play in their natural biological and existential forms is in imitation and measure-out mandate of God.

children, sons and daughters of his. He still remains Father, ever faithful, trusting, loving, merciful, concerned and caring. In the verdict prefigured in the woman and her seed in Genesis 3:15, he provides a New Covenant in the Incarnation to redeem, restore, renew and reinsure his special filial relationship with humans. Sin fatally defiliates (defiles), but the Son of God gracefully refiliates.

Incarnation as Filiation '*In Christo*, *Per Christo Et Cum Christo*'

In the New Covenant, through the mission of evangelization (the Word of God) and the sacraments, God shows himself Father in a deep and supreme manner (a) with the Incarnation of God the Son when the Word took flesh to become human (*et Verbum caro factum est*), and (b) with the graceful adoption of humans in and with Christ by the power of the Holy Spirit to become children able, like and with Christ, to call God Abba Father. All this is in accord with God's loving intention and attention to redeem and realize for humans his original filiation project which they lost through the original sin of our first parents Adam and Eve.

Incarnation is, *primo*, the filiation of Jesus Christ himself. Jesus Christ God the Son comes down ("descends", "condescends") from his heavenly abode into our world and human condition, taking our human flesh, and conceived by the power of the Most High and the Holy Spirit, and born the Only-Begotten "Son of God" of the Blessed Virgin Mary Mother of God (*theotokos*). While still remaining God the Son and the "Son of God" his heavenly Father, the historical Jesus of Nazareth, Emmanuel, also becomes the "Son of Man". He comes down from heaven to be like us humans and to be with us, sharing in our humanity, that we may in turn be like him in sharing in his divinity (*kenosis*, Phil. 2); he came to us in order to show us that God is Father, his Father and our Father[16] ("descendental"-Vertical Filiation). In his coming in the Incarnation event (ministry, passion and resurrection), God recreates humanity, indeed all creation, this time, in

---

16 See A. J. V. Obinna, *Uju Nwa: Afurj Uwa Niile*, Odenigbo Lecture Series (Owerri: Assumpta Press, 2002). Jesus comes to show us that God is Father. See also, Harcourt Whyte (1956): "*O si n'igwe bia bu Onye nw'ay Jisus, O si n'igwe bia n'uwa bu Jisus; O si n'igwe b'okwu nke ghoro madu, O si n'igwe bia n'uwa bu Jisus. O si n'igwe ya n'udo nke Chukwu, O si n'igwe izi na Chukwu bu Nna. N'ihi ihe ndia na ihe ndi ozo, O si nigwe bia n'uwa, emesiakwa, O si n'uwa la n'igwe.*"

the image and likeness of Christ (*in imago Christi*);[17] in other words, God refiliates humanity and creation through his Incarnate Son.

The Incarnation filiation of Jesus is revealed by God himself and through his messengers (angels, prophets, apostles, disciples). For St. Mark the evangelist, the Gospel is the Gospel of Jesus Christ the Son of God (cf. Mk 1:1). At the annunciation, God sent his angel to reveal the Immaculate Conception and Birth of a child, the Son of God, made possible by divine love, divine grace and by the power of the Holy Spirit (cf. Lk 1:26-35; Mt 1:18ff.). And at the baptism and transfiguration, God identifies Jesus Christ as his "beloved Son" (Mt 3:17; 17:5; 2 Pet 1:17). The infancy and temptation[18] narratives help to further buttress Christ's incarnation filiation. A special case to note is the extraordinary confession of St. Peter identifying Jesus as "Son of the living God" (Mt 16:16). To this Jesus replied, "Blessed are you, Simon son of Jonah. For flesh and blood has not revealed this to you, but my heavenly Father." (Mt 16:17).

Jesus also reveals much on his divine filiation and God's Fatherhood. Excepting on rare occasions,[19] he hardly addressed himself directly as the Son of God. He would use the simple single form "Son"[20] as he did in reference to God as Father and the Father as God. Jesus mostly preferred calling himself the "Son of Man",[21] yet he did not reject the "Son of God" title when others used it to identify or address him.[22] While his "Son of God" title gives precedence and prominence to the divinity of his sonship relation with God the Father, his "Son of Man" title turns to the humanity of his Person in his divine sonship relation with humans. He acknowledged them all.

---

17   See the filial anthropology of Real Tremblay in his *L'homme qui divinise*, op. cit., 152f.

18   Cf. Mt 4:3, 6; even the devil addressed Jesus Christ as the Son of God.

19   Cf. Jn 1:8; 3:18; 5:22; 10:36; 11:4.

20   Cf. Jn 3:36; 5:20f

21   Cf. Mt 8:20; 9:6; 10:23; 11:19; 12:8, 32, 40; 13:37, 41; 16:13, 27f.; 17:9, 12, 22; 19:28; 20:18, 28; 24:27f.; 25:31; 26:2, 24,45, 64. There are many more such instances in the other three Gospels.

22   "For instance, by John the Baptist (Jn 1:34), St. Peter (Mt 16:16), St. John the Evangelist (Jn 20:31), his disciples (Mt 14:33; Jn 1:49; 11:24), the devil (Mt 4:3, 6), the demoniacs (Mt 8:29; Lk 8:28;. 4:4), the thieves on the cross (Mt 27f.), the Jewish high priest, chief priests, scribes, elders and Jews (Mt 26:63; 27:41f.; cf. Lk 22:69f.; Jn 19:7), the centurion at the resurrection (Mt 27:51), unclean spirits (Mk 3:11; 5:7). St. Paul also used it severally in Acts 9:20° Rom 1:4,9; 5:10; 8:3; 1 Cor 1:9; 2 Cor 1:19; Gal 2:20; 4:4; 6:13; Heb 4:14; 6:6; 7:3; 10:29; 1 Jn 3:8; 4:9; 4:15; 5:5, 9-13, 20; 2 Jn 1:9; and Rev. 2:18.

The Incarnation is not only the filiation of Christ (*"in Christo"*), it is also filiation of humans with him (*"cum Christo"*). Through him, in him, with him and like him, humans are also children, sons and daughters of God. Christ's filiation parables (the Prodigal Son Lk 15:11f. and the Two Sons Mt 21:28) also bear eloquent testimonies. God offers all humankind the grace of filiation despite our human imperfections, limitations, weaknesses and sinfulness.[23] His Sermon on the Mount can rightly be called his declaration of his filiation **Magna Carta**; He enunciates the behavioural qualifications of those to be called children of His heavenly Father, those who bring glory to the Father and who would receive His blessings (cf. Mt. 5-7). The categorical imperatives constituting the filial behaviour of humans and of Christians especially include: their faith, hope and love, their modest prayer, piety, trust, forbearance, sacrifice, generosity, penitence, mercifulness, firmness and fruitfulness. These are the major ways to filial holiness, to being perfect like their heavenly Father (cf. Mt 5:48).

In the Gospel according to St. Matthew, Christ enunciates fraternal filiation of His Incarnation and makes it an inevitable visa to heaven. On the last day, it will be filial judgment; the key to open or close the doors of heaven depends on what each person does or does not do to Jesus in his fellow sons and daughters, his brothers and sisters (Mt 25:35f). If anyone wants to be member of the family of Jesus, that is, anyone filiated to him as his mother, father, brother and sister, that person must heed the qualification Jesus sets: be hearer and doer of the word of God - like his natural family members, His Mother Mary, His kith and kin, His apostles (cf. Mk 3:32f.; Lk 8:20f).

---

23 Without being fussy about it, the mother-image and attributes of God can be contemplated and factored-in. A story tells of a heated-up controversy, in those early beginnings, between an expatriate "missionary and a traditional Igbo on the latter's proposal for a preferable Igbo logic of a Trinity of God the Father, God the Son and God the Mother. Without any gender exaggeration, it was in the Igbo traditionalist's bid to make a case for what would not be unusual on the family mother image and role of the divine. In the insights of apophatic theology, the mystery that God is moderates any contentious tendency that pretends a total positive grasp of the divine essence, nature and attributes. Closet bu ama-ama- amacha-amacha: "the known-and-knowable-but-not-completely-known-and-knowable".

Christofiliation

"Christofiliation" is Archbishop Obinna's special terminology for the Christly and Christlike sonship-to-sonship relationship of humans with God the Father in his Church-family. It also concerns other creatures in their order and degree, in their mode and manner of being and relating. Since the Incarnation, Christofiliation is the main and only channel of "Theofiliation", the filiation of humans and creatures to God as Father and to the other Two Persons in God, In Christofiliation, we distinguish with the Archbishop three main types, namely, Christian "Confiliation", General "Cofiliation" and "Re-Confiliation".

(a) Christian 'Con-Filiation'

Divine filiation is confiliation for humans who, by God's special grace and power, respond positively and resolutely to the invitation to believe in him and to follow him through Christ His Incarnate Son. These are Christians filiated to Him through His word and sacraments in Jesus Christ (cf. Jn 3:16f; Mk 16:15f; Mt 28:19) and who are members of His community or family of followers, the Church our Mother - like the mother we have in our Mother Mary, the Mother of Jesus Christ, the Mother of God and the Mother of the Apostle.

In the fourth Gospel, John the Baptist testified that "to those who did accept Him He gave power to become children of God, to those who believe in his name, who were born not by natural generation nor by human choice nor by a man's decision but of God (Jn 1:12-13). These are those who are born again from above with water and the Spirit (Jn 3:3f); those (children) who are enabled by the power of the Holy Spirit (by adoption) to, like Christ and in imitation of Christ, call God "Father!" (cf. Rom 6:15). "And because you.ate sons, God has sent the Spirit of his Son into our hearts, crying, 'Abba! Father! (Gal 4:6).[24] In the sacrament of Baptism, as of Confirmation, Eucharist, Penance, Matrimony, Anointing and Priestly Ordination, God constitutes and claims us as his children, sons and daughters.

---

24   See also Paul's teaching on adoption or filiation in Rom 8:15, 23.

(b) Catholic 'Confiliation'

This is Christian confiliation in its complete requirement. It is the sonship and daughtership of Christians fully Christofiliated by sacramental constitution and character. Sacramental filiation identifies those who, by the Word and Sacraments of God are responsible, and in unity and communion with the Church-family of God founded by Christ under the apostolic succession headed by St. Peter (cf. Jn 21:17). These are Christians who come what may never despair, but keep faith willingly, resolutely and actively, who are regular and constant in being sons and daughters of God the Father, fellow brothers and sisters of Christ, member children of the one, holy, apostolic and Catholic Church-family (ecclesial filiation).

As we learn from the magisterial teaching of Blessed Pope John Paul II, divine filiation constitutes:

> the deepest mystery of the Christian vocation: in the divine plan, we are indeed called to become sons and daughters of God in Christ, through the Holy Spirit.[25] The culminating point of the mystery of our Christian life. In fact, the name Christian indicates a new way of being, to be in the likeness of the Son of God. as son in the Son, we share in salvation, which is not only the deliverance from evil, but is first of all the fullness of good: of the supreme good of the sonship of God.[26]

(c). Ecumenical 'Confiliation'

This is Christian confiliation yet to be fully actualized. It is the sonship and daughtership of those partially or defectively, i.e., insufficiently Christofiliated. There are categories in this dimension. They include (a) those who, contrary to all biblical prescriptions and proscriptions, found

---

25 Pope John Paul II, "Message of the Holy Father for the VI World Youth Day, 15 August 1990" (Vatican City: Editrice Liberia Vaticana, 1990), §. 1, available at http://w2.vatican.va/content/john-paul-ii/en/messages/youth/documents/hf_jp-ii_mes_15081990_vi-world-youth-day.html [accessed, October 2012].

26 Pope John Paul II, "Homily, Solemnity of Mary Mother of God: World Day of Peace, 1 January 1997" (Vatican City: Editrice Liberia Vaticana, 1997), §. 3, available at http://w2.vatican.va/content/john-paul-ii/en/homilies/1997/documents/hf_jp-ii_hom_19970101.html [accessed, October 2012].

their own "churches"; (b) who by their "church proliferation", divide the true one Church-family of God founded by Christ; (c) those who are selective in what they believe, preach and do and (d) those who are heretical or syncretistic in what they believe, preach and practice about Christ and His Gospel. This situation defiliates for it gravely falls short of Christ's prayer testament of filiation for all who believe him: that they may be so filiated into substantial bond of unity and community, in full accord with and in imitation of the divine relationship between Him the Son and God the Father, His Father and their Father (cf. Jn 17:20-26).

(d). General 'Cofiliation'

This is the filiation of humans who are not yet Christofiliated by any sacramental constitution and confession, but who live in the time and mission of Jesus the Son of God. It also describes the relationship of other creatures with Christ as the one through and for whom God made all things and to whom God destined them. In spite of divergent views, the saving Gospel of the Incarnation of Christ is God's free gift and open invitation to all humankind, everywhere, every time.

> For God so loved the world that he gave his only Son, so that everyone who believes in him might not perish but might have eternal life. For God did not send his Son into the world to condemn the world, but that the world might be saved through him. Whoever believes in him will not be condemned, but whoever does not believe has already been condemned, because he has not believed in the name of the only Son of God.[27]

Also, from Christ's evangelization commission, we learn more about the universality of divine filiation when he mandates his followers to: "Go into the whole world and proclaim the gospel to every creature" (Mk 16:15). As Matthew's version has it: "Go, therefore, and make disciples of all nations, baptising them in the name of the Father, and of the Son, and of the Holy Spirit..." (Mt 28:19).

Despite human reservations, objections and rejections, God is ever faithful in playing his path. Filiation is for all humankind, believers

---

27   John 3:16-18; Mark 16:15f.

and non-believe alike including atheists, agnostic, sceptics, secularists, indifferentists, ignorant, etc., who are yet to come to any or full filiation in Christ and His Church. By divine providence, Christ also came for those metaphorically classed as "lost sheep", "the sick", "sinners", "the fallen and "the ignorant" (Mt 9:12; Mk 2:17; Lk 5:31; Mt 10:6; 15:24). In all these references, we learn about the universal dimension of filiation in principle, by divine providence and plan: God's will of filiation is for all humans to be his sons and daughters in Christ.

(e). Human 'Cofiliation'

This describes the sonship and daughtership relationship of humans by God's providential acts of universal creation and as re-enacted in the Incarnation as God's plan and offer, but such persons are not christianly confiliated, Christofiliated. Out of love for humanity and in keeping with his original will and plan since eternity, God promised and sent his Only Begotten Son Jesus Christ to redeem, without exception, all human beings (Jn 3:16, Mt 28:19, Mk 16:15), old and young, male and female, saints and sinners, rich and poor alike, the prodigal, the lost or strayed, the sick, fallen, ignorant, etc., all.

(f). Ecological Filiation

St. Paul in his letter to the Ephesians helps us appreciate the implication and application of divine filiation for all creation, for nature and its other creatures as well. As we explained earlier on, our Christian concept of filiation applies not only to humans alone but also to nonhumans, to the entire creation. Archbishop Obinna sees divine filiation as "the new integral kinship of creation in Christ". He connects with what we call St. Paul's filiation hymn: that God the Father set forth a purpose in Christ as a plan for the fullness of time, to unite all things in him, things in heaven and things on earth (Eph 1:10). The Eucharistic Doxology in Igbo brings our more poetically this share of nature in divine filiation: *"Ihe niile ekere eke na-eso yabu Kristi, na-esikwa n'ime Ya na waka Ya, na idiko n'otu nke Mmuo Nso, na-enye Gi bu Nna ji ike niile, nsopuru na otito niile, site n'uwatuwa niile."*

(g). Re-Confiliation: Eschatological Filiation of All Things 'In Christo'

As said above, at the fullness of time and according to divine plan, everything in heaven and on earth will be united in Christ, all humans and other creatures will return to God in Christ (Eph 1:10). With God (Rev 21:6), Christ is *Alfa* and *Omega,* the beginner and finisher (Rev 22:13) who will reconcile all things on earth and in heaven (Col 1:20; Eph 1:10).

Concluding Section

This part one of our centenary paper on the Fundamental Theology of Divine Filiation leaves us with a doctrinal message: to consider one another as sons and daughters of God in Christ, as brothers and sisters of Christ and as members of the same family of God. More than any other, Christianity is a filiation religion. It is the Good News of our filiality with God through Christ and in Christ, of our filiality with Him, our fellow humans and all creation, locally and globally. Christ is and has laid the foundation for us; the Church extends this divine filial invitation and grace to us all. What remains is for us to express our response to the offer and call to be like him and with him and with one another, sons and daughters of God his Father and our Father, and brothers and sisters, children of the same one Catholic family of God.

As we enter the second century, divine filiation is a special gift of our Christian first centenary for our local Church as for the universal Church. The centenary 1s urging us to, clearly and strongly, understand this major doctrine of our faith, to take it to heart, to preach it and, what is more, to live it out, the Archbishop will say, as a rectifying and fructifying principle of our daily Christian life - as our spiritual and moral code of conduct in our religious and social relationships with God, with other human beings as with other creatures that come under the Fatherhood and family of our Three-in-One God. How we can practically live out this doctrine in our Christian life is the scope of the part two of this paper.

Part Two
The Gospel of Divine Filiation: In Christ We are All Sons and Daughters of God the Father, Our Father, Brothers and Sisters of the Church-Family of God

At the Close of the Provincial Centenary

The Catholic Church in Owerri Ecclesiastical Province has clocked a hundred years (1912-2012), but the memories of the first centenary celebration will linger, and the events that marked these years will continue to echo far into the future. The theology of Divine Filiation is one such emerging fruit of these years of Christianity in the province. This second part of this paper concentrates on the Pastoral Theology of Divine Filiation. The first part is dedicated to the fundamental theological dimension of divine filiation. Given the title above, we shall explore the practical pastoral implication of Archbishop Obinna's Theofiliation. We aim to argue that divine filiation is the heartbeat of the ultimate mission of Christ and how his Theofiliation can serve as an interpretative key to understand how we can be truly Christi-animated as people who have received the gospel of salvation in Christ.

Centenary of Evangelization for Establishment of The Church and Conversion of the Peoples

Our Province celebrated 100-years of European missionary propagation of the Gospel of Jesus Christ among our people. The main preoccupations of that expatriate mission were: (a) establishment of the Catholic Church here in our Igbo area and (b) sacramental conversion of our people from our ancestral Igbo traditional religion to Christianity, to become Christian, believers in the true Trinitarian God.

Centenary of Evangelization for Divine Filiation

The paper strongly affirms that filiation is at the core of evangelization as its soul and driving force, its content and intent. Evangelization is all about filiation: to evangelize is to filiate, as much as to be evangelized is to be filiated. This is the sense of evangelization our paper promotes:

proclamation of the Gospel of divine filiation of Jesus Christ Son of God the Father (cf. Mk 1:1) in whom humans are in turn filiated. Divine filiation expresses, principally and at the transcendental level, the Trinitarian relationship in the Godhead, between the Three Persons of the Blessed Trinity, God the Father and God the Son and God the Holy Spirit. This pre-eminent reference also expresses the intimate historical relationship which the Incarnate Jesus Christ who is Son has with God who is his Father in the community of the Holy Spirit. Still sublime and at the "descendental" level, divine filiation also expresses the filial relationship which the filiator Son of God, "brings down" for humans who, like him, vertically with God the Father and horizontally with one another, become sons and daughters, children of the same God his Father and thus their Father.

Option for the Gospel of Divine Filiation

As we give thanks to God for a successful celebration of the centenary and congratulate the Bishops, clergy, religious and laity of our Province, including our guests and well-wishers from far and near, we acknowledge the Most Rev. Anthony J.V. Obinna, our Metropolitan Archbishop, for making divine filiation a choice topic and a core message of the centenary. This paper is a response to the Archbishop's clarion call for divine filiation to "be critically examined and welcomed as a rectifying and fructifying dynamic". He is, among us, a chief proponent who accords the doctrine the prominence and popularity it is increasingly receiving. The Archbishop wants us to, henceforth, turn our gaze and focus more on divine filiation as the fundamental theological and pastoral option for anchoring and animating our Christian live of faith and mission of evangelization, individually and collectively, valid for us locally as for others globally. The Gospel of divine filiation, as the Archbishop asserts, is "the new integral kinship of creation in Christ". Our Christianity is essentially a filiation religion, our Church like our life of faith all about filiation.

On the Doctrine of Divine Filiation

Ordinarily, filiation is about child-parent relationship; it is about being son or daughter to father and mother. It is an existential connection, an intimate tie, bond, rapport, unity or community existing between them as is the case with our natural and biological, but relative, sectional, problematic, contentious and unsatisfactory human family filiation (of *"nneji, nnaji, nwanne, nwannaa, nwaafo, onye uzo ulo,"* son/ daughter of the soil).

This second part talks of another realm and type of filiation, the divine, supernatural, most supreme and original, the true and major one. Divine filiation is typically a Christian doctrine at the core of our Christianity. As divine, it originates from God the principal, efficient and sufficient cause, the Fatherly generator or engenderer of all creation, including humans. It is an essential attribute of God and describes how filiation is expressed in God's very manner of being, and causally in its historical extension and expression in creation and recreation.

The Gains of Divine Filiation

Inspired and enabled by the old-age authoritative teaching of the Church drawn from and founded on the Scriptures and the meditations of her saints and theologians, our option for divine filiation both locally and globally, sees it as a new evangelization focus and highlight, as a return to our Christian foundational sources and resources. We return to the essential status quo and instruments of our faith to be able to re-launch our evangelization life and mission. It is a veritable new form of spirituality, a new catechetical thrust and a psychological disposition. For the new era of evangelization as for the year of faith inaugurated this year by Pope Benedict XVI, divine filiation occupies a prominent place and plays a determining role in the life and mission of the Church and Christians.

With the Universal Church, we enhance our means and tools, our concepts and language and our religious pedagogy and psychology. We do so in view of renewing, refortifying and sustaining the faith of those of us who believe, that we may be truly holy Christians, members in full union and communion in the true Church-family of God, that we may be more effective evangelizers and courageous witnesses to Christ in our era. Our option is also in view of having an efficient way of proclaiming and communicating the faith to: (a) those who are weak in faith though they may still be in the true Church- family of God; (b) those who,, whatever their reasons, have lost the faith and have left the Church for some other Christian denominations or non-Christian religions; these are those who do not fully believe and belong, who are yet to; (c) those of African

Traditional Religion, Islam, Buddhism, etc; it includes even (d) those who do not believe at all, who are not ready and willing to change: Catholics or Christians totally fallen, agnostics, negative sceptics, indifferentists, atheists, anti- religionists, anti-Christs and anti-Christians.

Family, father and mother, sons and daughters, brothers and sisters, kinsmen and kinswomen, these are, for our people, special terms, the homeliest, dearest and sweetest, the most inviting, touching and moving, as well as the most compelling, disarming and compassionate. Of all the metaphors describing God's relationship with us humans, these family concepts are among the most appropriate, intimate, personal, sacred and prominent. It makes a whole world of difference of impact on us to know that Christ is the Son of God who is Father, His Father and our Father, my Father — like it is for human beings to see themselves with Christ as fellow sons and daughters of this God, fellow brothers and sisters in Christ and children of the one family of God our Father.

As hinted at, divine filiation speaks more than the language of our natural-biological family designations and ties. As divine, it refers and takes us back to the supreme origin, primordial source and ultimate summit and destiny of our being children to a God who is Father to Christ His Son and to us through Him who is our brother. In Genesis and the Incarnation, God plays the Fatherly role that brings us his offspring to life. He is our creator, begetter, provider, nurturer, educator, protector, leader, assurer, sustainer and redeemer. He is The Father as such, the archetype from whom all fatherhood, all family, all existence takes its origin and title (Eph 3:14f); for it is from Him that we live and move and have our being (Acts 17:28).

Dimensions of Divine Filiation

From Archbishop's terminologies, we discern the following forms or dimensions of divine filiation:

1. Trinitarian Filiation is divine filiation in the Godhead. It is of God's eternal transcendental nature and attribute, the mysterious manner of relating, the unique bond of unity and community between the Three Persons of the Blessed Trinity: the First Person God the Father and the

Second Person God the Son Jesus Christ in the "communion" of the Third Person God the Holy Spirit who "proceeds" from the Father and the Son. As expressed in the credo formula, Trinitarian filiation is about Jesus Christ who is God the Son, the only eternally begotten Son of God the Father —born before historical time, before the first creation by God, the Incarnation of Christ and the Descent of the Holy Spirit at Pentecost. Because intrinsically of God, Trinitarian filiation is the archetype, source, sustenance and summit of all the other forms of filiation.

2. Creation Filiation: At the appointed time, God fatherly created everything including and especially humans he made in his image and likeness (Genesis). In this, humans and other creatures came to share in the grace of his father-child or genitor-offspring relationship. Unfortunately, the original sin of our first parents defiled (broke) the bond and consequently defiliated humankind from that special relationship. Despite sin and evil, God ever remains the faithful and loving Father He is. After the fall, He compassionately promised to renew His filial covenant with humans in the Redemptive act of the Incarnation of Jesus Christ His Son.

3. Incarnation (Re-creation) Filiation: The emphasis here is on this-worldly historical expression of Christ's filiation and God's Fatherhood. The Incarnation is the divine filiation of the person of Jesus Christ of Nazareth, of "Emmanuel" who is the Son of God and the Son of Man as He prefers to call Himself. By His providential Fatherliness and by the power of the Holy Spirit, God ordained that Jesus Christ be conceived and born of the Virgin Mother Mary as His only begotten Son. By taking our human nature, the Son of God and Son of Man who is God the Son con-descends from His transcendental divinity into our earthly humanity to take on our mortal flesh and to be like us in all things but sin (descendental or kenotic filiation). In this condescension (*katabasis*), Christ the Son came down to us from heaven to teach us that God is Father, his Father and our Father, and that we are like him sons and daughters of God.

4. Christofiliation: Confiliation, Cofiliation, Reconfiliation: The Advent, Incarnation (birth), Ministry and Passion (death and resurrection) of Christ the Son of God, the Son of Man has a human filiation dimension and purpose. One such purpose is to redeem human beings from sin that defiles and alienates, that defiliates them from God and from one another. Christ's divine filiation is a graceful act of reparation, redemption, restoration and renewal of the filial relationship we humans have with God His Father our Father. Our Provincial Centenary prayer and anthem makes so much clear: God refiliates us with Himself and with one another by sending His Son into the world; in and through Christ, He makes us His sons and daughters and builds us up into His one Church-family. This refiliation of ours is confirmed by the Holy Spirit who enables us humans to become God's adopted children, who like Christ (Mk 14:36) call God Abba, Father (cf. Rom 6:15; Gal 4:6).

In tandem with his messianic mission, we can correctly reread or reinterpret Christ's evangelical commission to his followers (Mt 28:19; Mk 16:15) to mean: go into the whole world and make all the nations sons and daughters (disciples) of God the Father in the Son and through the Holy Spirit. The core point is that, for those already evangelized as for those to be re- evangelized, including also those yet to be evangelized, evangelization is all about being, in Christ and like Christ, with Christ and with one another, sons and daughters or children of God the Father his Father and our Father.

5.1. Christian Confiliation is the sonship and daughtership of all those born again of God and not of natural generation, neither of human choice nor of human decision (Jn 1:12f.). As the Church teaches in keeping with Christ's will, Christian confiliation is the relationship of those sons and daughters of God sacramentally constituted in their belief, assent, worship and witness for Christ and his Father. These are those who, in truth and in spirit, willingly become and regularly remain Christian by the sacraments: by baptism in the name of the Trinity; by anointing (confirmation) in the Holy Spirit (Jn 3:3ff.); by the Eucharistic Body and Blood of Christ (Jn 6:1ff.); by the reconciliatory-reconfiliatory forgiveness of sin that defiles, alienates and so that defiliates humans (Mt 18:15ff., 19ff.; Jn 20:21ff.). Matrimony plays its role, for by it humanity have the graceful privileged to participate in God's mysterious power of fathering and filiating (procreation). Paradoxically, not all Christians are fully Christian by the word and the sacraments, that is to say, not all are fully Christofiliated. In other words, there are those who are Christian in a manner christianly partial or defective and so insufficient.

Conclusion

This reflection on the Pastoral Theology of divine filiation covered by the current article leaves us with the doctrinal message of our divine filiation through Christ, in Him, like Him and with Him. More than any other religion, Christianity is essentially a religion that enables us to understand God's filiation with creation and in a special manner with the human beings. It is the Good News of our filiality with God, with all humans and with all creation, locally and globally. Christ is the foundation and has laid it for us. The Church extends this filial invitation and grace of God His Father to all of us human beings. All that remains is for us to make our express fiat in effective response to the divine offer.

SELECTED LITERATURE ADDITA

- Benedict XVI. Encyclical Letter, Deus Caritas Est on Christian Love, 25 December 2005,"
- _____. *Jesus of Nazareth: From the Baptism in the Jordan to the Transfiguration*. Translated by Adrian Walker. New York, NY: Doubleday, 2007.
- Ciampa, R. E. "Adoption," in *New Dictionary of Biblical Theology*. Alexander Desmond T. & Rosner Brian S., eds. Leicester: Inter-Varsity Press, 2000.
- John Paul II. "Post-Synodal Apostolic Exhortation, *Christifideles Laici:* On the Vocation and the Mission of the Lay Faithful in the Church and in the World, 30 December 1988." Vatican City: Editrice Liberia Vaticana, 1988.
- _____. "Encyclical Letter, *Redepmtor Hominis*: On the Redeemer of Man, 4 March 1979."
- Osuagwu, I. Maduakolam. "The Church is the Family of God in Ekei." In *Church and Family in Africa*. John, Anosike, John & Nwanna Joseph. eds. Awka: Fab Educational Books, 2009.
- Palmer, F. H. "Adoption in the New Testament." In *New Bible Dictionary*. Wood, D. R. M. ed. Downers Grove, IL: Inter-Varsity Press, 1996.
- Ratzinger, Joseph. *Introduction to Christianity*. San Francisco, SA: Ignatius Press, 2004.
- Schmaus, Michael. *Dogma 3: God and His Christ*. London: Sheed & Ward, 1971.
- Scott, J. M. "Adoption and Sonship." In Dictionary of Paul and His Letters, Gerald, F. & Raph P. M., eds. Downers Grove, IL: Inter-Varsity Press, 1993.
- Selman, M. J. "Adoption in the Old Testament." In *New Bible Dictionary*. Wood, D. R. M., ed. Downers Grove, IL: Inter-Varsity Press, 1996.
- Stinton, B. Diane. *Jesus of Africa: Voices of Contemporary African Christology*. Nairobi: Pauline Publications African. 2004.
- Tremblay, Rial. *L'Homme qui Divise: Pour une Interpretation Christocentrique de l'Existence*. Montreal: Editions Paulines, 1993.

Chapter Seven

The Theological Anthropology of Archbishop Anthony J. V. Obinna

Michael Nnamdi Konye

Abstract

The neologism theofiliation is accurately credited to His Grace Archbishop Anthony J. V. Obinna. This concept captures a central kaleidoscope through which his theological oeuvres can be succinctly appraised. In this article, I wish to highlight its import in the field of theological anthropology. I argue that, in the main, the concept of theofiliation opens up a Christologico-ecclesiological trajectory within systematic theology, which fits harmoniously within the church's long-standing accent on the need for deepened pastoral catechesis on the revelatory sources of our Christian faith in view of the redemptive mission of the person of Jesus Christ, 'true God and true Man' (Cf. Nicean Creed; John 1:1, 14). In fact, I will also show in sketches what basic presuppositions on the relational concept of human person are imbedded in this theological project. Philosophical assumptions in these building blocks are shown to follow the age-old description of philosophy as *'ancilla theologiae'* (Clement of Alexandria, *Stromata*, 1, 5).

In pursuit of the above stated objective, I will show, from the Christological standpoint, how the concept of theofiliation can be used to demonstrate the theological anthropology of Archbishop A. J. V. Obinna. The one example of such a demonstration would draw insights from the church's understanding of the divine person of Christ, who is Himself, as the Son of God. Accordingly, this will form the foundational basis upon which a theofilial structure of the human person can be grafted. On the other hand, from the ecclesiological standpoint, the same human being, who, when baptized in Christ and grafted into His body (the church), becomes at once a coheir with Christ (Hebrews 2:11–17) and also made to become a 'joint-heir' (Romans 8:17) with all the baptized, the whole body of Christ, within which community he shares in the salvific graces made available through Christ, the Head of His Body (the church). In sum, the theofiliation trajectory of Archbishop A. J. V. Obinna, with its many dimensions, allows for a blend of various dimensions of systematic theology in such a way that an organic theological anthropology can be readily drawn from this same conceptual resource while retaining its ever-expansive theological richness.

Introduction

Between March 3–4, 2016, Birmingham Mayor William A. Bell, Catholic Bishop of Birmingham Bishop Robert J. Baker, and the Dean of Beeson Divinity School Timothy George of Stanford University, Birmingham, Alabama, USA, hosted a National Racial Reconciliation Conference titled 'Black and White in America: How Deep the Divide?' At that conference, Archbishop Anthony J. V. Obinna had presented an application of his concept of theofiliation to the theme of re-confiliation wherein he distinguished *reconfiliation* from the more common terminology, *reconciliation*. This is only one dimension of the applicability of the concept of theofiliation, which he has been developing in various other such presentations, including his reinGodment thesis on inculturation at the beginning of the third millennium during the Tenth CIWA Theology Week in March 1999.

Besides projecting theofiliation on papers presented in symposia and conferences both on the African continent[1] and beyond[2], Archbishop A. J. V. Obinna is practically involved in the pastoral application of this theme in relation to the breaking down of religio-cultural barriers in the Igbo society with specific reference to the *diala-osu-umeh* caste system. In a sense, the theologian of theofiliation has carved for himself a niche in the domain of systematic theology, which new frontier I intend to highlight in this short piece in commemoration of his twenty-fifth episcopal anniversary. In doing so, I want to invite readers to reflect with me on the efforts of the archbishop in pointing out to all of us the deep sense of rootedness in Christ the God-Man, which we all share as brothers and sisters in the one family of God. It is my view that the archbishop's concept of theofiliation highlights the Christological basis of the evangelical mission of the church aimed at our reinGodment as children of God as well as showcases the ecclesiological basis of our fraternity and sorority in Christ, the child of Mary the Virgin, and the Eternal Son of the Father.

My reflection will proceed in the following steps: first, under the subtheme 'Christological Affiliation', I shall lay out a Christological foundation for the theofiliation of an individual person through baptism. Next, I shall continue in the same thread, broadening this perspective in the context of the Christian community under the subtheme 'Ecclesiological Cofiliation'. Those two threads will be justified in terms of their philosophical presuppositions on the concept of the human person in the third section under the subtheme 'Archbishop A. J. V. Obinna's Relational Conception of the Human Person'. Based on the strengths of the arguments provided in the above segments, I shall then construct a thesis on theological anthropology using the tools provided by Archbishop

---

1   Anthony J. V. Obinna, 'Inculturation as Reingodment and Resplendouring the Great Jubilee Illumination', in *Inculturation in the Third Millennium: 10th CIWA Theology Week*, March 8–12, 1999, ed. Patrick Chibuko (Port-Harcourt, Nigeria, 1999). See also Anthony J. V. Obinna, Ujunwa: Anuri Uwa Niile: Odenigbo Lecture Series (Owerri, Nigeria, 2000); Anthony J. V. Obinna, 'Confiliatory Collaboration between the Church in Africa and Europe: A Theo-Filio-Logical Background' (Owerri, Nigeria, 2004); Anthony J. V. Obinna, 'African Cultures and Development: The Rectifying Challenge (A Colloquim on Culture and Development in African Theology)' (Abidjan, Ivory Coast, 2010).

2   Antony J. V. Obinna, 'Roots, Branches … Graftings and Fruits: The Reconciliatory Challenge to African-Americans and Humanity at Large' (Charleston, South Carolina, USA, 2003). Anthony J. V. Obinna, 'Confiliating Americans: Recti-Valuing One Another (2)', (Birmingham, Alabama, USA, 2016).

Obinna's concept of theofiliation. Finally, a short appraisal of what key issues were raised will bring the whole reflection to a modest conclusion.

Christological Affiliation

The person, nature, and mission of Jesus Christ forms the cardinal root upon which Archbishop A. J. V. Obinna's grafts his theology of theofiliation. This acknowledgment of a Christological ground is already present in the archbishop's own announcement of his own personal experiences as follows:

> My own lived experience of the Sacred [in the context of] a pre-nihilistic and post-nihilistic African Catholic Christian [culture] encourages me to confirm and share the new sense of the Sacred which the person of Jesus Christ has inaugurated and made available for the good of all creation and all humanity. Having felt in 1982 the crash of my primal cultural world in the face of the violent incursion of secularism and nihilism I remain eternally grateful for the new dawn in creation and in my being that links me directly to the Incarnation event. It is this Incarnation Event that enables me to re-advance the integral and global vision of creation and the earth in terms of theofiliance.[3]

It is thus evident that the default starting point of the analysis of the theo-filiation theology of the archbishop is the person of Jesus, the Christ, with whom all *affiliate* creatures are incorporated. First, we have to accentuate that with regard to the person of Jesus Christ, such a theofilial starting point masterfully overcomes the conventional distinction between high Christology[4] and low Christology[5] by its simultaneous grasping of the Catholic teaching on the divinity of Christ as the Second Person of the Trinity and the Incarnation event of the Son of God. In this way, theofiliation

---

3   Anthony J. V. Obinna, 'African Cultures and Development' (2010), 13.

4   High Christology refers to those theological interpretations of the person of Christ that emphasize His divinity, albeit in no way denying His humanity. In the gospel narratives, it is common to sample out the Johannine periscopes (1:1–2; 5:18; 10:34; 20:28) as examples of high Christology.

5   Low Christology refers to those theological interpretations of the person of Christ that emphasize His humanity, albeit in no way denying His divinity. This is more evident in the synoptics, among which it is more frequent for scholars to sample out the Marcan account as a repertoire of low Christology.

resonates with the theologies of the Middle Ages, which highlighted the hypostatic union of the two natures of Christ as truly God and truly man. The term *hypostasis* was already current in Greek philosophy before its adoption in the context of the Christological debates of the fifth century. It overlaps semantically with another Greek term *ousia*, both of which can translate as 'substance'. However, whereas *ousia* as substance can admit abstract entities, hypostasis implicates a rather concrete, actual, existing being. As concrete, hypostasis refers to concrete nature whereas *ousia* can pass for abstract or conceptual nature.

Hence, the significance of the phrase *hypostatic union* in reference to the union of the concrete (true) divine nature and the concrete (true) human nature in the one person of Jesus Christ in the First Council of Ephesus in 431[6]. Notably, the context of this council, wherein the hypostatic union was upheld, was the debate on the term *theotokos* (Mother of God). The title was meant for Mary, the mother of Jesus Christ. This historical exposition provides for us a necessary perspective of analysis of theofiliation because it is an interesting insight that highlights the alignment of the archbishop's theology of theofiliation with the more than two-thousand-year-old magisterium and tradition of the Catholic Christianity. Thus, in teaching about the event of the Incarnation as a moment in theo-filiation, the Archbishop points out simultaneously the place of Mary in his Christology as follows:

> The rein-Godment of creation, the re-radication of creation to God in the event of the incarnation which perfuses all of creation with God's grace, finds its luminous peak in the filiation of Jesus, the Word of God, to the Blessed Virgin Mary which in turn has effected the re-filiation of humans to God the Father, with the restoration to humans of God's image and likeness in which they were created.[7]

One notes how our theologian of theofiliation incorporates this Mariological thread, which encapsulates the highpoint of the divino-human hypostatic debate at Ephesus in the fifth century into his presentation of the significance of creation and Incarnation for theofiliation. The implication of the above foregoing analysis on the person and nature of Christ would

---

6   Gregaory of Nyssa, *Antirrheticus adversus Apollinarem.*

7   , Anthony J. V. Obinna, 'Inculturation as ReinGodment' (1999), 16.

become more evident in his application of these theological presuppositions in his interpretation of the mission of Christ as a 'reconfiliatory mission'.[8]

Archbishop Obinna announced his sources of inspiration as rooted in the familial kinship ties of fraternity and sorority, which is covivial to all human cultures. In his own words, such ties of fraternity and sorority are the 'shareable nature of life's experiences, dreams and reflections even with all the multiple particularity or specificity of our individual involvement and perspectives'.[9] These shared human lived experiences of kinship cutting across cultures and historical epochs form the primary context of a 'regeneratively reliable and resilient action-reflection prism' within which to make sense of the Christological *affiliation* moment as that of an awakening for all humanity irrespective of historical time and cultural place. In Christ, the *'Ujunwa'* (i.e., fullness of fraternal and sororal filiation to the Father), there is *'Anuri Uwa Niile'* (a joyous fulfilment of all creation).[10] Theo-filiation presents for us a theological anthropology suitable for the mission of animating all humanity with Christ-values, that is, a new vision of man 'in and through Christ'. In this kaleidoscope, therefore, the archbishop describes the mission of Jesus Christ as that of bridging kinship cleavages within and across cultures. While teaching about the significance of Christian baptism, the archbishop maintains that 'Jesus inaugurates his trans-cleaving breakthrough whose goal is re-dignification of humanity, the restoration of all children, all men and women to the status of beloved sons and daughters of God. This is the essence of re-filiation and re-confiliation which more concisely says so'.[11] It is evident that the archbishop intends that this transcleavaging mission of the Son of God be understood as a Christological affiliation of all humanity in Christ. In this sense, theofiliation becomes a missiological blueprint on the Christological canvass envisioned *ad gentes* (with respect to all peoples). This mission of Christ is also the mission of the church understood both *ad extra* and *ad intra*. The church herself is the sacrament of Christ[12] as her identity is

---

8   Anthony J. V. Obinna, 'Jesus Trans-Cleavaging Breakthrough: The Reconfiliatory Mission', in *Confiliatory Collaboration* (2004), 7–9.

9   Ibid., 1.

10   'Ujunwa: Anuri Uwa Nile' is the title of the 2000 Odenigbo lecture delivered by Archbishop Anthony J. V. Obinna at Owerri.

11   Obinna, 'Confiliatory Collaboration' (2004), 8.

12   Avery Dulles, *A Church to Believe In* (New York, NY: Crossroad, 1982), 5.

derived from her status as the Body of Christ. It is thus this ecclesiological dimension of theofiliation that I will explore in the next paragraphs.

Ecclesiological Cofiliation

That Christology is the foundation of ecclesiology is a given since a Christless church is a headless church. This truth is even made more evident when, hypothetically, a pope denies Christ (i.e., apostatizes) since as 'Vicar of Christ on earth', his vicariate derives from Christ, the Head of His Body. The *Catechism of the Catholic Church* makes it more eloquently clear when it teaches as follows: 'For it was from the side of Christ as he slept the sleep of death upon the cross that there came forth the wondrous sacrament of the whole Church.'[13] Thus, it follows that our foregoing Christological application of the archbishop's theology of theofiliation leads naturally to an ecclesiological dimension. Within this ecclesiological route, we can begin from the exploration of the flow of Christ's grace through the church's sacramental ministry.

In this specifically sacramental context, a basic starting point of reflection is the sacrament of baptism, the very moment when we become simultaneously affiliated into Christ and coaffiliated to one another as Christians, irrespective of our cultures (e.g., Jews, Samaritans, or Gentiles), races (e.g., Europe, America, or Africa), gender (e.g., male and female), social status (e.g., *osu, ume,* or *diala*) and so on. As cofiliates, sharing in the one theofiliance of Christ to God, the Father, all Christians are sons and daughters of God, the Father of all. On the other hand, the church as mother of believers also extends her maternal mantle to all humanity. Pre-eminent among the believers who share in the theofiliance mystery of Christ in the church is the virgin daughter of God, our Blessed Mary, graced by God Himself with the title of *theotokos.* However, this shareable theofiliance mystery of Christ is also extended through the evangelizing mission of the church to nonbelievers in consonance with her essential mark of Catholicity (universality), irrespective of anyone's sociocultural roles in the society. In a sense, the church as Catholic is open in degrees of theofilial incorporation to both the baptized and the not-yet-baptized

---

13 *Catechism of the Catholic Church* (London: Chapman, 1999), §, 766.

children of God since Christ, the theofilial foundation of the Church, came to save all of humanity (1 Tim. 2:4) and not just a selected few.

Even though we know that not all men are fully incorporated into this ecclesial (assembly) cofiliation of every human being to God, through Christ, we note with respect to non-Christian religions in particular in the context of the relationship of Christians to Judaists that both the synagogue and the church are irrevocable covenant assemblies of the chosen people of God (Rom. 11:29).[14] The Vatican II Council Fathers had noted such layered degrees of ecclesial cofiliation that extends across the varieties of theo-filiated persons, to wit, across the 'baptized believers'.[15] It is noteworthy that the Council Fathers' view on the central significance of the sacrament of baptism coincides with the archbishop's theology of theofiliation in Christ, even though they employ such other conciliar terms of description that were already rooted in the image of the Church as *corpus* Christ (Body of Christ) as 'full and partial *incorporation* with the Church'. A copious quotation of the conciliar presentation of this theme will make this resonance explicit (*Unitatis Redintegratio*, 2, 3, 22):

> the Lord Jesus poured forth His Spirit as He had promised, and through the Spirit He has called and gathered together the people of the New Covenant, who are the Church [i.e. the gathering of the people of the Old Testament is evidenced

---

14 Commission for Religious Relations with the Jews, 'The Gifts and the Calling of God Are Irrevocable (Rom. 11:29). A Reflection on the Theological Questions Pertaining to Catholic-Jewish Relations on the Occasion of the 50th Anniversary of *Nostra Aetate* (No.4)' (2015).

15 The phrase *baptized believers* can be theologically problematic as it is simply tautologous, but its opposite, *unbaptized believers*, overlaps with but is not entirely synonymous to such controversial descriptions of Karl Rahner as 'anonymous Christians'. In Karl Rahner, the focus is on those who may never have had the Christian gospel, but in my indirect use of the phrase (unbaptized believers) here, I imply an undeniably vague but subtle twofold distinctions betwixt Christians (as baptized believers within the ecumenical context) on the one hand, as well as between Christians and non-Christians (unbaptized believers as non-Christian theists in general but particularly to other monotheists, who not only have heard the Christian gospel but, even more, may also be baptized in their own religious rites of initiation—e.g., Judaists and Muslims, but who are not baptized in the Christian faith). It is important to note that non-theists (or atheists, as the case may be—anyone who has no religion at all) are not considered in this subtle distinction (baptized believers/unbaptized believers) for the very fact that an ecclesial assembly is essentially an assembly of theists, an assembly of believers, an assembly of godly people, a theofiliated assembly, or the 'whole universal community of believers' (See *Catechism of the Catholic Church*, §, 751–752), some of whom may have baptismal rites in their religious practices while some may not really have such rites.

in the Synagogic assemblies], into a unity of faith, hope and charity. ... The Church, then, is God's only flock; ... The brethren divided from us also use many liturgical actions of the Christian religion. ... It follows that the separated Churches and Communities as such, though we believe them to be deficient in some respects, have been by no means deprived of significance and importance in the mystery of salvation ... Whenever the sacrament of Baptism is duly administered as Our Lord instituted it, and is received with the right dispositions, a person is truly incorporated into the crucified and glorified Christ, and reborn to a sharing of the divine life [i.e. a Christological theo-affiliation]. ... Baptism therefore established a sacramental bond of unity which links all who have been reborn by it [i.e. ecclesiological co-filiation]. But of itself Baptism is only a beginning, an inauguration wholly directed toward the fullness of life in Christ. Baptism, therefore, envisages a complete profession of faith, complete incorporation in the system of salvation such as Christ willed it to be, and finally complete ingrafting in eucharistic communion. Though the ecclesial Communities which are separated from us lack the fullness of unity with us flowing from Baptism, ... especially because of the absence of the sacrament of Orders, nevertheless when they commemorate His death and resurrection in the Lord's Supper, they profess that it signifies life in communion with Christ.[16]

The above lengthy quotation from the Council Fathers encapsulates the rootedness of the ecclesial cofiliation in Christological affiliation, which expands the scope of theofiliation beyond the Roman Catholic fold as to incorporate our Christo-filiated brethren who in baptism are made cofiliates with all who profess the name of Christ, albeit in varying degrees. However, beyond the ecumenical context, the Vatican Council Fathers has also indicated a wider extension of the theofiliatory significance of the assemblies God's people who belong to other religions as most eloquently expressed in *Nostra Aetate,* with particular reference to Judaism. These variously expansive applications of the theology of theofiliation across

---

16   Vatican II Council, 'Decree on Ecumenism, *Unitatis Redintegratio, 7* December 1965,' in *Decrees of the Ecumenical Councils: Trent-Vatican II*, ed. Norman Tanner and Guiseppe Alberigo, vol. II (New York, NY: Costello Publishing Company, 1987), 908–909, 919.

various faith or religious communities is even made more extensive by the archbishop's trajectory of reflections based on transcultural indices to include all of humanity. The archbishop's approach, which goes beyond the specifically Christian purview, is coherent with the same etymological inspiration that gave rise to his seminal reflections on theofiliation. He traces the etymological roots of the operative concepts to the Latin words *filus* and *filia* in this wise:

> The root words from which Re-con-filiation is derived are *Filius* and *Filia*, the Latin for son and daughter. These words fuse into one as in filial expressing a relationship to father or mother. Filiation, affiliation are generally in use to describe belonging as a child, a son or a daughter, to a parent, to an institution or an organization. In my wider reflection on filiation in the context of the human family as well as in the church-religious context, words like re-filiation, confiliation, cofiliation, de-filiation, recti-filiation and re-con-filiation have surfaced.[17]

Beginning from this more generic context of theofiliation, the archbishop sets the ecclesiological blueprint of theofiliation on a broad base that gives the church's mission *ad gentes,* a field of action as far-reaching as the ends of the world, wherever humans live and coexist as social participants, whether this is a religious, political, economic, or any sort of cultural community of persons. In a positive appraisal of how this ecclesiological cofiliation mission of assembling all of humanity in Christ has been carried on by the apostles and their collaborators over the years as well as how it presents a continual challenge for the church of today and tomorrow, the archbishop succinctly avers that

> given the nearly two-thousand-year span of this apostolic mission of bringing Christ to people and people to Christ with a view to forming one family of humanity, one stands amazed at what has been achieved and at the apostolic vibrancy which the Holy Spirit continues to generate across the continents in contemporary apostles of Christ. Nevertheless, in the face of contemporary hate tendencies and acts that threaten us locally, nationally and internationally even among those who have

---

17   Obinna, 'A Theology and Practice of Reconfiliation' (2016), 2.

been sacramentally baptized into Christ, Jesus' confiliatory spirit needs to be personally and corporately internalized by us contemporary apostles of Christ in Nigeria if God's love for all mankind is to triumph over our reciprocal hatred and destruction.[18]

As a contemporary apostle himself, the archbishop has engaged in this mission of ecclesiological cofiliation of humanity in Christ by his concrete engagement in bridging the cultural cleavages of Igbos, as evident in his ideological polemics against the religio-cultural caste system practices that Igbo Catholic Christianism inherited from the pre-Christian indigenous religion of the Igbos. He understands his efforts as coherent with Jesus's mission of theo-confiliating Jews and Samaritans (John 4:4–42; Luke 10:25–35), the Apostles's mission of theo-confiliating Jewish Christians and Gentile Christians (Acts 15: 1–31), and the Vatican II Council Fathers mission of theo-confiliating all Christians *(Unitatis Redintegratio)* as well as theo-confiliating all covenanted people of God *(Nostra Aetate)*. This mission of ecclesiological cofiliation of humanity in Christ has become a veritable base for a plausible Christologico-ecclesial cum culturo-linguistic appraisal of the archbishop's inculturation project of the Odenigbo lecture series (from 1996 till date). I wish to conclude this section on ecclesiological cofiliation with the very words of Mbem Odenigbo, which captures this vision in poetic lines:

Jesu Odenigbo, Kristi Odenigbo
Nonyere anyi bu umu Igbo
Ka anyi jiri anuri na ihunanya
Kwuputa Gi, nnukwu Odenigbo anyi.
Chukwu kenyere anyi asusu Igbo iji fee ya
Ma kwusaa ozioma n'ime Kristi
Na n'aha Kristi nwa ya
Onye bu Nzoputa nke mmadu nile.
Ya bu ka anyi suo, guo, ma dee Igbo
Ka Igbo na Ozioma debanye n'ime anyi
Na-edeputa ezi mkpuru na Kristi

---

18   Obinna, 'Confiliatory Collaboration between the Church in Africa and Europe: A Theo-filio-logical Background' (2004), 10.

Odenigbo Nzoputa anyi.
Olu Igbo towe Chukwu Nna
Olu Igbo towe Chukwu Nwa
Olu Igbo towe Chukwu Mmuo Nso
Chi amamihe, ugbua na mgbe ebighiebi, Amen.

Archbishop A. J. V. Obinna's Relational Conception of the Human Person

The archbishop's theology of theo-filiation, as already indicated, is rooted in kinship affiliations, which are evident in all human cultures. Every human person is a child of another human person to whom he is related biologically either as a son or a daughter. This is a primary affiliation upon which other secondary affiliations of brotherhood and sisterhood can be subsequently established. Culturally, each human being also belongs to certain kinship network of relationships, all of which can be grouped into primary or vertical kinship and secondary or horizontal kinship ties. For example, in the family, which is the most basic of kinship ties, we find such vertical relationships as sonship and daughtership as well as such other horizontal relationships as brotherhood and sisterhood. One could not become a brother or a sister in a nuclear family set-up unless one is first and foremost a co-*filius* or a co-*filia* (i.e., co-filiates: co-son or co-daughter) of the same parent.

Extensions of sonship and daughtership beyond biological ties can be made through adoption, in which case, adopted sons and daughters become brothers and sisters thanks to their common affiliation to the same parent. Based on the biological and adopted affiliations, members of the nuclear family acquire such cultural roles as father, mother, son, daughter, brother, and sister. These roles also serve as referent structures of belongingness into one family. One may also point out the logical primacy of the relationship between parents (i.e., as husband and wife), but it has to be underscored that the subjects (a groom and a bride) of this *marital* relationship are not originally scions of the same stock (i.e., each of them come from different parents) whereas in *filial* relationships, the co-filiates (i.e., brothers or sisters or siblings) are scions of the same stock (same parents). The similarity of the marital bond and the filial bond is derived from their horizontality (i.e., a certain equality of status—as couples of same marital union or children of same familial parents). This horizontality in the case of filial bond is, however, completed by another vertical relationship of sonship and daughtership, which is absent in the marital union (i.e., the husband is not the son of his wife's parents, and the wife is not the daughter of the husband's parents) as the each of the marital partners belong to different parentage. Culturally, we speak of sons-*in-law* and daughters-*in-law*, but as far as the descriptions go, such filiations are created by the *law* rather than by *nature*. In Christian religion, as also in most other religions, God's most popular image is that of a Father to whom all humans are related as children and each human person thus becomes either a son-child or a daughter-child of God.

This is much more than religious metaphor since all human beings as creatures receive their sources of existence from God and as such belong to God as children belong to their parents (i.e., their biological sources of life).[19] In this sense, the theology of theofiliation is to be understood as the divine parentage of all human beings, having their sources of existence in God. In teaching us the eternal truths hidden in the mysteries of this divine parentage, Archbishop A. J. V. Obinna aims at highlighting the universal relatedness of all human beings to God, our Father; hence he reaffirms this relational conception of the human being as evidenced even from the nonreligious experiences of kinship, which all human cultures acknowledge. In a speech on reconfiliation, which is one of the applications of the theology of theofiliation, he argues for the corrective-redemptive dynamism of this rediscovery of our common filiation in God. He speaks of this rediscovered affiliation of all humanity to our Creator-Parent, (i.e., God), as a *reconfiliation* or, as he describes it elsewhere, as a *re-inGodment.* It is in this perspective that the archbishop writes of the primacy and the need to propagate the gospel of this reconfiliation (or reinGodment) as follows:

---

19 Note the difference between God as a source of existence and parents as biological sources of life. God gives existence to all creatures and as such is the Father of all creation. No parent can give existence to his or her child since when the child dies, no parent can return him or her to existence. Parents as sources of life is to be taken with a pinch of salt because no one gives what he or she does not have. No human being is a source of life, but parents collaborated with God in the creation of human babies, hence as pro-lifers, parents are said to procreate their children; but they do not create their children, only God creates.

Given the distortions in perceiving, reacting and relating to fellow humans across our extensive human family, reconfiliation serves and is intended to serve as a principle or dynamic re-affirming the primacy of sonship and daughtership for every human ahead of the still important category of brother and sister. The sociological or religious extension of brotherhood and sisterhood, fraternity and sorority, are secondary to the primacy of filiality, confiliality or cofiliality. Thus, reconfiliation serves as a rectifying or corrective force in assuring that the dignity of every son or daughter in the human family is upheld and defended.[20]

From the foregoing expositions, the prevalent philosophical assumptions in the conception of the human person in the theology of theofiliation is that of the relational. Every human being is ontologically related to God as a child of the Father of all creation. This relational conception is also operative in the earliest theological appropriation of the philosophical concept of person from its Greek roots. The Cappadocian Fathers[21] were quite influential in the final drafts of the definition of the Trinity of divine persons as 'one substance (*ousia*) in three persons (*hypostasis*)' in the First Council of Constantinople and the final version of the Niceno-Constantinopolitan Creed. This definition of the Triune God is structured on the relational conception of the divine persons, each of whose personhood is related to *one* divinity. It can be said that this is the first theological insights on theofiliation, whose context was the relationship of Jesus Christ as Son of God, the second person of the Trinity. In this relational conception of divine persons, Jesus Christ, being the Second Person of the Trinity is thus 'an image of the invisible God' as well as 'the firstborn of all creation' (Colossians 1:15), since in Him as Son of God, we share by virtue of our baptism, in the Sonship of the First Son and become related by *grace* to God our Father to whom we are ontologically related by *nature* in creation.

---

20   Obinna, 'Reconfiliation—A Corrective-Redemptive Dynamic,' in *A Theology and Practice of Reconfiliation* (2016), 2.

21   Tradition considers such Greek fathers Basil the Great (330–379), his younger brother, Gregory of Nyssa (332–395), and his close friend Gregory of Nazianzus (329–389) as the Cappadocian Fathers, thanks to their active doctrinal engagement in Christian theology in the region of Cappadocia, now in modern-day Turkey.

Moreover, each one of us becomes 'Though Him, With Him, In Him' images of the glory of God, the truth of which the Archbishop points out has been appropriately inculturated in the Eucharistic doxology.[22] From this trinitarian vantage point, a theology of theofiliation that is Christologically grounded becomes the bedrock of an ecclesiological cofiliation that unites all the many members of the church as one body in Christ, as Saint Paul severally announced in his epistles (cf. Rom. 12:4–5; 1 Cor. 10:17; 1 Cor. 12:12–14, 18–20, 25; Eph. 2:16). This Christian inspiration is the anchor upon which the relational concept of the human person in the theology of theofiliation rests. The archbishop's ingenuity is most expressed in his own engagement of his Igbo nation, whose cultural context is suffused with many religio-sociocultural cleavages in need of this rectifying intervention that theofiliation offers. The archbishop testifies that efforts at such a rectification has been ongoing, and frontline actors can be identified in this regard both from the political and religious spheres where he himself has made enormous contributions:

> On the 10th May, 1956 under the impact of Christianity and modern enlightenment the Eastern Nigeria House of Parliament legally abrogated the demarcation of Igbos into three alienatory groups – The Free Born (Di-ala), the Enslaved-Outcasts (**Ohu, Osu**) and the Prone-to-die (**Ume**). ... A close reading of Jesus' relationship with the Jews, Samaritans and Gentiles and his redemptive-filiative concern for each of these human groups opened my eyes, my ears, my inner heart and mind to a redemptive-filiative concern among my Igbo folks...By a combination of God's grace in Christ and by continued self-probing I found a new and unbelievable freedom and courage which I am offering to Igbos once enslaved by Igbo religio-cultural divides. ... Though I have been in the fore-front of this refiliative-confiliative mission, many others across Church groups and non-Church groups are pushing it forward and breaking down our centuries old inhuman customs, habits and barriers.[23]

---

22 Obinna, 'Inculturation as ReinGodment and Resplendouring the Great Jubilee Illumination' (1999), 17.

23 Obinna, 'A Theology and Practice of Reconfiliation' (2016), 3.

What is most evident in the above considerations on the theology of theofiliation, which the Archbishop presents is that a new consciousness of the relatedness of all human beings, is central in the evangelization mission that Jesus inaugurated. This new consciousness draws its inspiration from a relational conception of the human person with respect to our being created in the image and likeness of God, who is the Father of all creation; and through Jesus Christ, the grace of sharing in the divine life is offered to build on the platform of filiality already made present in nature. The theology of theofiliation in its acknowledgement of the relational concept of human person is thus an affirmation of Thomistic principle that grace builds on nature. In a commentary on Boethius *De Trinitate*, the angelic doctor writes of the relationship of the resources of divine grace to the givenness of nature as follows: 'Although man is inclined to an end by nature, yet he cannot attain that end by nature but only by grace because of the exalted character of that end'[24]. To be theofiliated is therefore to seek an exalted status of sharing the divine life, a status that requires the human person to be sanctified in order to enjoy the theofilial state. As created by God, we are already gifted by nature to be related to God, our Creator, but we need the redemptive grace of Christ Jesus to activate this natural relationship and for which activation we also need the sanctifying power of the Holy Spirit to cleanse us of our deficiencies and impurities that we constantly pick up along the way in our strivings towards God. Theofiliation is thus both a given of nature that human beings as persons share in relation to the divine persons, but it is also a work of grace that Jesus Christ, the first 'theo-filius'[25] offers us through the mysteries of His redemptive life, death, and resurrection.

---

24 Thomas Aquinas, *Commentary on Boethius 'De Trinitate'*, 6, 4, ad. 5, cited in Mullady, O.P. S.T.D., Fr. Brian, *Man's Desire for God* (Bloomington: 1stBooks, 2003), 19.

25 The word *theo-filius* should be distinguished from the proper name *Theo-philus*. *Theo-filius* is an amalgam of both Greek and Latin concepts. *Theos* in Greek means 'God' and *Filius* in Latin means 'son'. But the proper name Theophilus is a completely Greek name meaning 'lover of God'. Luke used it as an honorary title of the person to whom the Gospel of Luke and Acts of Apostles are addressed. *Philos* in Greek means 'lover, friend', hence we find it in such compound words as 'philosophy' or *Theophilos/Theophilus*. It is thus rendered differently in English as lover of God in contrast to the English rendition of *theo-filius* as 'God-son' (i.e., God-affiliate).

Theofiliation as a Thesis on Theological Anthropology

To consider theofiliation as a thesis on theological anthropology is to delineate some scientific features of such a proposal, which include its subject matter, its formal object, its methodological resources, and its goal of investigation. First of all, a thesis proposal in the context of a science of theological anthropology should share the same subject matter of any anthropological science, namely the human being. This is the same object of investigation for cultural anthropology, philosophical anthropology, linguistic anthropology, and so on. What differentiates any of these anthropological sciences would in fact be their specific formal objects, i.e., the perspective from which they investigate the subject matter of their sciences (i.e., the human being). In this wise, theofiliation as a thesis on theological anthropology also has the human being as its subject matter of investigation.

In its own specification of the formal object, it shares the theological presuppositions of all theological sciences. Theological anthropology is a branch of systematic theology, given that it overlaps with Christology since the understanding of the humanity of Christ is a central focal point of departure for the theological investigation of the human person, whose natural boundaries (human nature) is transcended by the supernatural grace of baptism, which opens for sinful man the redemptive-salvific pathways of a flourishing divine life in Christ. A flourishing Christian life thus becomes the intended goal of the science of theological anthropology, a life that is made accessible by visible signs of theofiliality with Christ and His Body, the church. In the previous segments of this reflective piece, I have tried to present veritable outlines of this theofiliance of the human person in the context of Christological affiliation and ecclesiological cofiliation.

Any scientific thesis, including the one under consideration, viz. theofiliation, can be made operative using specific methodological tools that are acceptable in the domain of science in which it is proposed. Theological scholars are at one in the ascertainment of such resources *Loci theologici* as are made available in revelation (e.g., sacred scriptures), the magisterium (e.g., *Catechism of the Catholic Church*), tradition (e.g., patristic sources), as well as ordinary human rational tools that confirm rather than contradict the deposit of revealed truths (e.g., As Thomas

Aquinas noted, there are two ways of knowing, namely reason and faith. Whereas reason can know what is accessible to it through the senses and intellect, for instance that there is an Absolute Being, which we call God, and as an Absolute Being, there can only be one God, hence monotheism); those truths that are beyond the capacities of the human senses and intellect can only be known by means of revelation from God Himself (for instance knowing that there is One God, monotheism is not enough, yet the knowledge of Three Persons in One God, or Trinity, has to be a knowledge from revelation. More so, the historical Jesus is God-Incarnate, fully God and fully Man; and as such, the Incarnation as the first theofiliance event has to be a revealed truth that is beyond the potentiality of ordinary human reason to discover on its own).

In the Benediction hymn *Tantum Ergo*[26] composed by the Angelic Doctor, this twofold sources of knowledge were highlighted thus '*Praestet fides supplementum, sensuum defectui*' (*Okwukwe na-enye ihe nke nti na anya enweghi ike inye* [Faith can give what the senses/intellect cannot reach]. The English rendition of the hymn has a slightly different translation as follows—Faith our outward sense befriending, makes the inward vision clear). On the count of the above arguments, the thesis of theofiliation also accepts sources and tools of the science of theological anthropology, which includes both faith and reason (*fides et ratio*).

Some elements of its truth are discoverable by reason in the context of the natural filiance of every human being to specific kinship contexts. These natural contexts form the base of its cultural justifications in Igboland, in Yorubaland, in Hausaland, in Bantulands, or other African cultures, not excluding African-American cultures, European, or Asian cultures. In a nutshell, its applicability is universally manifest in kinship ties all over the world. Some other elements of its truth are well grounded in supernatural filiance, which is the appropriate context of theofiliance in Christ, which highlights its theological significance and justifies its inclusion as a veritable thesis on theological anthropology. I have thus made a strong case of scientificity of theofiliation as a thesis on theological anthropology by highlighting its subject matter (the human being), its

---

26   Thomas Aquinas, 'Tantum Ergo', in the last two stanzas of *Pange Lingua Gloriosi Corporis Mysterium*, written at Orvieto, Umbria-Italy for the Vespers of Feast of Corpus Christi as commissioned by Pope Urban IV (1246).

formal object (a theological vision of the human being), its methodological tools and sources (faith and reason) as well as its goal (a flourishing Christian life grounded on the rectification of the appropriate vision of man for the purpose of making present in all human cultures the divine riches the redemptive-salvific mission of Christ Jesus).

Conclusion

In the above reflection on the theological anthropology of Archbishop A. J. V. Obinna, I expound the theological thesis of theofiliation, which has characterized the greater part of his episcopate in the last twenty-five years. I was emboldened to engage in this reflection, having been myself influenced by his zeal to fashion out a 'regeneratively reliable and resilient action-reflection prism'[27] that will serve as a basic theoretical framework for the pastoral implementation of what he has contemplated for a considerable length of years beginning from his days in the seminary. The archbishop has testified on the pre-1996 origin of the Odenigbo Project as follows:

> My own enthusiasm for inculturation which dates back to my post-war theological formation in the Bigard Memorial Seminary, Enugu and to my more critical studies in Europe and America, in the fields of Religion, Culture and Education, found a major stimulus in the Igbo cultural renaissance spear-headed by respected Igbo intellectuals and scholars, many of whom were Christians, but in varying degrees of disenchantment with the Christianity which they had received and imbibed.[28]

The archbishop's theology of theofiliation is thus a long-researched thesis. The history of which had spanned over five decades in the reflective mind of our silver jubilarian. Its pastoral implementation has also had a long incubation lifespan before the various visible projects came to fruition. In this claim also, we echo another testimony from the archbishop as follows:

---

27 Obinna, 'Confiliatory Collaboration', 1.
28 Obinna, 'Inculturation as ReinGodment and Resplendouring the Great Jubilee Illumination' (1999), 11.

> Long before the 1994 Synod of Bishops on the Church in Africa
> which took up the theme of 'Family' as a principle framework
> for building the church in Africa, I had between 1979 and 1984
> devoted research time and energy to developing a positive family
> principle for educating Nigerians morally and religiously in a
> volatile, pluralistic context. The principles of life-enhancement
> and convivialism were the outcome of that research.[29]

Given these testimonies from the jubilarian himself, one can appreciate the dexterity of the archbishop to keep the light of faith in Christ shinning amidst the daunting challenges of preaching a gospel of theofiliation to an Igbo-Nigerian-African-Universal world of today, where faith in technology has replaced faith in God, where the dictatorship of legal positivism has replaced the desire for common good in politics, where secularism has relegated the God-talk to the private life of individuals and fewer members of the society. No doubt, for the most part, a theofiliation gospel for an individualistic society is prone to be dead-on-arrival, suffocated by selfishness and clannish cleavages; yet in the archbishop's unrelenting witness to this gospel, we acknowledge the truth in the words of Isaiah (52:7), 'How beautiful on the mountain are the feet of those who announce the good news.' Timely and clearly, the archbishop's feet hasten to bring to us this good news of theofiliation. It is a good news for this critical period of our history of discords, disunity, and cleavages at various levels (within families and cultures, locally, nationally, internationally). Theofiliation is good news announcing the grace of God's adoption of each one of us in Christ, and one cannot but appreciate how joyfully the archbishop announces this gospel, teaching us to rediscover our theofiliance in Christ.

As we celebrate this joyful and rectifying good news today, we also celebrate the messenger of this good news, Most Rev. Anthony John Valentine Obinna, who in the course of these twenty-five years of episcopate has impact on our lives in more ways than we can considerably enumerate in this short piece of reflection. Your Grace, we make our own once again those words of Isaiah, how beautiful are your reassuring feet that bring us this good news of theofiliation. Perhaps this short reflection of mine is an acknowledgement of a minuscular fraction of the many fruits of grace we have reaped from your theology of theofiliation. Even so, on this occasion of

---

29   Obinna, 'Confiliatory Collaboration' (2004), 1–2.

your episcopal silver jubilee celebration, it is my prayer that these valuable seeds you have sown in our lives blossom for the glory of God and the salvation of all humankind. May your episcopal silver jubilee celebration also bring you more graces of theofiliation in Christ, for the greatest reward for serving God and His people is the grace of a theofilial union with God.

References

- Aquinas, Thomas. *Commentary on Boethius 'De Trinitate'*, 6, 4, ad. 5 (1250). Cited in O.P. S.T.D. Fr Brian Mullady, *Man's Desire for God*, Bloomington: 1stBooks, 2003.
- Commission for Religious Relations with the Jews. 'A Reflection on the Theological Questions Pertaining to Catholic-Jewish Relations on the Occasion of the 50th Anniversary of *Nostra Aetate* No.4.' Accessed October 15, 2017. http://www.vatican.va/ roman_curia/pontifical_councils_/chrstuni/relations-jews-docs/ rc_pc_chrstuni_doc_20151210_ebraismo-nostra-aetate_en.html.
- Dulles, Avery. *A Church to Believe In*. New York, NY: Crossroad, 1982.
- Obinna, Anthony J. V. 'Inculturation as Reingodment and Resplendouring the Great Jubilee Illumination.' In *Inculturation in the Third Millennium: 10th CIWA Theology Week*, edited by Patrick Chibuko, March 8–12, 1999, Port-Harcourt.
- ——— '*Ujunwa: Anuri Uwa Niile.' Odenigbo lecture series*, Owerri, 2000.
- ———. 'Roots, Branches … Graftings and Fruits: The Reconciliatory Challenge to African-Americans and Humanity at Large.' Charleston, South Carolina, 2003.
- ———. 'Confiliatory Collaboration between the Church in Africa and Europe: A Theo-Filio-Logical Background.' Owerri, 2004.
- ———. 'African Cultures and Development: The Rectifying Challenge.' (A Colloquium on Culture and Development in African Theology), Abidjan, Ivory Coast, 2010.
- ———. 'Confiliating Americans: Recti-Valuing One Another (2)', Birmingham, Alabama, 2016

Chapter Eight

Advancing Interreligious Dialogue and Inculturation through the Owerri Archdiocesan *Odenigbo* Religio-Cultural Project

Patrick Mbarah'

1. Introduction

The need for advancing interreligious dialogue and inculturation in the various dioceses and provinces in Nigeria remain an urgent task. Interreligious dialogue and inculturation are aspects of evangelising mission of the Catholic church. They are like the strong wings of the soaring eagle that lead to a very great stride in the spirit of grassroot evangelisation. They are parts of the indispensable effort of the church to incarnate the message of Christ. Thus, considering the obviousness of religious pluralism of our time, the fact that the kingdom that the gospel announces is lived by men and women profoundly linked to a culture, and the fact that the building of this kingdom cannot be dispensed from the daily interaction of peoples of various religious backgrounds and cultures,[1] promoting dialogue and inculturation remains a duty for the church.

---

1   Michael Ukpong, *Igbo Culture and Gospel: Empirical-Theological Research into*

In his address to the Symposium of African Bishops, Pope Paul VI pointed out the richness of African values and how they can be harnessed for a deeper assimilation of the gospel message and towards the promotion of a rich African Christian identity. He puts it thus:

> You may, and you must, have an African Christianity. Indeed, you possess human values and characteristic forms of culture which can rise up to perfection such as to find in Christianity, and for Christianity, a true superior fullness, and prove to be capable of a richness of expression all its own and genuinely African. This may take time. It will require that your African soul become imbued to its depth with the secret charisms of Christianity, so that these charisms may then overflow freely, in beauty and wisdom, in the true African manner.[2]

Thus, Owerri Archdiocesan *Odenigbo* Religio-Cultural Project seems to be one of those 'charisms of Christianity' that the Holy Father had indicated in the above statement. The aim of this article is to examine and highlight how this noble project of African Igbo origin of ecclesial birth can, in the spirit of the Second Vatican Council (1962–1965), contribute to the deepening of interreligious dialogue and inculturation within the ecclesial communities in Owerri Province and beyond.

2. Understanding the Owerri Archdiocesan *Odenigbo* Religio-Cultural Project

Odenigbo Religio-Cultural Project is the brainchild of His Grace Most Rev. Anthony Obinna, the metropolitan of Owerri Ecclesiastical Province. He instituted this project to commemorate the elevation of Owerri diocese to the status of an archdiocese and, consequently, the seat of the Owerri

---

Inculturation in Nigeria (Zurich: LIT Verlag GmbH & Co., 2015), 264. In this statement, Ukpong is referencing Pope Paul VI apostolic exhortation *Evangelii Nuntiandi*, 20. He reasons that the pope is challenging the Africans to adapt to the Christian faith with their African identity. Cf. Pope Paul VI, *Evangelii Nuntiandi: Apostolic Exhortation to the Episcopals, to the Priests and to all the Faithful of the Entire World*, 8 December 1975 (Maryland: The Word Among Us Press, 1975), 22.

2   Pope PAUL VI, 'Address to the Symposium of African Bishops', Kampala, July 31, 1969 in *Insegnamenti*, (1969), VII, 535–536.

Ecclesiastical Province.[3] Archbishop Anthony J. V. Obinna, a seasoned scholar, having gained mastery of various languages, was propelled to return to his own native language for fruitful evangelization. The coinage *Odenigbo*, in the Igbo language, does not mean absolutely writing in Igbo or a mere promotion of Igbo language but rather, resounding and transmitting the gospel in the native language of the people, Igbo language, to permeate the fabrics of Igbo culture. It further depicts Jesus Christ as one who speaks to his people in their own language for a deeper grasping of his salvific message.

This religio-cultural project is a new creation symphony that serves as a local and global trumpet calling on all Igbo sons and daughters to rise and worship the almighty God in spirit and in truth through Jesus Christ Our Lord in their God-given gifts of Igbo language and culture.[4] The *Odenigbo* serves as an annual gathering to regenerate and recreate the participants in a wholesome and delightful way by drawing into celebrative communion a variety of cultural heritages. The *Odenigbo* Lectures, which is the apex of this religio-cultural project, demonstrates an eloquent development of ideas, vigorous research, and cultural values orchestrated with the Igbo language as the sole medium of lecture presentation by erudite scholars of Igbo extraction.

Moreover, since the Second Vatican Council, the church has continued to emphasize the need for the promotion of inculturation of the gospel of Christ to be brought to every nook and cranny of the world. Thus, Archbishop Obinna considered it paramount to promote the Igbo language, which was in the danger of imminent extinction, given its abandonment and undue preference to foreign languages. He advocates that Igbo language is used in the worship of God and should also serve as a veritable tool in the spread of the gospel to the grassroots in Igboland. Furthermore, the *Odenigbo* lecture series serves as a splendorous dynamic in a relentless

---

3   The *Odenigbo* Lecture Series was instituted in 1996. It is part of the Owerri Archdiocesan Day celebration. This festive gathering takes two days, usually the first Friday and Saturday in September. The first day, known as the *Odenigbo* Eve, of the celebration is spiced with a variety of cultural performances—drama, choral dances, cultural exhibitions, traditional wrestling, and sometimes masquerading. The second day, which is the penultimate celebration is commenced with a concelebrated Holy Mass. Then comes the *Odenigbo* Lecture, which is delivered in Igbo language and is broadcasted live on the radio stations.

4   Anthony J. V. Obinna, 'Religion and Culture in the Modern Igbo Context: The Chukwu-Kristi Dynamic'. An Address to the Alaigbo Development Foundation, 25 May 2016.

quest to savour and realign the Igbo language, cultures, and traditions towards the embrace of God.

For the past two decades and half of the existence of the *Odenigbo* Religio-Cultural Project, the themes for the lectures has cut across culture, religion, philosophy, theology, morality, politics, science, and technology. Since its inception, the lecture aspect of this project has touched on many pertinent issues and various facets of Igbo life in a global setting by renowned lecturers and erudite scholars of various professions and faiths. As a public lecture that is delivered in the mother tongue of the people, it is an outstanding avenue to inculturate and bring evangelisation to the grassroot. It remains a model for teaching and educating Christians both lettered and unlettered, for dialogue and mutual relationship especially, with followers of African Traditional Religion and Islam. The *Odenigbo* celebration serves as a possible avenue to promote and practice inculturation and interreligious dialogue, considering the fact that some of the lecturers who had delivered the *Odenigbo* lectures were not Catholics.

In its literary meaning, the coinage *Odenigbo* will stand for 'resounding in Igbo language' and, in our case, resounding the gospel of Christ in Igbo language. God speaks to his people in the way they can understand, thus through their language, signs, symbols, and their cultural values. In the light of the Second Vatican Council, *Odenigbo* is one of the outstanding responses of the archdiocese to the use of the mother tongue in the sacred liturgy and worship.

The Second Vatican Council Fathers adopted the principle that the use of the mother tongue, whether in the Mass or other parts of the liturgical worship, may be of advantage to the people; and the limits of its application may be extended.[5] The worthy reforms of the council has extended not only to the Holy Mass, the rituals, and the Liturgy of the Hours[6] but also to some other *fons ecclesia* that could serve as sources of nourishing the souls of *Christifideles. Odenigbo* Religio-Cultural Project occupies a high pedestal of prominence in Owerri Archdiocese in fulfiling this desire of the Catholic church. This worthy enterprise reinvigorates the life of the people while permeating and inculturating the cultural values with the ardour

---

5   Vatican II Council, 'The Constitution on the Sacred Liturgy: *Sacrosanctum Concilium*, 4 December 1963', in *Vatican Council II: The Conciliar and Post-Conciliar Documents*, ed. Austin Flannery, §. 36, 1–36 (New York, NY: Costello Publishing Company, 1987), 13.

6   Vatican II Council, *Sacrosanctum Concilium*, §. 36, 54, 63a, 76, 78, 101.

of wholeness and sanctifying power of the teaching of the church. The various disciplines, facticity of life, and human conditions that *Odenigbo* examines gives boost to the annual longing of the celebration. It revives yearly, like 'a New Pentecost', the spirit of inculturation of Igbo cultures, arts, and entertainments into the liturgical life of the local church, thus creating an occasion of celebrative communion as one people of God in their God-given Igbo language.

3. Interreligious Dialogue and Inculturation in the Mission of the Church

Some of the documents[7] of the Second Vatican Council give eloquent testimony of the place of interreligious dialogue and inculturation in the mission of the church. The Second Vatican Council noted that the church takes to herself 'in so far as they are good, the ability, resources and customs of each people. Taking them to herself, she purifies, strengthens and ennobles them'.[8] Dialogue has become a household terminology since after the Second Vatican Council. Pope Paul VI was the first to refer to the concept of dialogue as we understand it today in his encyclical on the church, *Ecclesiam Suam.*[9] The term was controversial in that *'dialogus'* was a neologism in Latin. The Latin text of the encyclical of Pope Paul VI employed the term 'colloquium' for dialogue, although 'colloquium' can also mean discussion or conversation. Thus, *'dialogus'* and 'colloquium' are translated as dialogue.

The Holy Father's reflection on dialogue in this encyclical could be described from two purviews: vertical and horizontal. The vertical level he called the dialogue of salvation, which stems from God out of his love. This relationship demands a responsibility on the part of those to whom this salvation is directed. The second understanding is the relationship between the church and the world and among individuals. Thus, dialogue is seen

---

7   *Lumen Gentium, Nostra Aetate, Ad Gentes, and Dignitatis Humanae.*

8   Vatican II Council, 'Dogmatic Constitution of the Church: *Lumen Gentium,* 21 November 1964', in *Vatican Council II: The Conciliar and Post-Conciliar Documents,* ed. Austin Flannery, §.13, 350–426 (New York, NY: Costello Publishing Company, 1987), 393.

9   Pope Paul VI, *Ecclesiam Suam: Encyclical Letter on the Church, 6 August 1964* (Vatican City: Liberia Editrice Vaticana, 1964) was a ground-breaking document that placed on a high pedestal of prominence the need for the church to engage in dialogue (dialogue of salvation) with different persons and institutions in the world.

in this sense as a way of fulfiling and realising the apostolic mandate, an integral part of her openness to and solicitude for all persons.[10] It is 'an art of spiritual communication,'[11] which presupposes the freedom to relate and communicate with other people to foster friendship and neighbourliness.[12] Dialogue is different from debate; it involves two or more individuals or parties with various views aiming at learning from one another. This knowledge enriches and helps each party to grow.[13]

Nostra Aetate used *dialogue* in a narrow sense and in a broader sense. In a strict sense, as the main way for Catholics to engage the followers of other religions and in a wider understanding, it endorsed dialogue as a new beginning for relations with Jews.[14] Dialogue, therefore, is the name the church uses to express her positive attitude toward non-Christian religions or its relationship with them, a sign of her maternal care to all human beings. Dialogue is not just a mere curiosity to know about other faiths or an academic study of world religions. It is not just an exchange of information about religions but rather an engagement that is all involving. Thus, 'when believers of different religions dialogue, there takes place an event much more profound than verbal communication: an encounter between human beings with respect to the end toward which each one tends, bearing the weight of his own human condition.'[15] Dialogue becomes an 'indispensable step along the path towards human self-realization, the self-realization both of each and of every human community'[16] that 'has become an outright necessity, one of the Church's priorities'.[17] It is more than an exchange of ideas; it is also an 'exchange of gifts' individually and

---

10   For the different definitions of dialogue and in the context of religion, see Patrick Chinedu Mbarah', 'Education for Interreligious Dialogue: Towards an Interreligious Directory for the Archdiocese of Owerri, Nigeria' (PhD Diss., Rome: Angelicum University, 2018), particularly pp. 81–89.

11   Pope Paul VI, *Ecclesiam Suam*, §.72–75.

12   Ibid.

13   Leonard Swidler, 'The Dialogue Decalogue: Ground Rules for Interreligious Dialogue,' *Journal of Ecumenical Studies* 20 (Winter 1983): 1.

14   John Borelli, 'Dialogue, Religion and the Catholic Church' in *Mission in Dialogue: Essays in Honour of Michael L. Fitzgerald*, eds. Catarina Belo and Jean-Jacques Pérennès (Louvain-Paris: Institut Dominicain d' Études, 2012), 26.

15   International Theological Commission, *Christianity and World Religions-Preliminary Note*, http://www.vatican.va/roman_curia/congregations/cfaith/cti_documents/rc_cti_1997 [accessed January 13, 2019].

16   Pope John Paul II, *Ut Unum Sint: Encyclical Letter on Commitment to Ecumenism* (Vatican City: Libreria Editrice Vaticana, 1995), §. 28.

17   Ibid., §. 31.

collectively.[18] Thus, dialogue based on mutual esteem among believers of the great monotheistic religions leads to safeguarding and fostering social justice, moral values, peace, and freedom among all peoples.[19]

Interreligious dialogue is not a private enterprise, although it is 'connatural to the Christian vocation. It is inscribed in the dynamism of the living tradition of the mystery of salvation, whose universal sacrament is the Church'.[20] Therefore, in the light of the mission of the Church, 'it is not the Christians who are sent, but the Church; it is not their ideas that they present but Christ's; it will not be their rhetoric that will touch hearts but the Spirit, the Paraclete. To be faithful to the "sense of the Church", the interreligious dialogue begs for the humility of Christ and the transparency of the Holy Spirit'[21].

Inculturation on the other hand[22] is the term that church theologians have used in recent decades to denote a process of engagement between the Christian gospel and a particular culture. The issue of engagement with the world, and with it inculturation, would be significant elements in the Council documents especially, *Gaudium et Spes* (Pastoral Constitution of the Church in the Modern World), *Lumen Gentium* (Dogmatic Constitution on the Church) and *Ad Gentes* (Decree on the Missionary Activity of the Church). *Lumen Gentium* emphasized the positive relationship between the gospel and cultures, pointing out that through the work of the church, 'whatever good lies latent in the religious practices and cultures of diverse peoples is not only saved from destruction but is also cleansed, raised up and perfected unto the glory of God, the confusion of the devil and the

---

18   Ibid., §. 28.

19   *Nostra Aetate*, §. 3.

20   The International Theological Commission, *Christianity and the World Religions* (Vatican City: Libreria Editrice Vaticana, 1997), §. 114.

21   Ibid., §. 116.

22   The Pontificate of Pope John Paul II did give boost to the development and practice of inculturation in the different diverse cultures. Pope John Paul II referred to inculturation as a neologism. For him, inculturation is synonymous with acculturation, and he often used them interchangeably. The intention here is not to be preoccupied with the different nuances on the term *inculturation* or the diverse opinions of creating local theologies and liberation theologies, but rather to demonstrate the appropriation of inculturation in the mission of the Church. For further readings, see Robert J. Schreiter, *Constructing Local Theologies* (Maryknoll, NY: Orbis Books, 1985); Aylward Shorter, *Toward a Theology of Inculturation* (Maryknoll, NY: Orbis Books, 1988); Emmanuel Martey, *African Theology: Inculturation and Liberation* (Maryknoll, NY: Orbis Books, 1993).

happiness of man'[23]. *Ad Gentes* stressed especially the connection between culture and evangelization. *Gaudium et Spes* highlighted equally the crucial theme of the development of culture.

In her missionary activities, the church encounters diverse cultures and, while permeating and inserting the gospel message into these cultures, introduces them into the life of the church.[24] This will involve 'the opening of culture' that long and careful listening to discover the principal values, needs, interests, directions, and symbols.[25] Pope John Paul II in this direction encouraged African bishops on the essence of inculturating African cultural values into the life of the church in these words:

> The 'acculturation' or 'inculturation' which you rightly promote will truly be a reflection of the Incarnation of the Word, when a culture, transformed and regenerated by the Gospel, brings forth from its own living tradition original expressions of Christian life, celebration and thought. By respecting, preserving and fostering the particular values and riches of your people's cultural heritage, you will be in a position to lead them to a better understanding of the mystery of Christ, which is to be lived in the noble, concrete and daily experiences of African life. There is no question of adulterating the word of God, or of emptying the Cross of its power, but rather of bringing Christ into the very centre of African life and of lifting up all African life to Christ. Thus, not only is Christianity relevant to Africa, but Christ, in the members of his Body, is himself African.[26]

Thus, inculturation involves an ongoing dialogical relationship between diverse cultures and the gospel message.[27] It is a fact that in 'many ancient cultures religious expression is so deeply ingrained that religion often represents the transcendent dimension of culture itself'[28].

23 *Lumen Gentium*, §. 17.

24 Pope John Paul II, *Slavorum Apostoli*, §. 21, in *AAS* 77 (1985): 802.

25 Robert J. Schreiter, *Constructing Local Theologies* (Maryknoll, NY: Orbis Books, 1985), 32.

26 Pope John Paul II, 'Address to The Bishops of Kenya Nairobi *Wednesday*, 7 May 1980' http://w2.vatican.va/content/john-paul-ii/en/speeches/1980/may/documents/hf_jp-ii_spe_ 19800507 [accessed 14/1/2019].

27 Aylward Shorter, *Towards A Theology of Inculturation*, (Maryknoll, New York: Orbis Books, 1988), 11.

28 Francesco Gioia, ed., *Interreligious Dialogue: The Official Teaching of the Catholic Church from the Second Vatican Council to John Paul II (1963–2005)*, 122–123.

This is the case with the African (Igbo) Traditional Religion, where the religious tenets and practices highlights the customs and cultures where the anthropological and cosmological world views are intertwined. From this purview, it becomes necessary that inculturation should necessitate an open dialogue that is not in opposition to the mission *ad gentes* and that does not dispense from evangelization[29]. To say that interreligious dialogue and inculturation have a role to play in the missionary activity of the church cannot be over emphasised, given the fact that the church is on mission, encountering not only people of different religious backgrounds but also the different cultures in all corners of the earth. Furthermore, documents from the Pontifical Council for Interreligious Dialogue (PCID) speak eloquently of the connection between inculturation and dialogue in the mission of the church. The church is committed to exalting what is good and noble in human cultures and other religions, which she rightly acknowledges 'as a preparation for the Gospel'.[30]

Therefore, the church, on a mission, has to go out to meet and incarnate those good values 'found sown' in the minds and 'rites and customs of all peoples'[31] and as such engage them in dialogue. Henri de Lubac was of this opinion when he said that 'the Church can find in the very shrines of the devil things to beautify her own dwelling; that particular miracle is always something new and unforeseen ...'[32] It implies that the church, through her missionary mandate, is ready to encounter and engage in dialogue with people of other religions, including traditional religions. Thus, she infuses the gospel message and purifies through her sanctifying powers some cultural elements, thereby raising them into a status of wholesomeness for the praise and glory of God who sees everything that he created as good.[33]

Moreover, there are complexities and challenges that some aspects of traditional Christian cultures pose to the local cultures of other religious traditions. Nevertheless, interreligious dialogue at the level of culture aims at eliminating tensions and conflicts and confrontations. Thus, contributing to purifying cultures from any dehumanizing elements, and thus, be an agent of transformation and it can help in upholding certain traditional

---

29   Pope John Paul II, *Redemptoris Missio*, §. 55.

30   *Lumen Gentium*, §. 16.

31   *Lumen Gentium*, §. 17.

32   Henry De Lubac, *Splendor of the Church* (London: Sheen and Ward, 1986), 281.

33   *Genesis* 1:31.

cultural values which are under threat from modernity.[34] This aspect of interreligious dialogue and inculturation is evident in the *Odenigbo* Religio-Cultural Project as a means of safeguarding some Igbo cultural values facing the threats of modernism.

4. *Odenigbo*, Interreligious Dialogue and Inculturation: Any Connection?

The Fathers of the Special Assembly for Africa of the Synod of Bishops did consider inculturation as an urgent priority for a firm rooting of the Gospel in Africa. Inculturation is seen in this light as a 'requirement for evangelization,' and 'a path towards full evangelization'.[35] Pope John Paul II, speaks of the two dimensions of inculturation; the transformation of authentic cultural values through their integration in Christianity and the insertion of Christianity in the various human cultures.[36] While interreligious dialogue remains 'an integral element of the Church's evangelizing mission',[37] *Odenigbo* emerges as an archetypal approach of integrating the Igbo cultural values into the life of the local Church. It stands out as a channel through which the salvific message can be inserted deeply and fully into the Igbo culture. Thus, looking at the *trio* (*Odenigbo*, Interreligious Dialogue and Inculturation), there is a web of interconnectivity.

The *trio* are related and ontologically connected in the sense of their being avenues of incarnating the word of God and bringing about his kingdom among his people. In the light of the Second Vatican Council, *Odenigbo* offers the opportunity of inculturating our cultural values, philosophising, theologising, reflecting and praising God in the vernacular. Igbo culture embraces the Gospel message in *Odenigbo*, thus, opening up a dialogue of mutual encounter with followers of Igbo Traditional Religion whose religious tenets are entwined with the Igbo customs and culture. As a celebration which convokes the people of God; priests, religious men and women, Catholic Christians, Christians of other denominations, members

---

34 See Pontifical Council for Interreligious Dialogue and Congregation for the Evangelization of Peoples, *Dialogue and Proclamation*, §. 46.

35 Pope John Paul II, *Ecclesia in Africa*, §. 59.

36 Pope John Paul II, *Redemptoris Missio*, §. 52.

37 *Dialogue and Proclamation*, §. 38.

of African (Igbo) Traditional Religion, in an arena of divine worship and praise, depicts that image of the Church as *Mater et Magister.* A mother who opens wide her arms to embrace her children and a noble teacher who impacts knowledge and wisdom to her children in the language of their birth, thereby raising them from the dungeon of darkness and ignorance to a wonderful mystery of light and transformation.

Therefore, through the *Odenigbo* Religio-Cultural Project of Owerri Archdiocese, inculturation is no longer to be seen as a 'defence' of culture but a transcendence to wholesomeness, exaltation of the African (Igbo) identity and the purification of the deposits of the wealth of culture that God had embedded in the Igbo church for his glory and joy of his people. Thus, *Odenigbo* challenges the blurred vision of our Missionaries whose lenses saw our culture as emanating from the citadel of the underworld as well as the religious practices of the people, an impression that created a distance between the 'new faith' and the ancestral religion.[38] Pope Paul VI in his *Africae Terrarum* was swift in correcting this impression surrounding the culture and even the traditional religious practices of Africans that link directly to their culture, as he stated:

> Here we have more than the so-called 'animistic' concept, in the sense given to this term in the history of religions at the end of last century ... In this spiritual concept, the most important element found is the idea of God, as the first or ultimate cause of all things. This concept, perceived rather than analysed, lived rather than' reflected on, is expressed in very different ways from culture to culture, but the fact remains that the presence of God permeates African life, as the presence of a higher being, personal and mysterious.[39]

The significance of his appraisal resides in the fact that it is the first time that such an official recognition by the church has ever been made, particularly of traditional religions of Africa. This recognition that African people do have a religious expression that is uniquely African is in line with the desire of the Second Vatican Council with its theological

---

38   This statement does not intend to ridicule anyone. We cannot thank enough the early missionaries who laboured to bring us the gospel message. Nevertheless, many of them did not see any value in our culture and customs. Surely, not everything in our Igbo culture is admissible. But the noble ones must not be allowed to phase out.

39   Pope Paul VI, Apostolic Message *Africae Terrarum*, §. 8.

awareness and openness to non-Christian religious traditions and cultures. Thus, *Odenigbo* stands as a bridge and never a wall to bring dialogue of life, dialogue of action, and dialogue of religious experiences[40] to the fore. Followers of the traditional religion are not left out in this embrace of openness and rendering worship to the almighty God. *Odenigbo* is open to all Igbo sons and daughters and to all men and women of goodwill. It is like Wisdom that has prepared a meal and calls on her children to come and eat to their delight. Thus, as a rich harvest of deeper reflections about God, humanity, religion, culture, ethics, sociopolitical well-being of the people, care and concern for creation, and the exaltation of our cultural values in the very language of the people, *Odenigbo*, therefore, stands out as an ecclesial celebration for our social nourishment and spiritual well-being.

5. *Odenigbo*: A *Chukwu-Kristic* Celebration

The founder of *Odenigbo*, His Grace Most Rev. Anthony J. V. Obinna, refers to this religio-cultural project in most of his writings on *Odenigbo* as 'a *Chukwu-Kristic* Celebration'.[41] According to him, '*Odenigbo* is to new-validate and new-create Igbo Identity with the riches of God's fullness in Christ and with the riches of our Igbo heritage.'[42] This 'fullness in God (CHUKWU) and in Christ (Kristi) is the fulcrum of the celebration. This is expressed in the day's liturgy of the Holy Eucharist, which evokes awe and reverence heavily spiced with Igbo tunes and reverential rhythmical movements, revealing the elatedness of the people of God for the gift of language and culture. The *Odenigbo* Anthem expresses these sentiments thus: 'God gave us the Igbo language that with it we may worship Him and spread the Gospel in Christ and in the name of Christ His Son who is the

---

40   See *Dialogue and Proclamation* n. 42, enumerated the various forms of dialogue.

41   *Chukwu-Kristic* is just a coinage of the two Igbo words—*Chukwu* for God and *Kristi* for Christ, indicating that the *Odenigbo* celebration is a godly celebration in Christ our Saviour. See Anthony J. V. Obinna, 'Religion and Culture in the Modern Igbo Context: The Chukwu-Kristi Dynamic', anniversary lecture for Alaigbo Development Foundation, Emene Enugu, May 25, 2016; 'Celebrating the Gift of Creation-A Chi-Christic Persuasion', a keynote address at the Thirty-First Annual Conference of the Catholic Theological Association of Nigeria, Umuahia Abia State, March 30, 2016.

42   Anthony J. V. Obinna, 'Religion and Culture in the Modern Igbo Context: The Chukwu-Kristi Dynamic', anniversary lecture for Alaigbo Development Foundation, Emene Enugu, May 25, 2016.

Saviour of all people[43]. The anthem points out this aspect of *Odenigbo* that aims at integrating every good and noble aspects of life, traditional and contemporary, into a harmonious communion under the graceful persuasion of our 'God-*Chi* who is our Christ-*Chi*'.

The public lecture, which is another highlight of the day's event in full Igbo language, fills the yearnings for new knowledge and provokes thoughts for a continuous reflection for our spiritual, moral, psychological, and sociopolitical growths. The *Odenigbo* Lectures no doubt opens up the minds of the people to new horizons concerning Igbo culture, anthropology, and cosmology through theological reflections. Thus, God the creator is celebrated through Christ the Redeemer of humanity in the Holy Spirit the Sanctifier. Consequently, 'obnoxious beliefs and customs, modern waywardness and secular nonsenses, unhealthy religious practices among us have equally been confronted through these lectures ...'[44] Thus, God (Chukwu) is at the centre of this religio-cultural project. He is revered and adored by the people redeemed by his only begotten Son (Kristi) through the gifts of the native language and cultural values. This project apparently serves as a 'dynamic in a relentless quest to re-splendour and re-align the Igbo cultures and traditions' towards the embrace of God.

6. Recommendations and Concluding Remarks

Odenigbo Religio-Cultural Project has existed for more than two decades, promoting Igbo language and cultural values of Igboland. It is a capital-intensive project given the economic situation of the country. However, Owerri Archdiocese remains resolute in sustaining this project for the simple reasons of grassroot evangelization, of deepening the faith, of promoting the Igbo language in the evangelizing mission, of inculturation, of saving our cultural values from the divulging fists of modernism, and for posterity. Therefore, this project should be all involving for the good of the church in Igboland and for her progenies.

---

43 '*Chukwu kenyere anyi asusu Igbo iji fee ya, ma kwusaa Ozioma n'ime Kristi na n'aha Kristi Nwa Ya onye bu nzoputa nke mmadu niile*' (Nchikota Nkuzi Odenigbo, 2015), 6.

44 Anthony J. V. Obinna, 'Celebrating the Gift of Creation-A Chi-Christic Persuasion', a keynote address at the Thirty-First Annual Conference of the Catholic Theological Association of Nigeria, Umuahia Abia State, March 30, 2016.

The religious leaders of Igbo extraction should support the founder and the archdiocese of Owerri in promoting and fostering this project because it is for the good of the Igbo sons and daughters irrespective of their dioceses of origin. It should be a project that ought to unite all the provinces in Igbo nation, given the fact that the choice of guest lecturers of *Odenigbo* for more than twenty years has cut across the various provinces and ecclesiastical denominations in Igboland.

Furthermore, an outstanding autonomous commission under the auspices of Owerri Ecclesiastical Province should be inaugurated. It should comprise of scholars—priests, religious men and women, and the lay faithful from different academic fields especially—of theology, religion, culture, philosophy, and others. The members of this commission should as well have representations from other dioceses, making it all inclusive in collaboration with the inculturation commission to ensure that this project receives the required ecclesial boost.

The church, through this project, is not only evangelizing but also teaching and salvaging the deposits of our cultural values. To this effect, the state government through the ministry of culture should show concrete support to the church. This is a needful task in encouraging the church in advancing the growth of Igbo language and sieving out odious elements from our culture. This noble task should not only be acknowledged by the government but should receive a commensurate support that it deserves.

In conclusion, the *Odenigbo* Religo-Cultural Project remains an outstanding visible approach to inculturating our cultural values in the light of the Second Vatican Council. Through this project, the mother tongue that was facing nearly extinction has received an elaborate attention and appreciation. More attention is being paid to translating our liturgical books and prayers in the Igbo language for a deeper understanding. Priests preach and present their homilies and reflections in the language of the people. Liturgical music and sacred songs in Igbo language are trending in such a high rate that people now appreciate Igbo melodies. The seeming shyness of speaking the mother tongue in public schools is now given way to the boldness of cherishing what God gave to us in our language and culture. This does not impede the zeal to learn foreign or other ethnic languages.

Moreover, more openness to members of other faiths has been witnessed since the inception of this project. The celebration is open to all men and women of goodwill to come and worship God and share in the joys of the exhibition of various talents and skills, especially on the eve that precedes the lecture. Through this way, the local church extends hands of friendship to members of other religious traditions. It is a gradual but steady process to achieve the desire of the church in maintaining mutual relationship *ad intra* and *ad extra*. The local church of Owerri needs **Odenigbo** as it desires inculturation and dialogue.

Chapter Nine

Discerning the Interculturality and Ecumenical Framework in Archbishop A. J. V. Obinna's Reconfiliation and ReinGodment

Kenneth Ameke and Emmanuel Obi

Introduction

With the resurgence of the religio-cultural conflicts that trail the burning down of centuries-old traditional shrines, the cutting down of the ancestral trees in Igbo communities[1] in Nigeria by some members of a firebrand Christian prayer groups, and the persistent tension that exists between the mainline churches and the firebrand churches have remained a strong challenge to the Christian-dominated context. When one examines the deep spirit of hospitality and room for guest naturalization of the Igbo culture, it is difficult to reconcile them with the manifestation of this intrinsic resistance to Christianity as well as the inter-church disharmony they created. This disharmony, to some extent, presents Christianity as an unwelcomed guest in spite of the vast adherents and the impacts

---

1   Onyekachi Eze, 'Shrine Demolition: Anambra Traditional Worshippers Threaten Reprisal on Churches', *New Telegraph*, January 21, 2018, https://www.newtelegraphng.com [accessed November 11, 2018].

of Christianity. However, there seem to be negative experiences from the encounters with European explorers of the pre-missionary era that affected and are repeated by the European Christian missionaries in the postcolonial time. Besides, it is pertinent to question the neutrality of the Christian message at the heart of this broken trust on the culture of the people that brought the good news of salvation to the mission land.

In light of the above, this essay explores the anthropological framework that reconciles the negative mindset of the people evangelized towards the European foreign missions. Exploring the theological principle of Anthony J. V. Obinna's reconfiliation[2] and reinGodment,[3] this paper investigates why almost a century and a half years after its arrival in the Eastern part of Nigeria, Christianity seems to be perceived not just as a stranger but sometimes even as an enemy of the Igbo traditional ways of life.[4] The question this paper seeks to address is to what extent does/ can an indigenous articulation of the Christian faith and practice yield key insights into establishing harmony between Christianity and the Igbo indigenous culture and tradition as well as providing a model for inter-church relationship? Through a historic-analytical approach, this paper also contends, however, that uncritical romanticism, as a way of defending the Igbo culture against the 'cultural arrogance of the bringers of the good news', remains inconsistent with the soul of the Igbo culture itself.

---

2   According to Anthony J. V. Obinna, 'the word "Reconfiliation" with verb forms refiliate, confiliate and reconfiliate, describes and defines the fact of effecting and regaining the right of sonship and daughtership in a family in fellowship with other sons and daughters of the family. Though reconfiliation is closely related to reconciliation it adds an absolute dimension to the peace-making and harmonizing thrust of reconciliation by emphasizing the equal dignity of all humans from creation and by redemption' (cf. Anthony J. V. Obinna, 'Root Branches ... Grafting and Fruits: The Reconfiliatory Challenge to African-Americans and Humanity at Large', at the Black Catholic Heritage Celebration, Diocese of Charleston-South Carolina, USA, Saturday, June 21, 2003, 2. Also in, Anthony J. V. Obinna, 'Confiliating Americans: Recti-valuing One Another, A Theology and Practice of Reconfiliation' (unpublished paper, US, 2016), 4.

3   ReinGodment according to Obinna refers to the human re-experience of the Incarnation of Christ who continuously perfuse creation with the grace of God from the human state of nothingness to the beauty and splendour of God. Cf. Anthony J. V. Obinna, 'Inculturation as ReinGodment Resplendouring the Great Jubilee Illumination', in *Inculturation in the Third Millennium*, eds. Patrick Chibuko and Simeon Eboh, 10–18 (Portharcourt: CIWA Press, 1999), 16.

4   The claim is that there appears to be an 'invader-triumphalist' attitude that the bringers of the good news of salvation left many Igbos in a cultural limbo as well as breeding fanatical religiosity in some others. This religious fanaticism is strongly seen among the fire-brand Pentecostals.

This essay comprises three sections. The first section begins by illustrating the narrative of suspicion created by the Western colonizers' approach and attitude. The second section deals with the reconstructive theology of Obinna in the face of the disinGoded context. The third section analyzes the significance of Obinna's reconfiliation and reinGodment method and concludes with a reflection of the findings. We launch into the problematics that elicited the narrative of suspicion.

Situating the Conflicts: Creating the Divide in the Missionary Era in Igboland

This section provides the historical narrative that led to the positive and negative effects of the advent of Westerners in the Igbo context. The Igbo encounter with the European explorers/colonizers left an ambivalent experience in their consciousness as a people. On the one hand, the experience was full of suspicion, and on the other hand, it marked the moment of human reformation that awakened a set of values of the human person and his/her activities. In the first instance, Anthony Obinna points out one aspect of this experience in the role played by the Arab and the European slave traders 'as middlemen in the terrible and systematic enslavement of humans in Igboland and other parts of Africa. This enslavement turned out to be intimately connected with Europe's imperial design and colonial scramble for Africa with a view to taking over, exploiting and controlling the entire resources of Africa.'[5] There was also an unhappy experience in the minds of the indigenous people with the British military (especially Ekumeku movement (1893–1914) of the Anioma people).[6]

---

5   Anthony J. V. Obinna, 'Confiliatory Collaboration between the Church in Africa and Europe: A Theo-Filio-Logical Background' (unpublished lecture, June 2004), 4. Suffice it to note that slave trade began as early as from the 1500 by some Igbo dealers in the Bight of Biafra and Benin. This was a corruption of the fact that the precolonial Igbo enterpreneurs were basically traders, merchants, craftmen and women, and owners of cottage industries. Cf. Don C. Ohadike, 'When Slaves Left, Owners Wept: Enterpreneurs and Emancipation of the Igbo People', in *Slavery and Colonial Rule in Africa*, eds. Marin Klein and Suzanne Mierst (London: Routledge, 1999). See also Suzanne Mierst and Martin Klein, 'Introduction', in *Slavery and Colonial Rule in Africa*, 1–21 (London: Routledge, 1999), 7.

6   Oblong Media, 'The Ekumeku War: On Reason the British Hates the Igbos', available at https://oblongmedia.net/2019/03/22/the-ekumeku-war-one-of-the-reasons-the-british-hates-the-igbos/ [accessed March 25, 2019]. This military invasion was in accordance with the 1804–1805 Berlin Conference resolution that gave the European nations the right to lay

This fierce and violent confrontation hardened the negative impression
and resistance of the people against the Europeans.[7] In other words, these
moments of encounter with the Europeans created some form of distrust
towards them.[8] One cannot dismiss the fact that this shaped the perception
of the indigenous people when the white missionaries came to evangelize in
the nineteenth century. Obinna observes that this suspicion made the Igbos
perceive the Europeans as invaders into their land.[9] Consequently, it was
not simple then to distinguish between the explorers and the missionaries.[10]
Elizabeth Livingstone underlines an identical mode of occupation that
made it difficult to differentiate the colonizers from the missionaries when
she states that 'missions came with the scramble and partitioning of Africa
in which missions were established everywhere according to the colonizers'
colonies'.[11]

---

claim to lands and resources in Africa. The British adopted two approaches in this regard.
They came with the gun and with the preachers.

7   Chika J. B. Okpalike and Kanayo Nwadialo, 'The Missionary Twist in the Development of the
     Igbo Identity: The Dialectics of Change', a paper presented on the Thirteenth International
     Conference of the Igbo Studies Association in Marquette, Wisconsin (2015), 18.

8   Ako Adjei, 'Imperialism and Spiritual Freedom: An African View', *American Journal of
     Sociology* 50, no. 3 (1944): 189. What triggered this distrust is captured by Adjei, who
     contends that 'the establishment of Christian missions in Africa has been an act of spiritual
     aggression, they operated on the principle that everything African and indigenous is contrary,
     while everything European and foreign is acceptable to the Will of God'. Ibid. From a non-
     African perspective, it seemed to be an attempt to change the African society and to some
     extent changing the political and economic structure of the indigenous people. Cf. Dmitri
     van den Bersselaar, 'Creating "Union Ibo": Missionaries and the Igbo Language', *African
     Journal of the International African Institute* 67, no. 2 (1997): 273.

9   Obinna, 'Confiliatory Collaboration between the Church in Africa and Europe', 4. The idea
     behind this invasion is seen as coming to conquer, subdue, and exploit the land. It is clear that
     Europe has experienced several wars and manufactured sophisticated weapons and military
     tactics that gave them an edge over any territory they intend to capture. For example, the
     invasion of the African and Caribbean islands. Cf. Ibid. Elizabeth Isichie, also in this line
     of thought, remarks on the perception of the indigenous Igbo's perception of the Europeans
     thus: 'But for centuries, inland peoples had heard rumours of strangers from the spirit world
     who purchased Africans in order to feed on their life force, who dyed cloth with their blood
     and processed their bones into gunpowder'. Cf. Elizabeth Isichie, *A History of African
     Societies to 1870* (Cambridge: The Press Syndicate of Cambridge University, 1997).

10   C. N. Ubah remarks in his study of the missionary penetration of the hinterland by
     distinguishing themselves from the colonizers who employed or had a different motive from
     them. Ubah, 'Religious Change among the Igbo during the Colonial Period', 80.

11   Elizabeth A. Livingstone, *The Concise Oxford Dictionary of the Christian Church*,
     revised 2nd edition, (Oxford: Oxford University Press, 2006), 9. The credibility of this claim
     is that some missions were sponsored by the government/colonial rule that sent them to
     represent their interest too. At the same time, some missionaries disassociated themselves
     with the abuse by the colonizers.

From its advent into the Igbo cultural environment, mutual denigration, suspicion and sometimes full-blown conflicts have marked the interaction between Christianity and the Igbo indigenous way of life in general and its religious[12] expressions in particular. C. Ubah aptly captures these sentiments in the following words: 'The dominant role in the religious change among the Igbos was adaptation and accommodation. It also contends that during the period under consideration, traditional religion still ruled the minds of most Igbos to a greater extent than has generally been realized, notwithstanding the outward manifestations to the contrary.'[13] This evidently reveals a silent internal resistance or the ambivalence of the Igbos to the approach of the bringers of this new faith even during the missionary era. To this end, one can infer that it could be that the Igbos were not fundamentally transformed by the European missionaries in the real sense. Thus, there remain residues of strong loyalty and attachment to their cultural and traditional religious beliefs. The consequences of this double loyalty are playing out in diverse forms in contemporary time.

For instance, there was a protest in 1910 against the 'Union Ibo' that attempted to translate the Bible into one dialect of the Igbo nation.[14] This protest supports the fact that one basic component of the peoples' identity is threatened, in that it breeds the superiority of one dialect over the others among the people. Therefore, linguistic injustice is entailed in this

---

12   In the subsequent parts of this paper, I use the abbreviation ITR to mean Igbo Traditional Religion.

13   C. N. Ubah, 'Religious Change among the Igbo during the Colonial Period', *Journal of Religion in Africa* xviii, no. 1 (February 1988): 71. Richard Burgess, in the same vein, points out this dissatisfaction of the mission spirituality, especially among the Igbos. This led to the emergence of the indigenous church by the Igbos and the Yorubas (who formed Church of the Lord [Aladura] and the Christ Ascension Church with its base in Enugu). The reason for this protest was to ease the impasse of the bipartite loyalty to the church and the traditional cult. Cf. Richard Burgess, *Nigeria's Christian Revolution: The Civil War Revival and Its Pentecostal Progeny '1967–2006'* (UK: Regnum Books, 2008), 76.

14   Bersselaar, 'Creating "Union Ibo": Missionaries and the Igbo Language', 284. In fact, 'Union Ibo' was a newly created dialect the missionaries employed in their translation of the Bible to Igbo language. This translation encountered opposition, especially since the Bonny Igbo believed that their dialect should be used rather than Onitsha and Owerri. The Catholic mission used the Onitsha dialect in 1899 and in 1904 published the Igbo grammar and dictionary. Cf. Ibid., 283, 284. In another case, a traditional converted into Christianity was chastised by fellow traditional rulers. For example, Chief Samuel Idigo of Aguleri was penalized for it. Cf. F. Anyika, 'The Roman Catholic Mission and Traditional Rulers in Igboland in the Nineteenth Century', *Africa: Rivista trimestrale di studi e documentazione dell'Istituto italiano per l'Africa e l'Oriente Anno* 44, no. 2 (1989): 211.

effort of the missionaries. Another strong resistance against the mission
by the Igbos was the condemnation of polygamy, which for the Igbos was
connected to the economy and social status of a man. Hence, polygamy was
not a religious issue before the coming of the missionaries to Igboland.[15]
Moreover, the Igbo nation resisted the missionaries' downplay of the
relevance and value of their traditional and ancestral worships. This was
an affront to the Igbo-African cosmology.[16] This means that the indigenous
beliefs, sacrifices, affairs, and connection between the living and the dead
means nothing. Therefore, the new faith rejected and denied the tangibility
of such a belief.[17] This also informed the perception that some missionaries
used Christianity as a tool of Western cultural imperialism in Igboland.
Chinua Achebe represents one of the earliest outstanding voices against
the perceived treacherous and divisive intrusion of the 'white man' with his
religion into the 'once harmonious' Igbo communities. He writes:

> The white man is very clever. He came quietly and peaceably
> with his religion. We were amused at his foolishness and
> allowed him to stay. Now he has won our brothers, and our clan
> can no longer act like one. He has put a knife on the things that
> held us together and we have fallen apart.[18]

---

15 Ubah, 'Religious Change among the Igbo during the Colonial Period', 77. The Igbos also
confronted the missionaries' attempt to abrogate the *Ozo* title. This was resolved by the
1914 Anglican conference in Onitsha, which underlined that *Ozo* titleship was not anti-
Christian. Cf. Okpalike and Nwadialo, 'The Missionary Twist in the Development of the Igbo
Identity', 21.

16 By Igbo-African cosmology we mean that the missionaries did not pay adequate attention
to the fact that the Igbo's perception of the world plays a role in the attitudes and actions.
In this regard, M. I. S. Onyibor asserts that "the concept of the world whether sensible or
supra-sensible held by a people in a given culture has a vital influence on their attitude
to and evaluation of life and death'. Cf. M. I. S. Onyibor, *Death in Igbo Cosmology:
A Hermeneutical Investigation* (unpublished doctoral dissertation, Nnamdi Azikiwe
University Awka, 2012), 36. In the same vein, F. U. Okafor notes that 'cosmological and
metaphysical ideas determine the basic notions underlying our (Igbo) cultural religious
and social ontology. In fact, these notions necessarily though, sometimes covertly shape
our behaviour and thus guide our actions'. Cf. F. U. Okafor, Igbo Philosophy and Law
(Enugu: Fourth Dimension Pub., 1992), 13. See also, F. U. Okafor, 'Igbo Cosmology and the
Parameters of Individual Accomplishment in Things Fall Apart', in *Emerging Perspectives
on Chinua Achebe, vol.1. Omenka: The Master Artist* (Trento, NJ: African World Press
Inc., 2004).

17 Ubah, 'Religious Change among the Igbo during the Colonial Period', 77. It appears to be the
case that the European missionaries viewed the indigenous people as lacking civilization.

18 Chinua Achebe, *Things Fall Apart* (London: William Heinemann Ltd., 1958), 124–125.
Achebe actually tried in his novel to be fair and nuanced in his evaluation of both the Igbo

Another form of this protest in the present time is the unprejudiced criticism of the contemporary indigenous theologians against the fanatical missionary methods and policies that operated with the mindset of coming *'from the best to the rest'*. These indigenous theologians are also on the mission even in the land of their early missionaries. Thus, the indigenous theologians and missionaries critique the old mission style that discredits indigenous cultures and traditions from the perspective of discovering all positive values in the religious thoughts, life, and practices of the people they are encountering.[19]

However, despite the Christian missionary's overt victory in claiming already an overwhelming majority of the Igbo population for itself, in a way that tear the people away from their cultural roots,[20] scholars have continued to wonder whether Christianity has been able to provide satisfying answers

culture and the activity of the early missionaries in Igboland. He recognized the positive contributions of some missionaries while decrying the fundamentalism of the others. This is partly due to the mentality where the European missionaries viewed the indigenous people as lacking civilization. Therefore, the imposition of Christianity seemed to be an imperative. In a similar view, Ako Adjei trenchantly expresses this idea that 'so far as Africa was concerned, it was alleged that the continent was backward, and that Africans were groping in the darkness of ignorance and superstition. They did not have any religion, nor any morals not did they have any character. Therefore, Christian mission in foreign land was an act of spiritual aggression and spiritual imperialism.' Cf. Adjei, 'Imperialism and Spiritual Freedom: An African View', 190. On a critical view, Achebe was fair about the Igbo culture, presenting it both in its light and in its shadow sides. The unfortunate lingering incidences of resistance, which this paper focuses on, demands a redress. The reason is that they represent a misconception of enormous works of the Christian missionaries in Africa. As indeed they are, while we cannot underestimate the persistent and subtle dissensions highlighted in this paper, they clearly do not represent the full account of the Igbo-Christianity relationship, neither during the missionary era nor at the present.

19 James L. Barton, 'The Modern Mission', *The Harvard Theological Review* 8, no. 1 (1915): 4. Also, recently in Igboland, we see the IPOB members burning their Bibles and demanding answers for fundamentals questions that challenge the role of the church in advocating for the freedom of the oppressed people. The claim is that since the church was not advocating enough to the liberation of the people from the indirect colonial rule, therefore, she must be an accomplice with the oppressive government. In view of discovering the positive values in people's culture and life, the Fathers of the Second Vatican Council acknowledge this perspective in evangelization. Cf. Vatican II Council, 'Pastoral Constitution of the Church in the Modern World, Gaudium et Spes, December 7, 1965', in *Decrees of the Ecumenical Councils: Trent-Vatican II*, vol.2, ed. Norman P. Tanner, 1069–1135 (London: Sheed & Ward Press, 1990), §. 57, 1108.

20 We discover that the education and the religious instruction of the Christian missionaries was easier among the young people of the time. These young people were believed to be not rooted in the ideas, practices, and the traditional beliefs of their fathers. Cf. C. C. Ifemesia, 'The Social and Cultural Impact of Christian Missionaries on West Africa in the 19th and 20th Centuries', *West African Religion* 12 (1972): 70.

to specific existential questions that confront the Igbo man and woman daily.[21] In view of the certain existential problems and challenges from nonliteracy as well as the negative views of the Europeans[22] made the nineteenth-century missionaries adopt a new strategy in the mission land.

This brings us to the positive aspect of the missionary enterprise in Igboland that flourished the *humanum* of the Igbo person. Obinna describes this as the new creation dynamics in which Christianity embodies and dispenses the fullness of life to creation. Through the Christian's sacraments and holy instructions, the church 'converts and reforms humans into holy delightful sons and daughters of God in Christ'. Thus, this new dynamic reshapes mentalities, forms consciences, and educates attitudes that make us Christianimated families.[23] In this view, the church continues to manifest herself as the bearer of the fulfilment of the splendour of life to both the human person and human cultures. In his words, the human person and his/her cultures[24] thus have received theofiliatory and theoglorificatory orientation and imprint.[25] In order to achieve this, the missionary employed modern education and educational systems, medical services (by building

---

21 F. Hale, 'Debating Igbo Conversion to Christianity: A Critical Indigenous View', Acta *Theologica* 26, no. 2 (2006): 116–135. See also Akuma-Kalu Njoku and Elochukwu Uzukwu, eds., *Interface between Igbo Theology and Christianity* (Newcastle: Cambridge Scholars Publishers, 2014), 142.

22 Either as the failed earlier mission (by the Portuguese) or as an explorer coming under similar government or country.

23 Anthony J. V. Obinna, 'Culture, Human Development and the New creation Dynamic' (a keynote address at the Fourth Annual Convention of the Catholic Biblical Association of Nigeria, Seat of Wisdom Seminary Owerri, 20th October 2011), 4.

24 By culture, we refer to the 'set of means used by mankind to become more virtuous and reasonable in order to become fully human'. Cf. Joseph Cardinal Ratzinger, 'Christ, Faith and the Challenge of Cultures', Meeting with the Doctrinal Commission in Asia, Hong Kong, March 3, 1993, § 1. See also Francesco Follo, 'Inculturation and Interculturality in John Paul II and Benedict XVI', Religion and Society, available at www.oasiscenter.eu/en/inculturation-and-inculturality-in-john-paul-ii-and-benedict-xvi [accessed, March 28, 2019]. The Fathers of Vatican II Council (GS, 53) comprehensively expresses this term thus, '*Culture* in its general sense indicates everything whereby man develops and perfects his many bodily and spiritual qualities; he strives by his knowledge and his labor, to bring the world itself under his control. He renders social life more human both in the family and the civic community, through improvement of customs and institutions. Throughout the course of time he expresses, communicates and conserves in his works, great spiritual experiences and desires, that they might be of advantage to the progress of many, even of the whole human family.' Vatican II Council, 'Pastoral Constitution on the Church in the World of Today, *Gaudium et Spes*', in *Decrees of the Ecumenical Councils: Trent-Vatican II*, ed. Norman Tanner, 1069–1135 (London and New York, NY: Sheed & Ward Press, 1990), 1106.

25 Obinna, 'Culture, Human Development and the New creation Dynamic', 5.

hospitals), aids, and social welfare.[26] One cannot exclude the fact that the exemplary lives of some missionaries also generated a set of values in the life of the people.[27] These made a lasting impact in the lives of the people, in the sense that it brought about the transformation in the ideals and the thoughts of the people. Therefore, these factors facilitated the widespread of the Christian sentiment and atmosphere in the region.[28]

Consequently, this Christian sentiment was marked with the spirit of competition among the missionaries. We recall that the Church Missionary Society (CMS) led by Samuel Ajayi Crowther under John Christopher Taylor (a Sierra Leonian of Igbo descent) was first to arrive in Onitsha (1841). By 1885, the Holy Ghost Fathers led the Roman Catholic Mission (RCM) to Igboland.[29] From 1903, more Christian missions penetrated Igboland, beginning with Mary Slessor to Arochukwu under the United Free Church of Scotland Mission. CMS equally set up a base in Awka and Egbu in 1905. Moreover, Fr Dan Walsh led the RCM to establish a mission in Emekuku. The Methodist came to Oron in 1910 and at Uzuakoli in 1915.[30] While these missionaries of Christian denominations arrived in Igboland and its environs, they were accepted warmly, and lands were offered to them. At the initial stage, there was a cordial functional relationship among them.[31] One can imagine that these occupations of the allotted lands and space evolved into colonies or territories of a certain Christian denomination. For instance, the Methodist controlled from Aba through Uzuakoli to Umuahia. CMS occupied the riverine areas along the Imo and Niger River to Udi. The Presbyterians dominated in the Cross River and the Efik-speaking region. The Catholic under Shanahan was revolutionary in approach, and dynamism dominated the entire Igboland.[32] What this means is that each territory of a Christian denomination has influence over the people

---

26 Okpalike and Nwadialo, 'The Missionary Twist in the Development of the Igbo Identity', 3.

27 Okpalike and Nwadialo, 'The Missionary Twist in the Development of the Igbo Identity', 3.

28 Barton, 'The Modern Mission', 7.

29 Ubah, 'Religious Change among the Igbo during the Colonial Period', 75. It is important to note that these missionaries concentrated at the riverine areas before the colonial occupation and penetration of the hinterland. This occupation was delayed because the European trade outposts were at the coastal areas. Ibid., 76.

30 Ubah, 'Religious Change among the Igbo during the Colonial Period', 76.

31 Okpalike and Nwadialo, 'The Missionary Twist in the Development of the Igbo Identity', 7.

32 Okpalike and Nwadialo, 'The Missionary Twist in the Development of the Igbo Identity', 7. Shanahan was most successful because of 'his initiative, foresight, courage and lively dynamism.' Ibid.

hosting them. Hence, there is the possibility that rivalry ensued among the missionaries. One could perceive that the Christian sectionalism or denominationalism that characterized the church in Europe has stepped into the African continent. The ripple effect of this scandal of division in the church is now more pronounced in the African context through the new wave of the firebrand Pentecostals.

Hence, there exists the elements of a radical tendency to 'churchianity'[33] rather than Christianity.

The teachings and approaches of the missionaries with different voices created a division in the lives of the indigenous people since there was no form of denominationalism in the Indigenous Traditional Religion (ITR). Hence, when the missionaries undermined the cult of religious worship and the Igbo-African cosmology, the identity of the indigenous people was twisted as well. In other words, the indigenous identity as a people remained elusive after embracing Christianity, especially with the new wave firebrand Christians (Pentecostals). One discovers the problem of Christian anthropology in these charismatically inclined Christians. Meanwhile, the missionaries having despised the cult of the deities and regard for the ancestors created a serious gap in the lives of the indigenous people in two ways, namely, (i) the disruption or twist of the indigenous identity and (ii) the detraditionalization of the traditional authorities. On the latter, the new converts began to pay more allegiance to the newly found faith, perhaps due to the fact that the traditional sanctions had been weakened by the missionaries.[34] To this effect, the charismatically inclined Christians developed a strong resentment to the indigenous religion by devaluing some traditional cultures and ways of life and destroying the trees and forests designated as evil forests.

Furthermore, the consequences of these are that the indigenous traditional religion lost its charm and appeal to the indigenes, and the new converts developed a poor view of their identity in favour of the biblical

---

33   By *churchianity*, we refer to the devolution of Christianity into a mutual admiration society that embraces the church subculture with emphasis on the social aspects and stresses adaptation to the modern world. It is a form of a religious system that attempts to confine Christ to an enclosed space. Cf. The Evangelical Herald, 'Churchianity or Christianity', available at www.evangelicalherald.com/christianity_or_churchianity.htm. Also, Urban Dictionary, s.v. 'Churchianity', [accessed March 15, 2019], https://www.urbandictionary.com/define.php?term=Churchianity.

34   Adjei, 'Imperialism and Spiritual Freedom an African View', 195.

patriarchs. Already, one can sense a tension created by this new wave Christians between the biblical patriarchs and the indigenous ancestors. With these extreme disregard of the indigenous customs and norms, there exists some form of division among the Christians, especially between the historic churches and the Pentecostal/charismatic churches on what to accept about the indigenous religion, customs, and norms. Therefore, it is discernible that some forms of the missionary approaches created division and ambivalence among the indigenous people and their cultures and among the Christians between the mainline churches with the later firebrand churches.

Hence there are persistent complaints about a noticeable crisis of identity, spiritual schizophrenia, and syncretic dualism in many Igbo Christians. Capturing this view, Onuora Nzekwu writes:

> Go among the grown-ups who profess Christianity. The moment they can afford it they become polygamists and take *Ozo* and other traditional titles. When they think it will do them good, they consult fortune-tellers, make charms and wear them, and do a thousand and one other things which to their tens of African priests, who themselves mimic their white brother clerics, are purely 'idolatrous and un-Christian'.[35]

Nzekwu's remark is not only revealing in highlighting the kind of spiritual and cultural 'limbo' in which Christianity seems to have thrown many of its members in Igboland. It goes further to indicate why the relationship between the culture and Christian religion sometimes turns violent and irreconcilable. Nzekwu blames not only those fundamentalist missionaries who subjugated the Igbo culture but he also castigates the overzealous Igbo successors who currently perpetuate the subjugation and the disruption of the traditional customs, sanctions and norms.

Beyond these studies that focused on the past, Chukwuma Okeke and others, using qualitative and comparative methodologies, recently studied the nature, the pattern, and the rationale of these recurrent conflicts.[36]

---

35   Onuora Nzekwu, *Wand of Noble Wood* (London: Heinemann Educational Books, 1961), 76 as cited in Akuma-Kalu Njoku and Elochukwu Uzukwu, eds., *Interface between Igbo Theology and Christianity*, 142.

36   Chukwuma O. Okeke, Christian N. Ibenwa, and Gloria Tochukwu Okeke, 'Conflict between African Traditional Religion and Christianity in Eastern Nigeria: The Igbo Example', *Sage Open* 7, no. 2 (2017), https://journals.sagepub.com/doi/pdf/ [accessed November 12, 2018].

According to them, the issue is complex; the conflicts between the ITR
and Christianity in addition to the disharmony/proliferation of churches in
Igboland are not just religious; they are moral, ideological, and physical.[37]
In the light of these, the problem of invasion created a twisted mission
style, the disruption of indigenous identity, an imposition of culture on
another, and the undermining of cultural and religious values of the people.
Cognizant of these complexities, we turn to Obinna's ideas of reconfiliation
and reinGodment as theological models to reflect on these conflicts,
which responds to the tension between the culture and religion as well as
interfaith disharmony as each (culture and religion) tries to influence the
peoples' process of meaning-making within their immediate environment.

Assessing Obinna's Reconfiliation and ReinGodment Theological Framework

Having seen the events that led to some form of disinGodment among
the indigenous people, this section examines the meaning of Obinna's
reconfiliation and reinGodment as a theological principle for establishing
relation marred by human disinGodment. The interruptions by the
downside of European colonialism and the indignity to humanity and the
indigenous people in particular challenge Obinna to a renewed inspiration
in re-experiencing creation's original beauty.[38] This re-experience led
him to the formulation of his reconfiliation theology. He describes
reconfiliaiton as 'the filiation of Christ into Mary and into humanity has
triggered a confiliation thrust which draws us humans into one family of
fellow sons and daughters in Christ. At the same time, it leads us to God
Our Father thus making us theofiliates and compatriation in Christ.'[39]
Obinna's reconfiliation is imbued with Christological directedness that it
incorporates a cultural narrative that integrates people from their different
background into a family in Christ. In his pioneered project, Odenigbo,
Obinna brings us to the interculturation perspective of his Christological
new resplendouring. The high point of his argument is that through (re)

---

37 Ibid.
38 The event of personal encounter on the twenty-fifth of March 1988 being the solemnity of
the Annunciation brought him to a new awareness of the person of Christ and what this new
awareness portends for the Christian faith. Cf. Obinna, 'Roots, Grafting and Fruits', 7.
39 Obinna, 'Culture, Human Development and the New Creation Dynamics', 6.

confiliatory and theofiliatory mission, humanity and the entire creation are brought into a saving-healing anchorage in Jesus.[40]

By focusing on Christ, Obinna bridges the cleavages of the culturation intrusion and subjugation of the colonizers. In this optimism, he trenchantly affirms, 'Given the restless spirit of humans and observable legacies of goodness in every human culture, fresh hopes of a better future and a better life have continued to be enkindled in many a heart and in many communities.'[41] What Obinna set to achieve by his theofiliological theological enterprise is to underpin the reconciliatory significance of this theological paradigm for the entire humanity and the reconciliation of the fault lines of the European mission enterprise in Africa.

Moreover, through the Christological lens, Obinna emphasizes the reconciliatory mission of Christ to humanity. The word *reconciliation*, which literally means 'to bring together again' is enshrined in his reconfiliation. However, Obinna examines reconciliation as the therapy for the human disintegrated being (through wars, oppression, and destruction of the fundamental values). It is Christ who brings together again into humanity the beauty of creation and redignification. This restoration of the original relation in Christ is significant in that Christ becomes central as well as the medium for attaining this redignification. Exploring Obinna's reconciliation through the idea of Christopher Schwöbel fulfils twofold identification roles, namely, (i) the up-downward perspective of the sinless Christ identifying with our sinful humanity and (ii) the down-upward perspective in which by redignifying humanity, Christ identifies us with the righteousness of God.[42] In this regard, Obinna states this as the mission of Christ who has come to inaugurate the trans-cleaving breakthrough whose goal is redignification of humanity.[43] The intrahuman unificatory goal is the restoration of all to the status of beloved sons and daughters of God. This is the essence of Obinna's refiliation and reconfiliation, such that there will no longer be barriers to mature interaction of humanity

---

40 Obinna, 'Culture, Human Development and the New Creation Dynamics', 6.

41 Obinna, 'Confiliatory Collaboration between the Churches in Africa and Europe: A Theo-Filio-Logical Background', 5.

42 Christopher Schwöbel, 'Reconciliation: From Biblical Observation to Dogmatic Reconstruction', in *The Theology of Reconciliation*, ed. Colin E. Gunton, 13–38 (London: T & T Clark, 2003), 17.

43 Obinna, 'Confiliatory Collaboration between the Churches in Africa and Europe: A Theo-Filio-Logical Background', 7.

among themselves. In other words, through his reconfiliation thesis, we can transcend this man-made disposition that creates a divide among us and thus build humanity into a family of God in Christ.[44] Viewed thus, one can underline that Obinna's reconfiliatory mission has a universal character such that it will be problematic when a culture appropriates the Christian faith as a particular heritage they can give or not give to others.

Furthermore, from an anthropological dimension, Obinna emphasizes the role of the human person in this reconfiliatory mission of Christ, which opens up the discussion for the interchurch relationship. Obinna admonishes for the internalization of the confiliatory Spirit of Jesus when he emphatically states,

> But because all five components (proclamation, inculturation, dialogue, justice and peace, and means of social communication) are means of building up the family of God on earth with the target of turning men and women into sons and daughters of God through Christ the crucified and risen Son of God and of humanity, I see in the confiliatory spirit and outreach the dynamic that will sustain the family mission in each evangelization programme and build up the family circle in every area of life, while keeping the person of Jesus at the heart of the entire mission.[45]

Being pneuma-filiated, we become an agent of this unificatory role of Christ for humanity to God and to one another. Thus, through pneuma-filiation, we are empowered to continue this confiliatory mission of Christ across our church boundaries.[46] In this sense, Obinna's reconfiliation entails the reconstruction of the human person in Christ. This reconstruction of the human person further attends to the anchoring of our identity in Christ. There is a personal experience perspective to this anchorage in which the resplendouring beauty of Christ evokes. In this experience, a new creation status is granted to humanity. Obinna's Annunciation re-experience of the beauty of creation eloquently attests to this in his testimony: 'Out of

---

44 Obinna, 'Confiliatory Collaboration between the Churches in Africa and Europe: A Theo-Filio-Logical Background', 7.

45 Obinna, 'Confiliatory Collaboration between the Churches in Africa and Europe: A Theo-Filio-Logical Background', 10.

46 Obinna, 'Confiliatory Collaboration between the Churches in Africa and Europe: A Theo-Filio-Logical Background', 8.

my nightly shed I stepped out gazed heavenward and stood arrested by sky-blue beauty ... I had caught that moment when God took a look at everything He made it was so beautiful[47].' In this direction, (re)confiliation as a personal encounter invites Catholics to engage the charismatic-oriented denominations. This shows the importance of personal experience dimension for interchurch dialogue and fellowship. Hence, dialogue becomes a diafilial exchange of people sharing an experience of God in the Spirit.

Moreover, Obinna's reconfiliation theology through its Christological focus deals with the intercultural reconciliation. Obinna exonerates the Christian missionaries even though they were not different from the colonizers from the perspective that the European colonizers came with the domineering spirit, while the missionaries sought to upgrade the human status, although the missionaries' activities diluted and weakened the traditional sacredness of the religious world of the indigenous people. However, their mission provoked a new independent force attempting to substitute the pre-existing indigenous sacred and religious tradition of the people.[48] For Obinna, reconfiliation becomes the welcome development for an African cultural self-rehabilitation and renewal of confidence interrupted by the European invasion and denigration of African values and customs. Given this, his reconfiliation envisages 'the re-acquisition of Africa's human dignity [which] has been done and is being done in the face of centuries long and on-going depletion and pollution of Africa's ecologies human and material'.[49] By this statement, one infers that his reconfiliation theology is part of the revelation of God embedded in our African cosmology which has been punctured by the European missionaries as well as the colonizers.[50] In this way, our indigenous identity, which is not

---

47 Obinna, 'Roots, Grafting and Fruits', 8. Also in Anthony J. V. Obinna, 'African Cultures and Development: The Rectifying Challenge', at the First Colloquim, Culture and Development in African Theology, in Abidjan, Ivory Coast, September 27 to October 1, 2010, 14.

48 Obinna, 'African Cultures and Development: The Rectifying Challenge', 8.

49 Obinna, 'African Cultures and Development: The Rectifying Challenge', 4.

50 Obinna, in this regard, notes that 'each component of the earth or of the entire worlded in traditional African eyes shares in the sacredness, awesomeness or mystery of the Creator Being. That is why myths, sacred stories of origin, exist for almost every element in existence'. Cf. Obinna, 'African Cultures and Development: The Rectifying Challenge', 5. See also, Ikenga E. Metuh, *Comparative Studies of African Traditional Religions* (Onitsha: IMICO Publishers, 1987), 125–144. Metuh reaffirms this African cosmology and its impact in the ethics of the Africans.

easily separable from the world we live in, is respected; and the dignity of
an indigenous person is appreciated. Therefore, his reconfiliation attests
to the one-human-family consciousness that runs across multiple cultures
of God's diverse revelation to humanity.[51] He optimistically remarks in
this regard:

> Happily, the theme of integral human development and
> emphasis on it resonates with Africa's integrationist vision of
> life and culture. Through this consonance the best in African
> cultures can be harnessed, cherished and further developed,
> while what is dangerous and disadvantageous will be pruned,
> minimized or eliminated. A rectifying dynamic undergirds my
> engagement with culture and development a provocative fertile
> terrain.[52]

Consequently, Obinna subscribed to a Christologically based aspect
of mission in his reconfiliation as a way of rectifying the intercultural[53]
relation between the European heralds of the gospel to Igboland and the
African people. He explores St. Paul's approach to the mission, which
demonstrates the love of God to every people destined to be redeemed
by Christ as the driving force. This mission approach has an element of
pastoral directedness. The reason is that it concentrates on the human
person who is the subject of conversion and not on the substitution of a
culture that encounters Christianity. He writes,

> Bearing and sharing intimately the fact and the conviction
> that God loves every people and every land Catholic pastor-
> missionaries free ourselves of baggage of racial, ethnic, class,
> cultural superiority or inferiority and approach any people and
> every setting with the only superior possession of gift that we
> bring, namely God's love and care for everyone, for every people
> for every location, for every context, for every land.[54]

---

51   Obinna, 'African Cultures and Development: The Rectifying Challenge', 1.

52   Obinna, 'African Cultures and Development: The Rectifying Challenge', 1–2.

53   We shall describe this term in the next section for its proper relevance to the entire discussion.

54   Anthony J. V. Obinna, 'St. Paul and the New Areopagi: Christi-Animated Missionaries in
Humanity's Multidimensional Settings', 3.

This Christological underlining of the mission accomplishes two tasks: (i) it vouches for the human person as the primary target of mission and (ii) mission should not be Church denominationally oriented. By underlining the human person, interculturality[55] can be mutual since all humans are made in the image of God or by the fact that we are *imago-Christi*, who is the image of the unseen God (Col. 1:15; 2:9–10). In fact, this reconfiliatory dimension of the mission, on the one hand, should be the mainspring for contemporary mission. Obinna describes it as the 'anima and re-enlifting energy in the life and mission of Catholic Pastor-Missionaries'.[56] This constitutes a missionary intention designed with the aim to enrich life in fullness (John 10:10). On the other hand, missions should not be seen as/nor subject Christianity to an exclusively Western expression superior to the context of the global South. Invariably, Obinna reconstructs this idea through his reconfiliatory theology. However, Obinna's theology of reconfiliation cannot be reduced simplistically as a theology of liberation nor like the black apartheid theology of South Africa. His reconfiliation is not aimed at blaming the limitations of the missionaries to Africa. On the other hand, he invites us to a proactive engagement of the good news through the theological and existential categories meaningful to the people and which pays attention to the concepts and symbols comprehensible to the people.

To buttress this further, insistent on the impotence of listening and creative entrance into the symbolic world of the local cultures, Robert Schreiter blames paternalistic and invader attitude of both the earlier foreign and later indigenous leadership for the rough relationship between Christianity and some local cultures.[57] Schreiter contends that without embracing the host culture, which the theology of Incarnation demands, Christianity continues to run the risk of being introduced and maintained

---

55 *Interculturality* refers to the 'cross cultural dialogue and challenging self-segregation tendencies within culture'. Cf. John Nagle, *Multiculturalism's Double-Bind: Creating Inclusivity Cosmopolitanism and Difference* (Farnham: Ashgate, 2009), 169. 'It is based on the recognition of both differences and similarities between cultures.' Cf. Hans van Ewijk, *European Social Policy and Social Work: Citizenship-Based Social Work* (UK: Routledge, 2010), 136.

56 Obinna, 'St. Paul and the New Areopagi: Christi-Animated Missionaries in Humanity's Multidimensional Settings', 3

57 Robert Schreiter, 'The Study of Culture' in *Constructing Local Theologies* (Maryknoll, NY: Orbis Books, 1985): 39–75.

as 'an alien body in a culture'.[58] He concludes that the studying of culture
is the point of departure towards constructing a local Christianity that the
people can identify with.[59]

Similarly, R. S. Sugirtharajah explores the story of the encounters
between the Third World countries and the Bible from the perspective
of their colonization experience.[60] Without yet the support of imperialist
impositions, the Bible did have the reception in precolonial Africa and Asia
but simply as one minor book, which found and took its place among the
many religious texts of other traditions. Then, the Bible neither threatened,
claimed to surpass, nor attempted to subsume other texts. Under the watch of
colonial powers, however, the once-inaccessible text becomes ubiquitously
diffused, enthroning scriptural imperialism, with the effect that the Bible
becomes interpreted often within a rigid colonizer-colonized dialectics
positions. However, within the postcolonial encounter, local rejection gives
way to a nuanced reclamation, where the locals begin to creatively reclaim
'the Bible text by galvanizing their own cultural resources to illuminate
biblical narratives'.[61]

Sugirtharajah's narrative about the various forms of an encounter of
the Bible by people in the Third World countries, in general, has several
similarities with the Igbo story of its encounter with Christianity as a whole.
The critical difference, however, is that the Igbo experience of a precolonial
(that is, the humble presence of) Christianity is little. Christianity's initial
entrance in the Igboland was at the highpoint of colonial imperialism, and
it was to a greater extent denigrating and imposing. Unfortunately, these
attitudes have not completely disappeared. The unbecoming development
to this is seen among the firebrand, charismatic, inclined churches who
are perpetuating the denigration of the African cosmology.

Some constructive efforts are being made to bridge the gap between
Christianity and the culture across the Igboland; unfortunately, reactionary
and negative responses are getting popular daily. Nkem Chigere declares
that there is an 'unprecedented war against self-annihilation and cultural

---

58   Schreiter, 'The Study of Culture', 39.
59   Schreiter, 'The Study of Culture', 39–75.
60   R. S. Sugirtharajah, *The Bible and the Third World: Precolonial, Colonial and
     Postcolonial Encounters* (Cambridge: Cambridge University Press, 2001), 4–9.
61   Sugirtharajah, *The Bible and the Third World: Precolonial, Colonial and Postcolonial
     Encounters*, 7.

demise'[62] going on in Igboland. While some unsatisfied Christians tend towards uncritical syncretism or indiscriminate fusing of Christian faith with culture, some concerned traditionalists revert to naive romanticism, which, like Nasoom Kang's description of 'culturalist alibi', ultimately leaves a local culture stagnant, fossilized, and uncritically stuck to an idealized past.[63] In his 2011 pastoral letter, Hilary Okeke criticizes these tendencies as ultimately backward and unhelpful.[64] Obinna's reconfiliation and reinGodment make explicit the implicit richness and values in the African concept and symbols. The significance of his ideas can be compared to what Elochukwu Uzoukwu describes as the 'ministry-with-Large-Ears'.[65] This designates a theological articulation from the perspective that pays attention to the grammar and language of the people.

Theological Appraisal of Obinna's Reconfiliation and ReinGodment

Studies have shown that the success of the early missionaries to the hinterland of the Igboland was credited to the commitment and contribution of the indigenous people.[66] Besides, the task of rectifying the deflated Igbo identity and meanings acceptable to Igbo religio-cultural norms, values,

---

62 Nkem Hyginus M. V. Chigere, *Foreign Missionary Background and Indigenous Evangelization in Igboland* (Berlin: LIT Verlag, 2002), 570.

63 Nasoom Kang, 'Whose/Which World in World Christianity? Towards World Christianity as Worldly-Responsibility', in *A New Day: Essays on World Christianity in Honor of Lamin Sanneh*, ed. Akintunde E. Akinde (New York: Peter Langs Publications Inc., 2010), 41.

64 Hilary Peter Odili Okeke, *Pastoral Letter on Faith Rooted and Built on Christ* (Nnewi: CathCom Publishers, 2011), 86, 87, 96 *passim*. On these pages, the bishop comments: 'This cultural reawakening and affirmation has led some people in Igbo land to view Christianity as an imported religion that came to destroy their cultural heritage. [It is] increasingly evident that many Christians are longing for the fleshpots of Egypt [that is, giving in] to the temptation to return to the old ways.'

65 Elochukwu E. Uzoukwu, *A Listening Church: Autonomy and Communion in African Churches* (New York, NY: Orbis, 1996), 127.

66 We recall the contribution of Sierra Leonian of the Igbo descent (Christopher Taylor) and the invitation of the missionaries by the warrant chiefs even though with a different intension, which is identified as desiring their community to progress due to the fact that the presence of the missionaries brings development. For instance, Abanobi Ekwebelum, chief of Okwelle, went to Egbu to invite the missionaries and Chief Osuala Ndiribe of Isunjaba led a delegation to Ozubulu to bring the missionaries to mention but a few. Cf. Ubah, 'Religious Change among the Igbo during the Colonial Period', 80, 81.

and practices with the message of the gospel becomes an onus of the indigenous theologians.[67] So also, in the present time, if the Igbos should have a proper understanding of themselves as Christianimated persons, then it is paramount to have a perception of Christianity not shaped by the Church-based-orientation but Christologically-based. The question we seek to address is, From which perspective can the Igbos understand the engagement between the gospel and their culture, Christianity or Church point of view? The response to this question will clarify the Igbo ambivalent attitude toward the type of Christianity of the Europeans that Obinna's theological reflection alludes to.

In order to maintain the balance between being Igbo Christian who is rooted in Igbo culture, there is a need for a re-imaging of theology from an indigenous perspective. In this regard, the observation of Kanyandogo (one of the prominent African theologians) 'that an African who has been uprooted from their religious heritage cannot be truly Christian. Theologically, it cannot be stated emphatically that an African cannot be an authentic Christian without affirming their African heritage. The African personality is the raw material for the transforming action of the Spirit'[68] becomes pertinent for the healing of memories and proactive to the message of the gospel. Given this mandate, Obinna's chifiliation is kairotic for its rectifiliatory and reinGodment goal. It addresses the area of the identity of the indigenous people, the ideal of mission, and its dialogical dimension, which offers reconciliation to the cleavages between the gospel and the indigenous traditional, cultural, and religious beliefs.

---

67   This point resonates with the recommendation of Bishop Shanaham that 'future missionary work in Igbo land should be left to the natives themselves'. Cf. Okpalike and Nwadialo, 'The Missionary Twist in the Development of the Igbo Identity', 10. The significance of the involvement of the indigenous Christian thinkers is further emphasized by Pope Benedict XV, who remarked that 'lined as they are by bonds of origin, character, feeling and inclination, they (the indigenous missionaries) possess exceptional opportunities for introducing the faith to their wards, and is endowed with powers of persuasion for superior to those of any other man'. Cf. Joan F. Burke, *These Catholic Sisters Are All Mamas: Towards the Inculturation of the Sisterhood in Africa, an Ethnographic Study* (Leiden: Brill, 2001), 18. See also I. R. A. Ozuigbo, *Igbo Catholicism: The Onitsha Connection 1967-1984* (Onitsha: Africana Feb., 1985), 39.

68   Kanyadago A. Chepkwong, 'Development and Challenges of Pastoral Care in Africa', in *African Theology Comes of Age: Revisiting Twenty Years of Theology of Ecumenical Symposium of Eastern African Theologians*, ed. L. Magesa (Nairobi: Pauline Pub., 2010), 71.

In the first instance, the Second Person of the Trinity is at the heart of Obinna's Chifiliation[69] theology. By this very foundation, Obinna reconstructs how an indigenous person can perceive his/her identity. One of the consequences of the transformation of the indigenous people's identity through school and education by the missionaries is the development of a flexible and unstable identity of the people. There is a common perception by authors that the missionaries exploited the propensity of the people towards the foreigners to impose their culture. Ozuigbo notes that the sentiment of the people was seduced by the cultural pleasantness of the Westerners that they craved to acquire their dressing mode and learn their language and their cuisine.[70] For Okpalike, the Western education isolated the individual into the conditioned territory of training, which created a sort of social gap between the individual and his/her community, such that the educated person is regarded as one who was no longer in touch with and/or has repudiated one's traditional beliefs and customs.[71] These claims are not aimed to discredit the humanization education carries with it. Obinna identifies two intrinsic and contradictory tendencies in this form of *de facto* enlightenment, namely the religio-materialistic and secular-materialistic tendencies.[72] The consequences are that these tendencies exposed and entrap the people in the dilemma of the yet-to-acquire full European identity and the haven-repudiated identity (who is no longer

---

69 In Obinna's theological paradigm, the concepts of Chi and Christ are two indispensable dynamics that shape and continue to form the life of the indigenous people of Igbo even in the present time. The reason also is that there is an intrinsic historical connection the two concepts evoke in the world of an Igbo person today. Cf. Obinna, 'Root, Branches … Grafting and Fruits', 2, 3.

70 Ozuigbo, *Igbo Catholicism: The Onitsha Connection 1967–1984*, 34. *See also*, Okpalike and Nwadialo, 'The Missionary Twist in the Development of the Igbo Identity', 13.

71 Okpalike, 'A Critique of Western Education and Search for a Functional and Environmental Based African Education', *Journal AIJCRNET* 4, no. 11 (2014/2015): 184.

72 Anthony J. V. Obinna, 'Inculturation as ReinGodment and Resplendouring: The Great Jubilee Illumination' (a lecture delivered on the occasion of the Tenth CIWA [Catholic Institute of West Africa] Theology week, March 8–12, 1999), 1, 3, 4. This is also contained in the conference proceedings titled *Inculturation in the Third Millennium*, edited by Patrick Chibuko and Simeon Eboh. See also Luke Mbefo, *Christian Theology and African Heritage* (Onitsha: Spiritan Publications, 1996), 94–95. Mbefo emphasized how the materialistic perspective with the accompanied cultural trends drove people away from their indigenous cultures. This is not exclusive of the impact of the urban life in the life of the people that disassociated them from their village communal lifestyle. Cf. Okpalike and Nwadialo, 'The Missionary Twist in the Development of the Igbo Identity', 17.

grounded in his/her religious systems, life and symbols, social structures
and stratification, and the traditional customs and values).

Given this, Obinna's chifiliation rectifies the indigenous understanding
of Christianity, which does not entail altering or replacing one's identity
with that from another culture (Western orientation). Rather, it reinforces
an acknowledgement of the plenitude identity in Christ offers us in the good
news. Thus, as Christians, we are *imago Christi*. The remarkable aspect
of Obinna's chifiliation in this regard is the anthropological focus of the
union between the redemptive work of Christ with the individual person.
He invites us to a penitent anthropology in need of reconfiliation to Christ.[73]
In this way, there is no fear of a foreign superimposition of culture on an
indigenous identity. So African Christian or Christian African intersect
and are mutually exclusive.[74] Therefore, one can proudly affirm one's Igbo
identity as a Christian without the fear of losing one's original culture,
which has imprints of the Christological character and spirituality.

Secondly, Obinna's chifiliation advocates for the ideal of mission in
the manner of Christ (*missio Dei*). While Obinna demonstrates critical
sympathy for the missionaries, he does not undermine their glorious works
and achievements in Igboland. Evidently, he redirects the Igbos to focus on
the effects of the good news in our lives. This means that the indigenous
people can reconstruct and connect themselves to the standard established
by Christ and not by the European missionary standard.[75] Focusing on
the missionary standard of Christ will rectify the Western missionary
inadequacies that led to their disdain of the culture of the people they
evangelized. The outcome is the need to respect the culture of the people
to be evangelized. Thus, there is the idea of interculturality in Obinna's
reinGodment.

---

73   Obinna, 'Inculturation as ReinGodment and Resplendouring: The Great Jubilee Illumination', 5.
74   Thus stated, our African identity and a new belief with its culture, knowledge, law, morals,
      arts, and customs will not constitute a confusion with our origin as a people with history
      in a given context and modus vivendi. Cf. Victor I. Ezigbo, 'African Christian or Christian
      African? Identity Relations in African Christianity', in *Sources of the Christina Self: A
      Cultural History of Christian Identity*, eds. James M. Houston and Jens Zimmerman,
      664–682 (Grand Rapids, MI: Eerdmans, 2018), 667, 668.
75   The argument is to distinguish as much as possible the identity of the European Christian
      missionaries from the European colonizing techniques in foreign land. This distinction will
      enable an understanding that the content of the missionary message of salvation of Christ
      speaks to every context. We are also aware of the fact that the message of salvation has a
      historical background from which we can understand its universal relevance.

Thirdly, Obinna's theology of chifiliation makes the good news of salvation reinGoded in the life and culture of the indigenous people. This points to the inculturation thesis of reconfiliation. Evidently, Peter Schineller's insignificant understanding of inculturation, which clamours for the 'de-westernization' and 'indigenization' of Christianity in Nigeria particularly is not a helpful model. For him, authentic inculturation of gospel values into Nigeria demands the stripping down of Christianity to its 'essentials'.[76] Schineller's elaboration on inculturation seems to suggest that he understands it in terms of Stephen Bevans's so-called translational model.[77] In the case of Obinna's reconfiliatory approach, reinGoding Christ in the Igbo culture seeks to purify and elevate the values of the culture. This reinGodment also argues that the Igbo cosmology: indigenous beliefs and religious cults are not in themselves evil. For instance, he reiterates the beauty of the Igbo culture in his brainchild project of Odenigbo.[78] Thus, Odenigbo resonates well with the Fathers of the Second Vatican Council's (*Gaudium et Spes*, 58) idea of inculturation, which advocates for the safeguarding of the integrity of the gospel in its encounter with the culture.[79] Obinna's Odenigbo project also fits well with the line of thought of Pope John Paul II on the re-evangelization of culture by focusing on cultures that had traditionally been Christian, but which are now not clearly so.[80] Hence, theologically speaking, inculturation denotes a process

---

76 Peter Schineller, *A Handbook on Inculturation* (New York: Paulist Press, 1990), 11.

77 Stephen B. Bevans, *Models of Contextual Theology, Revised and Expanded Edition* (Maryknoll, New York: Orbis Books, 1992 2002), 37–53.

78 It is pertinent to reiterate here how this led to the origin of the Odenigbo project as a way of revoking the consciousness of the splendour of the Igbo culture. Obinna observed the growing disregard among the Igbo Christians who have Chukwu consciousness. This consciousness has a negative perception of the Ahiajoku as paganistic. Ahiajoku is a deity who belongs to the Igbo Pantheon charged with stimulating hard work in the noble field of yam cultivation and with protecting all the values associated with yam, especially the new yam festival, which is a popular feast in Igboland. Hence, celebrating Ahiajoku is equivalent to return to its patronage rather than the Supreme God. In the light of this development, Obinna initiates the Odenigbo, which literally means 'sounding or resounding in Igbo the language in Igboland or among the Igbo'. Odenigbo thus sets to reverberate the Igbo language, values, cultures again in our present time. Cf. Obinna, 'Inculturation as ReinGodment and Resplendouring: The Great Jubilee Illumination', 2.

79 Vatican II Council, 'Pastoral Constitution on the Church in the World of Today, *Gaudium et Spes*', 1109. In the real sense, the concept inculturation was first appeared in *Catechesi Tradendae* § 56, October 1979.

80 'Inculturation: John Paul II and the Third World', *East Asia Pastoral Review* 32 (1995), 277–290. See also, Dennis M. Doyle, 'The Concept of Inculturation in Roman Catholicism: A Theological Consideration', *Religious Studies* 30, no. 1 (2012): 1–13.

of engagement between the Christian gospel and a particular culture.[81] Therefore, Obinna's Odenigbo project is a path to reinGodment of the Igbo culture.

Thus established, Obinna's reinGodment as inculturation is not an encounter in which there is fear of superiority of European Christianity over another culture (Igbo); rather like Reinhard Niebuhr notes,[82] it is an awareness of the Christian faith in culture. The reason is that the gospel of salvation that Christianity communicates is not a culture; it goes beyond culture. The issue with this encounter is identified with the agency of communication of the gospel of salvation. In this way, we have to separate the interaction of the gospel with culture and the communication of the gospel through a cultural perspective to another culture. The former offers and discovers the values of the culture it encounters and enriches it such that people of that culture welcoming the good news are fulfiled, while the latter always attempts to impose a culture on the culture it encounters. To this effect, we should not allow the subjectivity/particularity of a culture overshadow the objectivity and the universality of the gospel. The gospel links with the destiny and life of the culture it engages. Paul Tillich regards this approach as a correlation of the gospel with the human experiences. Hence, through Obinna's reinGodment one differentiates the gospel from the culture of the 'gospel bringers' (often with mix-orientation and packages). This saves the internal contradiction of the concept of inculturation, whereby reinGodment and reconfiliation express the union between the gospel and the culture in a relationship akin to the 'flesh of my flesh and bone of my bones' (Gen. 2:23).

Buttressing further, the interculturality in Obinna's reinGodment also reveals a culture of mutual respect characteristic of Christianity. This is explicit in his statement that 'the European of Western cultural pride is gradually yielding a more human hearts to a sober acceptance of cultural differences accompanied with respect'.[83] This immediately points to the dual movement of inculturation,[84] which Pope Benedict XVI in 1993

---

81   Doyle, 'The Concept of Inculturation in Roman Catholicism: A Theological Consideration,' 1.

82   Richard Niebuhr, *Christ and Culture: An Overview of a Christian Classic* (New York, NY: Harper Collins, 1951).

83   Obinna, 'Inculturation as ReinGodment and Resplendouring: The Great Jubilee Illumination', 6.

84   The dual movement of inculturation are the dialogical and the incorporational movement. By dialogical, the gospel is incarnated in the culture it meets, while the incorporational

suggests to the Asian bishops for a new understanding of the relationship between the gospel and culture. Benedict's idea of the relationship between the gospel and culture is an invitation to the original attitude of Christianity towards other cultures she encounters. In this way, the gospel of Christ is not seen as interrupting the soul of the culture of the people; rather, the gospel purifies it. This is termed the culture of faith.[85] It is in this interaction of the gospel with a culture that the divine beauty radiates to the people. This interaction in the light of reinGodment enables an understanding of Christianity as God's redemptive presence among us and the experience of the resplendouring of God in our culture. Therefore, the church, as a bearer of this good news, not only accompanies the people but also becomes an agency of filial and grateful service of God to humanity. Thus, harmony is seen to exist in the Christian and public life of the indigenous people.

Finally, reinGodment in Obinna's chifiliation also has a sociolinguistic dimension, which is an encouragement to reflect and theologize in concepts that are meaningful to the indigenous people. The use of peculiar cultural concepts to theologize is thus seen as part of the universal Christian tradition. This reveals an element of continuity between the particular understanding of the Christian faith with the universal expression of the Christian faith. This has the prospect of clarifying and establishing points of contact with between Christianity and the Igbo indigenous religious beliefs and understanding of the Igbo cosmology.[86] This is one of the fruits

---

movement, Christianity, the agent of this good news, incorporates the values of the culture she encounters and enriches it from within. In John Paul II's view, it is the 'evangelization of culture and the cultural understanding of the gospel'. This means that inculturation is not an action but a process that unfolds in time. Cf. John Paul II, *Redemptoris Missio: Encyclical Letter on the Permanent Validity of the Church's Missionary Mandate, December 7, 1990*, available at http://w2.vatican.va/content/john-paul-ii/en/encyclicals/documents/hf_jp-ii_enc_07121990_redemptoris-missio.html, § 52 [accessed March 28, 2019]. It is pertinent to note that John Paul II's idea of inculturation in this encyclical was informed by Pope Paul VI's *Evangelii Nuntiandi: Apostolic Exhortation to the Episcopate, the Clergy and to all the Faithful of the Entire World, December 8, 1975*, § 20.

85 Joseph Cardinal Ratzinger, 'Christ, Faith and the Challenge of Cultures', Meeting with the Doctrinal Commission in Asia, Hong Kong, March 3, 1993, § 1. See also Francesco Follo, 'Inculturation and Interculturality in John Paul II and Benedict XVI', Religion and Society, available at www.oasiscenter.eu/en/inculturation-and-inculturality-in-john-paul-ii-and-benedict-xvi [accessed March 28, 2019].

86 It is pertinent to illustrate the four parts of the Igbo cosmology. M. Onwuejeogwu points outs these four components thus: *Okike* (refers to creation), *Alusi* (deals with the supernatural forces and deities), *Mmuo* (spirit), and the *Uwa* (means the world). Cf. M. Onwuejeogwu, *An*

of his Odenigbo lecture series, which allows people to theologize beyond the confines/limits of a foreign language. In other words, theology being universal expects particular linguistic articulation of a culture. This is not an attempt to dethrone the Western theological patriarchy, rather expressing the values and revelations of God from an indigenous encounter of God since theology is not particularized or reserved for a certain context. Hence, Christian theology has its constant in Christ (Trinity).

Conclusion

This paper set out to investigate how an Obinna's theofiliation theology reconstructs the broken trust that led to the misperception of the gospel as a culture imposing itself on the culture it encounters. We discovered that the persistent struggle of the Igbo culture and tradition to become one flesh with the Christian mode of thought and approach is due to the distrust in the approach employed by the Westerners in Igbo context. His theofiliation has Christological imperative that disrupts the twisted historical narrative and unhappy experiences of the people. Hence, we observe that his cognates—reconfiliation and reinGodment—are not a means of advocating for the emancipation of the Igbos from the Christian faith; rather, these concepts point towards making the indigenous people Christifiliated because we are fundamentally Chi-istic and Chi-phoric peoples. We have shown that through Obinna's theological articulation of theofiliation, the Igbo people can see themselves as people who worship God in truth and in spirit. We note that the errors of coldness and hostility to the Igbo culture and identity by the European foreign mission are addressed in the reconfiliation dynamics and reinGodment ideas of Obinna, which reaffirms the redignification of the Igbo identity as well as the bond of continuity between the Igbo culture and tradition with the Christian faith. Thanks to Obinna, the deeply traditional Igbo person does not need to experience the dilemma of being a true Christianimated cultural/traditional person. It is clear that the current 'unwelcomed guest'/'foreigner' status of Christianity in Igboland, even after almost hundred and fifty years of neighborhood, is very unusual given the deep spirit of hospitality that defines the traditional Igbo cultural soul.

Igbo Civilization: Nri Kingdom and Hegemony (London: Ethnographical Ltd., 1981).

This paper has shown that the Igbo culture and tradition have been open and welcoming to the non-Igbo cultures she encounters. Christianity, therefore, can certainly become Igbo. It can naturalize itself among its Igbo host.[87] Igbo culture, on its part, needs to stay self-critical, particularly with its reactions against Christianity. It must remain open rather than recoil and gets fossilized, either through uncritical syncretism or through naive romanticism of some idealized past. To remain hospitable and open is just the best way the Igbo culture stays authentic to itself.

Through Obinna's idea of reconfiliation and reinGodment of Igbos, one can perceive the continuity and no longer as conquering of culture between the indigenous culture and tradition with the Christian faith. This understanding also creates fertile ground as a model for interecclesial relation. In the sense that being Christifiliated, we can understand Christianity according to the redemptive work of Christ in our lives rather than as a European culture into African soil. Therefore, our discussion reveals that the indigenous resistance to the presence of the Europeans (especially Christian missionaries) were not mainly or directly against Christianity, but rather, it was directed against the spirit of invasion and substitute mentality of the colonizers. Obinna's chifiliation serves as a theology that put the indigenous narrative into perspective. This indicates the optimism that acceptance of Christianity in Igboland is not submission to another culture but a proactive theology that has the ingredient to endure for generations.

The transformation of the human person is also at the heart of Obinna's theological discourse. Reconfiliation and reinGodment are not inclined towards protection of the institutional culture or religion. They reveal a different model entails in mission towards radiating Christ, whereby the life of the human person draws people to Christ through witness to the gospel.

---

87   Here again, I am already alluding indirectly to the central Christian theology of Incarnation, especially in its kenotic sense as God's *self-emptying* into humanity. This is the vision of theology of Incarnation.

Section Three

Pastoral, Mission, and Management

Chapter Ten

Theofiliance and the Reconfiliation Dynamic: Healing Humanity's Divisions through the Memory of the Cross

Bede Uche Ukwuije

Archbishop Obinna defines *theofiliance* as *'creation's new and integral sense of kinship with God derived from its relationship with the Son of God who has become the Son of Man'*.[1] In that sense, *theofiliance* is the event of the redemption of humanity and the entire

1   Anthony Obinna, 'African Cultures and Development: The Rectifying Challenge', in *Cultures and Faith* vol. XVIII, no. 4 (Rome, 2010), p. 321–333. See also his other reflections: 'Roots, Branches … Graftings and Fruits: The Reconfiliatory Challenge to African-Americans and Humanity at Large' (Charleston, USA, 2003); 'Confiliatory Collaboration between the Church in Africa and Europe: A Theo-Filio-Logical Background' (Owerri, 2004); 'Confiliating Americans: Recti-valuing One another. A Theology and Practice of Reconfiliation' (un published); 'Chi and Christ in Igbo Salvation Experience—An Explication', in *God, Bible and African Traditional Religion*, ed. Bede Ukwuije (SIST International Missiological Symposium 2009, Enugu, SNAAP Press, 2010), 5–14; 'The Pastoral Approach to the Challenges of Caste Systems', in *Beyond Frontiers* (Spiritan International School of Theology, Attakwu, 2011/2012), p. 14–18; 'Celebrating the Gift of Creation—A Chi-Christic Persuasion' (a keynote address at the Thirty-First Annual Conference of the Catholic Theological Association of Nigeria, March 30, 2016, Umuahia); 'Religion and Culture in the Modern Igbo Context. The Chukwu-Kristi Dynamic' (anniversary lecture for Alaigbo Development Foundation [ADF], Enugu, May 25, 2016, unpublished).

creation through the self-donation of Jesus on the cross. ***Reconfiliation***, therefore, is the pastoral project that aims at the restoration of the dignity of every human person as son and daughter of God and the unity of humanity wounded by sin and divisions. In this homage to the theological thoughts of Archbishop Anthony Obinna, I would crave the indulgence of the reader to first briefly give a personal testimony about how I became a disciple of the pastoral theology of *theofiliance*. Then I will expose the concept of *theofiliance*, with particular attention to the sociocultural context of its emergence as well as its theological framework. Finally, I will sketch out the project of *reconfiliation*, which is the practical pastoral implementation of the *theofilial* event.

1. How I Became a Disciple of *Theofiliance*

My theological conversation with Archbishop Obinna started, God-incidentally, to borrow his expression, on 26th September 2010 at the Murtala Muhammed International Airport, Lagos. I was then teaching at the Spiritan International School of Theology, Attakwu, Enugu. I was travelling to Abidjan, Ivory Coast, with Sr. Prof. Theresa Okure of CIWA, for a Symposium on Culture and Development, organised by the Pontifical Council for Culture and the Congregation for the Evangelization of Peoples (27 September -1 October 2010).

When we arrived at the departure gate on that 26th September, NEPA (National Electric Power Authority) took light as usual. We heard a loud shout in Igbo, and immediately identified the voice as that of Archbishop Obinna. When light came back few minutes later, we located him. To his and our great delight, he was heading to the same symposium. Like the Ethiopian Eunuch on the way to Gaza, he was struggling with his paper on 'African Cultures and Development: The Rectifying Challenge.' He immediately asked me to bring out my laptop and help him type his paper. I gladly complied while he continued thinking aloud, manufacturing concepts, *theofiliance, Christofiliance, cofiliance, rectifiliance, covivance*, etc. As the dialectic of grace and contradiction would have it, our flight was delayed for three hours. So, I enjoyed almost a four hours course on *the pastoral theology of theofiliance*.

After he had presented his paper at the symposium, I suggested to him that his concept of theofiliance would need a dogmatic-trinitarian framework. He spontaneously said, 'Take it and develop it. You are a theologian. I am a pastor.' This is how I became a *griot* of theofiliance. Our theological conversation culminated in several publications, the summit of which is my book, *The Trinitarian God, Contemporary Challenges and Relevance*,[2] which consecrated the entire part three to the sociopolitical and anthropological implications of the Trinity using theofiliance as guiding concept. I remain grateful to His Grace for this unmerited opportunity he gave to me to deepen my understanding of Trinitarian theology, exploring its pastoral relevance. Let us now examine the meaning of theofiliance with special attention to the sociocultural and anthropological context of its emergence and its theological framework.

2. The Pastoral Theology of Theofiliance

The Context of the Emergence of the Concept of Theofiliance

The pastoral theology of theofiliance is a response to present-day anthropological crisis in contemporary societies, precisely the fact that 'there are distortions in perceiving, reacting and relating to fellow humans across our extensive human family'.[3] This has resulted in violence to the sacredness and preciousness of the human person all over the world. However, this crisis is fundamentally connected to a form of secularism, the loss of the sense of God.

---

2 Bede Ukwuije, *The Trinitarian God, Contemporary Challenges and Relevance* (Mumbai, 2013). My other publications include 'Retrieving the Sacredness of the Human Person in Nigeria', *Encounter: Journal of African Life and Religion*, 12 (2017), pp. 99–111; 'Theofiliance: Our Kinship in God through Jesus Christ', in *Beyond Frontiers* (Spiritan International School of Theology, Attakwu, 2011/2012), 11–13; *Faith in Africa in the Context of the New Evangelization SEDOS Bulletin* volume 45, nos. 9/10 (Rome 2013), pp. 212–221; Innocent Maduakolam Osuagwu and Bede Uche Ukwuije, 'Evangelization Locally and Globally: The Filiation Dynamic' (a joint paper at the international seminar on November 8, 2012, at the Obiri Odenigbo, Assumpta Cathedral, Owerri, organized to Mark the Centenary Jubilee of the Establishment of the Catholic Church in Owerri Ecclesiastical Province, unpublished).

3 Anthony Obinna, 'Confiliating Americans: Recti-valuing One another ...', 4

The Loss of the Sense of the Sacredness
of the Human Person

The loss of the sense of the sacredness of the human person is visible through different abnormal happenings, which unfortunately have become a routine in Africa, especially Nigeria. They include allowing dead bodies to decay on the road, exposing the bodies of accident victims on the social media; jungle justice; rampant killings by military and police; kidnappings; and human trafficking. I analysed these in detail in a recent article.[4] Suffice it here to dwell on the phenomenon of geogamy/geolatry, which is expressed in the *osu/diala* castes discrimination, as well as in the present exchange of hate speeches by the different militant groups— IPOB, Arewa, Oduduwa, Niger Delta—and their respective intellectuals.

Geogamy/Geolatry

The thorny and complex question of the *osu/diala* superstition continues to destroy relationships and people in Igboland. In a Lenten pastoral dedicated to this issue in 1977, Bishop Mark Unegbu, the then ordinary of Owerri, officially launched a campaign for the abolition of this superstition. The custom, he explained, stared in an undated past *'by some form of human sacrifice in which an individual was offered, or more rarely, offered himself to some idol. He was then henceforth regarded as property of the god and was supposed to act as its cult slave or even as priest.'*[5] This individual is referred to as *osu*, 'slave of a god', while the rest of the people are the *diala*, literally, 'husbands of the land'. *Diala* can also be translated to mean 'free born'. Following this sacrifice, the *osu* was ostracized by the society and could not relate with others who regarded him with awe. It was also believed that this status was transmitted from parents to their children. Hence, if either parent is *osu*, the children all ipso facto become *osu*. Consequently, marriage between *osu* and *diala* is regarded as taboo. Surprisingly, despite a great level of development and Christianization in Igboland, this ancient pagan practice continues to impact on relationships among people in the Igbo society. People could be Christians and Catholics in the same church, sharing the

---

4   Bede Ukwuije, 'Retrieving the Sacredness of the Human Person in Nigeria', 100–105.

5   Mark Unegbu, *The Osu/Diala Scandal* (Lenten pastoral, Owerri, 1977), 4.

kiss of peace, receiving communion together; but when they want to marry one another, their families tell them that it is not possible because one is *osu* and the other one is *diala*.

Unegbu's successor, Archbishop Anthony Obinna, continuing the fight against the depersonalization involved in this pagan practice, sees it as a form of *geogamy*, a marriage to the land. It is also a form of idolatrous worship of the earth. Hence, its designation as *geolatry*. This comes out clearly from the fact that *diala* literally means 'husband of the land, married to the land'. This means that the *diala* no longer sees himself as freedom and possibility, since his destiny is permanently tied to the land. On the one hand, the *diala* lives permanently with fear and insecurity; on the other, the *osu* is pushed to live permanently with the stigma and sentiment of rejection and dehumanization. In many Igbo kindreds, villages, and towns, they are denied of social and political responsibilities.

Archbishop Obinna notes that the self-definition of the Igbo as *diala* or *osu* or *umeh* or *ohu* as 'crippling and paralyzing'.[6] They are 'ancestral-diabolic distortions of our sacred identity—*Umu Chukwu*—God's children'.[7] Earlier, in their pastoral letter for the Centenary of Catholic Faith in Owerri Ecclesiastical Province 2012, the Bishops of the Province described the *osu-diala* divide as *'one of the darkest hangovers of traditional religion. It discriminates unfairly between members of a community and entrenches 'apartheid' in the center of our so-called traditional communism. This offends every civility and Christian living standards'.*[8]

Hate Speeches

Other forms of geogamy and geolatry are the hate speeches that keep escalating as different groups—IPOB, AREWA, ODUDUWA, NIGER DELTA—fight for their autonomy and declare their dissatisfaction with the Nigerian State and government. The wrong perception of one another is subtly diffused in jokes made through the corruption of the meaning

---

6   Anthony Obinna, 'Religion and Culture in the Modern Igbo Context. The Chukwu-Kristi Dynamic' (2016), 9.

7   Anthony Obinna, 'Religion and Culture in the Modern Context …', 10.

8   *Upholding the Faith, A Pastoral Letter of the Bishops of Owerri Ecclesiastical Province, for the Centenary of Catholic Faith in Owerri Ecclesiastical Province 2012* (Assumpta Press, Owerri, 2012), 9.

of names. For example, Igbo becomes 'I Go Before Others'; NAIRA, 'Never Allow Igbo's Rule Again'; HAUSA, 'House Animals Using Seat of Authority'; APC, 'Association of Past Criminals'; PDP, 'People Deceiving People'; etc.

One would claim that these are jokes, but they translate what people really think about others and shape their behaviour towards them. These circulate worldwide through the social media. Once, during a conference in Dakar, I introduced myself as an Igbo. After the conference, someone from another African country came to me and smilingly said, 'Are you also "I Go Before Others"?' We laughed together, but reflecting on it later, it dawned on me that I had been judged and categorized. The corruption of language imprints lasting impressions on the self-definition and world vision of children and youths as they grow up, and it determines how jobs and responsibilities are shared across Nigeria. This fact comes up in different arguments for or against the possibility of keeping Nigeria together as a nation.

Hate speeches contributed to the Rwandan Genocide in 1994. The hate radio operated by the Hutus designated the Tutsi as *cockroaches*. They called on the Hutu everywhere to sweep off the *cockroaches* that had invaded their streets. This propaganda created chaos in peoples' minds and distorted their perception of others.

The relationship between Africans and Westerners, Europeans and Americans, is also distorted by memories of violence to the sacredness of the human person through slavery and colonization. The European who bought Africans considered them as merchandise and not human beings. At the same time, Africans who sold their brothers and sisters considered them as non–human beings. Some traditional rulers settled their internal quarrels by selling their opponents or potential challengers. People used the opportunity of slavery to deal with their enemies, debtors, or creditors, etc. There were and are still in some cultures some stories and myths, rituals, and social structures, which teach children from their age of initiation to disregard people from the other ethnic groups or villages or social strata. All these played a significant role in determining who was sold. What of the Arochukwu politics, which used the name of *Chukwu*, the god of the Aro, to confuse people and finally sell them to the white man?

Africans need to take time to evaluate the impact of the anthropological crisis that is ruining their cultures and traditions and societies. In these acts, it is humanity that is wounded, and distorted. Sometimes, people tend to think that there are, on the one hand, perpetrators and, on the other, victims. In reality, all are victims. Desmond Tutu, analysing the devastating effect of apartheid, said:

> In a real sense we might add that even the supporters of apartheid were victims of the vicious system which they implemented and which they supported enthusiastically. This is not an example for the morally earnest of ethical indifferentism. No, it flows from our fundamental concept of *ubuntu*. Our humanity is intertwined. The humanity of the perpetrator of apartheid's atrocities was caught up and bound up in that of his victim whether he liked it or not. In the process of dehumanizing another, in inflicting untold harm and suffering, inexorably the perpetrator was being dehumanized as well.[9]

We can only see our history and cultures in a new way and, by consequence, assume it if we courageously accept that we are taken up in this crisis. Before we move to the corrective response of theofiliance, we need to unveil another dimension of the anthropological crisis Africa is facing.

The Loss of the Sense of God

A deep cause of the anthropological crisis Africa is experiencing is the subtle development of secularism, which in reality is a crisis of God. Normally associated with Western industrialized countries, secularism has deeply eaten into the cultural fabrics of Africa. In Western traditions, secularism is the suppression of religion in order to make sure that it does not play a determining role in social, moral, cultural or political life.[10]

Paradoxically, in Africa, secularism is expressed through a form of functional religion. While people in the Western tradition declare openly that they don't need God in order to be human, Africans invoke God for the achievement of their human strategies. There is less an emphasis on

---

9   Desmond Tutu, *No Future without Forgiveness* (New York, NY: Doubleday, 2000), 103.

10   Patriciu Vlaïcu, "The Consequences of the Enlightenment, from the Perspective of the Orthodox Communities in France', in *International Review of Mission*, ed. J. Matthey, vol. 95 (Geneva: The Commission on World Mission and Evangelism of the World Council Churches, 2006), 299.

the personal and transforming relationship with God and more and more emphasis on what God can do to improve the material condition of the worshippers.

A deep dimension of secularism is the eclipse of teleology. The idea of salvation is domiciled to the here and now. *'The after-life which is ultimately what gives meaning and solace is hardly ever remembered in normal day to day life. In real terms therefore, the world remains a summum bonum to be sought by all means.'*[11] This secularism is being marketed by a disturbing crossless Christianity under the influence of Pentecostalism, which proposes the 'gospel of material prosperity'.

The resurgence of witchcraft by people seeking relevance, especially the new political elite in search of cultural and traditional authenticity and power, belongs to this functional religion. The different militarized ethnic factions maintain their power through magical practices and beliefs and witchcraft, which are fundamentally anticultural and antireligious. Political leaders belong to secret cults through which they flee to the patronage of one deity or another. They go through occult practices in hidden shrines. They offer human sacrifices like the famous Okija Shrine uncovered in 2014. Here, it is no longer question of African Traditional Religion but a perversion and manipulation of religion for personal, economic, and political strategies.

Surprised by the persistence of the *osu/diala* discriminations in Igboland, even among those who are considered as staunch Catholics, Bishop Unegbu asked a pertinent question. Could it be that people who claim to be Christians still believe in the gods they claim to have renounced? If not, *'is the "osu" status a purely social stigma (...) maintained by those who derive social advantage or personal satisfaction by pretending that some others are their inferiors?'*[12] I am convinced that for many people, the 'gods' and God don't mean anything anymore. What matters is their personal survival strategies. When God does not matter or becomes an instrument for the achievement of personal survival strategies, then the human person becomes very cheap and can easily be sacrificed

---

11 Josephat Oguejiofor, 'The Resilient Paradigm: Impact of African World View on African Christianity', in *God, Bible and African Traditional Religion,* ed. Bede Ukwuije, 99–112 (Enugu: SNAAP Press, 2010), 110.

12 Mark Unegbu, *The Osu/Diala Scandal,* 7.

for the same goal. The pastoral theology of theofiliance responds to the anthological crisis herein explored.

The Theological Framework of Theofiliance

Theofiliance, as stated above, is 'creation's new and integral sense of kinship with God derived from its relationship with the Son of God who has become the Son of Man'.[13] Theofiliance is closely related to two other neologisms coined by Archbishop Obinna: *confiliance/confiliation* and *cofiliance/cofiliation.* While cofiliation or *cofiliality* refers to the natural relationship of people by birth, *confiliation* designates our adoption as children of God in Jesus Christ. *Theofilance* includes and transcends both realities; it is *'humanity's new kinship with God, through His Son Jesus Christ born of the Virgin Daughter Mary, which makes of humans new sons and daughters of God endowed with the Spirit of Christ'.*[14]

Theofiliance was achieved through the Jesus's self-donation on the cross, the event in which God totally identified himself with Jesus Christ and revealed him to the world as his son and the universal brother of all. In that sense, theofiliance is intimately connected with Christofiliance, which articulates creation's kinship and humanity's sonship in and with Christ who has filiated himself to creation and humanity.[15] While it is a fact that humans participate in Jesus's filiation to creation and humanity through baptismal-conversional experience, the filiation and radiation of Christ in creation is a historic, cultural given that continues to attract and reach persons and cultures not yet visibly reached. Hence, theofiliance is also made possible through the activity of the Holy Spirit, since it is the Spirit that brings us into the intimate union of the Father and the Son. The entire theology of theofiliance-Christofiliance constitutes a dynamic of

---

13   Anthony Obinna, 'African Cultures and Development: The Rectifying Challenge', in *Cultures and Faith*, Vol. XVIII, no. 4 (Rome, 2010), 321–333; 'The Pastoral Approach to the Challenges of Caste Systems', in *Beyond Frontiers to the End of the Earth* (Attakwu: Spiritan International School of Theology, 2011/2012), 14–18; Bede Ukwuije, 'Trinitarian Relation and Theofiliance', in *The Trinitarian God, Contemporary Relevance and Challenges* (Mumbai: Paulines, 2009).

14   Anthony Obinna, 'African Cultures and Development', 328.

15   Anthony Obinna, 'African Cultures and Development', 328.

grace that could rightly be designated as trinifiliance because theofiliance is the activity of the Trinity.

God's fatherhood is expressed through his immense love for humanity. This is primarily designated as the act of creation (Gen. 1, 1–2, 2). God made human beings in his image and likeness, that is, as relation and community. Hence, every human being is *chukwukere* (created by God). God rejoiced over his creation because he saw that it was good. Therefore, every human being is *chukwukeziri, mmandu,* created good by God.

The sin and evil that eat into the fabric of humanity's relationship with God do not prevent God from loving us. The event of the death and resurrection of Jesus Christ is the perfect expression of the eternal love of God the Father through which he reconciled the whole of humanity. First, it must be noted that the cross of Jesus is at the same time his exaltation, his resurrection, and the effusion of the Holy Spirit. It is precisely through this event of Jesus's self-donation that God justified humanity with himself. Jesus accepted *cruci-mortification* and reconciled humanity with God.

Christofiliance has ecclesial extension because the church was born from the cross. Although the Lukan tradition has it that the church was officially born at Pentecost (Acts 2:1–13), nonetheless, the logic of faith shows that Pentecost is the clearer revelation to the church of the mystery that was accomplished on the cross as well as the actual sending on mission of the church. The teaching of the intimate connection between the church and the cross of Jesus Christ runs throughout the church's tradition. It comes from her interpretation of the significance of the blood and water that came out from the pierced side of Jesus (John 19:33–35). Origen, the Alexandrian father of the second century, stated that '*Christ has flooded the universe with divine and sanctifying waves. For the thirsty he sends a spring of living water from the wound which the spear opened in His Side. From the wound in Christ's side has come forth the Church, and He has made her His Bride.*' Later, John Chrysostom, bishop of Constantinople in the fourth century was more elaborate in his instructions to catechumens.

> If you desire further proof of the power of this blood, remember where it came from, how it ran down from the cross, flowing from the Master's side. The gospel records that when Christ was dead, but still hung on the cross, a soldier came and pierced his

side with a lance and immediately there poured out water and blood. Now the water was a symbol of baptism and the blood, of the holy eucharist. … From these two sacraments the Church is born: from baptism, 'the cleansing water that gives rebirth and renewal through the Holy Spirit', and from the holy eucharist. Since the symbols of baptism and the Eucharist flowed from his side, it was from his side that Christ fashioned the Church, as he had fashioned Eve from the side of Adam.[16]

Another African ancestor and great father of the church, St Augustine wrote, *'There it was that the gate of life was opened, from there the sacraments of the Church flow; without these one does not enter true life.'*

This conviction was reaffirmed by Vatican II in its dogmatic constitution on the church, *Lumen Gentium 3*: *'The Church, or, in other words, the kingdom of Christ now present in mystery, grows visibly through the power of God in the world. This inauguration and this growth are both symbolized by the blood and water which flowed from the open side of a crucified Jesus.'*[17] The council connected this interpretation with Jesus's affirmation in John 12:36: *'And I, if I be lifted up from the earth, will draw all things to myself.'* Hence, the event through which God reconciled humanity with himself is the event that inaugurated the community that will perpetuate the memory of grace (*LG* 3).

As often as the sacrifice of the cross in which Christ our Passover was sacrificed, is celebrated on the altar, the work of our redemption is carried on, and, in the sacrament of the eucharistic bread, the unity of all believers who form one body in Chris is both expressed and brought about. All men are called to this union with Christ, who is the light of the world, from whom we go forth, through whom we live, and toward whom our whole life strains.[18]

---

16   John Chrysostom, Cat. 3:13–19: Office of Readings, Good Friday.

17   Vatican II Council, 'Dogmatic Constitution on the Church, *Lumen Gentium*, 21 November 1964,' in *Decrees of the Ecumenical Councils: Trent-Vatican II*, ed. Norman Tanner and Guiseppe Alberigo, vol. II, 848–900 (London: Sheed & Ward and Georgetown University Press, 1990), 850.

18   Vatican II Council, 'Dogmatic Constitution on the Church, *Lumen Gentium*', *850.*

Therefore, the church is called to embody this mystery of reconciliation of God and humanity. In fact, *Lumen Gentium* (1) presents the church as *'a sacrament ..., a sign and instrument of a very closely-knit union with God and of the unity of the whole human race'*.[19]

The criterion of admission into the new community formed from the death and resurrection of Jesus is conversion. This means self-dispossession, the obligation to dispossess oneself of the dictatorship of the flesh, which includes cultural limitations. Paul affirmed later that this new community was founded not on debt but on the liberality of God, grace, and is called to live through mutual exchange, communion, and collective creativity. This love must be ready to encounter death—the proliferation of evil force. That is why faith lives through hope (*Spe Salvi*, 7).[20] The *Letter to the Hebrews* 11:1 defines faith as *'the substance (hypostasis) of things hoped for; the proof of things not seen'*. Hebrews 10:34 testifies that the early Christians were persecuted because of their faith. Thanks to their faith, they were able to accept the plundering of their property: *'For you had compassion for those who were in prison, and you cheerfully accepted the plundering of your possessions, knowing that you yourselves possessed something better and more lasting.'* Because Christians had in them the *substance*, the basis for life, they could accept the destruction of the normal source of security (material possessions). They could give up material basis for life because they have found a substance that endures. As it were, they have gained a new freedom. Faith, grounded in the event of the death and resurrection of Christ, establishes us in the freedom of the people of God.

The community born from the cross has the capacity to change the society from within. This is evident in the way it handles the internal divisions of the Jewish community that are transported into the Christian community as well as the relationship between the Jews and others, the Samaritans and people of Greek origin. The way the new community handles these divisions becomes a model for the global society. The community offers healing to the wounded humanity through the celebration of the *memoria passionis et resurrectionis Christi* dramatized in the

---

19　Vatican II Council, 'Dogmatic Constitution on the Church, *Lumen Gentium*', 849.

20　Benedict XVI, *Encyclical Letter: Spe Salvi, to the Bishops, Priests and Deacons, Men and Women Religious and all the Lay Faithful on Christian Hope, Rome, 30 November 2007* (Vatican City: Libreria Editrice Vaticana, 2007), 13–15.

celebration of the sacraments, especially the Eucharist and the sacrament of reconciliation. In the sacrament of reconciliation, the memory of sin is turned into salvation history; the memory of race and disgrace is transformed by the memory of grace. Meditating on the immensity of God's grace, Paul came to this conclusion: *'All have sinned and fall short of God's grace'* (Romans 3:23). He notes, however, that God took it upon Himself to reconcile humanity with Himself through the blood of His Son, Jesus Christ. This is what he calls the message of justification.

> For when we were still without strength, in due time Christ died for the ungodly. For scarcely for a righteous man will one die; yet perhaps for a good man someone would even dare to die. But God demonstrates His own love toward us, in that while we were still sinners, Christ died for us. Much more then, having now been justified by His blood, we shall be saved from wrath through Him. For if when we were enemies we were reconciled to God through the death of His Son, much more, having been reconciled, we shall be saved by His life. And not only *that*, but we also rejoice in God through our Lord Jesus Christ, through whom we have now received the reconciliation (Romans 5:6–11).

Paul makes it clear in Ephesians 2:13–19 that through His cross, Christ broke down the barriers separating peoples and restored universal peace. Because of that, the gentiles *'are no longer aliens or foreign visitors'* but *'citizens like all the saints and part of God's household'* (Eph. 2, 19). Paul joyously declared that there is no more distinction between Jew and Greek, slave or free, male or female (Cf. Gal. 3, 28). This is the good news of confiliation.

One of the achievements of the Holy Spirit at Pentecost Acts 2, 2–11 is that he banished ethnic divisions and created a community of differences. The Spirit realized a communion of cultures and languages. The universal *confiliance* of peoples is recognized; unity in diversity is confirmed. This conviction will be defended by Peter in Acts 10:34–35 at the House of the Gentile, Cornelius. *'The truth I have come to realize...is that God does not have favourites, but that anybody of any nationality who fears God and does what is right is acceptable to him.'* It is precisely this confiliation that is distorted by the anthropological crisis analysed above. Hence the pastoral project of *reconfiliation*.

The Reconfiliation Dynamic

Reconciliation is the project of the new evangelization that flows logically from the correct understanding of theofiliance. Archbishop Obinna defines reconfiliation as a *'corrective-redemptive dynamic'*, the rectifying or corrective force that assures that the dignity of every son or daughter in the human family is held and defended beyond all biological, cultural, or religious divides. Reconfiliation, he writes, affirms *'the primacy of sonship and daughtership of every human ahead of the still important category of brother and sister'.*[21] In that sense, *'the sociological or religious extension of brotherhood and sisterhood, fraternity and sorority are secondary to the primacy of filiality, confiliality or cofiliality'.*[22]

Reconfiliation as a redeeming and healing dynamic aims at the liberation and redignification of humanity. This work, says Obinna, requires a confrontation *'with persons, groups, ideas, practices, customs, institutions and systems that distort and assault the dignity of humans in so many places on earth'.*[23] Obinna has other neologisms that express the same dynamic of reconfiliation: the *recti-valuing* one another, that is bringing people to think of one another correctly; *new-joining, con-joining,* or *new-kinning* of humans into fellow sons and daughters in equal dignity. Let us examine some concrete ways through which this new-creating, recti-valuing project can be achieved.

Rediscovering Our Divine Filiation

Our lives will become more meaningful if through Christ we rediscover our common humanity in Christ and if through Christ we become sons and daughters of God beyond our sociocultural origins. The memory of theofiliance celebrated in the sacraments shows its effectiveness when we

---

21   Anthony Obinna, 'Reconfiliating Americans', 5.
22   Anthony Obinna, 'Reconfiliating Americans', 5.
23   Anthony Obinna, 'Reconfiliating Americans', 5.

experience *the church as family of God* as strongly advocated by the two African Synods *Ecclesia in Africa (1994)* and *Africae Munus(2009)*.[24]

This reality is already embodied by African missionaries all over the world. African missionaries, religious and diocesans alike, are carrying the gospel of theofiliance to the ends of the earth and are gradually confiliating people of different cultures and languages. In my book, *The Memory of Self-Donation*,[25] I tried to explain the mystery of self-donation of African priests who work in foreign lands as a mystical expression of divine filiation in the church. I explained that Owerri Archdiocese has two sons who were missionaries buried in foreign lands, Rev Fr Valentine Nnaji, CSSp, and Msgr Fidelis Anunini, both from Amasa Ngugo, Ikeduru. Fr Nnaji died on December 10, 2003, in Congo Brazzaville at the age of thirty-five and was buried there, according to the Spiritan tradition. Msgr Anunini died on January 16, 2004, in L'Aquila, Italy, at the age of forty.

A reflection from the point of view of the paschal mystery gives us the full dimension of the filiation dynamic involved in the act of self-donation of these our brothers. The church in Brazzavile-Congo and the church in L'Aquila, Italy, remain grateful to the church in Nigeria for allowing these witnesses of the universality of the gospel to be buried in their lands. I recounted a touching moment during the funeral of Msgr Fidelis Anunini. It was marvellous to hear the choir of Italian youths sing in Igbo, '*Kelenu Maria, n'ihi n'ona eme ezi ihe, Kelenu Maria n'igwe n'uwa nile. Ekele diri Nne nke Chukwu, onye ihunanya ya di mgbe nile.*' ('Let us thank the Virgin Mary in heaven and on earth because she works marvels. Thanks to Mary, Mother of God whose love endures forever.') Msgr Anunini taught them this song together with other Igbo hymns. Here are Italians thanking the Virgin Mary in Igbo. From the point of view of the Christian faith, the Mother of God was being thanked here because her love endures forever. The youth in L'Aquila understood that as through Mary, God's love was lavished on us, so did God's love travel from Nigeria to their small village in Italy. They were thanking God for having sent them a young man who recognized them as children of God whose love endures forever.

---

24   John Paul II, *Post-Synodal Apostolic Exhortation, Ecclesia in Africa* (September 14, 1995), n. 39–40; Benedict XVI, *Post-Synodal Apostolic Exhortation, Africae Munus* (2012), n. 7. See also Elochukwu Uzukwu, *A Listening Church, Autonomy and Communion in African Churches* (New York, NY: Orbis Books, 1996).

25   Bede Ukwuije, *The Memory of Self-Donation*, 51–56.

Nigerian missionaries serve in different parts of the world. In the Holy Ghost congregation alone, Nigerians are superiors in two Spiritan provinces of Europe and North America, Belgium, Germany, British Province, Philippines, Mexico, South Africa, Zimbabwe, etc. Nigerian prelates are papal nuncios (pope's ambassadors) in Nicaragua, Benin/Togo, and Ireland. Recently, a Nigerian whose parents took to Gabon as refugees during the Biafra Civil War was appointed Bishop of Port-Gentil, Gabon. They are welcomed and loved by the people they are sent to. On the other hand, the rejection of African bishops appointed by the pope in some African dioceses on the ground that they are not from those dioceses or do not speak the dialect of the people of those dioceses is a counter witness to the confiliation dynamic. It is a symptom of the crisis of faith in contemporary African societies.

The reconfiliation dynamic invites all to conceive the church in the image of the Trinity, which has as basis the relationship of communion and love. If Christians want to be taken seriously as partners in the construction of peace in the contemporary society, they must question themselves on their relationship with one another and with people of other religions and cultures. If Christians ask the world to live out the invitation to forgiveness and reconciliation, they most show that that is possible in Christian communities. If they want the world to practice fraternity, there must be exemplary Christian communities. A *church family of God* in which people love themselves in the Trinitarian manner—love as self-dispossession—will be a credible partner for the construction of peace in the society.

Critical Re-Evaluation of Our Cultures

The reconfiliation dynamic involves also a critical re-evaluation of our different cultures. This will also bring to question the disturbing growing ethnocentrism in Nigeria, Africa, and worldwide. There is no doubt that ethnicity helps in structuring the human person and contributes to development in different parts of the world. There is nothing wrong for someone to identify oneself as Igbo, Hausa, Yoruba, Fulani, Eve, Asante, etc. The more situated the human person is, the more he/she is empowered to act in the world, locally and globally. However, ethnocentrism is a form of cultural and anthropological crisis that contributes to the division of humanity.

Vatican II Council's Pastoral Constitution on the Church in the World, *Gaudium et Spes* 53 defines culture as a system of values that shape a people's mode of life.[26] The heart of every culture is the humanization of the human being and the society. It means that culture is fundamentally connected to morality. It is the vocation of culture to help to surmount the anarchy of human instincts and the violence that inhabits every human person in order to create conviviality in the society. However, as a living system, every culture is in the process of adapting to the changes of times because individuals who are architects of culture are constantly changing their plans for a successful life.[27] This is also where a culture runs the risk of being dominated by a particular group or ideology that imposes a particular interpretation of its symbols and values. People should be able to be critical about their cultures and values because they are necessarily marked by limitations, violence, and sin.

The role of intellectuals in this rectification dynamic is vital. In a lecture, 'Intellectualism and the Development of a People'[28], delivered at the Federal University of Technology Owerri on February 8, 2016, Godfrey Onah, the Catholic bishop of Nsukka, offered an illuminating definition of an intellectual. Borrowing from Theophilus Okere,[29] he defined the intellectual as one who *'makes a business of intellecting'*.[30] All human beings use the intellect and are intelligent, even intellectual beings. But 'an intellectual is one who makes the cultivation of the intellect and the acquisition of intellectual knowledge his or her own vocation in life.'[31] More profoundly, *'the intellectual is a minister … at the altar of truth; one who sees as his main obligation to humanity the diakonia of*

---

26 Vatican II Council, 'Pastoral Constitution on the Church in the Modern World, *Gaudium Et Spes*, 7 December 1965', in *Decrees of the Ecumenical Councils: Trent-Vatican II*, ed. Norman Tanner and Guiseppe Alberigo, vol. II, 1069–1135 (New York, NY: Costello Publishing Company, 1987), 1106.

27 Luis Lutzbetak, *The Church and Cultures. New Perspectives in Missiological Anthropology* (New York, NY: Orbis, 1988).

28 Godfrey Onah, 'Intellectualism and the Development of a People' (Thirty-Third Public Lecture of the Federal University of Technology [FUTO] Owerri, Imo State, February 8, 2016).

29 Theophilus Okere, 'The Mission of the Intellectual', in *Philosophy, Culture and Society in Africa: Essays* (Nsukka: Afro-Orbs Publications, 2015), 130–138, 132

30 Godfrey Onah, *Intellectualism and the Development of a People*, 11.

31 Godfrey Onah, *Intellectualism and the Development of a People*. 10.

truth.[32] This means that the intellectual is not to seek recognition of his society or popularity because that would lead him/her to prostitute his/her skills. Onah wrote again, borrowing from Richard Hofstadter,[33] that *'to be faithful to their intellectual vocation, they must avoid all 'undignified prostrations' before wealth and a surrender of their freedom of expression through an undue attachment to the seats of power'.*[34]

The pathetic collapse of liberal Protestant theology in the twentieth-century Germany was due to the fact that intellectuals and theologians lost a critical distance from their culture and allowed themselves to be mobilised by the Nazi government. As at 1914, liberal theologians in Germany were convinced that God's cause and the German cause were identical.[35] Great theologians like Adolf von Harnack, Friedrich Gogarten, Wilhelm Herrmann, Ernst Troeltsch, and Hermann Cohen did not resist the fascination of the Nazi cultural propaganda. They joined the *Deutsche Christen* (German Christian) movement, which provided theological arguments and grounds to the nascent national socialism. Marc Lilla reports that when the German leader Kaiser Wilhelm decided to address the German nation in early August 1914 after declaring war on Russia and France, he sought the help of the theologian Adolf von Harnack. 'Harnack graciously complied, turning in a discourse that defended German war aims without concession.'[36]

Mark Lila notes also that Adolf von Harnack and Wilhelm Herrmann, together with a total of ninety-three leading intellectuals and scholars, signed petitions in favour of the Nazi cause. One of the declarations reads:

> It is not true that the combat against our so-called militarism is not a combat against our culture, as our enemies hypocritically allege. Without German militarism, German culture would long ago have vanished from the earth. The former grew out of the latter for its protection ......We call out to you: believe us, believe that we shall fight this fight to the end as a people of

---

32 Godfrey Onah, *Intellectualism and the Development of a People*, 10.

33 Richard Hofstadter, *Anti-intellectualism in American Life* (New York, NY: Vintage Books, 1962), 397.

34 Godfrey Onah, *Intellectualism and the Development of a People*, 13.

35 Mark Lilla, *The Still Born God. Religion, Politics and the Modern West* (New York: Vintage Books, 2007), p. 244.

36 Mark Lilla, *The Still Born God ...*, 244.

culture to whom the legacy of Goethe, a Beethoven, a Kant is
as holy as its hearth and soil.[37]

It is also very interesting to read a declaration made by Ernst Troeltsch
in Heidelberg:

> Since yesterday we are one people in arms ... The flames of
> unreason and malice, of hate and envy, the puzzle of dark
> conflicts of interest and mass moods, all strike us to the ground
> and remind us that all human culture is a house that sits upon
> volcanoes. So, chat is to be done? Only one thing, the call: to
> arms, to arms! ... Today, and especially in these hours, when
> we feel and have, not only the Kaiser and Reich, but also the
> living breath of God, when out of a mix reverence and hope,
> care and faith, the feeling of God's omnipotence flows through
> us, in these hours we pray this deep, serious, passionate, and
> firm vow, with God, for Kaiser and Reich.[38]

It took a courageous theologian, the Suisse Calvinist Karl Barth, to
address an unequivocal *nein* to the collaboration between the church and
Nazism. Dietrich Bonhoeffer and many others followed suit. This gave
rise to the famous Barmen Declaration 1934.[39] Worthy of note also is the
resistance of the great Christian philosopher Dietrich von Hildebrand,
recounted in his powerful autobiography, *My Battle against Hitler:
Faith, Truth, and Defiance in the Shadow of the Third Reich*.[40]

This may sound far away from Nigeria or Africa, but a great danger
facing Nigeria and other African countries is the facility with which
intellectuals and university professors join the chorus of cultural and
ethnic propaganda against other ethnic groups. Oftentimes, social media
circulate texts from intellectuals who are pro/against Biafra, pro/against
IPOB, pro/against Arewa, majority of which tow the same line of cultural

---

37   Mark Lilla, *The Still Born God*, p. 245, quoting 'To the Civilized World by the Professors
      of Germany', in *Current History* 1, no. 1 (New York, 1915): 25.

38   Marc Lilla, *The Still Born God*, 245–246.

39   Reproduced in Eberhard Jüngel, *Christ, Justice and Peace. Towards a Theology of the
      State* (Edinburgh: T & T Clark, 1992).

40   Dietrich Von Hildebrand, *My Battle against Hitler: Faith, Truth, and Defiance in the
      Shadow of the Third Reich* (New York, NY: Image, 2014).

propaganda. During the Rwandan genocide, the Tutsi and the Hutu had their own intellectuals and theologians.

Intellectuals who embrace the reconfiliation dynamic will help their people to promote what is noble in their cultures and question the violence and sin inherent in them. Archbishop Obinna gives an example of healthy theological approach to culture through the promotion of Odenigbo lectures. These are meant to help the Igbo welcome Christ and express the mystery of humanity's kinship with Christ through the Igbo language. He writes, 'Under the impact of Christ recti-filiating Incarnation and liberative creation-redemption dispensation in Christ is becoming vigorously operative. It is embracing what is noble in Igbo culture and confronting what is idolatrous and demonic in the Igbo preconscious, subconscious, and conscious reflexes.'[41]

I strongly believe that all theologians should adopt this posture. The theologian, as an intellectual, does not belong to public opinion. He is at the service of the Truth, who is Jesus Christ. Theologians should not allow themselves to be recuperated by cultural nationalism and propaganda. Theologians and intellectuals should remain critical of their cultures and traditions and every political or social ideology.

Articulated Sociopolitical Critique

The reconfiliation dynamic grounded on the memory of theofiliance also has sociopolitical implications. The interventions of Archbishop Obinna in the social and political debates in Nigeria are motivated by this conviction. Some people, especially politicians, are worried that a bishop is setting the pace of governance in Imo State. One recalls his vehement intervention that led to the repeal of the Abortion Law. The law was packaged in a *Reproduction Life Bill* purported to be in favor of women and signed into law by the state governor, Rochas Okorocha, on May 29, 2013. In an article on this issue, a journalist, Nneka Victor Okoro, responding to the critiques, noted that the bishop as a citizen has the right to contribute to debates in his society. *'All of us are aware that every human being is a political animal. Again, politics in its contextual meaning connotes the process of structuring the polity of a society. From this bearing, it is clear that each and every one of us has*

---

41   Anthony Obinna, 'Celebrating the Gift of Creation—A Chi-Christic Persuasion', 13.

a quota to contribute in assuring that the structure of the city or society where we live is rightly organized for the betterment of all.[42]

Reconfiliating humanity through the celebration of the *memoria passionis et resurrectionis Christi* calls for the articulation of a form of political theology.[43] It does not mean that the church should draw political programs from Christian dogmatic expressions. The reconfiliation dynamic brings theologians and pastors to understand the church as *an institution of social critique* that is situated neither besides nor above the social reality. Such a church will avoid the trap of aligning with a particular political ideology. This sets her free for a possible cooperation with the different institutions and groups in the state and society.[44] In that sense, even if the church does not issue political laws or decrees to the civil state, she continues '*to make demands on law-givers from a gospel perspective*'[45] and to urge Christians to participate actively in the construction of the civil society.

Pope Francis' apostolic exhortation, *Evangelii Gaudium*, is an act of political theology. Even if he does not use this expression, he underlined clearly '*the profound connection between evangelization and human advancement*'[46] which flows from heart of the gospel itself. Hence this affirmation:

> The Church's pastors, taking into account the contributions of the different sciences, have the right to offer opinions on all that affects people's lives, since the task of evangelization implies and demands the integral promotion of each human being. It is no longer possible to claim that religion should be restricted

---

42   Nneka Victor-Okoro, 'Evil is Infectious, Avoid it', *The White Paper*, vol. 5, no. 066 (Monday, September 2, 2013–Tuesday 3, 2013): 10.

43   Johan Baptist Metz, 'Théologie politique et liberté Critico-Sociale', *Concilium*, no. 36 (Juin 1968): 9–25; Bede Ukwuije, 'Existe-t-il une théologie politique en Afrique?', in *Laval Théologique et Philosophique* 63, no. 2, (June 2007): 291–303. See also, Michael Kirwan, *Political Theology, A New Introduction* (London: Darton-Longman and Todd, 2008).

44   Johan Baptist Metz, 'Théologie politique et liberté critico-sociale', 24.

45   Eberhard Jüngel, *Justification, the Heart of the Christian Faith* (T & T Clark, 2001), 276.

46   Pope Francis, *Apostolic Exhortation, Evangelii Gaudium, to the Bishop, Clergy, Consecrated Persons and the Lay Faithful on the Proclamation of the Gospel in Today's World, 24 November 2013*, §. 178, http://w2.vatican.va/content/francesco/en/apost_exhortations/documents/papa-francesco_esortazione-ap_20131124_evangelii-gaudium.html#I.%E2%80%82Communal_and_societal_repercussions_of_the_ kerygma, n. 178 [accessed July 2018].

to the private sphere and that it exists only to prepare souls for heaven.[47]

Describing the prophetic role played by Archbishop Obinna in the line of others like Cardinal Okogie and Desmond Tutu, Sam Onwueodo wrote: '*The issue is that any society without such men who can offer such spirituality oriented political leadership is just existing and not living.*'[48]

Conclusion

The pastoral theology of *theofiliance*, promoted by Archbishop Anthony Obinna, is a response to the present critical context of anthropological crisis. This crisis is crystalized in the distortions in the way fellow human beings perceive, react, and relate to one another. The consequence of this anthropological crisis is the growing violence to the sacredness and preciousness of the human person as well as the negation of the humanity of the other. At the depth of the anthropological crisis is the more critical crisis of faith—the loss of the sense of God that is eating into the fabrics of Western and African cultures alike.

Theofiliance, therefore, is the memory of humanity's kinship with God and the kinship of human beings with one another through the justifying event of the death and resurrection of Jesus Christ. It celebrates the divine confiliation of all human beings beyond ethnic groups, cultures, and biological affiliations.

The memory of theofiliance is translated through the evangelization project of reconfiliation dynamic—that is the *new-joining, new-kinning* of humans into fellow sons and daughters of God in equal dignity. First, the entire church should be mobilized to become an 'institution of narration' that joyously tells the world about our common humanity and our belonging to the same family. Second, this project pushes the church to confront cultures, ideologies, and practices that promote exclusion, violence, and the negation of the humanity of the other. This work begins from within the church. If the church tells the story of the divine confiliation of the whole

---

47   Pope Francis, *Evangelii Gaudium*, §. 182.
48   Sam Onwuemedo, 'Archbishop Obinna, Ohakim, Rochas and the 2011 Election', *The White Paper*, op. cit., 16.

creation through the death and resurrection of Christ, she is the first to subject herself to the judgment of this history. She will first of all seek to control the tendency to violence, domination, and cultural discrimination within Christian communities before extending the same to the society at large.

Chapter Eleven

The Leadership Approach of Archbishop Anthony J. V. Obinna as Animated by His Theology of Confiliation

Samuel Uzoukwu

Introduction

It is quite spectacular and joyous moving from last year's twenty-fifth anniversary of the episcopal ordination of Archbishop Anthony Obinna to this year's silver jubilee celebration of his elevation as the metropolitan archbishop of Owerri. In the face of these historic events, one is moved, appreciatively, to ponder on the dynamics of His Grace's leadership style and engagements and on the theological model upon which they are driven in order to understand the vision and the impetus behind his pastoral labours. This reflection proves pertinent in the face of the present-day interdisciplinary interest on leadership, which, *inter alia*, seeks in the ingenious thoughts, instructive attitudes, and valiant efforts of some leaders (ecclesial and secular alike) inspirations and models for improving human conditions, confronting life's challenges, and enriching leadership studies. Such reflection also proves relevant amidst the efforts today, within the Catholic circle, to reconsider managerial themes (including leadership) within the moral framework of the church's social teaching, in order to draw principles for reflection, criteria for judgment, and guidelines for action, and be able to approach concrete life situations with gospel spirit.[1]

In this case, we shall, in an interdisciplinary manner, ponder on Archbishop Obinna's theological, pastoral, and leadership response to the social questions. This, as we shall see, tells of his commitment in fidelity to the grace and task of humankind's *refiliation* in God through Christ and his profound and galvanizing vision to rectify, rekindle, and reconfigure (globally and locally) the crisis-ridden social order, so as to reclaim its *reinGodment* and to influence and coalesce others towards the same goal. It also tells of the courage, wholeheartedness, and perseverance with which he exercises his episcopal mandate in order to speak the gospel truth to power, to business, to families, to culture, to law, to structures, to the faithful, and to all hearts in ways that benevolently promote human flourishing, restore human dignity, and aid the salvation of souls. In this reflection, we shall discover within the archbishop's pastoral insights and engagements an administrative frame characterized by a human resource model and a shepherding style marked by transformational and servant leadership. We shall also realize that His Grace's insights and approaches to issues of religious, spiritual, ethical, anthropological, and social kinds are informed by the theological model of *confiliation*, the model from which his human resource pattern of leadership is ensouled and on which his transformational and servant leadership styles are shaped. This is the model he has proffered passionately, developed consistently, launched persuasively before the magisterial circle, and endorsed proactively for further theological advancement. To this model we now turn.

Confiliation: The Foundation of Obinna's Leadership Strides

The leadership thrust of Archbishop A. J. V. Obinna is theoretically anchored on and empowered by the theology of *confiliation*, which His Grace articulates and develops 'as a redeeming and healing dynamic

---

1 Pontifical Council for Justice and Peace, *Compendium of the Social Doctrine of the Church* (Washington, DC: Liberia Editrice Vaticana-United States Conference of Catholic Bishops, 2004), n. 7; *Catechism of the Catholic Church*, n. 2423.

that served and continues to serve the cause of humanity's liberation, redignification and newkinment'[2]. Before the Synod Fathers in Vatican, Obinna proposes *confiliation* as 'our share in Jesus' sonship that makes us sons and daughters of God'.[3] He beckons that it be embraced as 'a one family-building dynamic', a model that has the capacity of resolving family skirmishes and social clashes, restoring people's dignity, rectifying interpersonal relations, and ensuring the integral well-being of every person even in the midst of suffering.[4]

Explicating creatively some of the neologisms that convey his enduring and deep thoughts, and that are basically drawn from the concept of *filiation*, meaning belongingness to a parent or an institution, as a son or daughter, as derived from the Latin *filius* (son) and *filia* (daughter),[5] he states: '*Re-filiation* would mean restoration to the status of son or daughter. *Confiliation* would mean a mutual share in the status of son or daughter from a common kinship or stock. *Confiliation* would equally imply a reciprocal recognition of equal sonship or daughtership. *Cofiliation* is the basic appreciation that humans across all differences and divides are fellow sons and daughters in the human family.'[6] Elucidating further, he continues: '*De-filiation* would mean a refusal or denial of sonship or daughtership. *Recti-filiation* is the corrective inclusion of excluded humans into the one family of sons and daughters. *Reconfiliation* would imply a return to right or deserved relationship as son and daughter...It would also mean the new joining or conjoining or new-kinning of humans into fellow sons and daughters in equal dignity.'[7]

Confiliation embodies a substantive reawakening of our common *filiation* in God in order to set aright, restore, and defend the equal dignity

---

2   Anthony J.V. Obinna, 'A Theology and Practice of "Reconfiliation"', (Beeson Divinity School, Sanford University, 2016), https://www.youtube.com/watch?v=qG947DVYrqE [accessed March 3, 2019]. Anthony J. V. Obinna, 'Confiliating Americas: Recti-valuing One Another', in *The Leader Online*, accessed May 1, 2016. https://theleaderassumpta.com/2016/05/01/confiliating-americans-recti-valuing-one-another-2/, [accessed May 20, 2019].

3   Anthony J. V. Obinna, 'Intervention at the Tenth General Congregation of the Second Ordinary Special Assembly for Africa of the Synod of Bishops, Vatican', accessed March 3, 2009. http://www.vatican.va/news_ services/press/ sinodo/documents/bollettino_23_ii_ speciale-africa-2009/02_inglese/b16_02.html, [accessed March 3, 2019].

4   Obinna, 'Intervention at the Tenth General Congregation of the Second Ordinary Special Assembly for Africa of the Synod of Bishops'.

5   Anthony J.V. Obinna, 'A Theology and Practice of "Reconfiliation"', 2016.

6   Obinna, 'A Theology and Practice of "Reconfiliation"', 2016.

7   Obinna, 'A Theology and Practice of "Reconfiliation"', 2016.

of Africans and non-Africans and of all individuals, families, and peoples within the human societies, nations, and the universe. It is a model that seeks to provide an ennobling platform for interpersonal, intertribal, and interracial reconciliation and crises resolution; and it's a remedial drive against disorder, hatred, discrimination, and bigotry. As a new term, thanks to Amarachi Obinna, *confiliation* rearticulates dynamically and intensely and presents in a new currency, urgency, and reach the gratuitous gift and the historical realities that redefine us as *theofilians* (adopted sons and daughters of God) and the corresponding responsibilities therein, to which it reawakens our individual and social consciousness. *Confiliation* is not an ideology; it is a theology, one grounded especially in Christology, with trinitarian and pneumatological corollaries. The discovery of our common *filiation* in God tells of the Christocentric character of *confiliation*, as we are drawn both by the pulsation of the heart in faith and the creative enquiry of the mind through reason to the reality of the *Confiliator*, who is no other than Jesus Christ, who reveals the Father, the initiator of *reconfiliation*, to whom we are *reconfiliated*, and who gives us the Holy Spirit, the grace of reconfiliation (recreation) and the transmitter and perfecter of our *refiliation*.[8]

Thus, the theology of *confiliation* which Archbishop Obinna proposes, centres principally, but not exclusively on *Christofiliation*. It is through Christ that we become adopted children, sons and daughters, of one Father, the God who is love (1 John 4:8). Christ is the one sent by the Father in love to redeem humankind. Drawing from the argument of St. Thomas Aquinas, it most fittingly behoves on Christ, who relates by filiality to the paternity of the Father, being himself the eternal Son of the Father, to undertake such salvific mission, in order to let us participate by filial adoption to the likeness of his divinely natural filiation.[9] It is through Christ, through his *reconfiliatory* mission, that God the Father reconciles us to himself. Thus, *confiliation* implicates and accentuates *theofiliation*. Christ's

---

8   *Compendium of the Social Doctrine of the Church*, no. 38, 46; Kevin E. O'Reilly, *The Hermeneutics of Knowing and Willing in the Thought of St. Thomas Aquinas* (Leuven-Walpole, MA: Peters, 2013), 28.

9   Thomas Aquinas, *Summa Theologiae* III, q. 3, a. 8 (hereafter *ST*), https://dhspriory.org/ thomas/ english/summa/TP/TP003.html#TPQ3OUTP1 [accessed May 18, 2019]. See also Dominic Legge, *The Trinitarian Christology of St. Thomas Aquinas* (Oxford: Oxford University Press, 2017), 82–83. Thomas G. Weinandy, *The Father's Spirit of Sonship: Reconceiving the Trinity* (Eugene, OR: Wipf and Stock Publishers, 2010), 29.

confiliatory work gives rise to our *refiliation* in the triune God, such that, in the word of the Archbishop Obinna, we attain a *reinGodment* as merited for us by Christ's redeeming act, which began with the event of his Incarnation (*infiliation*), underwent the critical stage of crucifixion, and attained consummation in his glorious resurrection. Through his passion, death, and resurrection, Christ 'bears within himself the action of God who reconciles us with himself effectively'.[10] By acknowledging that we have a common adoptive *filiation* in God as *theofilians*, we are led to the acceptance of the fraternal bond that girdles us as sons and daughters of God and ties us with a deeper cord of solidarity that transcends, unites, and harnesses differences.

In the light of Obinna, *confiliation* is linked to *crucifiliation*, which, I would think, buttresses the fact that the *confiliatory* redemptive act by which Christ, the incarnate Lord, wrought our *refiliation* in God was by way of the cross, through which he became the crucified Lord. By his Holy Cross, he accomplished our *theofiliation*. Thus, the archbishop notes that 'the filiation of the Son of God unto Mary, the daughter of humanity, reached its bloom in *crucifiliation*'.[11] *Crucifiliation* reveals the cruciform character of divine love. Christ's passion, for which he willingly underwent excruciating torture and humiliating sufferings in atonement for our sins, and his death on the cross, by which he sacrificed his life in order to instate our hope for eternal life, were for love's sake. Both express Christ's ecstatic love, love that goes beyond itself. His passion and death on the cross were products of that plenitude of charity that characterized his human will, diffused in the mystery of the cross, in loving obedience to the Father and in intense loving desire for the reparation of sinful humanity. *Crucifiliation* shows that Christ's *reconfiliatory* mission is an act of ecstatic love. In beholding his passion and crucifixion, we are drawn to realize how much God loves us and are moved to love him in return.

This cruciformity of divine ecstasy, which also inspires us to perceive the wisdom of the cross, explains why we continue to seek grace at the foot of the cross. On the cross, where he let his humanity be crucified, Christ manifested a supreme love by assuming our condemnation, atoning for our

---

10   Thomas Joseph White, *The Incarnate Lord: A Thomistic Study in Christology* (Washington, DC: The Catholic University of America Press, 2015), 306.

11   Anthony J. V. Obinna's speech during his meeting with Owerri Archdiocesan Priests in the United States (OAPUS), held at the Blessed Sacrament Church Newark, New Jersey (July 14, 2017).

sin through sacrifice, and putting to death our sinful humanity, in order to earn for us the grace of adoptive filiation, to present us anew to the Father, and to have us *refiliated* in God as *theofilians*.[12] The cruciform character of God's diffusive love has made the cross a source of healing and hope to all those who are laden with sufferings, miseries, and infirmities, such that rather than feeling forsaken by God when it hurts or perturbed by his apparent silence, one may feel accompanied and loved by God even in moments of sorrow. Instead of separating us from God's cruciform love, the cross draws us closer to that mysterious love through which we are *theofiliated* and by which we can be comforted, healed, and saved.

More so, *crucifiliation* calls our attention to the fact of what Archbishop Obinna calls cruci-humiliation. This means that in that human obedience to the Father and in that loving desire to make reparation for condemned sinners, for which he suffered and died to make us *theofilians*, Christ's humanity that journeyed *via crucis* was exposed to untold humiliation by denial, betrayal, ingratitude, calumny, severe torture, mockery, and hanging, all of which he still bore for the sake of love. The cruci-humiliation of Jesus, therefore, becomes a source of consolation, endurance, and joy to all those who suffer persecution or calumny while witnessing to the truth or abiding by right conducts; for Christ suffered the same. In *cruci-humiliation*, we feel the need to stand in solidarity with those who suffer unjustly and see our own undeserved humiliating experiences, in whatever way they emerge, as a participation in Christ's own cruciform debasement in order to draw therefrom the steadfastness for ceaseless prayer, the strength of endurance, the infused fortitude of the martyrs, the joy of genuine witnessing, and the confidence to persevere amid the sorrows of life. In all, by recognizing themselves in the incarnate, crucified, and risen Christ, through whom they have been made *theofilians*, with whom they are *patrifiliates*, in whom they remain *Christofilias*, and by whose cross they have become *crucifilians*, men and women 'rediscover their sonship and daughtership in Christ and open themselves to the re-glorification of their negated and dehumanized beings'.[13]

---

12 Thomas Joseph White, *The Light of Christ: An Introduction to Catholicism* (Washington, DC: The Catholic University of America Press, 2017), 169. See also, Kevin O'Reilly, 'Lecture note, *Angelicum* Rome' (November 15, 2018). Thomas G. Weinandy, *Jesus the Christ* (Hungtington, Indiana: Our Sunday Visitors, 2003), 106–116.

13 Anthony J. V. Obinna, *Roots, Branches … Graftings and Fruits: The Reconfiliatory Challenge to African-Americans and Humanity at Large* (Owerri: Assumpta Press,

As it undertakes the tasks of rectification and restoration, *confiliation* imposes certain moral obligations that are not only local in scope and in application but are likewise universal, especially in its dynamic of *reconfiliation*.[14] The awareness that in Christ we are all filiated to our common divine origin, endowed with common dignity as earthly pilgrims, and communally implicated in the events of history as those who must work for the common good of the entire human family, with openness towards our eternal calling, brings us to experience a reawakening of the moral forces necessary for building a just and fraternal society, for making a right configuration of social life, and for realizing lasting and balance solutions amidst global crises and disorder. As the dynamic for what Archbishop Obinna calls *covivance*, that is, brotherly celebrative existence, *confiliation*, in its globalism, demands a rediscovery of our niche in the order of existence. Such discovery helps us to live truly as *theofilians*, not in isolation but socially, in 'a world that has not been created by us but has been given to us as a home to share in brotherhood'.[15] It also helps us to recognize one another as a cotenant and a copal in the habitation of the world, without any of us, either as individuals or as groups, deserving extinction or tolerated presence. Being vertically solidarios in nature, *confiliation*, at the same time, imposes a demand of horizontal solidarity by which all of us—irrespective of colour, race, tongue, or faith—need to develop a deep sense of fellow-feeling and strive to live harmoniously as members of one human family.[16] It summons us to struggle together with others, far and near, rich and poor, as *cofiliated* brethren and neighbors, neither against them for the just ordering of society nor without them in uprooting structures of injustice.

On the natural and human ecological terrain, *confiliation* demands a renewed consciousness to the goodness of all things, which are recreated

---

2003).

14 Anthony J.V. Obinna, 'Confiliating Americas: Recti-valuing One Another', in *The Leader Online*, accessed May 1, 2016. https://theleaderassumpta.com/2016/05/01/confiliating-americans-recti-valuing-one-another-2/, [accessed May 20, 2019].

15 Benedict XVI,' Letter to Cardinal Peter Kodwo Appiah Turkson on the Occasion of the Plenary Assembly of the Pontifical Council for Justice and Peace' (November 3, 2010), http://w2.vatican.va/content/benedict-xvi/en/letters/2010/documents/hf_ben-xvi_let_20101103_giustizia-pace.html [accessed May 20, 2019].

16 Benedict XVI, *Caritas in Veritate*, June 29, 2009: *AAS* 101 (2009), 11. Benedict XVI, address to participants in the 14th session of the Pontifical Academy of Social Science, May 3, 2008: *AAS* 100 (2008), 384.

in Christ, and a new sense of wonder that realizes the beauty of created realities.[17] Such realization shows that humans, animals, and plants are all beauty-filled creatures in that creative work of God, for which it is, therefore, forbidden to distort, disfigure, or idolize the beauty impacted upon creatures or to engage in any idolatrous veneration of the earth and in the deification of creatures (lands, minerals, animals, trees, mountains, oceans, bar beaches, etc.) and artifacts. The new vision of creation introduced by Christ's *reconfiliatory* gift has exposed the nothingness of other gods and led to the illegitimacy (using the word of A. J. V. Obinna) of any *geogamous* enslavement of humans. All artistic masterpiece, in manifesting a mysterious and sudden spark of the divine, should prompt the mind towards openness to the transcendent rather than demean and spur it into apotheosis.[18] Preserving the beauty of God's creation within the human ecology, *confiliation* opposes discrimination, cultural supremacy, and blood superiority, since, as the archbishop notes, all racial colours not only constitute parts of the holistic form of human creatural beauty in their different outer aesthetic appearances but also experience the disappearance of such aesthetic disparities below the outer layers of the human skins. Within the family dimension of human ecology, Christ's *reconfiliatory* work impels us to reject the institutionalization and exaltation of all antisocial and unnatural relations (such as same-sex and de facto unions), for these not only mock the family, the church in miniature, and the very foundation of human society, they also trigger moral debasement.

Reawakened by the dynamo of *confiliation*, we feel within a deep impulse to reject the false security of darkness with all its iniquities and wickedness, for Christ, our *Confiliator*, is the light of the world, *Lumen gentium* (see John 12:46; Luke 2:32). We also feel empowered to refuse being susceptible to hopeless anxieties amidst crisis, since with faith that opposes fear, with love that drives away fear, and with courage that entertains no defeat, we shall always hear Christ, the cause of our *theofiliation*, say to us, 'Do not be afraid!'

---

17 Benedict XVI, *Post-Synodal Apostolic Exhortation Verbum Domini* (September 30, 2010), n. 108, http://w2.vatican.va/content/benedict-xvi/en/apost_exhortations/documents/hf_ben-xvi_exh_20100930_ verbum-domini.html [accessed May 21, 2019].

18 See *L'Osservatore Romano* English language edition (May 2, 1999), 6

Having, thus far, drawn from and built upon Archbishop Obinna's theology of *confiliation*, we shall now consider how this theological model is transformed into pastoral care and leadership visions. This will be our focus in the next two headings, beginning in the first succeeding heading with some of his pastoral insights.

Pastoral Insights

Led and informed by the grace of *confiliation*, Obinna engages and approaches various issues affecting and confronting peoples in ways that instruct, rectify, restore, and reform. Let us consider five of such issues.

a. Honest Democracy

The democratic life of Nigeria is a matter of great concern for Archbishop Obinna. He recognizes that the country has started once more to experience the return of democracy since 1999, after twenty years of military regime that disrupted its postindependence democracy. He, however, describes what Nigeria has since the last twenty years of her second democratic dispensation as a violent and fraudulent democracy, one marked by unbridled elitist greed, driven by excessive quest for power and wealth, unscrupulous plundering of common funds, and waste of human and natural resources. The same elitist greed, he continues, is driven by indifference and lack of compassion for citizens' welfare, political brutality and crime, untold disregard for moral discipline and virtuous leadership, and the erroneous view of politics as a dirty game, one irreconcilable with uprightness and authenticity.[19] According to him, a country where leaders are thus driven cannot claim to be practicing real democracy.

In his genuine desire to overhaul the nation's political status quo, Obinna calls for the enthronement of a compassionate and honest democracy, to whose realization he proposes three basic principles. The three principles include (a) protecting the life of every Nigerian citizen and fostering a safe and free environment, rather than limiting security to rulers who are usually escorted by soldiers and policemen; (b) letting the leadership of Nigeria *confiliate* every Nigerian by fostering filial fellowship that

---

19   Anthony Obinna, Easter interview (August 24, 2008), *The Leader*, Easter edition, 20.

will enable us to see, appreciate, relate, and treat one another as fellow
sons and daughters of Nigeria; and (c) instilling a culture of patriotism
among Nigerians so that everybody, the leaders and the led, will serve the
nation with honesty, dedication, and love.[20] Aware of the indispensability
of a reliable judiciary in the realization of an authentic democracy, the
archbishop writes: 'If Nigeria's violent and fraudulent democracy must
be finally healed, the judiciary must play a prophetic-martyral role: truth
must become a drum major in the band of judges and lawyers; justice, the
sword of truth, must replace the compromises that mammon has induced
judges and lawyers to make from the military days until now.'[21] Rectifying
the nation's widespread misapprehension of politics as a dirty game, he
stresses that politics is a noble art that provides opportunity for organizing
the community so as to better life and things.[22]

The ideal democracy that Obinna proposes for Nigeria is drawn from
his theological model of *confiliation*. He advocates for a *confiliatory*
democracy, one in which 'all of us, every one of us recognizes one another as
a child of God, and we treat one another with respect, with appreciation'.[23]
If implemented, he argues, *confiliatory* democracy that leads to the
realization of a *theofilial* society, one in which everybody recognizes the
other as a son of God and a daughter of God, fosters people's flourishing as
is subservient to their supernatural goals.[24] While being informed by the
gospel principles, Archbishop Obinna's *confiliatory* democracy remains
practicable in a multireligious and multicultural country like Nigeria, since
it advances values that are also in line with the precepts of the natural law,
which, as such, appeal to everyone irrespective of faith tradition, tribal
origin, and political affiliation.

---

20   Anthony Obinna, Press briefing at Villa Assumpta (May 27, 2004), *The Leader* (June 13,
     2004), 11.

21   Anthony Obinna, Discussion on the pope's message for the 2006 world day of peace (January
     22, 2006), *The Leader* (January 29, 2006), 1.

22   Anthony Obinna, Address at the inauguration of Owerri Archdiocesan Youth Council (May
     12, 2007), *The Leader* (June 3, 2007), 3.

23   Anthony Obinna, Exclusive interview, *New Searchlight* 7 (2007/2008): 32.

24   Obinna, Exclusive interview, *New Searchlight*, 32.

b. Good Governance

Archbishop Obinna's outspokenness concerning the state of the nation Nigeria is driven by a genuine desire for the realization and sustainability of good governance in the country in order that the common good be served and individuals' and communities' welfare achieved. Only this can explain the persevering passion and fortitude with which he often encourages and admonishes those in political leadership position to be honest in the exercise of their duties. To foster good governance, he insists, leaders must rectify their motives, transcend tribalism and ethnic nationalism, show real concern for human and national development, encourage efforts, preserve our chivalrous legacies, and harness ingenuities. He regrets that days are gone when leadership was manifested as people-oriented service with governance founded on laws and principles. Today, he observes, governance is anchored on patronage, to accord good turns to relatives, friends, and supporters, those in good book. The church, on her part, he says, has become more proactive and vocal in political matters, not with party or political interest but for the sake of justice, peace, and development and on the conviction that people and society deserve good governance.[25] The archbishop's insistence on good governance is based on the obligations that the status of people as *theofilians* imposes on leaders, namely that citizens of the state be appreciated as humans, that their dignity as persons be respected, that their needs and their share of democratic dividends be benevolently provided, and that their integral human development be fostered through commitment to social justice, the social virtue that demands the promotion of the good of the whole, guaranteeing therefrom the good of each person, and that regulates the just ordering of a *confilial* society.[26]

c. Corruption

The remedying passion with which Archbishop Obinna advocates for good governance in Nigeria parallels with the pastoral concern he manifests over the high rate of corruption in the country. Aware that

---

25 Obinna, Exclusive interview, *New Searchlight*, 32.
26 Pius XI, *Divini Redemptoris*, March 19, 1937: *AAS* 29 (1937), 92; Benedict XVI, *Deus Caritas Est*, December 25, 2005: *AAS* 98 (2006), 28–29.

corruption is part of the major factors responsible for the lack of good governance in Nigeria, he laments that the country has hit the deepest level of corruption considering the pervasiveness of murder, oppression, examination malpractices, and embezzlement of public funds that have not only eaten deeply into the political terrain of the society but have also penetrated into intermediary institutions such as families, schools, and even churches.[27] He notes that the celebration of corruption is more glaring in the country during electoral activities. During such periods, the electoral tribunal becomes so gullible to bribery that it makes some winners and some losers based on corruption. Those who triumph in corruption resolve to 'giving glory to God in corruption and going for thanksgiving for corruption'.[28] He describes the above situation as the tragedy of Nigeria and appeals to women and men of good will, those who care about the future of the country, to toe the path of justice, honesty, and rectitude rather than the path of corruption. He charges his priests to stand above board in trappings and never allow that truth and integrity be compromised by the lures of corruption. He appeals to young people to reject the baton of corruption and to refuse to be used as cosowers of corruption, for such can only damn and distort their life and future.[29] The archbishop's prophetic voice against untold and prevailing corruption in Nigeria is empowered by the dynamo of *confiliation*, which finds in corruption the cankerworm that destroys the very foundations of social harmony, undermines the possibility of peaceful social *covivance*, institutionalizes social injustices, and creates an environment unworthy of *theofilians* by ridiculing the formation of a newly oriented, coresponsible, caring, and disciplined humanity.

d. Youth Unemployment

The extreme high rate of unemployment tormenting the Nigerian youth is a matter of great concern for Archbishop Obinna. He is moved by the agonizing faces of young people, some of whom have been traumatized by prolonged joblessness in a country where political leaders neither have any plan for job creation nor feel morally bound to eradicate unemployment

---

27   *The Leader* (February 20, 2005), 1.

28   Anthony Obinna, Easter interview, *The Leader*, Easter edition (2008), 20.

29   Anthony J. V. Obinna, exclusive interview, *The Catholic Informer* (April/May 2002), 13–15.

crises and see to it that the right to work is promoted. His Grace is greatly concerned by the fact that unemployment not only ruins the state, tortures families, causes civic disorder, and collapses social economy but that it so often drags the youth into destructive and depressive exploits. At the inauguration of Owerri Archdiocesan Youth Council, he says to young people: 'I am interested in your education, in your employment, in your welfare. We hope to find practical solutions to your problems.'[30] He appeals persuasively to graduates among them who are jobless not to yield to immoral mindset, antisocial behaviours, and existential hopelessness, and reminds them that Nigeria still needs a youthful populace who will tomorrow help to redignify the society and rescue the country from those elements of corruption that have kept many jobless. He pleads with the youth not to give up in life and asks their forgiveness for the faults of the aging generation. He urges the youth to be wiser during election periods by voting according to the dictates of their conscience rather than according to the influence of money or car gifts. They need to look out for those with right values and manifestos, those who have their good at heart, who will respect their right to have a job and rescue them from joblessness through job creation and empowerment.[31] In these words, he expresses to the youth words driven by a *confilial* vision, Archbishop Obinna locates *theofilians* at the centre of the employment question. He buttresses the fact that the lack of work for those who are capable of it—which easily leads to a feeling of alienation, marginalization, and failure and to a loss of the sense of self-fulfilment and self-worth of which young people, full of laborious energy and productive capability, are most hit—maims and debases victims' integrity and innate dignity as *confiliated* persons and frustrates their natural quest for decent livelihood and human development.[32]

---

30   Anthony Obinna, address at the inauguration of Owerri Archdiocesan Youth Council (May 12, 2007), ibid.

31   Anthony J.V. Obinna, interview, *The Touch* (December 2008), 18–20; *The Leader* (February 25, 2007), 5. *The Leader* (June 8, 2003), p. 2.

32   See John Paul II, address to workers of Ivrea diocese (March 19, 1990), n. 2, *L'Osservatore Romano* English language edition, March 26, 1990, 7; John Paul II, address to labour representatives in Civita Casteliana, Italy (May 1, 1988), *The Pope Speaks*, (1988), 294–295; John Paul II, *Laborem Exercens*, September 14, 1981: *AAS* 73 (1981), no. 9.

e. The Idolatrous *Diala-Osu* (Freeborn-Slave) Divide

The earliest official arrival of Catholic Christianity in Igboland (South-Eastern Nigeria) was in 1885, precisely at Onitsha. In 1912, that light of faith settled formally at Emekuku Owerri, the very hometown of Archbishop Obinna. In 2012, Owerri Ecclesiastical Province, under the metropolitan headship of Archbishop Anthony Obinna, celebrated the centenary of the Catholic faith in that region. While still experiencing the dispersing joy of that centennial faith, His Grace remains greatly worried about the sustained presence of *osu* caste system (and the like, such as *ohu* and *ume*) in many parts of Igboland, a region highly dominated by Christians. He condemns such obnoxious practice (similar to the caste of untouchability in India) for degrading a section of people as slave-born (the so-called *osu*) and parading the other section of people as freeborn, with superior blood (the so-called *diala*). Tracing the origin of such a dehumanizing practice to the negative element of Igbo culture, Obinna insists that such a detestable, idolatrous system must be uprooted in the mindsets, impulses, and lifestyles of all and sundry. He rejects the appeal to let this sociocultural discrimination die a natural death, insisting that what is needed is a sweeping and urgent transformational approach that will rapidly end the enslavement and oppression of fellow humans and *theofilians*.[33]

Making a catechetical description of the *osu* caste system as the original sin of Igbo people (*Njo ekereigbo*), one handed over by our ancestors, the outspoken prelate, in ways unprecedented, calls upon people of different walks of life, including traditional rulers, priests, journalists, knights of the church, parents, and young people, to unreservedly eradicate within their minds the residual fears that have sustained the *osu* caste system and to join forces in the work of dismantling this age-long contemptuous practice that has perpetuated exclusion, bitterness, marital difficulties, pride, and duplicity in Igbo families and communities. Informed by the gospel precepts that narrate Christ's *reconfiliatory* mission; motivated by St Paul, to whom there are no more Jews, Greeks, and Gentiles; and backed by the law of the Federal Republic of Nigeria, which officially abolished the *diala-osu* (freeborn-slave) divide more than sixty years

---

33   Anthony J. V. Obinna, exclusive interview, *Ekwe Magazine* (2012 edition), 26–28; Anthony Obinna, Exclusive interview, *Beyond Frontiers Magazine* (2011 edition), 14–18.

ago, Obinna undertakes, with prophetic courage and without delay, some practical measures to integrally eradicate this sociocultural ill. According to him, the *osu* caste system 'does not die a natural death; it can only die a redemptive death'. Unhindered by oppositions, calumnies, and threats, while finding joy and strength in Christ's own *cruci-humiliation*, he reaffirms his readiness to suffer and even to lay down his life, if that is the price needed to dismantle the demeaning *osu* caste system that is as vicious and senseless as apartheid. With that martyrial fortitude, he reaches out restoratively and persistently to safeguard the integrity of our collective *refiliation* in God and to raise greater awareness about the inviolable ontological equality of our *newkinment*, which *osu* caste system abuses.[34]

Tackling the matter from the root, Obinna locates the cause of this horrible '*osucizing*' heritage to a change in Igbo ontology, anthropology, and cosmology, which moved away from the centrality of the concept of *Chi* (God), recognized as existing eternally as Creator and as Provident, to an emphasis on *Ala*-divinity (earth goddess). This, he says, dominated Igbo mindset and worldview and led to the superstitious intimacy with *Ala* (earth) as goddess and necessitates the enchaining of humans to the service of earth goddess.[35] Applying his theological model of *confiliation* to the issue of *diala-osu* divide, an issue that has already become one of the major focuses of his pastoral addresses, homilies, scholarly writings, exclusive interviews, and interventions, the archbishop argues that the *diala-osu* (freeborn-slave) dichotomy we have inherited originally from our pre-Christian ancestors is totally incompatible with the redignified status that Christ's *recti-filiatory* action has effected upon all persons and with the 'new family kinship that has been inaugurated by God in Christ'.[36] He therefore challenges all those who really follow Christ wholeheartedly to reject in their minds, hearts, and souls, in words and in deeds, the furtherance of *osu* caste practice. *Confiliation* explains the alacrity with which Archbishop Obinna wages war against the *diala-osu-ume* and

---

34 *The Leader*, December 4, 2005, 9; Anthony Obinna, exclusive interview, *Beyond Frontiers Magazine* (2011 edition), 14–18. Anthony J. V. Obinna, 2013 *Christmas message: From enemies to family members and neighbors, The Leader News Online* (December 23, 2013), http://theleaderassumpta.com/2013 /12/23/from-enemies-to-family-members-and-neighbours-a-2013-christmas-message/ [accessed May 24, 2019].

35 Anthony J. V. Obinna, exclusive interview, *Ekwe Magazine*, 26–28.

36 Anthony Obinna, exclusive interview, *Beyond Frontiers Magazine* (2011 edition), 26–28.

amadi-ohu cultural divides among the Igbos. Having pondered deeply on humanity's redignified status as restored by Christ, he confronts with zero tolerance any system or practice that dares to reduce and *defiliate* some *theofilians* from that equal and transcendental dignity, since such system or practice mocks God's handiwork and the essence of Christ's *cruci-filial* undertaking.

Having seen the pastoral insights of Archbishop Obinna and how these are informed by his theological model of *confiliation*, we shall now consider how the same model is reflected in his pastoral actions, some of which I now consider.

Practical Milestones

Three months after his episcopal consecration in September 1993, Obinna celebrated his Christmas Eve with prisoners at the state's central prison in Owerri. At that historic visit, the prisoners, touched by his fatherly and consoling presence, presented to him a gift of a wooden crozier, which one of them had skilfully caved. Keeping aside his golden crozier, Archbishop Obinna, till date, has continued to use that particular wooden crozier from prisoners as an expression of his spiritual solicitude with those behind bars, as a way of appealing to authorities to make the prison a place of rehabilitation rather than a place of dehumanization and brutality and as a way of encouraging the exercise of corporal works of mercy towards prisoners.

Ordained a bishop one year after the Second National Eucharistic Congress that took place in Owerri in 1992, Obinna, in 1994, established an outreach called Eucharistic Care for the Needy (*Eu-Care*) in honour of that historic grace-filled event. He was propelled by the conviction that the Eucharist stimulates and sustains deeper care for the poor. *Eu-Care*, which has become a household name in Owerri Archdiocese, has continued, till date, to feed uncountable poor mouths, to cloth numerous indigent persons, to care for people with disability, to engage significant number of employable hands, and to empower young people. The overall target of the *Eu-Care* charity services includes modest loans to individuals to encourage self-supporting economic ventures; scholarship assistance to indigent talented students; a job scheme that funds skills acquisition training for youths and provides tool for those trained for a job but lack tools; a relief program for immediate material assistance to distressed persons which involves little hand-outs of money for food, medical and transport needs, extending to needs of prisoners, hospitalized and motherless babies; assistance to poor parishes carrying big projects.[37]

As an extension of the Eu-care outreach, Archbishop Obinna instituted the *Chikum* microfinance bank in order to empower young, unemployed, and poor people by offering them noninterest loans, with the hope that they would be spurred to engage in agro-related activities, create job for themselves, harness their talents, and become self-reliant, rather than be frustrated by unemployment and hard conditions.[38]

As an apostle of social justice and an advocate of good governance, one of the challenges that has continued to confront Archbishop Obinna and to which his fidelity has remained constant is to remain the prophetic voice of the masses amidst the anti-democratic (military and civilian) juntas that have continued to highjack the political leadership of Nigeria. In 1999, he drew the attention of the then military administrator of Imo State to some of the publicized governmental decisions that will not serve the best interest and legitimate concern of the masses. His pastoral intervention was met with intimidation, blackmail, and ultimatums. Responding to a query from the military administrator, Archbishop Obinna declared: 'In fact I would be reneging on my spiritual prophetic responsibility in Imo State and beyond, if I did not address myself to the anxieties and concerns of the people, especially the weak and the voiceless.'[39]

In the year 2000, he initiated an open forum for the people of the state, as part of his propeace efforts, and invited all and sundry to come and air their views and make helpful suggestions that could assist in moving the country forward. The forum was, for him, a practical means of reculturing and rehumanizing both individuals and government by

---

37   Innocent Aguwuom, 'Monuments of the 1992 Eucharistic Congress', *The Leader* (November 8, 1998), 8.

38   Anthony Obinna, exclusive interview, *New Searchlight*, (2007/2008 edition, vol.7), 32.

39   See *The Leader* (Easter 1999), 8.

providing a platform that spurred the silent majority to speak and a medium that signaled political leaders to be listeners and to be open to feedbacks and criticisms. The event, which was well attended, provided the people veritable opportunity to speak and pour out their worries, at a time when outlets of such kind were nonexistent due to violation of press freedom.[40]

In his peerless efforts to break the idolatrous yoke of caste divide existing in most part of Igboland, Archbishop Obinna, in 2005, gathered the whole traditional rulers within his ecclesiastical territory, those of them who are Catholics, and motivated them to channel their cultural powers and leadership positions towards the eradication of the fabricated and inhuman *diala-osu* system. He assured them of his constant readiness to complement their efforts in this regard. The same year, he participated in a three-day parish exercise tagged 'Spiritual Reconciliation-Purification-Reconfiliation Exercise', an exercise that took place in a rural community where it was offensive and risky to talk about the *diala-osu* (freeborn-slaveborn) divide. He lauded the pastoral bravery of the parish priest in Umuawuka-Emii Owerri who initiated the exercise and praised the over one thousand parishioners in attendance on their willingness to repudiate the idolatrous system and to accept conversion, reconciliation, and mutual forgiveness.[41] The archbishop's outstanding pastoral effort to eradicate this age-long discriminatory tradition among the Igbos is generally acknowledged. Having spoken the gospel truth to culture, through the awakening force of *confiliation*, his effort has inspired some liberating cultural renaissance across Igboland, as recently seen in Irete Owerri (July 2018) and as was spectacular in Nri Kingdom in Anambra State (December 2018). To mention but a few.

Back to 2005, precisely in the month of October, Archbishop Obinna joined a peaceful rally in Owerri organized by labour and civil society coalition under the auspices of the Nigeria Labour Congress to protest the ugly escalating prices of fuel that have generated untold hardship and chaos in the society. Leading at a prayer section that inaugurated that orderly and peaceful protest, he said, 'We have gathered here against greed, injustice, and misuse of the resources of our land.'[42] His expression

---

40   See *The Leader* (March 5, 2000), 13.
41   Anthony J. V. Obinna, Homily during mass for the celebration of World Day of Peace (January 1, 2006).
42   *The Leader* (Christmas 2005), 3.

of solidarity in this regard boasted the morale of the suffering masses and empowered the efforts of human right advocates.

Through his provincial organ, the Justice, Development, Peace/Caritas Committee, an open political forum was organized prior to the Nigerian elections of May 2011. At that forum, the archbishop stood so prominently like a mother pelican feeding her children with the blood of truth, justice, and right conducts. Through that successful forum, he prophetically and strategically enlightened, awakened, and revitalized the consciences of the masses: an effort that proved heroic when at the dawn of the gubernatorial phase of that election, the vote of the majority could not be stolen by money. This development spurs the nurturing of a critical and scrupulous masses and remains a milestone in the history of political elections in Imo State and in Nigeria, even as the search for good governance continues.

In October 2012, just before the grand finale of the centenary celebration of the Catholic faith in Owerri Province, Archbishop A. J. V. Obinna persuaded the CEO of Zinox Technologies (one of the leading info-tech firms in Africa), who belongs to his archdiocese, to create jobs for our looming unemployed youths. The CEO looked inwards into his firm and discovered that the company needed about sixty employees. Applications and CVs of enlisted candidates were submitted as demanded by the company's HR, and interviews were afterwards conducted by the recruitment officer. Twelve out of sixty candidates made it after some rigorous interviews and were suddenly rescued with attractive salaries from over eight years of joblessness. His Grace's inspiring concern for our looming jobless graduates, demonstrated in this regard, was significantly applauded as the audience were moved with admiration when this encouraging effort of our archbishop was recounted during our seven minutes' diocesan intervention at the National Pastoral Congress held in Abuja in November 2012.

These selected instances of the archbishop's noteworthy actions are also animated by his *confiliatory* theology. In each of these pastoral feats, he seeks to defend the integrity and inalienable dignity of human persons whose cast-down status is restored and elevated in Christ through that redemptive act by which we are *refiliated* in God. In keeping aside his best quality crozier and subjecting to frequent usage the wooden crozier he received as a gift from a prisoner during one of his pastoral visits to the prison, he demonstrates that life behind bars is still human, has an innate personal dignity that is not loss because of chains, and deserves, even in matters of retributive justice, the fulfilment of rehabilitative needs and the provision of care. Through his *Eu-Care* outreach, he extends to the poor, the destitute, and the handicapped, through practical charity, that diffusive love of Christ that was shared at the Last Supper, stretched on the cross, and is re-enacted daily on the altar in order that they be constantly encouraged to always reclaim their *cofiliated* integrity that the humiliating experiences of poverty, homelessness, and disability do not take away. His interventions against governmental policies that are not people-oriented are meant to speak for and defend the basic rights of those whose human dignity are mocked through appalling neglect for both common and private needs. It is the same rights that he defends by identifying with peaceful civil demonstrators in advocacy for better human conditions (security, job, basic amenities, wealth, etc.) for the masses, while imploring the people to pray and to always eschew violence and hostility that do not befit *theofilians.*

More so, the archbishop's unbiased open political forum, which is educational and nonpartisan, gives voice to the silent majority and embodies the church's tasks of evangelizing the field of politics by, among other things, forming right political consciences, reforming public opinion, and reviving in people's hearts those moral values essential for good governance, for preserving just structures, and for promoting the elements of the common good in order that the *theofiliated* dignity of persons be served and enhanced. His liberating war against *osu-ohu-ume* segregating and enslaving caste system in Igboland aims at restoring the equal dignity of our culturally and socially wounded *cofilians*, eradicating the age-long superstitious assaults on their precious existence, and fostering their holistic and equitable integration in the society. He solicits for job opportunities for the youth in order that these professionally equipped graduates can share in that basic right that work expresses and acquire that title of nobility that work confers. He believes that rather than letting their sense of human fulfilment be threatened by prolonged joblessness, young people who are intellectually and technically ready for work should be assisted to participate in that metaphysical, existential, social, creative, ethical, spiritual, toiling, and salvific values that work conveys,[43] values that celebrate human *refiliated* dignity and fulfil the renewed dignity of being human.

---

43   John Paul II, *Encyclical Letter, Laborem Exercens, on Human Work on the Ninetieth Anniversary of Rerum Novarum*, September 14, 1981: *AAS* 73 (1981), no. 14.

So far, I have explored the insights and actions of Archbishop Anthony Obinna as informed by his theology of *confiliation*. I will now, in the two proceeding sections, consider how these have contributed towards defining his model and pattern of leadership. I will make this consideration through a rereading of Bolman and Deal's *Reframing Organizations* and Northouse's *Leadership Theory and Practice*.

Obinna's Leadership Model in the Light of Bolman and Deal's *Reframing Organizations*

Drawing from the social sciences, L. G. Bolman and T. E. Deal champion a four-frame organizational model in which leadership perspectives are considered. The model includes the structural frame—noted for its factory metaphor and characterized by rules, authority, objectives, systems, and chain of command—and the human resources frame, which 'sees an organization as an extended family, made up of individuals with needs, feelings, prejudices, skills, and limitations' and which recognizes the importance of security and trust for deeper organizational participation of individuals. There is also the political frame, denoted with jungle, which is marked by power dynamics, struggles, competition, and conflicts of interest and of expectation; and finally the symbolic frame, with its temple and theatrical view of organization, which 'depicts organizations as cultures, propelled by rituals, ceremonies, stories, heroes, and myths'.[44]

In the light of the above frames, the thoughts and actions of Archbishop Obinna reflect the human resource frame of leadership since they exude family principles and are characterized by great concerns about human needs, including spiritual, moral, social, cultural, economic, and political needs. He instituted the Eu-Care to respond to the needs of the poor, the destitute, and the handicaps and joined in nonviolent match in order to stimulate greater consciousness for attending to the legitimate needs of the people. He also supported and participated in open political forum as a way of educating consciences and raising awareness about the legitimate desires of common people and the just expectations of the electorates for free and fair election, upright electoral counting, and accurate declaration

---

44   Lee G. Bolman and Terrence E. Deal, *Reframing Organizations: Artistry, Choice and Leadership*, 5th edition (San Francisco: Jossey-Bass, 2013), 16.

of electoral results. He not only inquired about job opportunities for youths who are jobless in order to care about their employment needs, he also provided zero interest loans through his diocesan microfinance bank (*Chikum*) in order to help nonworking youths to become creatively engaged and be able to fulfil personal and social needs.

Heading a divinely instituted faith tradition as a metropolitan archbishop, Obinna, in line with the human resource model, invests on people. Once he fishes out latent talents among young people, he encourages them to develop such talents. Being himself multitalented, he supports talents wherever they are. He likes to empower people too. He exhorts priests to fight against systemic corruption in the land, challenges the knights to reject *osu* caste system, mobilizes both rural and urban-minded youths to patronize agriculture, persuades government officials to be servant leaders, and appeals to the masses to let the dictates of their conscience determine who gets their electoral votes.[45]

Relationship remains very important for Archbishop Obinna, thanks to his human resource leadership frame. This explains why he wants all men and women, irrespective of color, gender, race, tribe, and creed, to regard themselves as *cofiliated* brothers or sisters and as creatures in God and to relate as friends and neigbours and not as enemies or un-equals. Little wonder he proposes the theology of *confiliation* as 'a one family-building dynamic'. *Ndaa Anto* (as he is fondly called in his native town) brings the church closer to the people, aligning her to the integral needs of the people. In addition to religious and spiritual concerns of the church, he lets the church address, morally and pastorally, all aspects of the social questions, convinced that the church can neither remain indifferent to social problems nor be at the periphery of efforts geared towards promoting human flourishing and the good of the society.

---

45   *The Leader* (October 5, 2008), 3. Anthony J. V. Obinna, Sermon during a non-denominational service for the inauguration of Governor Emeka Ihedioha (May 26, 2019), *The Leader News Online* (June 2, 2019), https://theleaderassumpta.com/2019/06/02/ihediohas-inauguration-imo-needs-true-servant-leader-archbishop-obinna/ [accessed June 3, 2019].

Obinna's Leadership Pattern in the Light of Northouse's *Leadership Theory and Practice*

In the compilation of leadership approaches by P. G. Northouse, as developed by different authors, a significant number of leadership theories was identified, some of which include the trait approach, skills approach, behavioural approach, situational approach, path-goal theory, leader-member exchange theory, transformational leadership, servant leadership, adaptive leadership, and psychodynamic approach. Northouse's work also examined leadership issues and styles as they concern ethics, teams, gender, and culture.[46] When studied in relation to these leadership approaches, Archbishop Obinna's leadership insights and engagements reflect transformational and servant leadership.

Transformational Leadership

'Transformational leadership is a process that changes and transforms people. It is concerned with emotions, values, ethics, standards, and long-term goals. It includes assessing followers' motives, satisfying their needs, and treating them as full human beings.'[47] It is a follower-oriented pattern of leadership in which the good of the whole, which guarantees the welfare of each, is promoted, while exploitative and self-serving activities born of leader-egocentric interests are avoided. Transformational leadership manifests certain factors. It shows idealized influence, one in which a leader sets inspiring standard, is seen as a role model, and spurs others into action with visions. It also shows inspirational motivation, which entails that a leader motivates others to achieve common goals. Transformational leadership features intellectual stimulation, for which the leader challenges others to be creative and to apply critical thinking over long-held opinions and customs. It also features individualized consideration in which a leader offers active listening to specific needs.[48] Leaders who are transformational

---

46   Peter G. Northouse, *Leadership: Theory and Practice* (Thousand Oaks, CA: Sage, 2016), 19–324.

47   Northouse, *Leadership: Theory and Practice*, 161.

48   Bernard M. Bass, 'From Transactional to Transformational Leadership: Learning to Share the Vision', *Organizational Dynamics* 18, no. 3 (1990): 18–31. Peter G. Northouse, *Leadership*, 167–171.

are said, in certain catchphrases, to 'model the way,' to 'inspire a shared vision', to 'challenge the process', to 'enable others to act', and to 'encourage the heart'. Transformational leaders 'model the way' by being clear of their own value, 'inspire a shared vision' by helping in the actualization of people's legitimate desires, 'challenge the process' by prompting positive change, 'enable others to act' by making others to participate and to feel coresponsible, and 'encourage the heart' by lauding committed efforts.[49]

One finds in the words and deeds of Anthony Obinna the features of transformational leadership. As a transformational leader, he exudes lots of charisma. His deep thoughts, detailed knowledge, invigorating eloquence, and unrivalled articulacy make his arguments convincing and his truth-serving ideas sellable. His power of words and his semantic dexterity account for the ease with which he coins striking and catchy concepts and develops neologisms, as he uses these to advance his transforming and enriching visions. His poetic, singing, and multilingual competences diversify and flavour his charisma. In his idealized influence, he stands as a fearless prophet of truth, an outspoken architect of social justice, an apostle of practical charity, a rectifier of culture, and the initiator of the theological model of *confiliation*. He continues to inspire and empower many, including clerics, professors, and lay people in these ways. As an inspirational motivator, Archbishop Obinna, with significant and noticeable success, continues to persuade traditional rulers to reject the discriminatory *osu* caste system, an age-long idolatrous tradition inherited from our Igbo ancestors. He continues to influence and to support unemployed youths to be self-creative. Lots of marriages between the so-called freeborn and the so-called slave-born, which would have been hindered or severed because of fear, pride, and discrimination, finally came to be through mutual resolves stirred by the unifying force of his *confiliatory* vision.

More so, displaying intellectual stimulation as a transformational leader, Obinna has challenged lots of Igbo and African cosmo-visions that are neither in line with the gospel precepts nor compatible with the precepts of the natural law. For instance, he has awakened the intellectual curiosities of many Igbo scholars into deeper reflection and research about an issue that can never be overemphasized: the *osu* caste system, the original sins of Igboland. Such a reawakening has given rise

---

49   J. M. Kouzes and B. Z. Posner, *The Leadership Challenge*, 3rd Edition (San Francisco: Jossey-Bass, 2002), 9–13.

to many publications, conferences, debates, and concrete actions on the issue, all geared towards eradicating this societal scourge. Because of his individualized consideration, as a leader that transforms, which has made him a compassionate listener and the voice of the voiceless, he is usually approached by people and professionals of different walks of life who lay their complaints about unjust governmental actions and policies while asking for his timely and objective pastoral interventions. Among these include civil servants, when embittered by months of salary arears; pensioners, after prolonged years of non-payment of pensions by the government; the disabled, after years of governmental apathy and neglect; and journalists, after reoccurring instances of abuses of press freedom by the government. His commitment to such just causes, as a forthright defender of human rights, has been consistent.

In line with the elements of transformational leadership, the archbishop is clear about his personal values and philosophy. He strongly believes in the brotherhood and sisterhood of all men and women and spreads the same belief through his theological model of *confiliation*, which on the moral terrain provides the Christological foundation for the principle and the social virtue of solidarity. He shares with optimism a vision of honest democracy through his ideals of *theofilial* democracy, aware of what is urgently needed to heal Nigeria from the wounds and anomalies of long years of militarism and from the structural poverty enthroned through recurrent empty political promises, political looting, untold nepotism, and wanton disregard for the provision of basic amenities as seen in both military and civilian regimes in Nigeria. He also continues to stress on the value of authentic education, aware that ignorance, which sustains superstitious mindset and misplacement of values, is greatly responsible for the continued sociocultural enslavement and underdevelopment in our land. Resolute then to foster quality education and to make the church an active agent of educational transformation, being himself a professional educator, he criticizes the intolerable dilapidation of the nation's educational system, establishes more mission schools, promotes the rehabilitation of government-returned mission schools, and embarks in training many priests for advanced specialization in education. His personal lifestyle also exudes steady detachment and devout simplicity, which are inspiringly noticeable. These exemplary personal values, chosen in imitation of Christ, our *Confiliator*, enables him to advance in the pursuit of eternal values and interior greatness, to be better disposed for contemplative exercises, to instruct a materialistic and extravagant world, and to be more devoted to the service of the poor, the needy, and the marginalized.

As a transformational leader, His Grace has greatly challenged the process, determined to change the status quo by rectification and rehabilitation. Against the conventional mentality of usurping the national cake once in power for self and sectarian interests, he continues to challenge political leaders to be servant leaders and to place their priority on being people-oriented and on promoting the common good. Against an age-long pagan practice of *diala-osu* divide in Igboland, which many think can only die a natural death even as its residual elements continue to permeate deeply among Igbo Christian families, he takes the bull by the horn by exorcising and overhauling Igbo superstitious mindset. He spearheads the application of a redemptive death on such obnoxious and inhuman practice so that the shared ontological integrity of redignified *theofilians*, long culturally partitioned and socially disorientated, can be *recti-filiated* to enable the reinstatement of the common equality of all *confilians* and the furtherance of the good of each and every one in equity, fairness, and charity.

Servant Leadership

Servant leadership is a leadership theory that is anchored on the ethical value of service. It involves the character of being other-serving rather than self-serving or power-serving and of making the development and the good of others one's priority. A servant leader directs power to the service of the people for whom he has received in trust the mandate to lead, and to the edification of the institution (secular or religious) under which he leads. Such a leader sees every level of position as providing an opportunity and imposing a responsibility to serve. A leader committed to service feels indebted and accountable to the people, equips oneself with all that will enable him or her give the people his or her best, empower them, fosters their holistic development, and helps everyone be as God desires. A leader who serves shows concern for the needs of his subjects and exercises a genuine sense of fellow feeling for the poor, the disadvantaged, the defenceless, and the vulnerable among whom he serves.

The characteristics of a servant leader include the ability to listen, to be empathetic, to heal and be healed, to be aware, and to convince. A servant leader manifests vision, foresight, a sense of stewardship, and is committed to fostering individual and community welfare and integral development.[50] These characteristics reflect in the leadership approach of Archbishop Obinna, some of which we shall highlight.

His Grace is both an active and a reflective listener. Actively, he listens with enthusiasm and serenity to the cries and concerns of others, a disposition that encourages people to run to him to express their struggles, lamentations, frustrations, complaints, criticisms, and social anxieties, while seeking for his consolation, counsel, and intervention. His active listening connects him communicatively with his subjects, increases his awareness of situations and events, disposes him to value, and let him be open to other people's ideas. His capacity for reflective listening, on the other hand, enables him to carefully analyse information received, inquire further, and differentiate between imagination and reality, facts and opinions, truth and all forms of non-truth such as lies, prejudiced or manipulated information, selective indignation, crafty insinuation, sectarian propaganda, blackmail, etc. before taking further steps so that his actions will favour proper discernment, application of wisdom, and right conscience.[51]

In practical term, Archbishop Obinna's commitment to works of charity, for instance, through his *Eu-Care* outreach to which he empties his purse, represents his empathetic and compassionate care for the afflicted and the needy; and this speaks of servant leadership. Affirming the humanity of indigent persons as *cofilians*, he extends helping, empowering, and consoling hand of solidarity in honour and at the service of their *reconfiliated* dignity. In the same vein, his peerless, relentless, and sincere efforts to break the idolatrous yoke of *diala-osu* divide in

---

50 Robert K. Greenleaf, *The Servant Leader* (Westfield, IN: The Greenleaf Center for Servant Leadership, 2012), 5–10. Larry C. Spears, 'Character and Servant Leadership: Ten Characteristics of Effective, Caring Leaders', *The Journal of Virtues and Leadership* 1, no. 1 (2010): 27–29. See also Peter G. Northouse, *Leadership*, 225–229. B. M. Ledbetter, R. J. Banks, and D. C. Greenhalgh, *Reviewing Leadership: A Christian Evaluation of Current Approaches*, 2nd ed. (Grand Rapids, MI: Baker Academic, 2016), 106–107.

51 Alexandre Havard, *Virtuous Leadership: An Agenda for Personal Excellence*, 2nd ed. (New Rochelle, NY: Scepter, 2007), 59. See also, John Paul II, Message for 1980 World Day of Peace, n. 1, http://w2.vatican.va/content/john-paul-ii/en/messages/peace/documents/hf_jp-ii_mes_19791208_xiii-world-day-for-peace.html [accessed May 30, 2019].

Igboland, as part of his redemptive efforts to heal families and peoples of an age-long tribal wound and to reconcile human relationships, reflects the mark of a servant leader who seeks the good of others by insisting on the recti-valuing of their humanity and the integration of their existence.[52]

Taking up for his episcopal coat of arm the maxim 'To Serve God and His People', Archbishop Anthony Obinna operates with a distinguished sense of stewardship and has let this service-oriented principle form the framework for his pastoral engagements. During our ordination as deacons, he said to us: 'As you rejoice that you are being ordained deacons remember that you are only ordained to serve, to become servants. And the more you progress in this path the more a servant you become. As priests, you will become elder-servants; as bishop, one becomes a big servant; as an archbishop, I (referring to himself) see myself as arch-servant. Cardinals are royal servants, while the pope is servant of the servants of God.' That message lives on. It reflects not only his own approach to leadership but also his proposal for everyone in leadership position (political, traditional, organizational, and ecclesial).

Another feature of servant leadership is vision—the ability to conceptualize and to proffer lasting models, principles, or ideas that can feed thoughts and inform actions. This is precisely what Obinna's *confiliation* expresses. It is a theological model that provides authentic guides with spiritual, ontological, and moral import for all men and women living in the local and global society as *theofilians* who are journeying towards the ultimate goal of our *reconfiliation* (eternal life); who are dependent beings and creatures made to the image of God[53] with the faculty to know and to love the One to whom we are *refiliated*; and who have basic responsibilities to be holy and virtuous, to be open to grace for the perfection of the image, and to strive for the just ordering of the temporal order as conducing to the supernatural end. It is also a theological model that reawakens us anthropologically, culturally, and socially in order to refocus our consciousness to the truth of our being as people endowed by God with equality of personhood and whose innate dignity, once wounded by the Fall, has been redeemed and elevated by Christ, our *Confiliator*; as people whose human nature, though revealed by culture, transcends culture, constitutes the measures of culture, and

---

52 Northouse, *Leadership*, 228,

53 Gen 1:26, *New Jerusalem Bible* (NY: Doubleday & Company Inc., 1985).

possesses a redignified transcendent status that should be served and not be subjected to enslavement by culture;[54] and as *co-filians* called naturally to a communal rather than isolated existence in the *confilialed* society of equals.

We shall now consider in the final section that follows how this vision not only informs the archbishop's mission but also surfaces in his actions.

Vision to Mission to Action

The theology of *confiliation* that Archbishop Anthony Obinna envisions for humanity remains the dynamic force that propels his leadership role in the church and in the society and is further translated into the practical milestones that concretize his vision. Being an uplifting, humanizing, and shared vision, the archbishop's theological model of *confiliation*, principally driven by charity, by his restorative love for persons and society for the sake of God, expresses, *inter alia*, magnanimity of spirit and humility of being. Expressing a contagious magnanimity, his *confiliation* strives theologically to the heights by exploring the greatness of being, on the conviction that 'there is in man something great which he possesses through the gift of God'.[55] Envisioning magnanimously his *confiliatory* theory, Obinna extols the worth, grandeur, and transcendence of the human person as ordained to eternal happiness and as being inviolably a reflection of God. He lauds the greatness of human dignity as resonant of divine splendour and as endowed with a treasure of freedom. He extols the beauty of human nature as endowed with infinite faculties for knowing and loving God, as redeemed and elevated by Christ, and as constantly being purified and transformed by grace. He further wonders on the mystery, preciousness, and sacredness of human life as honoured and divinized by the Incarnation (*infiliation*).

Deeming human persons as gratuitously worthy of this greatness, in gratitude to God, the source of human greatness, the theology of *confiliation* strives always to transform persons, structures, and systems. Driving a path to a mission, this transforming proclivity imbedded in

---

54 Pontifical Council for Culture, *Towards a Pastoral Approach to Culture* (May 23, 1999), n. 2, http://www.vatican.va/roman_curia/pontifical_councils/cultr/documents/rc_pc_pc-cultr_doc_03061999_pastoral_en.html [accessed May 31, 2019]

55 ST. II-II, q. 129, a. 3, ad 4.

the magnanimous feature of Obinna's theological model of *confiliation* accounts for his transformational approach to leadership. This explains, as his actions concretize, the passion with which the archbishop appeals for the conversion of hearts and the rectification of mindsets in order to repair and appease deformed image of God on faces disfigured by abject poverty, faces humiliated by discrimination, faces disenchanted by political criminality, and faces terrified by persecution.[56] It also explains, as his persistent moves have shown, the fortitude with which he identifies and seeks for the eradication of all structures of injustice and all *defiliating* sociocultural systems. It also explains the high morale with which he challenges peoples of all walks of life, common people and professional, to embrace transformational and redemptive change in favour of integral human development.

In addition to its magnanimous feature, Obinna's theology of *confiliation* manifests a sense of humility of being. Such humility does not undermine that greatness of being that draws magnanimity but complements and demands it, since 'humility is the proper attitude towards all true greatness, including one's own greatness as a human being, but above all towards the greatness which is not one's self, which is beyond one's self'.[57] This element of humility rooted in the theology of *confiliation* expresses the fact that other than possessing a greatness conferred on him gratuitously by God, man, in Thomistic terms, has 'something defective which accrues to him through the weakness of nature' that makes him 'think little of himself in consideration of his own deficiency'.[58] Humility rapports with magnanimity by acknowledging human capability and strength while at the same time complementing the latter by recognizing human deficiency and weakness. While striving respectfully towards the grandeur of being, the theological model of *confiliation* equally recognizes the limits of man's divine image, nature, beauty, dignity, and life. It asserts man's imago Dei as imperfect and participatory of the perfect image of God who is Christ, our *Confiliator*. It recognizes man's nature as wounded by original sin, for which, despite Christ's redemptive act, man is still inclined

---

56   John Paul II, *Post-Synodal Apostolic Exhortation Vita Consecrata, on the Consecrated Life and Its Mission in the Church and in the World, March 25, 1996*, AAS 88, no. 75 (1996).

57   Karol Wojtyla, *Love and Responsibility*, trans. H. T. Willetts (London: Harper Collins Pub., 1981), 172.

58   ST. II-II, q. 129, a. 3, ad 4.

to sin and is often trapped in the net of sin, which makes him in constant need of grace as he undertakes the daily struggle to do good and avoid evil.

Confiliatory theology recognizes that the beauty of *theofilians* is only a reflection of the divine, original, exemplary, and everlastingly satisfactory beauty that is God; and unless he is filiated to this pure and incorruptible beauty, man dissipates in beauty, dries up in dignity, and diminishes in true greatness. The theology of *confiliation* recognizes the life of every person as a gift to which men and women are not masters but are assigned to serve as administrators. It also recognizes the appalling reality of life's earthly mortality that makes death inevitable and its anxiety existentially inescapable, even while it opens wide on eternity.[59] Also buttressed in the theology of *confiliation* is the fact that men and women are thrown into neediness. Men and women are not self-sufficient; they indispensably need God, who keeps and sustains us in being. They also need others as a logic of our natural sociality for which we are destined for life in the society as affirmed by the precepts of the natural law.

In expressing the basic and objective truth about the human person, exposing *inter alia* human finiteness, defects, insignificances, imperfections, and weaknesses, the theological model of *confiliation* locates humility in the depths of human personality and draws attention to why the human person should be cared for and administered to rather than be downgraded or apotheosized. It also tells of the need for us to convert all our humiliations to humility, mindful of Christ's own cruci-humiliation. Despite his or her metaphysical, existential, anthropological, social, and personal limitations, the human being is loved by God, has a nature tested by God without sin, and remains God's image. These reveal the need to reverence what is best and what is of God in every creature and spurs the altruistic desire to serve God in others, a desire that is substantiated by proactively cultivating the habit of service, by seeing men and women as persons rather than objects of use, and by helping every human being to develop, reintegrate, succeed, and be fulfiled. The integral neediness of the human person, which *confiliatory* theology indicates, not only calls attention to the logic of interdependence but also presses upon leaders the

---

59   Benedict XVI, General audience (August 29, 2007), http://w2.vatican.va/content/benedict-xvi/en/audiences/2007/documents/hf_ben-xvi_aud_20070829.html [accessed July 1, 2019]. John Paul II, *Encyclical letter Evangelium Vitae, on the Value and Inviolability of Human Life* (March 25, 1995), n.97. John Paul II, *Post-Synodal Apostolic Exhortation, Ecclesia in Asia* (November 6, 1999), n. 35.

duty to sincerely foster the accomplishment of these needs. It is in these ways, thanks to its feature of humility, that *confiliatory* theology informs the archbishop's servant approach to leadership. This explains the ardour with which he beckons upon all those in any level of leadership position to be servant leaders, leaders who build, create, rehabilitate, enhance, and contribute, and not tyrants, ego-centrists, self-idolizers, and mass murderers who only deceive, loot, waste, debase and destroy. This also explains his interventions against all idolatrous practices, which violate the right order of existence by subjecting man to the service of things rather than letting things serve man and letting man serve God and what is God in man. The same is the case with his social criticism against placing self-interest and party interest above the common good, since no leader can achieve genuine stewardship without recognizing the primacy of the common good, which alone safeguards the dignity of persons and guarantees the fulfilment of private goods.

Indeed, the theological vision of *confiliation*, animated by love for God, person, and society, which informs, empowers, and unfolds the mission of transformational and servant leadership, by embodying a magnanimity that extols persons' divinely endowed greatness and a humility that restores and enhances the inalienable and equal dignity of persons, is greatly relevant. More than ever before, it is needed today in the moral field to reawaken the pursuit of virtuous and authentic leadership as the archbishop has demonstrated. It is needed to perseveringly engineer both the liberation of oppressed persons and enslaved mindsets and the refinement and humanization of native cultures and sociopolitical systems from oppressive and discriminatory elements. *Confiliatory* theology promises to be a great contribution to a spiritual, moral, cultural, and political renaissance that will harmonize and reconcile interpersonal and family relations; transform Igbo society and Africa into a land of true unity, equality, respect, communion, and humanistic governance; and enthrone a civilization of integral and inclusive humanism, in which all men and women will have a sense of *refiliation* and, as *theofilians*, will feel respected and served for the sake of God, to whom we are all not only *reconfiliated* but also accountable.

Conclusion

In this write-up, we have combined theological, managerial, and leadership perspectives in exploring the leadership models of Archbishop A. J. V. Obinna as driven by his theology of *confiliation*. We have undertaken this meditation, especially, in appreciation of the silver jubilee anniversary of his arch-episcopal elevation as the metropolitan archbishop of Owerri Ecclesiastical Province.

Reflecting on Obinna's leadership style whose growing edge, if any, is beyond the competence and focus of this article, we have realized that when placed on the crucible of leadership studies, his (pastoral) leadership reflects the human resource frame that considers everyone, irrespective of differences, as constituting a single family, the united family of *theofilians*. In the same vein, we realized that the archbishop's outstanding commitment to a charity-animated just cause takes the shape of transformational leadership that seeks to rectify morals and conducts and to reform structures and systems. It also takes the shape of servant leadership, which is other-oriented in guiding, overseeing, and caring for the realization of a redignified and an interactive humanity. Both contribute greatly to contemporary and interdisciplinary leadership studies as the models he has positively employed to make a rehabilitative prophetic stride into the fields of politics, education, culture, business-economy, human family, natural ecology, communication media, and church life.

Behind the transforming and liberating force of Archbishop Obinna's leadership style and pattern is his Christological model of *confiliation*, which he proposes as 'a one family-building dynamic' for the integral restoration of persons' dignity, for societal remedial ordering, and for global *covivance*. Informing and invigorating his leadership thrust, his theology of *confiliation*, which ethically awakens human consciousness towards that truth of faith that it embodies, has become, in itself, a veritable and solid foundation for that transformational and servant leadership that the archbishop exemplifies and through which he fosters the principles of reform, equality, integrality, stewardship, care, solidarity, community, and eco-morality that are greatly needed today. Indeed, his model of *confiliation*, which appeals to all and sundry, locally and globally, defends its cause as the irreplaceable point of departure for any authentic and ethical leadership project geared towards the rectification and restoration of persons and structures and speaks for itself as timely and tropical for theological reflection. His transformational and servant leadership approaches, which his *confiliatory* theology has inspired through its elements of magnanimity and humility, proves relevant for serious exploration not only for leadership studies and for other disciplines but also for every person, leaders and the led alike.

Chapter Twelve

Pastoral Implication of the Theology and Practice of Reconfiliation in Christ: A Challenge to Christianity in Nigeria

Andrew C. Nkwocha

Abstract

Drawing from some of the articles of Archbishop Anthony J. V. Obinna since his twenty-five years' episcopate, this article attempts to show the passion and zeal in this seasoned good shepherd and academic. He used his position as the chief shepherd of Owerri Catholic Archdiocese to bring hope to degraded and devastated humanity. As a theologian, he also proposes the *theology and practice of reconfiliation* as a way forward. This new insight, if implemented in its pastoral undertone, will help us realize that we are one global family of fellow brothers and sisters. This article traces the scriptural origin of human dignity and how our dignity and our environment have been abused by human activity. It also discusses the pastoral implications and its challenges to Christians in Nigeria and sees the implementation of *theology and practice of reconfiliation* as a way to restoring human dignity at every level.

Preamble

Humanity is degraded, decimated, and abused by division, greed, power, and violence. It is not uncommon to see a group of people who claim superiority over others. From our knowledge of the scriptures, all men and women are created equal. To subject human beings to undignified treatment because of political, racial, social, or cultural affiliation is contrary to the divine order.

There is global insecurity today due to nuclear warheads, the ethno-religious fight between Christianity and Islam in many countries, and poverty across nations both developed and undeveloped. The gap between the poor and rich continues to widen. Uncontrolled industrial emissions from the developed world threaten human life and earth's other inhabitants because of climate change. Archbishop Anthony J. V. Obinna describes this situation as 'Creation is in Ruin'.[1] 'I see the evil weapons of hatred, violence and war ripping through humans or exploding unto destruction whether in Nigeria, Iraq, Israel, Palestine, India, Pakistan, Spain, England, America or Haiti, I re-experience with deep sadness the crash of creation into ruins and wonder: are we fated to nihilistic self-destruction.'[2]

Pained by this self-inflicted injury on humanity, Archbishop Anthony Obinna did not only condemn these inhuman behaviours; he also proposes a new theological insight that seeks to address the damage done to humanity and the creation as a whole. His *Theology and Practice of Reconfiliation in Christ* was born out of his 'living experience' as a pastor, manifesting his ministerial and intellectual prowess. His concept of *Theo-Filio* (God-Son) paves way to *confiliation* (fellow sons and daughters) and *reconfiliation* (bringing new the broken relationship with Father as sons and daughters) in Christ has taken centre stage in many theological discussions. Being both theocentric and Christocentric in his

---

1   Anthony J. V. Obinna, 'Confiliatory Collaboration between the Church in Africa and Europe' (June 3, 2004), 3.

2   Anthony J. V. Obinna, "Confiliatory Collaboration between the Church in Africa and Europe', 6.

reflections, he sees God as creating a new world/humanity in Jesus Christ through the Incarnation leading to Jesus' reconfiliatory death on the cross.

This article, which is written in honour of Archbishop Anthony J. V. Obinna, makes use of his various talks and argues that broken humanity is in need of rectification and revaluing one another, hence the importance of *theology and practice of reconfiliation* in our time. I will first establish the theological concept of human being from the scriptural perspective, the reality of human situation especially in Nigeria, and ask, What does *theology and practice of reconfiliation* look like? I will then discuss the pastoral implications/challenges posited by this theology and conclude with an evaluation of this new insight.

Theological Concept of Human Being

From the first account of the creation story, the Bible tells us that man and woman were created in the image and likeness of God:

> Then God said, let us make humankind in our image, according to our likeness; and let them have dominion over the fish of the sea, and over the birds of the air, and over the cattle and all the wild animals of the earth, and over every creeping thing that creeps upon the earth. So, God created humankind in his image, in the image of God he created, male and female he created them.Gen.1:26–27.[3]

From this account, to be made in the image and likeness of God means that we are God-like, implying that life is sacred and precious. To be in the image of God also bestows on every human being some dignity and honour. This dignity does not depend on human thinking, culture, colour, or tribe. Our dignity as humans derives from the Creator—whether black or white; Igbo, Yoruba, or Hausa; *osu* or *diala*—makes no difference. It is an inalienable right from nature. This is why every person deserves respect, even the unborn child. *Catechism of the Catholic Church* teaches that 'the dignity of man rests above all on the fact that he is

---

3   *The New Oxford Annotated Bible, New Revised Standard Version*, 4th edition (New York: Oxford Press, 1998). All scriptural references in this paper are from *The New Oxford Annotated Bible, New Revised Standard Version*, 4th edition.

called to communion with God. This invitation to converse with God is addressed to as soon as he comes into being. For if man exists, it is because God created him through love and through love continues to hold him in existence'.[4] Our dignity and the sacredness of life make it morally evil to violate human dignity in any form. Explaining further, Pope Francis teaches that 'every man and woman is created out of love and made in God's image and likeness. This shows us the immense dignity of each person who is not just something but someone'.[5] Therefore, to create division among men and women, killing of a person, group, tribe, or race violates right to respect and honour as well as right to life.

The above account also indicates that humankind came from one stock: 'in the image of God, he created them male and female'. If we are from one source, it means that humanity is one global family; therefore, we are brothers and sisters of equal rights and dignity. Pope Francis has this to say: 'As part of the universe, called into being by one Father, all of us are linked by unseen bonds and together form a kind of universal family, a sublime communion which fills us with a sacred, affectionate and humble respect.'[6] Killing or degrading others either because of an ethnopolitical or religious reason and forgetting that we are a global family of brothers and sisters makes no sense.

Creating male and female in a sense also portrays a sense of communal life. This imagery is also reflected in what God said, 'Let us make humanity'. God is in community and works in community, which is evidenced in the Trinity. The mystery of the Incarnation revealed to us the unity and relationship between God the Father, God the Son, and God the Holy Spirit, which should be a good metaphor for the unity and relationships between human persons, communities, tribes, race, or nations. One wonders why human beings cannot live communal lives without hatred, division, and senseless killings of one another. We may ask, What has happened to our sense of image and likeness of God? When did we lose the sight of our common origin that we prefer inhuman treatment to one and the other or even killing ourselves as if we were no longer created in the image of God? The Trinity is not only a mystery but more than that. It is also a

---

4   *Catechism of the Catholic Church*, 1ˢᵗ edition (New York: Image Book Doubleday, 1995), 27.

5   Francis, *Encyclical on Climate Change and Inequality, Laudato Si, May 24, 2015* (Brooklyn. London: Melville House, 2015), 89.

6   Francis, *Encyclical on Climate Change and Inequality, Laudato Si*, 89.

revelation of how we should live and relate with one another in love, unity, and communal life.

We are not animals, birds, or fish. 'In creating human beings, he has made them after his own image, giving them even a share in the power of reason, a kind of reflection of the wisdom of his Son.'[7] We were empowered by God to have dominion over the animals, birds, and sea creatures because we share in God's wisdom and reason; but this does not mean domineering or exploiting other creatures. We have to take care of these creatures because humanity is the closest to God's image and likeness. Being in the image and likeness of God does not necessarily mean physical appearance; rather, we resemble God more in the spirit because according to the second account of creation, God put his breath into Adam, 'Then the Lord God formed man from the dust of the ground and breathed into his nostrils the breath of life; and the man became a living being' (Gen 2:7). **Catechism of the Catholic Church** further explains it thus, 'The human person participates in the light and power of the divine Spirit, by this reason he is capable of understanding the order of things established by the Creator.'[8]

The power and authority over created things are not power to abuse. Pope Francis explained the concept of having dominion over created order: 'The biblical texts are to be read in their context, with an appropriate hermeneutic, recognizing that they tell us to "till and keep" the garden of the world (Gen 2:15). Tilling refers to cultivating, ploughing or working, while keeping means caring, protecting, overseeing and preserving.'[9] We should not only respect human beings but other creatures should be taken care of too, because we are sharing the same planet with them. Contrary to this, human degradation, wars, divisions, wanton spilling of human blood, environmental spillage due to oil exploration and industrial waste are what have befallen our world.

---

7   Francis Firth, 'Saint Athanasius: On the Incarnation of the Word', in **The Canadian Catholic Review** (March 1997): 35.

8   *Catechism of the Catholic Church*, 1704.

9   Francis, *Encyclical on Climate Change and Inequality, Laudato Si*, 67.

The Reality of Human Degradation in Nigeria

Since the 1914 amalgamation of Nigeria as a state, it has been synonymous with division, strife, and violence. This is due to tribes and religious affiliations, and the negative consequences of this stare at us today. They range from 'struggle for political power, resource control and indigeneship or citizenship'.[10] The 1966 coup, which was carried out by Nigerian military cutting across all regions and ethnic groups, was mischievously tagged 'the Igbo coup' because of ethnic and tribal bias. Since gaining independence in 1960, Nigeria and her people have scarcely known stable peace and harmony due to the coup and countercoup, tribal and religious clashes, as well as political upheavals.

The political and government appointments are based on tribal and religious affiliations as well as godfatherism, thereby sacrificing merit, integrity, hard work, and honesty at the altar of sectionalism and nepotism. In many instances, the attempt to get power controlled by one ethnic or religious groups leads to violent clashes. 'Ethno-religious conflicts have gained notoriety as the most violent crises in Nigeria, such conflicts are the Kafanchan-Kaduna crisis that occurred in the 1980s and 1990s, the Kaduna sharia riots of 2000 and the Jos riots in 2001.'[11] These conflicts have ripple effects on the citizens both young and old, especially on the vulnerable (children and women). Many Nigerians have died because of it, some are maimed, others are displaced, children are orphaned, and some drop out of school. Houses and other properties worth millions of naira are burnt and destroyed as the case may be.

Boko Haram insurgence in Nigeria has left thousands of lives dead, houses and schools burnt, and many women, including over two hundred Chibok schoolgirls, abducted since 2009, when it started its militia campaign. The recent military invasion of the South-East in the name of Operation Python Dance II has left many unarmed youth (IPOB agitators) dead. This has created fear and tension in the citizens of Nigeria. In one of his talks, Archbishop Anthony J. V. Obinna said, 'Between 1999 and 2002, three years into our apparent democracy thirty-nine episodes of

---

10   Canci Haldun & Odukoya A. Opeyemi, 'Ethnic and Religious Crises in Nigeria', in *Accord* (August 29, 2016), www.accord.org.za/ajcr-issues/ethnic-religious-crises-nigeria/ [accessed November 5, 2018].

11   Canci Haldun and Odukoya A. Opeyemi, 'Ethnic and Religious Crisis in Nigeria'.

inter-ethnic and interreligious conflicts involving numerous deaths and destructions were formally recorded in twenty three States of Nigeria.'[12] This number has definitely doubled, considering what has befallen Nigeria since the 2012 elections till date.

The tale of woes has not yet ended. The environmental degradation and human disaster is another monster that has not only affected standard of living but also claimed some lives. 'Virtually every Nigerian is vulnerable to disasters, natural or man-made. Every rainy season wind gust arising from tropical storms claim lives and property worth millions of Naira across the Country. In August 1988 for instance, 142 people died, 18,000 houses were destroyed, and 14,000 farms were swept away when Bagauda Dam collapsed following flash flood. Urban flooding such as the Ogunpa disaster claimed over 200 lives.'[13] Apart from flooding, water and air pollution have made life of the citizenry unbearable, especially people from Niger Delta area.

Most of these disasters are caused by human activities on the soil like deforestation, bush burning either by farmers or hunters, oil exploration, and industrial and domestic waste. In the beginning of his encyclical letter concerning the degradation of the earth, Pope Francis wrote: 'Praise be to you, my Lord, through our Sister, Mother Earth, who sustains and governs us, and who produces various fruit with coloured flowers and herbs. This sister now cries out to us because of the harm we have inflicted on her by our irresponsible use and abuse of goods with which God endowed her.'[14] Mother Earth is not only crying, but the negative effect of unbridled manipulation of the earth's resources is telling on humanity, especially on the poor and developing countries. Life is almost becoming unbearable in the world, and Nigeria is not exempted. Since the new administration in Nigeria came into power in 2015, the country has been in economic recession and acute inflation due to political looting of the national treasury by successive administrations. Many people are depressed, and others are dying due to conflicts, hunger, oil spillage, and other environmental

---

12   Anthony Obinna,. Confiliatory Collaboration between the Church in Africa and Europe', (June 3, 2004),1.

13   Angela K. Etuonovbe, 'Environmental Degradation in Nigeria and Human Disaster', in *Surveyors Key Role in Accelerated Development*, May 3–8, 2009, 8–9. *https:// www.fig.net/resources/proceedings/fig_proceedings/fig2009/papers/ts01d/ts01d_ etuonovbe_3386*

14   Francis, *Encyclical on Climate Change and Inequality, Laudato Si*, 1–2.

degradations. We count our woes daily because of these inhuman acts. One wonders if we are going to annihilation and extinction.

The above degrading human realities show that there is urgent need for rectifying and revaluing humanity. In many of his pastoral wrings, talks, and lectures, Archbishop Anthony J. V. Obinna argues that there is still hope for the crashing and ill-fated humanity. His assertion is based on his re-experiencing creation's original beauty on the Feast of Annunciation:

> In 1988, six years after the ruin of creation in my lived-reflective experience, I was beside myself with joy as the whole of creation re-appeared visibly around me, not far from this spot, in riveting splendour. I burst into celebration: Out of my nightly shade, I stepped out, gazed heavenward and stood arrested, By sky-blue beauty, I lowered my gaze, it was green beauty all over, I turned to the trees, it was chirping melody from coloured-spiced birds, I glanced earth-ward, my own colour-earth-colour, I shook my head in believing awe, I had caught that moment when God took a look at everything He made, it was so beautiful.[15]

This 'Upper-Room experience' fostered the birth of a new *theology of practice and reconfiliation in Christ*. In this new insight, Archbishop Anthony is of the view that the dehumanized and ripped-apart humanity can recoup her relationship with God, with one another, and with all created natures. This he affirms in the confiliatory and reconfiliatory mission of Jesus Christ.

The Theology and Practice of Reconfiliation

God has always taken the initiative to enter into a relationship with humanity. This is not because God wants relevance or because without us, he will no longer be God. He enters these relationships out of love and for our good. In the Old Testament, God entered into a relationship with Abraham: 'the Lord appeared to Abraham, and said to him, I am God Almighty, walk before me and be blameless. And I will make my covenant

---

15   Anthony J. V. Obinna, 'Confiliatory Collaboration between the Church in Africa and Europe', 6.

between me and you and will make you exceedingly numerous' (Gen 17:1–2). Humanity often breaks their relationship with God, but God's infinite mercy and love would not abandon men and women in ruins. The greatest show of love of God to us is the Incarnation. God did not only enter into a relationship as in the past, he decided to become one of us and to live with us for the purpose of saving the depraved humanity. 'Jesus is a concrete, historical, flesh-and-blood person, who, as such is known in and through his relationships: he is the Son of God, son of Mary, our Lord, brother, friend and *companero*.'[16] Through his confiliatory death on the cross, he made us fellow sons and daughters to His Father; and through it, Christ reunited us as brothers and sisters (reconfiliation).

Our inhuman behaviours negate this confiliatory and reconfiliatory mission of Christ. 'Taking off from the inhumanity of the *Diala-Osu* caste system and human sacrifices to spirits in Igboland, which increased exponentially. I come to realize how Nigerians on trade-routes looking towards North Africa and Nigerians living in the Atlantic Ocean Coast moved from being initially unwilling victims of Arab slave-raiders and European slave-traders to becoming willing middlemen in the terrible and systematic enslavement of humans in Igboland and other parts of Africa.'[17] This act is abominable and condemned by this new theological insight. 'Reconfiliation stresses the dignity of every human person, of every son, of every daughter irrespective of hurts and ill-feelings. It abhors violence to the sacredness and preciousness of the person.'[18] On the other hand, human woes, divisions, and devastations in the world seem endless. The theology and practice of reconfiliation calls for caution and challenges all, especially the church and her ministers, to take a clue from Jesus, who has started the work of confiliation and reconfiliation.

Pope Francis in '*Laudato Si*' put emphasis on the need to heal the wounds and division humanity has inflicted in the world. He called for an urgent step to address the issue of climate change that was caused by unguarded industrial revolution by developed nations. He also called for addressing the inequality among persons and between rich and poor

---

16   Roberto S. Goizueta, *Cominemos Con Jesus; Toward a Hispanic/Latino Theology of Accompaniment* (Maryknoll, New York: Orbis Books, 1995), 67.

17   Anthony J. V. Obinna, 'Collaboration between the Church in Africa and Europe', 1.

18   Anthony J. V. Obinna, 'Confiliating Americans: Recti-valuing One Another (2)' The Theology of Reconfiliation (talk delivered at Beeson Divinity School Sanford University, Birmingham, Alabama, USA), 4.

nations. 'Inequality affects not only individuals but entire countries; it compels us to consider an ethics of international relations.'[19] This is a wake-up call for the restoration and rebuilding, as well as recti-valuing of humanity and the degraded environment.

The act of reuniting us as brothers and sisters (reconfiliation) and recti-valuing humanity was the thrust of Jesus's mission on earth. This was God's design in the **Theo-Filio** initiative—God the Son restoring us back to our sonship and daughterhood to God's Kingship in the Incarnation. In Incarnation, Jesus reveals not only who God is (Love) but also who we are—relational beings with dignity. In his life, death, and resurrection, Jesus Christ made us sharers in his Sonship of God the Father. 'Jesus said to her, do not hold on to me, because I have not yet ascended to the Father. But go to my brothers and say to them, I am ascending to my Father and your Father, to my God and your God' (John 20:17). By his vicarious death, he reconciled us with the Father and with one another.

In the confiliation and reconfiliation dynamics, we still have hope for the broken world and humanity. Obinna strongly affirms this as 'my own re-experience of the Sacred a pre-nihilistic and post-nihilistic African Catholic encourages me to confirm and share the new sense of the Sacred which the person of Jesus Christ has inaugurated and made available for the good of all creation and all creation and all humanity'.[20]

The live experience of the creation on the Feast of Annunciation by Archbishop Anthony Obinna, which gave birth to this new theology, has a deep spiritual and theological tone. It means that God is still close to us communicating his love through the Holy Spirit to clear our worries and doubts. God still loves humanity even in their brokenness. God has created all things anew in the Incarnation (God-made-man through Mary by the power of the Holy Spirit). It could also mean that since creation is from one source, we are therefore brothers and sisters and Incarnation gathers all nations, races, tribes, or clans together. In him the chasm between the poor, marginalized, and the rich is bridged. 'There is no longer Jew or Greek, there is no longer slave or free, there is no longer male or female, for all of you are one in Christ Jesus' (Gal. 3:28). In view of this, 'the

---

19   Francis, *Encyclical on Climate Change and Inequality: Laudato Si*, 51.

20   Anthony J. V. Obinna, 'African Cultures and Development: The Rectifying Challenge', *The First Colloquium-Culture and Development in Theology* (Abijan, Ivory Coast, Sept. 27 to October 1, 2010), 13.

proposal is that Re-Confiliation and Confiliatory collaboration, be our life-engaging and life-orienting dynamo in making headway and sense in the varied family settings of our lives in the Church and society, in Africa and in our relations with the rest of the world'.[21] In the confiliatory dynamics, Archbishop Anthony strongly believes that 'by becoming sons and daughters of God and Humanity in Him we reposition ourselves to rectify our relationship with God, with one another and with the earth'.[22]

The reconfiliatory mission of Jesus Christ did not stop with his death and ascension. There was a great commission before His ascension. 'All authority in heaven and on earth has been given to me. Go you therefore and make disciples of all nations, baptizing them in the name of the Father, and of the Son and of the Holy Spirit, and teaching them to obey everything that I have commanded you' (Matt. 28:18–20). This empowerment forms the missionary trust for the church, the clergy, religious, and laity. All have a duty to perform in the healing process of the broken humanity and the earth.

Pastoral Implications/Challenges of Theology and Practice of Confiliation and Reconfiliation

Those who talk about God must also talk to God, as the saying goes. Theology is not a mere set of theories meant only for intellectual exercise. Even though it does not exclude intellectual reflection, it has a lot to do with praxis. Emmanuel Lartey observed that 'practical theology is not satisfied simply to end in an aesthetic statement but rather is transformational, aiming to make some difference in people's understanding and actual life situation. Practical theology is not only concerned with propositions and logic but also finds place for human emotions, the symbolic and even the irrational in addressing all of human experience.'[23] Christianity is not a mere theological ideology to be propagated; rather, it is a way of life. It is life to be lived and practiced daily in our different cultural settings. Terrence Tilley remarks in this regard in the following words: 'We Practice

---

21 Anthony J. V. Obinna, 'Confiliatory Collaboration between the Church in Africa and Europe', 2.

22 Anthony J. V. Obinna, 'African Cultures and Development: The Rectifying Challenge',16.

23 Emmanuel Lartey, *Pastoral Theology in an Intercultural World* (Eugene, Oregon: Wipf and Stock Publishers, 2006), 18–19.

our faith; faith is lived.'[24] The Apostle James had earlier testified to this claim, saying, 'For just as the body without the spirit is dead, so faith without works is also dead' (James 2:26).

How do we put into practice our religious beliefs and teachings? In the midst of the broken humanity ripped off by divisions and discrimination, wars and violence, how can the church play her role in such situation? How can the clergy and religious, even the laity, bridge these gaps and restore human dignity, equality, and a fair playing ground for all? What can we do for the black and white; *osu, diala*, and *ume*; poor and rich nations to see themselves as one global family and from the same God? All these are the pastoral implications and challenges of theology of practice of reconfiliation.

The church in her missionary role of evangelization has to rise up and preach against the great anomaly taking place in the world. It must rise to build bridges to heal the division between the rich and poor nations; the racism at every level between white and black; the *osu, ume,* and *diala* syndrome in Igboland; poor and rich; and low class, middle class, and high-class polarizations. It has to see for a genuine human development for a healthy community life built on love, equity, unity, justice, and peace—a community where the invisible and voiceless can be seen and heard. This will be more effective if the church plays a leading role in her faith communities.

The reconfiliation that Christ ensues may not have an impact if there is no genuine reconciliation among humans. 'Reconciliation, however, is unachievable without justice.'[25] For instance, during the Nigerian Civil War, about three million Biafrans were slaughtered by the Nigerian soldiers and all their means of livelihood destroyed. There has not been proper reconciliation, reconstruction, and rehabilitation of the people by the Nigerian government. Desmond Tutu captured the scenario well: 'Forgiving and being reconciled are not about pretending that things are other than they are. It is not patting one another at the back and turning a blind eye to the wrong. True reconciliation exposes the awfulness, the abuse, the pain, the degradation, the truth.'[26] The consequence of failing to do the above-

---

24   Terrence W. Tilley, 'Practicing the Faith; Tradition in a Practical Theology', in *Invitation to Practical Theology*, ed. Claire E. Wolfteich (New York/Mahawah, NJ: Paulist Press, 2014), 90.

25   Yvon C. Elenga, 'Toward a New Social Configuration', in *Reconciliation Justice and Peace*, ed. Agbonkhianmeghe E. Orabator (Maryknoll, New York, NY: Oribis Books, 2011), 89.

26   Desmond Tutu, *No Future without Forgiveness* (New York, London Toronto: Image

mentioned is the continuous agitations we see in Nigeria today by various groups. The church, 'founded on the love of the Redeemer, contributes toward the reign of justice and charity within the borders of a nation and between nations',[27] but more needs to be done as we are challenged by the theology of practice. 'While the Church has been addressing these issues for quite some time, it has not done so in a systematic and sustained manner, and definitely not at all levels.'[28]

The Church as agent of reconfiliation can do more through her hierarchy. For instance, in Nigeria, it can form a postconflict commission through the office of Justice, Peace, and Development Commission (JDPC). It should speak out to condemn all forms divisions, discriminatory behaviors, and humiliating treatment on people and on the environment. The church should compel the government to dismantle the unjust social structures used as the channel to perpetrate injustice on the vulnerable groups. Injustice is the root cause of environmental degradation, wars, and conflicts both religious and ethnic. If there is no injustice, there will be no human degradation.

The clergy, religious, and laity as well should not only preach love and equality; they should try more to identify with the poor, the discriminated, and the invisible in the society. This is what Jesus represents to all: he cured the sick; ate, drank, and mingled with the rejected; and reintegrated them into the society (Matt. 8:4). In this way, he restored their sense of human dignity. The spirit of confiliation and reconfiliation is breaking barriers of discrimination like *osu, ume* and *diala* syndrome; preaching equality of human; and restoring our degraded humanity. Archbishop Anthony Obinna expressed his commitment when he said, 'I had to break up with and break out of all conscious, reflexive and subconscious attachment to each and all three groups and their fears. By a combination of God's grace in Christ and by continued self-probing, I found a new and unbelievable freedom and courage which I am offering to Igbos once enslaved by Igbo-religio-cultural divides. Through pastoral rituals of filiation and confiliation, through public enlightenment on Radio and Television, through preaching ordination of priests, consecration of Rev. Sisters, celebration of marriages

---

Doubleday, 1999), 270.

27 Yvon C. Elenga, 'Toward a Social Configuration', 87.

28 Odomaro Mubangizi, 'Agent of Reconciliation, Justice, and Peace', in *Reconciliation, Justice and Peace*, 114.

without taking divisive identities into consideration, and through broad-based social programs, the reconfiliation of humanity already established and achieved in the life and ministry of Jesus Christ is causing a positive revolution in thinking of one another and in relating to one another.'[29] It is aberration of Christian values if we discriminate. It yields no positive result if we claim to be one Nigeria still. We cannot live in any part of the country and be treated equal. Christians are the visible representative of Christ's mission, and we are challenged to tackle frontally these problems that Jesus solved.

Evaluating Theology and Practice of Reconfiliation/Conclusion

The theology of reconfiliation is both theocentric and Christocentric because it is anchored on God's love and his Son, Jesus Christ, who took flesh by the power of the Holy Spirit in the womb of the Virgin Mary to make us sharers in his sonship to the Father (confiliation), thereby reconciling us with God and with one another as one family again (reconfiliation). This theology emphasises the love God has for humanity, which is visibly expressed in the Incarnation and culminated in the death and resurrection of Jesus Christ that restored our brokenness with God and with one another. This theology of practice calls to mind the sacredness of human life, which reaffirms the fundamental human right and dignity as an image of God. It is ethically and morally evil to abuse, discriminate, or dehumanize a person in any form no matter the race, colour, or gender. Confiliation brings us together as brothers and sisters, sharing in the Sonship of Jesus Christ. If we are fellow brothers and sisters (cofilians), we are one family of global community and should be given the same treatment.

Theology and the practice of reconfiliation is a call to revalue and rectifiliate one another in the reconfiliatory mission of Jesus Christ. It is, therefore, a call to advance the mission of Christ not only by the clergy and religious but by all humans. It calls for justice to all, freedom for the oppressed, and hope for the invisible and voiceless, the poor, and the marginalized. It is a new way of reconciling with God and with one

---

29   Anthon J. V. Obinna, 'Confiliating Americans, Recti-valuing One Another (2): A Theology and Practice of Reconfiliation' (2003), 5.

another. It brings to our focus the great work Jesus Christ did in restoring us back to our status. It is a great reminder that humanity is one family of God. The pedagogy of this theology—which includes but is not limited to pastoral rituals, preaching in the church, ordinations, consecration, marriages, public enlightenment on radio and television—is commendable and simple. It has to be emulated and applied easily as the case may be.

Pastorally, if we are to put in practice the new insight of this theology, we will have committed priests who will advance the mission of Christ on earth with the spirit of humility and sacrifice. We will have a situation where both clergy and laity will see themselves as one family, working for the actualization of God's kingdom. We will have a community of faithful and society where love and justice reign supreme. It will establish a society where every human person is respected and honoured regardless of ethnicity, nationality, and gender. It will encourage our being close to God and engendering holiness because emphasis will shift to those values that promote and respect life. To build a new world and new Nigeria, we need to embrace the theology of practice of reconfiliation.

Your Grace, the fruits of twenty-five years of your episcopal stewardship pastorally, morally, and intellectually speak volumes. Posterity will always remember you. Your new theological insights and terms will always resonate in the world of theological discussion. May God grant you more grace to forge ahead.

References

- *Catechism of the Catholic Church*. 1ˢᵗ ed. New York: Image Book Doubleday, 1995.
- Elenga, Yvon C. 'Toward a New Social Configuration.' in *Reconciliation Justice and Peace*, edited by Agbonkhianmeghe E. Orabator. Maryknoll, New York: Oribis Books, 2011.
- Etuonovbe, Angela K. 'Environmental Degradation in Nigeria and Human Disaster.' In *Surveyors Key Role in Accelarated Development*, May 3–8, 2009. https://www.fig.net/resources/proceedings/fig_proceedings/fig2009/papers/ts01d/ts01d_e_tuonovbe_3386.

- Firth, Francis. 'Saint Athanasius: On the Incarnation of the Word.' In *The Canadian Catholic Review* (March 1997).

- Francis, *Laudato Si* (encyclical on climate change and inequality). May 24, 2015, Brooklyn. London: Melville House, 2015.

- Goizueta, Roberto S. *Cominemos Con Jesus; Toward a Hispanic/Latino Theology of Accompaniment.* Maryknoll, New York: Orbis Books, 1995.

- Haldun, Canci and Odukoya A. Opeyemi. 'Ethnic and Religious Crisis in Nigeria.' In *Accord.* August 29, 2016. www.accord.org. za/ajcr-issues/ethnic-religious-crises-nigeria/

- Lartey, Emmanuel. *Pastoral Theology in an Intercultural World.* Eugene, Oregon: Wipf and Stock Publishers, 2006.

- Mubangizi, Odomaro. 'Agent of Reconciliation, Justice, and Peace.' In *Reconciliation, Justice and Peace*, edited by Agbonkhianmeghe Orobator. Maryknoll, New York: Orbis Books, 2011.

- Obinna, Anthony. 'African Cultures and Development: The Rectifying Challenge.' The First Colloquium—*Culture and Development in Theology*, Abidjan, Ivory Coast, September 27 to October 1, 2010.

- Obinna, Anthony. 'Confiliatory Collaboration between the Church in Africa and Europe.' Talk delivered in June 3, 2004.

- Obinna, Anthony. 'Confiliating Americans, Recti-valuing One Another (2): A Theology and Practice of Reconfiliation.' Lecture delivered at Beeson Divinity School, Sanford University, Birmingham, Alabama, USA.

- *The New Oxford Annotated Bible, New Revised Standard Version.* 4th ed. New York: Oxford Press, 1998.

- Tilley, Terrence. 'Practicing the Faith: Tradition in a Practical Theology.' In *Invitation to Practical Theology*, edited by Claire E. Wolfteich. New York/Mahawah, NJ: Paulist Press, 2014.

- Tutu, Desmond. *No Future Without Forgiveness.* New York, London, Toronto: Image Doubleday, 1999.

Chapter Thirteen

Strategic Orientation on Effective Interpersonal Pastoral Communication Skills in Parish Administration

Boniface Nkem Anusiem

Introduction

Organizations are people,[1] and the church is no different. Furthermore, organizations don't have needs nor feelings, but people do. People influence the ways organizations function through their proactive interactions, in addition to some of the organizational components. The organizational interaction, in turn, builds on the interpersonal communication and dispositions of the individuals in the organization. According to Karl Weick, interpersonal communication is the essence of organizations because it creates structures that affect what is achievable and by whom.[2]

---

1   Renee Robinson, 'COMM 7790: Instructor's Notes on Theories and Communication Phenomenon: Communicative Organization, Week 3'. College of Communication and the Arts, Department of Graduate Studies (New Jersey, NY: Seton Hall University, 2018).
2   Karl Weick, 'Organizational Culture as a Source of High Reliability', *California Management Review* 29, no. 3 (1987): 112–127.

Religion is essentially communication-based. It is therefore difficult to be religious without being communicative. In the Christian faith, God the Son is identifiable as the communicator par excellence[3] (*Communio et Progressio* § 11). In fact, communication is an essential characteristic of God *(Ecclesia in Africa* no. 71).[4] The entire Bible is essentially an advanced communication text with profound expressions of lateral and vertical communication activities and compelling narratives that have served as scripts for numerous dramas, movies, illustrations, and paintings. All religions exist to communicative values, doctrines, and practices to the adherents through instructions that could be written, orally transmitted, or received through symbols that are discernible as communication texts.

The purpose of this work is to develop a strategic orientation programme on effective interpersonal, pastoral communication skills in parish ministry. The idea is to equip pastors and pastoral collaborators with the necessary tools to communicate in profoundly humane and interpersonal ways beyond the current imploding misuse of modern means of social communication. The work would further serve as a practical recommendation for relational problems among people in the pastoral team and would also establish the parameters for strategic orientation program on effective interpersonal communication skills in parish communities.

Interpersonal Communication

Beyond the assertion that communication involves the passing of information from one person to another Keith Davis and Wilbur Schramm thought about a transaction between the sender and the receiver that brings them together for interactivity and sharing.[5] We shall understand

---

3   The Second Vatican Council, 'Pastoral Instruction, *Communio et progression: On the means of social communication*, 23rd May 1971', available at http://www.vatican.va/ roman_curia/pontifical_councils/pccs/documents/rc_pc_pccs_doc_23051971_communio_ en.html [accessed December 3, 2018].

4   John Paul II, *Post-Synodal Apostolic Exhortation, Ecclesia in Africa, to the Bishops Priests and Deacons Men and Women Religious and All the Lay Faithful on The Church in Africa and Its Evangelising Mission Towards the Year 2000* (Vatican City: Liberia Editrice Vaticana, 1995).

5   Keith Davis, 'Management Communication and the Grapevine', *Harvard Business Review* (September–October 1953): 43–49. See also Wilbur Schramm, 'Procedure and Effects of Mass Communication', in *Mass Media and Education*, ed. N. B. Henry (Chicago, IL: University of Chicago Press, 1954).

communication in this exposition as the sharing of ideas and meanings between individuals within an interactive context.

Communication is interpersonal when it involves two intentional and proactive individuals who switch places as senders and receivers in the same interactive framework. According to Peter Hartely, interpersonal communication is unavoidable as it involves the creation and sharing of meaning, which lubricates human interaction, though intrapersonal communication (self-communication) precedes interpersonal communication. The latter forms the foreground for small group and organizational communication.[6]

Interpersonal communication as a dyadic interaction is fundamental in the pastoral ministry of priests and their pastoral collaborators. The daily activities of the parish go beyond the ministry from the pulpit, which could qualify as small group communication.[7] They are also more profound than organizational communication, which involves the process through which groups of people connected by a shared mission, sets of goals, and culture design and share relevant information to achieve organizational goals and generate collective meaning.[8]

Modules for the Strategic Orientation Program

The orientation is designed in modular form to provide a systematic learning process that would be in-depth, trackable, and repeatable. The following highpoints are desirable for the orientation program.

Rationale

The purpose of the modules is to give professional guidelines on how priests and pastoral collaborators could rediscover themselves, their sociocultural environment, and others by building and maintaining effective interpersonal communication. The modules are educative as they

---

6   Peter Hartely, *Interpersonal Communication* (New York, NY: Routledge, 1993).

7   Stewart L. Tubbs, *A System of Approach to Small Group Interaction*, 11th edition (Pennsylvania: McGraw-Hill Education, 2011).

8   Theodore Avtgis, Andrew Rancer, and Corey Liberman, *Organizational Communication: Strategy for Success*, 2nd edition (Iowa: Kendall Hunt Publishing, 2012).

focus on developing communication skills that would be at the service of interpersonal relationship and for more fruitful pastoral ministry.

Explications and Implications of the Modules

The modules show an enlistment of vital elements that would help to structure how the priests and pastoral collaborators should interact with one another and with other people on lateral and vertical lines, especially in face-to-face but also in mediated communication. The awareness of these vital elements would have enormous implications for the future of interpersonal relationship and communication in the parish ministry. Priests and pastoral collaborators would learn how to be intentional and relational in their engagement with one another and others while paying attention to some intrinsic and extrinsic variables.

Organization/Participation

The orientation program would engage the various diocesan/archdiocesan departments of communication using skilled communicators or specialists in interpersonal communication. The program would be open to all priests and key pastoral collaborators like catechists and parish administrative secretaries and assistants. The reason for the broad engagement is to get all the members of the parish administration to a common learning ground with a unified reference source.

Frequency/Next Steps

The strategic orientation program on effective interpersonal communication would be a quarterly engagement and should be one of the certifications for parish ministering priests and pastoral collaborators. Every quarter would host two sessions: one at the beginning and the other at the end of the quarter. The first orientation would be the basics, while subsequent ones would gradually take the participants to the advanced steps that would be more of the evaluations of the participant's standing with the basic modules and the directions for the future. New persons in the pastoral team would undergo a special orientation on the basic modules and proceed to the advanced modules.

Conceptualization and Presentation of the Orientation Program Modules

Self-understanding. Communication is foremost intrapersonal before it becomes interpersonal. Intrapersonal communication involves self-talk and inner speech, which Donna Vocates, Roberts, Edwards, and Baker see as the conscious and unconscious processing of messages through the windows of self-perception.[9] Understanding the self requires honest attention and analysis of one's personality type, attitudes, and aptitudes. The following highpoints would constitute this module, which would leverage theories like Johari window by Joseph Luft and Harry Ingham,[10] Maslow's Hierarchy of Needs,[11] and the implicit personality theory by Cronbach:[12]

Personality-assessment
Self-concept development
Self-disclosure
Self-awareness
Self-esteem
Self-improvement

Message and messaging. A message in communication refers to the idea, meaning, or value a sender conveys to a receiver through a channel.

---

9   Donna R. Vocates, *Interpersonal Communication: Different Voices, Different Minds* (New Jersey, NJ: Lawrence Erlbaum Associate Publications, 1994). See also C. Roberts, R. Edwards, and L. Baker, *Intrapersonal Communication Processes* (Scottsdale, Arizona: Gorsuch Scarisbrick Publications, 1987).

10 Johari window is a technique that helps people better understand their relationship with themselves and others. This model of relationship was created by psychologists Joseph Luft and Harrington Ingham in 1955. Cf. Joseph Luft and Harry Ingham, *The Johari Window as a Graphic Model of Interpersonal Awareness* (Los Angeles, University of California, Proceedings of the Western Training Laboratory in Group Development, 1955).

11 Abraham H. Maslow, *Motivation and Personality* (New York, NY: Harper, 1943).

12 Lee J. Cronbach, 'The Counsellor's Problems from the Perspective of Communication Theory', in *New Perspectives in Counselling*, ed. Vivian H. Hewer (Minneapolis, MN: University of Minnesota Press, 1955).

The sender of a message follows the process of encoding the idea or meaning through a channel, and the receiver decodes the message to derive the meaning the sender wishes to convey.[13] From the above description, it is essential for the message to be adequately encoded to make the appropriate sense at the decoding end. The message and messaging module would include the following elements orbiting the goal-driven message production theory:[14]

Message content
Message context
Message tonality
Message delivery
Message intention
Message interpretation

Kinesics. Kinesics deals with the impact of body gestures in the process of interpersonal communication. According to Ray Birdwhistell (1952), kinesics includes facial expressions, posture, visible arm, and body movements that are interpreted as expressing some thoughts intentions and emotions.[15] Essentially, kinesics takes care of nonverbal clues in communication. The following typologies are reflected in kinesics:

Eye contact
Haptics (touch)
Proxemics (personal vs. social space)
Posture and mirroring

Listening skills. A good conversationalist is not the one who talks more than others during an interaction but the one who attends most. For Allison Daniel, active listening is vital for the creation of excellent communication.[16] Listening is primarily a skill that could enhance

---

13   David Berlo, *Process of Communication: An Introduction to Theory and Practice* (California, CA: Harcourt School, 1960).

14   James P. Dillard, 'A Goal-Driven Model of Interpersonal Influence,' in *Seeking compliance: The Production of Interpersonal Influence Messages* (Scottsdale, AZ: Gorsuch Scarisbrick, 1990).

15   Ray Birdwhistell, *Introduction to Kinesics: An Annotation System for Analysis of Body Motion and Gesture* (Louisville, KY: University of Louisville, 1952).

16   Allison Daniel, 'Active Listening Is Key to Good Communication', in *Organizational*

interpersonal communication when it is acquired. This module would draw mainly from the frameworks of emotional and social intelligence.[17] The module would consider the following elements:

Attending
Understanding
Remembering
Rephrasing
Responding

Interpersonal communication contexts and social variables. Communication takes place in a context, and the communication context could potentially affect the effectiveness of the interaction between communicating individuals. Significantly, every organization represents an enculturated context.

Further considerations would introduce the impact of some social and cultural variables on the effectiveness of interpersonal communication. The prevailing theoretical frameworks in this module would include organizational culture[18] and organizational structuration theory.[19] The module would explore the interaction and friction between individuals' socializing culture and the workplace culture.

Channels of interpersonal communication. The choice of the channel of communication has an impact on the effectiveness of the interaction, especially in dyadic contexts. The obtrusion of communication technology is gradually changing the landscape of interpersonal communication in organizational contexts.[20] In the contemporary organizational setting,

---

Behaviour, 6 (Homewood, IL: JAI Press, 2017), 191–233, retrieved from http://pearce. caah.clemson.edu/active-listening-is-key-to-good-communication/.

17 D. Goleman, *Emotional Intelligence: Why It Matters More than IQ* (New York, NY: Bantam Books, 1995). See also D. Goleman, *Social Intelligence: The New Science of Human Relationships* (New York, NY: Bantam Books, 2006).

18 E. H. Schein, 'Culture: The Missing Concept in Organization Studies',. *Administrative Science Quarterly* 41, no. 2 (1996): 229–240.

19 A. Giddens, *New Rules of Sociological Method* (New York, NY: Basic, 1976).

20 Boniface Anusiem, 'Followership Perception of Effective Leadership Communication' (unpublished manuscript, Department of Graduate Studies, College of Communication and the Arts, Seton Hall University, New Jersey, 2018).

interpersonal communication could be face-to-face or mediated by other channels like email, letters, memos, handbills, and others. Media richness theory would be very relevant in this module.[21]

Possible Limitations

Organizations differ regarding work engagement, scheduling, and timelines. These elements pose some potential limitations to the orientation program. Furthermore, it could get some pushback from some priests and pastoral collaborators who may find it too formal and tasking in addition to their job descriptions. The clustering of priests and pastoral collaborators in a joint orientation may potentially pose a problem as past experiences and conflicts could raise tempers and learning could be impaired.

Furthermore, the training could be cost effective as parishes would support the diocesan/archdiocesan departments of communication to settle the overhead costs, which would include lunch breaks and stationaries in addition to personal costs like transportation. The diocese/archdiocese could make a special budgeting for the orientation program, and to reduce costs, they could be linked up with the pastoral council plenary sessions.

Conclusion

Beyond the limitations, effective interpersonal communication is a desirable skill that every parish community should explore to help the priests and pastoral collaborators understand themselves more and realize their pastoral goals more seamlessly. An orientation program on effective interpersonal communication skills would help individuals to undertake the needful introspective examination of their personalities and work to understand others and the workplace environment more proactively.

---

21   Richard L. Daft and R. H. Lengel, 'Information Richness: A New Approach to Managerial Behavior and Organizational Design', in *Research in Organisational Behaviour*, eds. Larry L. Cummings and Berry M. Staw, vol. 6, 554–571 (Greenwich, CT: JAI Press, 1984), 191–223.

References

- Anusiem, B. 'Followership Perception of Effective Leadership Communication.' Unpublished manuscript, Department of Graduate Studies, College of Communication and the Arts, Seton Hall University, New Jersey, 2018.
- Baxter, L. A. 'Relationships as Dialogues: Personal Relationships.' In *Dialogue: Theorizing Differences in Communication*, edited by R. Anderson, L. A. Baxter, and K. N. Cissna. Thousand Oaks, CA: Sage Publications, 2004.
- Birdwhistell, R. *Introduction to Kinesics: An Annotation System for Analysis of Body Motion and Gesture.* Louisville, KY: University of Louisville, 1952.
- Cronbach, L. J. 'The Counsellor's Problems from the Perspective of Communication Theory.' In *New Perspectives in Counseling*, edited by Vivian H. Hewer. Minneapolis: University of Minnesota Press, 1955.
- Daft, R. L. and R. H. Lengel. 'Information Richness: A New Approach to Managerial Behavior and Organizational Design.' In *Research in Organisational Behaviour*, ed. L. L. Cummings and B. M. Staw, vol. 6, 1984.
- Daniel, A. 'Active Listening is Key to Good Communication.' In *Organizational Behaviour* 6, 191–233. Homewood, IL: JAI Press, 2017. Retrieved from http://pearce.caah.clemson.edu/active-listening-is-key-to-good-communication/
- Davis, K. 'Management Communication and the Grapevine.' *Havard Business Review*, September–October, 1953, 43–49.
- Dillard, J. P. 'A Goal-Driven Model of Interpersonal Influence.' In *Seeking Compliance: The Production of Interpersonal Influence Messages*. Scottsdale, AZ: Gorsuch Scarisbrick, 1990.
- Giddens, A. *New Rules of Sociological Method.* New York: Basic, 1976.
- Goleman, D. *Emotional Intelligence: Why It Matters More Than IQ.* New York: Bantam Books, 1995.
- Goleman, D. *Social Intelligence: The New Science of Human Relationships.* New York, NY: Bantam Books, 2006.

- Hartely, P. *Interpersonal Communication*. New York, NY: Routledge, 1993.
- Maslow, A. H. *Motivation and Personality*. New York, NY: Harper, 1995.
- Pope John Paul II. *Ecclesia in Africa: On the Church in Africa and Its Evangelizing Mission Towards the Year 2000*. Vatican: Libreria Editrice Vaticana, 1995.
- Roberts, C., R. Edwards, and L. Baker. *Intrapersonal Communication Processes*. Scottsdale, Arizona: Gorsuch Scarisbrick Publications, 1987.
- Robinson, R. 'COMM 7790: Instructor's Notes on Theories and Communication Phenomenon: Communicative Organization, Week 3.' College of Communication and the Arts, Department of Graduate Studies, Seton Hall University, New Jersey, NJ, 2018.
- Schein, E. H. 'Culture: The Missing Concept in Organization Studies.' *Administrative Science Quarterly*, 41, no. 2, 1996, 229–240.
- Schramm, W. 'Procedure and Effects of Mass Communication.' In *Mass Media and Education*, edited by N. B. Henry. Chicago, IL: University of Chicago Press, 1954.
- The Second Vatican Council. *Communio et Progression: On the Means of Social Communication*. 1971. Retrieved from http://www.vatican.va/roman_curia/pontifical_councils/pccs/documents/rc_pc_pccs_doc_23051971_communio_en.html. Accessed February 2019.
- Vocates, D. R. *Interpersonal Communication: Different Voices, Different Minds*. Hillsdale, New Jersey: Lawrence Erlbaum Associate Publications, 1994.
- Walter, H. L. 'The Emails in the Clinic Initial Services Department.' In *Case Studies for Organizational Communication: Understanding Communication Processes*, 2nd ed., edited by J. Keyton and Shockley-Zalabak. Los Angeles, CA: Roxbury Publishing Company, 2006.
- Weick, K. E. 'Organizational Culture as a Source of High Reliability.' *California Management Review*, 29, no. 3, 1987, 112–127.

Section Four

Philosophy, Politics, Postcolonial Reading and Psychology

Chapter Fourteen

A. J. V. Obinna's Concept of 'Filiation': A Resource for Political/Social Philosophy and Critical Theory

Donald Mark C. Ude

Abstract

This paper explores A. J. V. Obinna's idea of filiation, with a view to showing how it could become a resource for political/social philosophy and critical theory. Filiation, the paper maintains, is a veritable political/social philosophy and critical theory insofar as it provides inspiration for political/social behavior and furnishes a framework for the critique of society. The key argument is that a theory that underscores the kinship of all humanity in Christ could create and inspire a more responsible and solicitous sociopolitical atmosphere. The paper further argues that filiation, as a resource for critical theory, holds out the vision of the filiated society, not only as the standard or ideal for society but also as the framework to which all social critique must refer. In line with this claim, the vital question for all social critique becomes the question of the extent to which members of a given society love and value one another as brothers and sisters. A shortfall on this score would most assuredly be diagnosed as a filiation-deficiency, a social pathology that stands in need of a recti-filiation. The arguments sustained in this paper are all the more enriched with a brief discussion of A. J. V. Obinna's practical witnessing to the philosophy of filiation. In the author's judgment, Obinna's consistent role as the conscience of the politics of Imo State and beyond, his vehement denunciation of the *diala/osu* divide, and a number of archdiocesan charities and initiatives are certainly inspired by the *philosophy of filiation*.

Key Words: A. J. V. Obinna, Filiation, Political/Social Philosophy, Critical Theory, Society

1. Introduction

Filiation may rightly be regarded as one of A. J. V. Obinna's central ideas and the key that unlocks much of his theologizing. It is, as it were, the 'nucleus' around which such cognates concepts as confiliation, refiliation, cofiliation, re-con-filiation, and a host of others revolve. In its most basic sense, filiation, according to Obinna, is the simple state or fact of 'belonging as a child, a son or a daughter to a parent, to an institution or an organization'.[1] But beyond this basic fact of filial belongingness to a person or institution lies the deeper sense, namely, the sonship or daughtership of the entire humanity to God—Christ—the *Chi* 'who is both the creator and owner of humans and all creatures'.[2] Obinna's idea of filiation thus belongs to this deeper realm, a realm that necessarily situates it in Christ (*Chi*) and the twin events of Creation and Redemption. *Filiation* is a concept not only steeped in theology for the 'church-religious context'; it has also been employed in 'wider reflection ... in the context of the human family',[3] Obinna notes.

---

1   Anthony J.V. Obinna, *Confiliating Americans: Recti-valuing One Another*, 3. This pamphlet contains the text of a paper delivered by A. J. V. Obinna in Sanford University Alabama, USA. All references to this paper conform to the page number of the pamphlet format printed by Assumpta Press, Owerri.

2   Anthony J.V. Obinna, 'Celebrating the Gift of Creation—A Chi-Christic Persuasion', 14. This is a keynote address at the Thirty-First Annual Conference of the Catholic Theological Association of Nigeria, March 2016.

3   Anthony J. V. Obinna, 'Confiliating Americans: Recti-valuing One Another', 3.

In this paper, I explore its relevance to political philosophy and critical social theory. I argue that *filiation* is at once a political/social philosophy and a critical social theory insofar as it provides some inspiration for political behavior and furnishes useful resources for a critique of society's unjust structures. With respect to political/social philosophy, I propose that a notion that underlines the kinship of all humans could constitute the theoretical foundation for responsible and altruistic sociopolitical behaviors. Regarding critical theory, I argue that it holds out the vision of the filiated society as a yardstick or framework on which all social critique must be based. In this case, the vital question that every society must confront becomes the question of the extent to which it is filiated, that is, the extent to which individuals accept one another as brothers and sisters of the same Father-God. Any shortcoming in this regard is thus diagnosed as a social pathology that must be rectifiliated. Obinna has already pointed in this direction when he critiques the Igbo *diala-osu* caste system, taking hold of the fact of filiation of all humanity in Christ-Chi.[4] But this critique of society and politics must be enunciated in greater details and, with some philosophical rigor, so that *filiation* may rightly take its place in political/social philosophy and critical theory.

I proceed as follows. First, I attempt a brief description of the notion of filiation in Obinna's thought. Next, I provide, in a nutshell, the thrust of political philosophy and critical social theory. Thereupon, I show how *filiation* constitutes a useful resource for political philosophy and the critique of society. Finally, I briefly outline Obinna's personal witnessing to the *philosophy of filiation.* Here, I explore his consistent role as a 'gadfly' (in the positive sense) in the politics of Imo State and beyond, his proactive measures against the *diala/osu* divide, and some archdiocesan charities and programs that I judge to have been inspired by the philosophy of filiation.

Filiation and Cognate Concepts in Obinna's Thought

As has been noted earlier, the idea of filiation occupies a vital place in Obinna's thought. It is a fulcrum around which much of his theology (published and yet-to-be-published) revolves, and perhaps it is the

---

4   Ibid., 7–10.

backdrop against which other theological ideas of his could be situated. In the sense in which he uses it, 'filiation' refers to the fact of our being sons and daughters of God and brothers/sisters with one another in and through Christ, our Brother. In other words, this filial relationship is made possible in and through Christ, with whom we share the same Father-God. Filiation is thus a concept that represents our belongingness to God in Christ.

But this fact of belongingness (as sons/daughters) to God has nuances that intrinsically incorporate modes of standing in relationship with God and our neighbors—hence the 'con-', 'co-', and other prefixes that are conjoined with 'filiation': 'In my wider reflection on filiation in the context of the human family as well as in the church-religious context, words like **re-filiation, confiliation, cofiliation, defiliation, recti-filiation** and **re-con-filiation** have surfaced.'[5] These prefixes indeed point to the fact that our experience of God as Father bears some immediate implications for our relationship with other humans.

The Latin roots of the prefixes signal the state/situation applicable to the individual at any given moment vis-à-vis 'filiation'. At any given moment, an individual or a group of individuals may be said to be confiliated, reconfiliated, defiliated, etc. as the case may be. The following citation captures it all:

> Re-filiation would mean restoration to the status of son or daughter. Confiliation would mean a mutual share in the status of son or daughter from a common kinship or stock. Confiliation would imply a reciprocal recognition of equal sonship or daughtership. De-filiation would mean a refusal or denial of sonship or daughtership. Reconfiliation would imply a return to the right or deserved relationship as son or daughter. Re-con-filiation would mean the reconstitution or re-establishment of the status of son or daughter to any person whatsoever. It would also mean that con-joining or new-kinning of humans into fellow sons and daughters in equal dignity.[6]

The above passage brings out, in one fell swoop, most of the important elements of filiation. It has both the vertical and the horizontal dimension. The vertical dimension points to the filial relationship with God. The horizontal

---

5   Ibid., 3–4.
6   Ibid., 4.

dimension lays claim on our fraternal relationship with one another under a common kinship. This horizontal dimension is the domain of the social, which will be elaborated more in the subsequent sections. The passage further reveals that filiation could be compromised or even lost (perhaps temporally). When lost, it could—thankfully—be 'reconstituted', such that the person regains the fellowship of the 'new-kinning' of God's children.

Furthermore, Obinna's idea of filiation is decidedly Christo-centric. The filial belongingness of humanity to God is accomplished by Christ, the Son and Brother par excellence. The '*in* and ***through*** Christ' that usually accompanies much of the usages describing our filial relationship with God is a pointer to this Christo-centric character of filiation in Obinna's thought. He cannot overemphasize this dimension. He further enunciates this in one of his papers:

> Thus, the filiation of Jesus to our humanity has made it possible for us to be filiated to Jesus who is Chi-God. We thus become Chi-Christic as well as Christi-Chiic—created by God who is Christ and saved by Christ who is God. To be baptized in and converted to Christ tantamounts to sharing the Godness of Christ and the Christness of God. It is within the Chi-Christic communion that we live, flower and bloom to the full.[7]

It can be seen from the above that filiation is simultaneously an act of God who is Christ and an act of Christ who is God. Having been filiated, we have become both partakers and beneficiaries in the two great God-Christ/Christ-God events of Creation and Salvation. Since the aim of this paper is to establish the relevance of the notion of filiation to political/social philosophy and critical social theory, I shall now briefly provide their thrusts.

The Thrust of Political/Social Philosophy and Critical Theory

I do not intend to bother the reader with some supposed 'precise' or perhaps elaborate definitions of political/social philosophy and the critical theory. For our present purposes, I simply want to furnish an operative

---

7   A. J. V. Obinna, 'Celebrating the Gift of Creation—A Chi-Christic Persuasion', 15.

understanding and, more importantly, indicate their thrusts. Political philosophy, as a branch of philosophy, attempts to employ the critical tools of philosophy to reflect on the human being insofar as s/he is a political being. Aristotle's famous definition of man as *zoon politikon* (political animal) comes to mind here. Political philosophy, thus, tries to understand and flesh out what the fact of our being political beings presupposes and entails. Man's political essence must be seen in the light of his being both a social and a rational being. Humans form societies and rationally engage themselves on the leadership structures that would be best for everyone in society. On this note, political/social philosophy concerns itself with fundamental questions about society and political life, namely, the origins of sociopolitical organizations (hypothetically traced to the 'Social Contract' *a la* Hobbes and Rousseau), the source of legitimacy for the law and the constitution, the true source of legitimacy for constituted authorities, the question of citizenship, the rights and obligations of citizens, rights and obligations of leaders, issues of justice and its violation, sovereignty, and a wide range of other derivative issues. Political/social philosophy is a rather normative exercise in that it theorizes on what might be the ideal sociopolitical conditions for an optimal functioning of society and the realization of man's ultimate good; it does not necessarily engage in actual politics/politicking and the implementation of its prescriptions. The field is rapidly expanding, touching upon such contemporary issues as immigration, neocolonialism, globalization, terrorism, and several others. Despite the multifaceted issues that have recently caught the scholarly interest of political/social philosophers, I think that there is an underlying focus on man as a political and social being, capable of improving society qualitatively using the instrument of rationality.

In turn, critical social theory or, simply put, critical theory concerns itself with the critique of society—broadly speaking. I like to associate it with political/social philosophy insofar as this critique of society is carried out against the backdrop of some theoretical presuppositions of what the good society might look like. Some scholars have traced the presages of critical theory to the works of Kant and Hegel.[8] But it seems 'safer' to regard Nietzsche and Marx as the immediate forerunners of critical theory, given the particularly 'subversive' tenor of their philosophizing

---

8   S. E. Bronner, *Critical Theory: A Short Introduction*, 2.

vis-à-vis society. The latter especially engaged in a wide-ranging critique of the capitalist society in a manner that inspired and heralded what would come to be known as critical theory.[9] As an independent (so to speak) area of inquiry, however, Critical Theory is historically linked to the activities of the Frankfurt School in the 1930s, whose first-generation figures include Herbert Marcus, Theodor Adorno, Max Horkheimer, Walter Benjamin, and Erich Fromm. Being neo-Marxists and versed in other fields of enquiry, these figures brought philosophy and sociology to bear on their critique of the modern capitalist order. They are especially suspicious of the Enlightenment rationality that, despite bringing about some material progress to society, has, however, introduced social malaise as never known before. They caution against the overcelebration of the Enlightenment reason, pointing out that the freedom and emancipation it is supposed to bring have turned out to constitute new instruments of slavery and unfreedom to humanity. Modernity is thus shot through with inequality, violence, poverty, domination, wars—all traceable to capitalism and the Enlightenment reason.

The later generations of the Frankfurt School have continued the tradition of the critical diagnoses of the modern society, perhaps with varying degrees of optimism (or pessimism, as the case may be). Jürgen Habermas, who belongs to the second generation of critical theorists, famously speaks of the 'unfinished project of modernity'[10] as a recipe for some hope and optimism in modernity. If I may take the liberty to expand the scope of critical theory, there is a sense in which all shades of critique of the modern society and the ills of its capitalist culture may come under the name of a 'critical theory'. I shall presently situate Obinna's theory of filiation in this broader sense. The proviso here is that such a critique must be systematic and is expected to proceed from some disciplinary background.

---

9   Their Marxist heritage notwithstanding, the first generation of critical theorists refused to premise their theorizing on the two cardinal Marxist notions of economic determinism and the inevitable triumph of socialism.

10   On the occasion of his being awarded the Adorno Prize in 1980, Habermas gave a paper with the title 'Modernity: An Unfinished Project'. In the paper, he critiques the pathologies of modernity on the one hand but refuses, on the other hand, to side with the so-called post-modern thinkers who do not see any good in modernity. This paper lays a foundation for his *The Philosophical Discourse on Modernity* and some subsequent works.

From what has been said so far in this section, one may rightly maintain that both political/social philosophy and critical theory have a special interest in understanding the dynamics of society and diagnosing its anomalies—all with an eye on a freer and qualitatively better society. And this is exactly what they share with Obinna's thought on filiation, as I demonstrate in the next section.

Filiation as a Resource for Political/ Social Philosophy and Critical Theory

Having seen, in a nutshell, what the idea of filiation represents in Obinna's thought and having circumscribed the thrust of political/social philosophy and critical theory, an important question now confronts us: Does an idea that celebrates the kinship of humans furnish the resources (or itself constitute a resource) for a set of disciplines whose interest is the fostering of sociopolitical life and its emancipation through critique? The question is deliberately framed to elicit an affirmative response from the reader, and I frankly think that it has to be so.

First of all, when Obinna's notion of filiation was analyzed in section 2, I made mention of its dual dimensions—the vertical and the horizontal. On the one hand, the vertical points to heaven as it underscores our sonship/daughtership of God. The horizontal, on the other hand, refers to our relationship with other humans with whom we share a divinely rooted kinship and are, *eo ipso*, brothers and sisters in Christ. The latter is manifestly the domain of the *social*! At this point in my analysis, I doubt if anyone would fail to see the social relevance of an idea that is *essentially* social. By underlining the kinship of all humanity, filiation would provide the much-needed fillips to all social theories whose interest is the betterment of society and humanity. This, as has been explained, is the key concern of political/social philosophy and critical theory. The vision of kinship of all humanity no doubt supports a communitarian ethos that is now receiving attention among social and political philosophers. For instance, Michael Sandel founds his renowned theory of justice on communitarian principles as a challenge to the excessive individualism of liberal social theories.[11] In the domain of critical theory, the concept

---

11   Michael Sandel, *Liberalism and the Limits of Justice.*

of 'lifeworld', which is one of Habermas's most important concepts, is
decidedly communitarian.[12] The point here is that filiation, as a concept
that emphasizes kinship, could inspire political and social theories if
thoroughly explored.

Furthermore, filiation is a resource for political/social philosophy and
critical theory in the sense in which it could serve as a 'social imaginary',
to use Charles Taylor's expression. Taylor describes 'social imaginary'
in terms of 'the ways people imagine their social existence, how they fit
together with others, how things go on between them and their fellows, the
expectations that are normally met, and the deeper normative notions and
images that underlie such expectations'.[13] In other words, 'social imaginary'
embodies the vision of what a good society should look like, such that things
have to be measured against such expectations. If Obinna's filiation would
take its seat as a social imaginary, then we are looking at a social ideal
in which God is recognized as Father, Christ as Brother, we as brothers
and sisters. A society with such a 'filiated' imaginary of a 'human family'[14]
(as Obinna calls it) would inevitably be one in which people care for one
another's well-being and refrain from anything that might harm the other.
Now, critical theory, as earlier explained, has set itself the task of analyzing
society and critiquing its shortcomings. To do this efficiently, it operates
with (as least implicitly) some normative vision, standard, framework or, in
Taylor's coinage, 'imaginary', against which society is measured. *I argue
that filiation could be a veritable framework or imaginary against
which society might be evaluated. If filiation is taken on board,
a vital question for critical theorists would thus be the extent to
which a given society is filiated, confiliated, recti-filiated, etc.—as
the case may be.* For all practical purposes, the question of the extent
to which a society is filiated translates into that of the extent to which
individuals truly regard themselves as brothers and sisters in mutual love
and solidarity rooted in Christ. Any shortcoming in this regard becomes
a social pathology that must be corrected, perhaps through recti-filiation.

The fact that there could occur a filiation deficiency, a not-properly-
filiated society where individuals do not always recognize and appreciate
one another as brothers/sisters, leads to the next point I wish to explore:

---

12   J. Habermas, *The Theory of Communicative Action*, vol. II.

13   Charles Taylor, *Modern Social Imaginaries*, 23.

14   A. J. V. Obinna, *Confiliating America: Recti-valuing One Another*, 3.

namely, the question of social division. The pathology of social division finds expression in racism, tribalism, nepotism, caste system (like the *diala/osu* divide), class structure, etc. Freedom and social emancipation have been an important preoccupation for critical theorists right from the days of the foundational members of the Frankfurt School. Critical theory unearths the hidden elements in social structures, e.g., thoroughgoing capitalism that perpetuate the enslavement of man by man. *Similarly, Obinna's concept of filiation has been shown to have an emancipatory tenor. Using the notion of filiation as my point of departure, I have already interpreted the social malaise of racism, tribalism, and caste systems in terms of filiation deficiency*, a condition of **not-being-properly-filiated** that, therefore, stands in need of **recti-filiation**. A society that suffers a filiation deficiency is indeed malnourished and does not enjoy the wholesomeness and beauty of a genuine appreciation of one another as brothers/sisters in Christ. For the past couple of decades, Obinna himself has waged a frontal war against the *diala/osu* divide in his native Igboland. I shall dwell a little more on this in the next section. Suffice it, at the moment, to cite an important passage that recounts Obinna's struggle against the *Diala/Osu* divide.

> The so-called free-born Igbo would not associate with so-called enslaved-outcast Igbo not to talk of getting married to them ... The so-called slave-born ... were scared stiff by the so-called freeborn who with a superior air continued to humiliate and stigmatize the so-called Outcasts ... A close reading of Jesus' relationship with the Jews, Samaritans and Gentiles and his redemptive-filiative concern for each of these human groups opened my eyes, my ears, my inner heart and mind to a redemptive-filiative concern among my Igbo folks ... I found myself rejecting and renouncing ... break up with and break out all conscious, reflexive and subconscious attachment to each and all three groups and their fears.[15]

It is instructive to observe from the above citation that Obinna's commitment to the eradication of the *diala/osu* divide is primarily inspired by the philosophy of filiation. He speaks of the 'redemptive-filiative concern', and in the same page I quoted from, he makes reference

---

15   Ibid., 8–9.

to 'rituals of filiation and confiliation'.[16] My point is that the philosophy of filiation holds out the promise of inspiring social emancipation since it is suspicious of all essentialist/absolutist claims (e.g., of natural superiority). And this is in line with the very temperament of critical theory.

The final point I wish to make in line with the relevance of the idea of filiation to political/social philosophy and critical theory touches upon the very motive for sociopolitical actions and critique. Calling underlying motivations into question is very important, considering that apparently 'altruistic' social or political actions are frequently being undertaken for the wrong, nay, selfish motives. History has witnessed revolutions being carried out under the false pretenses of 'popular revolutions' that got eventually hijacked by a few who posed as 'messiahs'. George Orwell's *Animal Farm*, which depicts the oppressive situation of the Soviet Revolution, comes to mind here. To bring the example home to our country Nigeria, recent events have shown that the APC government that came to power under the banner of 'change' has dangerous ulterior motives after all. Further down home, the Okorocha government postured as a 'messianic' government and came to power in what the present writer had optimistically (but erroneously, now with the benefit of hindsight) referred to as the 'Imo Revolution' back in 2011. Tragically, Okorocha's government has turned out to be a colossal failure. It has become a failure because all the campaign propaganda was, in the first place, pathetically insincere and aimed at hoodwinking the masses. *The implication of the foregoing exposé is that any social or political action not actuated by the consciousness and sincere appreciation of our common kinship in Christ runs the risk of misfiring.* Philanthropy and charity, even when carried out with the best of intentions, could easily be diverted if it lacks the 'God-element'. For instance, NGOs and foreign aids frequently turn themselves into political tools in the service of the capitalist enterprise. Once again, it is the idea of filiation that would confer the much-needed 'God-element' to such otherwise altruistic gestures. In the next section, I give a concise account of Obinna's personal witnessing to what may now be rightly called the *philosophy of filiation.*

---

16   Ibid.

Witnessing to the Philosophy of Filiation: The Obinna Example

Inasmuch as the philosophy of filiation is essentially social, it cannot be confined only to the realm of theory. By its very nature, it calls for practical witnessing. On this note, I wish to point out just a few instances of such witnessing on the part of its proponent. For the sake of brevity, three suffice. This writer is aware that over the past couple of decades, A. J. V. Obinna has been a bulwark against oppressive leadership in Nigeria, but more particularly in Imo State. Successive governments, dating back to the military regimes of James Aneke and Tanko Zubairu, have never gotten it easy with him when it comes to demanding a people-oriented leadership. As he recounts, 'The Catholic Church, based on its own principles of justice, development and peace, also engaged the military with resonant effect. In Imo, it was not easy between the James Aneke and Tanko Zubairu Military Administrators and myself.'[17] More recently, the 'gadfly' role he has played in the Udenwa, Ohakim, and Okorocha regimes is still fresh in our minds. The erudite archbishop has consistently been the voice of the voiceless, speaking truth to power and refusing to be silenced by intimidation or financial gratification. In many ways, he is one of the last few bastions of sanity in a society where sanity has been thrown to the winds in almost all areas of life. From our earlier description of filiation, it goes without saying that all this would not have been possible without his firm vision of a free, just, and sane society where people see one another as children of the same Father-God.

In line with this vision of a filiated—and, *ipso facto*, free, just, and sane—society, Obinna has, for a couple of decades, waged a massive war against the *diala/osu* divide in Igboland. Filiation, as a social theory, would have no place for such an unjust and divisive structure. Critical theory aims at emancipating society from unjust structures. Obinna brings his idea of filiation to bear on the battle against the *diala/osu* caste system. He has written severally on the need to root it out; he sermonizes frequently on it; he has also designed pastoral policies in this regard, e.g., encouraging and endorsing the marriage of people from different so-called castes.

---

17 A. J. V. Obinna, 'Recti-Shaping Society with Hope-Bringing News', 4–5.

Finally, the present writer sees the charity works carried out by archdiocesan organs (like the EU-CARE), the recent amnesty/reintegration program for former kidnappers (through the JDPC), etc. as being inspired by the archbishop's philosophy of filiation. In the preceding section, I argued that otherwise altruistic acts like those performed by NGOs could easily become a political tool if not inspired by a sincere appreciation of our common kinship in Christ. The above-mentioned archdiocesan programs indeed exemplify charity motivated by nothing other than a filiative solicitude for the needy. There have been no reports of their being politicized or used as a tactic for tax cuts/outright evasion, as is common with 'nonfiliative' forms of charity. Once again, the genuineness in these programs could only stem from the archbishop's commitment to the philosophy of filiation.

Conclusion

From the foregoing discourse, there is no gainsaying that Obinna's theory of filiation holds out a profound promise for political/social philosophy and critical theory. I believe my paper would have achieved its stated goal if Obinna's theory of filiation gets widely recognized as a political/social philosophy and a critical theory in its own right. But beyond a mere recognition, the immense riches of the theory have to be explored in such a way that it begins to play a huge transformative role in society and politics.

References

- Broner, S. E. *Critical Theory: A Very Short Introduction.* Oxford: Oxford University Press, 2017.
- Habermas, Jürgen. *The Theory of Communicative Action.* Vol. II, translated by Thomas McCarthy. Boston: Beacon Press, 1987.
- Obinna, A. J. V., *Confiliating Americans: Recti-Valuing One Another.* Owerri: Assumpta Press. (This pamphlet is the text of a paper delivered by A. J. V. Obinna in Sanford University Alabama, USA. It was made into a pamphlet by Assumpta Press, Owerri.)

- ————. 'Celebrating the Gift of Creation: A Chi-Christic Persuasion.' A Keynote Address at the Thirty-First Annual Conference of the Catholic Theological Association of Nigeria, held at Umuahia, March 30, 2016.
- ————. 'Recti-Shaping Society with Hope-Bringing News: Some Thoughts Along Pope Francis' Message.' A Paper for the World Communications Day, May 28, 2017.
- Sandel, M. *Liberalism and the Limits of Justice.* Cambridge: Cambridge University Press, 1982.
- Taylor, Charles. *Modern Social Imaginaries.* Durham: Duke University Press, 2004.

Chapter Fifteen

From Colonialism and Slavery to Reconfiliation

Moses Chikwe

Introduction

According Webster's unabridged dictionary (1996), the word *colonialism* means 'the control or governing influence of a nation over a dependent country, territory, or people. It is the system or policy by which a nation maintains or advocates such control or influence.' It is the conquest and control of other people's land and goods by the dominating power. Philip Altbach describes it thus: 'Traditional colonialism involved the direct political domination of one nation over another area, thus enabling the colonial power to control any and all aspects of the internal and external life of the colony.'[1] There are varied resultant effects of colonialism from one country to another, determined in part by the policies of the colonialists and in part by the situation in the colony itself.

Overall, there is always a marked effect of colonialism on the colonized. As Wane observes: 'Any form of colonialism is bound to leave a mark of some kind. European colonialism in Africa left lasting marks on the

---

1   Philip G. Altbach, 'Education and Neocolonialism,' *Teachers College Record* 72, no. 4 (1971): 543–558.

landscape, as well as the political, social and economic organization of the African peoples.'[2] The colonialists felt it was their God-given 'duty' to Christianize the Africans and to bring them civilization. In that it was their avowed responsibility, they plundered and 'stole' everything they could from the colonized people. This damage done on both the landscape and psyche of the Africans has remained permanent. Africans, generation after generation, live to prove that they are no lesser humans to the whites who colonized both their land and spirit. The mental and emotional harm is beyond what anyone can quantify. From cradle or even from your mother's womb, you bear the mark of inferiority, your skin color. The religious images and symbols convey the same message. Black is the color used for Lucifer (the leader of rebel angels), while Michael (leader of the faithful angels) is painted the color of the white man. These forms of representations are seen everywhere, and every child grows up to see them and internalize the meaning.

Hence, Africans live with this burden of proof all the time that they are no lesser humans than white colonizers. 'Many colonized people … feel the need to prove that we are human beings; we did have a history before the colonizer and we did have meaningfully organized ways of living, educating and governing our societies.'[3] The emptying of African land and people has been done, among other ways, through 'Western systems of education, texts, and literature, thereby making the business of education and knowledge production contested terrain'.[4] It not only normalized Western conceptual scheme but also actively wounded the spiritual life of the people, leaving them both mentally and spiritually enslaved. It purveyed at its advent a Christianity that pulverized almost everything that was of value to the African religious being, a Christianity that did not acculturate into the already prepared soul of the African man.

Thus, education and religion were used as virile instruments to instantiate the hegemonic rule of the colonialists over the indigenous people. Wherever colonial rule invited itself, it never wanted to leave, even at the resistance of the natives. 'But the war goes on; and we will have to bind up for years to come the many, sometimes ineffaceable, wounds that

---

2   Njoki N. Wane, 'Is Decolonization Possible?' in *Anti-Colonialism and Education*, eds. G. J. S. Dei and A. Kempf (The Netherlands: Sense Publishers, 2006), 87.

3   Wane, 'Is Decolonization Possible?', 87.

4   Wane, 'Is Decolonization Possible?', 87.

the colonialist onslaught has inflicted on our people.'[5] We need to continue to find ways to remove the lingering negative impacts of colonialism as well as all the other similar wounds that Africans themselves have inflicted on one another. One of the ways, as suggested by Archbishop Anthony Obinna, is through theological process of reconfiliation, which allows us to better understand our common humanity and adoption in Christ.

In this paper, I am going to explore two of the major colonial tools in Africa and how it is perpetuated even after the colonialists have gone. I will look at the polar binarism of black and white, a strategic creation of colonialism to further subjugate the Africans. Finally, I will consider reconfiliation as a theological possibility out of slavery and colonialism and their ancillary ideologies of marginalization.

Colonial Use of Education

Education is the process of incorporating new members into the life of the society. Ngugi wa Thiong'o defines it as 'the process of integrating the youth into the entire system of social production, exchange and distribution of what we eat, wear and shelter under, the whole system of organizing the wealth of a given country.'[6] Colonial education succeeded in planting seeds for the expansion, growth, and sustainability of imperialism. 'In other words, education was an organized form of imperialism that allowed colonization to continue by indoctrinating new subjects. Unknown to me, the act of being schooled in the literary canons so valued in Europe caused me to be disassociated from and devalue the cultural knowledge and wisdom of my ancestors, my community, and my family.'[7]

There is always a deceptive tendency to assume that schooling is inherently liberating and holds the potential for social transformation. This assumption comes from the disregard of the compelling influence of the structural, social, political, and economic relations that shape school system. Martin Carnoy argues: 'The way society organizes formal schooling is a function of the economic and social hierarchy and cannot be

---

5   Fanon Frantz, *The Wretched of the Earth*, trans. Richard Philcox (New York, NY: Groove Press, 1963), 203.

6   Ngugi wa Thiong'O, *Barrel of a Pen: Resistance to Repression in Neo-Colonial Kenya* (New Jersey, NJ: Africa World Press, 1983), 88.

7   Wane, 'Is Decolonization Possible?', 90.

separated from it ... the school's function to reinforce the social relations in production.'[8]

While education is always a process of enlightenment, it does not always bring the promised liberation and social change. There can be what John Dewey would call a mis-education, whereby educative experience lacks critical quality and geared toward sustaining the status quo.[9] To underscore this form of mis-education in our contemporary society, Peter McLaren observes the invading of educational policy by the logic of transnational capitalism reducing education to a 'subsector of the economy'.[10] Education can always be used to oil the engine of oppressive system. History has shown how many totalitarian regimes have successfully used education as a hegemonic apparatus. Needless to say that it was largely and effectively used by the colonialists to keep the colonies aligned to the colonial ideologies, creating in them a rejection of their own being and an inferiority complex.

In the countries, such as Nigeria and India, where colonialists used direct colonialism, schooling was developed as an instrument of social control devised by the British in order to maintain and expand their colonial policies. Britain transformed India from a mercantile colony into a plantation extension of her economy. In this context of colonial domination, the British introduced schooling, which was organized to create Indian elite who served as intermediary bureaucrats between the colonizers and the colonized. With respect to Nigeria, though, the conversion of natives was the main goal of education by British missionaries in the early stages of colonialism; primary and secondary schooling was formed later by colonizers to maintain social control and to produce a bureaucratic elite as intermediary for the British.

Turning to internal colonialism, Carnoy examines structural relations existing in the economic, political, and educational systems between the bourgeoisie and the groups dominated by them. For instance, with the rise of capitalism in the United States, schooling became a vital institution of political socialization and training while functioning as an allocator of roles in the hierarchical system of a differentiated labor force. Formal education,

---

8   Martin Carnoy, *Schooling in a Corporate Society: The Political Economy of Education in America* (New York, NY: David McKay Co., 1975), 343.

9   John Dewey, *Experience & Education* (New York, NY: Touchstone, 1938),

10 Peter McLaren, *Che Guevara, Paulo Freire, and the Pedagogy of Revolution* (New York, NY: Rowman & Littlefield Publishers, Inc., 2000) 169.

Carnoy argues, was and is used to perpetuate the social class structure. 'Schooling for a hierarchical structure is ... a colonizing device'[11] since it serves to allocate social roles to individuals on the basis of the hierarchy's needs. Internal colonialism featured prominently in the social relations of political and economic systems between blacks and whites in the United States during the period of 1865–1930.[12] Similarly, Western education in many African countries was used by colonialists to create such internal hierarchical structure among the natives.

Education, therefore, was substantially used in various forms and different contexts as a tool of colonization. Moreover, colonial educational patterns in countries where direct colonialism was practiced were designed to serve the pleasure of the oppressors. For this reason, they were misplaced and did not focus on disciplines and areas of study that would engender autonomous technological and agricultural development. 'Most colonial powers, when they concentrated on education at all, stressed humanistic studies, fluency in the language of the metropolitan country, and the skills necessary for secondary positions in the bureaucracy. Lawyers were trained but few scientists, agricultural experts, or qualified teachers were available when independence came.'[13]

Because of their conscientious effort to perpetually dominate the indigenes, the colonialists craftily avoided any educational system that would bring independence and self-reliance to the people. Instead of building on what the people already knew, they jettisoned thousands of years of acquired wisdom of the people and replaced them with knowledge that would only facilitate the colonial machinery. During the encounter with colonialism, all these ways of dealing with life by Africans were destroyed and substituted with the Western mindset and frames of thought. They emptied the native brain of all form of content. As Fanon stated: 'The effect consciously sought by colonialism was to drive into the natives' head the idea that if the settlers were to leave, they would at once fall back into barbarism, degradation and bestiality.'[14] The colonialists fragmented and

---

11 Carnoy, *Schooling in a Corporate Society: The Political Economy of Education in America*, 346.

12 Nubuo Shimahara, 'Education as Cultural Imperialism,' *Teachers College Record* 76, no. 4 (1975): 688–690.

13 Altbach, 'Education and Neocolonialism,' 544.

14 Frantz Fanon, *Towards the African Revolution*, trans. Haakon Cheralier (New York, NY: Grove Press, 1994), 93.

destroyed thousands of years of African heritage. The entire project was to make the natives perpetually dependent on the colonial masters.

Consequently, there was a wholesale damage of the language and cultural heritage of the people. Language has been seen as a very crucial tool to preserve the cultural heritage and identity.[15] This preservation of cultural heritage and identity through language can happen when the teacher uses a culturally relevant pedagogy in teaching the students and when the teacher builds on the students' linguistic skills. Here we see the interdependency of language and culture, since according to Mercer, 'language is a creation of culture'[16] and conversely, culture is maintained by language. One of the early debates linking culture, language, and cognition surrounds the question, Do people who speak different languages think about and experience the world differently? Linguists Benjamin Whorf and Edward Sapir are noted to be the pioneer proponents of this line of thinking, which is known as the linguistic relativity hypothesis.[17] In this paper, the author contends that the attitude of the colonialist educational system was destructive toward heritage language, which bears the stamps of both the cultural identity and cognitive foundation of students; and I provide reasons why this was a serious crime to the indigenous people.

Research has shown that children begin to learn about themselves and the world around them through their home language (also referred to as heritage language, native or primitive language, or mother's tongue), which they pick up naturally from home.[18] This forms the foundation of children's linguistic life. Alim argues that the attempt to eliminate or destroy the heritage language is an attempt at the life of the speaker.[19] This attitude

---

15 Pamela L. Tiedt and Iris M. Tiedt, *Multicultural Teaching: A Handbook of Activities, Information, and Resources* (Boston, MA: Allyn & Bacon, 1990).

16 Neil Mercer, *Words and Minds* (New York, NY: Routledge, 2000).

17 Harry W. Gardiner, Jay D. Mutter, and Corrinne Kosmitzki, *Lives Across Culture: Cross-Cultural Human Development* (Boston: Allyn & Bacon, 2002).

18 Lev Vygotsky, *Thought and Language*, translated edition revised by Alex Kozulin (Cambridge, Massachusetts, MA: MIT Press, 1962). See also, Kenneth Rogoff, 'The Purchasing of Power Parity Puzzle', *Journal of Economic Literature* 34, no. 2 (1996): 647–668. Lucy Tse, 'Resisting and Reversing Language Shift: Heritage-Language Resilience among U.S', *Harvard Educational Review* 71, no. 4 (2001): 676–709. Samy H. in *Language in the USA: Perspectives for the 21st Century*, eds. E. Finegan et al., 387–409 (Cambridge, UK: Cambridge University Press, 2004). Ana Celia Zentella, *Building Strength: Language and Literacy in Latino Families and Communities* (New York, NY: Teacher's College Press, 2005).

19 Alim, 'Hip Hop Nation Language: Localization and Globalization'.

hits at the very 'being' of the students because the heritage language is the main cultural marker and identity of the students and the fulcrum of all they know about themselves and the world. As Rosina Lippi-Green notes: 'It is the most salient way we have of establishing and advertising our social identities.'[20]

Maina documents an account of how her language was assaulted when she was ten years old and in standard 4 in her rural village. According to her story, one of the most humiliating experiences was to be caught speaking Gikuyu in the vicinity of the school. They were given corporal punishments, several canes depending on the number of times a person had been caught speaking their native language. 'Denying us as children the right to use our language had one aim, to make us despise our language, hence the values carried by that language. ... By the same token, we would admire the English language and the values carried by that language and the people who evolve the language of our daily rewards and praise.'[21]

A focus on theories of teaching and learning further helps us to understand the extent of damage done to students when they are discouraged to use their primitive linguistic skills at school. Scholars, trained in such fields as psychology, anthropology, sociology, cognitive science, and sociolinguistics, have explored the question of how thinking processes, language, and cultural experiences interact in schooling situations.[22] They would all agree that the students' heritage language through which they first learned 'ways of taking from the world' plays a significant role in their cognitive and linguistic development.[23] It is crucial then for teachers to recognize these previous linguistic ways of students, encourage them, and build upon them.

Sociocultural theorists believe that our experiences are major ingredients of cognition and are inseparable from thought. Moment

---

20   Rosina Lippi-Green, *English with an Accent* (New York, NY: Routledge, 1997), 15.

21   Faith Maina, 'Disrupting Preconceptions: Postcolonialism and Education', *Teachers College Record* 106, no. 12 (2004): 2304.

22   Garcia, 2005.

23   Shirley B. Heath, *Ways with Words: Language, Life and Work in Communities and Classrooms* (Cambridge: Cambridge University Press, 1983). See also James P Gee, *Situated Language and Learning: A Critique of Traditional Schooling* (London and New York, NY: Routledge, 2004). Mercer, *Words and Minds*. Kenneth Rogoff, 'Globalization and Global Disinflation' (a paper prepared for the Federal Reserve Bank of Kansas City conference on 'Monetary Policy and Uncertainty: Adapting to a Changing Economy' at Jackson Hole, Wyoming, on August 29, 2003).

by moment, we construct reality. That process of construction and the understanding it generates depend on our previous understandings and our social experiences.[24] According to Vygotsky, language functions significantly as that tool of thought for constructing reality.[25] The mental frameworks (or schemas) by which children perceive the world around them are first constructed through children's home language. If language is a tool of thought, it follows that as children develop more complex thinking skills, their native language by which they formed the primal mental representations plays a significant role. When this is recognized and encouraged as the starting point or font of learning, students feel empowered to acquire the new linguistic abilities.

But this was not so with the colonialists. It was not an oversight by the colonialists that they failed to follow these sociocultural and linguistic theories of mental development. They never intended to build on the prior linguistic skills of the students. Their whole project was to wipe out or rather 'whiteout' the linguistic and cultural heritage of the people in order to gain a totalizing control over them. Ashcroft et al.'s work in *The Empire Writes Back* documents how language and literature were used as imperial weapons to dominate and subjugate colonized peoples. They contend that

> one of the main features of imperial oppression is control over language. The imperial educational system installs a standard version of the metropolitan language as the norm and marginalizes all 'variants' as 'impurities.' Language becomes the medium through which a hierarchical structure of power is perpetuated, and the medium, through which conceptions of 'truth', 'order', and 'reality' becomes established.[26] (p. 7)

This was aimed at controlling the people's ways of thinking and defining themselves. 'Embracing another person's language', Wane admits,

---

24 Garcia, 2005.

25 Vygotsky, *Thought and Language*. Michael Cole and Sheila R. Cole, *The Development of Children*, 4th edition (New York, NY: Worth Publisher, 2001). Paul B. Garrett and Patricia B. Lopez, 'Language Socialization: Reproduction and Continuity, Transformation and Change', *Annual Review of Anthropology* 31 (2002): 339–361. Mercer, *Words and Minds*.

26 Bill Ashcroft, Gareth Griffiths, and Helen Tiffin, *The Empire Writes Back: Theory and Practice in Post-Colonial Literature* (London, New York, NY: Routledge, 2002), 7.

'was the highest form of colonization. This is because one is denied what is essential to one's cultural growth.'[27]

Furthermore, colonial education created a dislike and lack of value for the indigenous language and culture and substituted it with the love for the Western culture and ways of knowing. 'With formal Western education and its inherent rewards, indigenous knowledges have been devalued in the minds and hearts of people, despite the fact that indigenous knowledge systems predate colonialism.'[28] It created dichotomy among the natives and made the 'elite'—those who were able to acquire the colonizers' language and cultural skills and look down on their culture, language, and people. It superiorized the colonialists and expanded grounds for domination of the indigenous people. As Cabral succinctly stated:

> The experience of colonial domination shows that, in the effort to perpetuate exploitation, the colonizer not only creates a system to repress the cultural life of the colonized people; he also provokes and develops the cultural alienation of a part of the population, either by so-called assimilation of indigenous people, or by creating a social gap between the indigenous elites and the popular masses. As a result of this process ... the urban or peasant 'petite bourgeoisie' assimilates the colonizer's mentality, considers itself culturally superior to its own people and ignores or looks down upon their cultural values.[29]

This manifests part of the divide and rule tactics of the colonialists. They always create a Manichaeism between themselves and the natives and between the natives themselves. They always position themselves as the subjects and creators of universal knowledge, while relocating nonwhites to objectified spaces of existence. This displacement of the nonwhites created them as only consumers of Western knowledge while elevating and arrogating the Europeans to the ownership of global knowledge production. As Linda Smith suggests, the commodification and 'globalization of knowledge and Western culture constantly reaffirms the West's view of itself as the centre of legitimate knowledge, the arbiter of what counts as

---

27 Wane, 'Is Decolonization Possible?', 95.

28 Wane, 'Is Decolonization Possible?'

29 Amilcar Cabral, 'National Liberation Culture' (memorial lecture series at Syracuse University, Syracuse, New York, under the auspices of the Program of Eastern African Studies), page 7.

knowledge and the source of "civilized" knowledge. This form of global knowledge is generally referred to as "universal'" knowledge, available to all and not really "owned" by anyone, that is, until non-Western scholars make claims to it.'[30]

Colonial education marginalizes and relegates the indigenous knowledge and worldview to the level of nothingness. It reinforces and assigns what counts as knowledge and who is capable of bearing knowledge. By this way, colonialism represents a potent and intentional destructiveness and willingness to detrimentally usurp and disregard the existence, purpose, and knowledge of others. It violates and disregards the right of nonwhite others to exist and define their lived experiences in their own terms. It represses the voices of others and basks in the assumed and fundamentally erroneous belief that others 'may be spoken for, about and to. It lingers through the tangible acts and discourses of hatred which consumed the colonists and presumed the worthlessness of "othered" lives'.[31]

Education as a colonial instrument remains very extant even today in the former colonies. Till date, the Western form of education and curricula and the use of colonial language pervade the entire continent of Africa and many Asian and Latin American countries. Even after the revolutionary literary works of many African writers—like Chinua Achebe, Ngugi wa Thiong'o, Albert Memmi, Wole Soyinka, Ashis Nandy, Aime Cesaire, to mention but few—to caution against the displacement of African indigenous knowledge and language by Western conceptual scheme, language, and culture, the educational system in Africa, India, and many other countries is heavily laden with colonial system.

Hence, even while the colonialists were gone, they maintain a telecontrol through education in what is now called neocolonialism. As Altbach points out, 'The continued use of European languages in many developing countries is one of the most important aspects of neocolonialism and the impact of the colonial heritage on the Third World.'[32] Sometimes by way of aids to the former colonies, the industrialized nations continue the control and regulation of the lives of the 'Third World' nations. This is not to say that what they offer is not useful to the underdeveloped countries,

30   Linda T. Smith, *Decolonizing Methodologies, Research and Indigenous People* (London: Zed Book, 1999), 63.
31   Ruck-Simmons, 2006, 276–277.
32   Altbach, 'Education and Neocolonialism', 543.

but it is always like the Greek gift, since the Western nations are not disinterested philanthropists.

Nevertheless, it is pertinent to note that there is today a growing awareness among the underdeveloped world regarding the inherent dangers in the offer of aids by the Western nations. Equally, there is a slow reversion to the giving of instruction in native languages and the untiring battle by indigenous scholars to minimize the damage by Western culture and thought process. For instance, Archbishop Anthony J. V. Obinna in 1994 initiated the *Odenigbo* lecture series, which celebrates the Igbo culture and language. This way, he rediscovers and rekindles the cultural values inherent in the Igbo language and encourages our youth to cherish and be proud of using their mother's tongue. It sanitizes the culture, removing the elements that do not respect the rights of each person as sons and daughters of God whose adoption in Christ has ennobled and entitled them to the highest respect.

These are but a drop in the ocean. The extent of damage seems irreparable and decolonization seems almost impossible because most of these colonies live and breathe in the social and linguistic frames structured and designed by the colonialists. 'Decolonizing oneself is the most difficult process. Most indigenous people who have been subjected to Western education have become a commodity of Western ideology.'[33] While this is true, we shall never resign to despair and hopelessness. There is a need to continue to push the boundaries from all fronts until complete liberation is realized. Another area to pay attention to is that of religion.

Religion as a Colonial Tool

As we discussed above the leitmotif of colonial domination was to make superior their ways of viewing the world by creating a binary. Christianity, which came in the same package with colonial education, was politicized and used as instrument of suppression. This collusion by Christianity with colonialists was underscored by Archbishop Obinna in the following statement: 'As I read into history, Christianity which I had seen as a saving grace in the harsh entry of European imperialism and colonialism into Africa, became increasingly compromised as a colluding agent in the

---

33   Wane, 'Is Decolonization Possible?', 98.

assault on Africa.'[34] The colonial method of evangelization was that of destruction of anything that indigenous people held as ways of worshipping the Supreme Being. It was done in the spirit of superiority over the natives regarding their former religious life as diabolical and animalistic. The point the colonial evangelizers missed was that Africans were deeply religious. They had already a potential for the Christian religion to take root without necessarily bulldozing the religious heritage that carried so much value and morals for the people. This damning mistake of the colonial missionaries have been acknowledged and corrected by many Christian denominations, especially the Catholic church. In the Vatican II 'Declaration on the Relationship of Church to Non-Christian Religions (*Nostra Aetate* 2)', the fathers of the council state the following:

> The Church therefore has this exhortation for her sons: prudently and lovingly, through dialogue and collaboration with the followers of other religions, and in witness of Christian faith and life, acknowledge, preserve, and promote the spiritual and moral goods found among these men, as well as the values in their culture and society.[35] 662

Similar statements are made in the 'Decree on the Church's Missionary Activity (*Ad Gentes*)', which admonishes that missionaries should insert themselves within the culture and social conditions of the people they are to evangelize in order to learn about them and their values just as Christ inserted himself into the human culture so as to transform it.[36] Unfortunately, prior to Vatican II, the damage has been done and remained a permanent presence of colonialism. Needless to list all the ramifications of the harm but suffice it to say that it slits the spiritual ligament and being of the indigenous people, allowing it to shrivel and die. This comes as no surprise since the entire enterprise of the colonialists was to dehumanize

---

34 Anthony J. V. Obinna, 'Confilitory Collaboration between the Church in Africa and Europe: A Theo-filio-logical Background' (a seminar workshop paper for the Nigerian-African Delegation in a meeting of the European and African Bishops in Rome, 2004), 6.

35 Vatican II Council, 'Declaration on the Relation of the Church to Non-Christian Religions, *Nostra Aetate*, 7 December 1965', in *Decrees of the Ecumenical Councils: Trent-Vatican II*, ed. Norman Tanner and Guiseppe Alberigo, vol. II (New York, NY: Costello Publishing Company), 662.

36 Vatican II Council, 'Decree on the Church's Missionary Activity, *Ad Gentes*, 7 December 1965', in *Decrees of the Ecumenical Councils: Trent-Vatican II*, ed. Norman Tanner and Guiseppe Alberigo, vol. II (New York, NY: Costello Publishing Company, 1987), 1011–1042.

and humiliate the natives and to suppress and relegate to the margin whatever they hold as true. The colonizers viewed indigenous knowledge and ways of being as uncivilized, primitive, and inferior as compared to their knowledge, education, religion, or ways of knowledge.[37]

However, it must be mentioned that while religion was used as an instrument of oppression by the colonialist and slave masters, Africans reconstructed it through black theology as a liberating force. Through black theology, which is a theology of liberation, blacks in South Africa persisted in defying apartheid and orchestrated their liberation. Even though the Christian churches promoted division and the suppression of the blacks, 'interestingly, they [blacks] did not dismiss the validity of Christianity but rather threw out the colonial distortions thereof. This process of decolonization was a rearticulation of their social predicament according to Scripture, not what white racists had dictated to them.'[38] Herein lies the paradox: the black church was able to recognize the liberating and emancipatory aspects of biblical Christianity and use it as an anticolonial tool, though it was used as a tool of colonialism and enslavement by the Europeans.[39] The Africans knew better and read a different Bible from that of the colonialists—a reading that brought them joy and hope in the midst of affliction. Therefore, black culture and religious spirituality have very strong affinities, and it is difficult to separate them entirely when discussing the struggles that blacks went through in the systems of slavery and colonialism.

Yet the traditional practice in the academy and western conceptual scheme is to fragment spirituality from the being of scholars. This according to many black scholars is a new way of colonialism. To some extent where religion was once used as a tool of colonization to breed compliance, domination, and control over the masses, secularism is the new colonial tool. In other words, secular-based theories like postcolonialism and postmodernism inculcate a 'politics of forgetting', which alienates us from our cultural experiences and, as a result, causes us to forget what kept our predecessors anchored and firmly rooted in their identities and

---

37 Mahia Munial, 'Indigenous Knowledge and Schooling: A Continuum between Conflict and Dialogue', in *What Is Indigenous Knowledge? View for the Academy*, eds. Ladislaus M. Semali and Joe L. Kinchele, 59–77 (London and New York, NY: Palmer Press, 1999).

38 Spencer, 2006, 118.

39 Spencer, 2006, 118.

culture.[40] So we claim religion as a deeply African thing that was part of our existence even before the advent of colonial Christianity, which was erroneously used to perpetuate white supremacy.

Nevertheless, it must be admitted that not everything in African religion and culture deserves credit or is worthy of sustainment. There were some cultural practices and beliefs that went against the intrinsic value and dignity of the human person—for instance, the killing of twins, the mourning rituals for widows, the caste system, and others. Obinna captures this in the following statement:

> Taking off from the inhumanity of the *Diala-Osu* caste system and human sacrifices to spirits in Igboland, which increased exponentially, I come to realize how Nigerians living on the Atlantic Ocean Coasts moved from being initially unwilling victims of Arab slave-raiders and European slave-traders to becoming willing middlemen in the terrible and systematic enslavement of humans in Igboland and other parts of Africa.[41]

African theologians have been doing the delicate and complex job of cleaning up the African culture and religion of the things that are opposed to the gospel values preached by Christ. One of such efforts is by Archbishop Anthony J. V. Obinna, who pushes against some of the Igbo cultural and religious beliefs and practices like the *Osu* and *Diala* caste system, which undermines the dignity of the human person. This effort will be discussed later in this paper. Let us now turn our attention to another oppressive ideology that colonialists used against the Africans: the black/white binary.

Whiteness

One of the great possessions of the West is their colour, which they use as a source of superiority to blacks and other coloured people. Whiteness is a colour of privilege and supremacy. It is a colour that many desires to have and still many would like to hate. Almost every woman wants

---

40 Spencer, 2006, 118.
41 Obinna, "Confilitory Collaboration between the Church in Africa and Europe: A Theo-filio-logical Background,' 5.

to change their hair colour to look blonde because that is the colour of power and domination, a colour that is admired by almost all because it was made so. There is therefore a lot of privilege attached to being white. 'White privilege is a system of benefits, advantages, and opportunities experienced by White persons in our society simply because of their skin colour.'[42] McIntosh sees it as 'an invisible weightless knapsack of special provisions, maps, passports, code books, visas, clothes, tools, and blank checks'.[43] The impact can be seen within various societal institutions, including education, government, finance and business, housing, and the criminal justice system.

Just by being white, one has all these privileges usually unearned and unrecognized. White privilege is so common and advantageous that most white persons are unaware of its existence. Unlike discrimination, which is a conscious act against another person, white privilege requires that no decisions be made, no premeditated actions taken. Within an ethnically diverse society such as ours, white privilege is a pervasive, but often unrecognized, social problem.[44] According to Frankenberg, whiteness has three dimensions of advantage: a structural advantage (racial privilege), a standpoint for viewing ourselves and others, and cultural practices that are unmarked or unnamed and thereby presumed to be normative.[45]

The first source of white privilege (structural advantage) is very invisible. In the US, most of the institutions were originally structured from the standpoint of whites to benefit them. Counting from the upper echelons of businesses, government, social services, the movie industries to the media, one would see a clear evidence of white domination. Many of the laws, business practices, and rules for social interaction were designed to privilege whites over people of colour. Although expressions of privilege resulting in outright discrimination are now illegal, subtle differences remain, which make it difficult for persons of colour to be truly equal in the United States and other countries where there is racial diversity.

Although most white persons are taught about racism (which is disadvantageous to others), they are not taught about white privilege,

---

42 Christi A. Donnelly, et al., Nature, 2006.
43 McIntosh, P. "White privilege: Unpacking the invisible knapsack. *Peace and Freedom*,' (July/August 1989): 10-12.
44 Christi A. Donnelly, et al., Nature, 2006.
45 Ruth Frankenberg, *White Women, Race Matters: The Social Construction of Whiteness* (Minneapolis, MN: University of Minnesota Press, 1993).

which puts whites at an advantage.[46] Prejudice and discrimination are easily identifiable, whereas white privilege remains hidden in Europe and America and other societies where whites are in charge. White privilege, like the air we breathe, is an unconscious and unthinking process. Thus, most whites are reluctant to acknowledge the privileges attached to whiteness and the discrimination that results from it. As Yancy observed, whites are not ready to face their racism. They always divert the issue away by dualistic thinking of 'good white' and 'bad white'. They are not ready to recount all the privileges that accrue to them as a result of being white. 'Whiteness does not speak its name, which is the function of both its power and its bad fate.'[47]

Outright prejudice and racism are seen as individual maliciousness and can be easily condemned, but acknowledging white privilege means admitting complicity and taking action against a whole social system that privileges whites over people of colour.[48] Whites, in other words, experience a number of mundane transactions as unproblematic, not realizing that this is the case because of their own whiteness, while others, bearing the burden of suspicion, encounter extra checks and questions.[49]

Another source of white privilege is that it provides a standpoint for viewing ourselves and others. White privilege is often masked behind the rhetoric of colour-blindness.[50] Colour-blindness is based on the assumption that if we do not notice colour, then everyone will be treated equally and held to the same standards. Certainly, this is a great goal, yet it fails to acknowledge that persons in racially diverse society do see colour and do react differently to people based on their skin tone. In fact, the first thing most Americans and people from other racially diverse nations notice about someone is their skin colour, making assumptions about the person's attitudes, behaviours, and their way of life.

Even in African nations, there is a wide gap in the perception of white engineers from Europe and America and those who are natives or blacks.

---

46   P. McIntosh. 'White Privilege: Unpacking the Invisible Knapsack' *Peace and Freedom* (July/August, 1989): 10–12

47   G. Yancy, ed., *What White Looks Like* (New York, NY: Routledge, 2004), 5.

48   Patricia Hill Collins, 'Reflection on the Outsider Within', *Journal of Career Development* 26, no. 1 (1999): 85–88.

49   Garner, 2006.

50   Frankenberg, *White Women, Race Matters: The Social Construction of Whiteness.* See also West, 1999.

Once the person is white, there is already an assumption and faith in the person as an expert in contradistinction to the African or black person. Even 'roadside' engineers in Europe and America are given more respect in Africa than the indigenous people. This perception pervades all aspects and facets of the black nations. There is always this white/black binary where the white phenotype is always the preferred and appealing colour. This was injected into the African psyche during the era of colonialism, when the white colonialists positioned themselves as superior race and colour. Hence, whoever has a light skin tone feels closer to the 'higher' race and appears more attractive than the dark skin. In several ways, the colour black or dark was used and is still used in English language to describe something that is evil or less desirable, whereas the colour white or light was used and continues to be used for something bright, good, and attractive. What a way to forever damage a race and people!

As mentioned above, some opine that being colour-blind can be a way to resolve this divide and white privilege. The colour-blindness argument is only useful to further privilege whites, because every other colour is subsumed under whiteness. Everyone then is judged by the measure of one colour—white. This would achieve nothing than further entrenching whiteness as the norm. Whiteness has always functioned as the norm or background against which others are viewed and judged. Toni Morrison sees whiteness (civilization, technology, and force) defining itself against nature (savagery, primitiveness, and weakness) characterized by otherness in the New World. She argues that a dominant theme in early American literature was 'the highly problematic construction of the American as a new white man'.[51]

The site of transformation of this new white man is within rawness; he is backgrounded by savagery. There were uncivilized 'others' in the American ideological landscape against whose shadowy cultures Europeans could aim to whiten themselves. Therefore, while whiteness became the norm, it could only understand itself against the background of the other. It cannot have an authentic ontological self without creating the other. To this Yancy asserts, 'It is here that white people (poor or not) live a kind of alienated selfhood, which means that they cannot be fully themselves (white) without dominating (or feeling better than) the Other (non-white).

---

51   Toni Morrison, 1993, 39.

Hence, white "superiority" thrives *vis-à-vis* black "inferiority." Whiteness is parasitic upon blackness.'[52] For whites to benefit, someone else must be disadvantaged—the people of colour.

Along with the normative advantage come fictions of equality based on the assumption that if everyone is treated the same, then outcomes will be similar for all groups. These fictions ignore diverse backgrounds, life experiences, cultural understandings, and opportunities. This type of thinking allows white persons to assume that racism does not affect their beliefs about or actions toward persons of colour and to pretend that inequalities no longer exist. What this position fails to consider is the impact of historical inequities, the cumulative effects of differential life experiences, and how racism is built into the very structure of the society.

We have so far pointed out the main and many areas and sources of oppression and subjugation of Africans and other coloured people by the West. Our question then is, Is there any way to heal ourselves from the incurable wound of slavery and colonialism and liberate ourselves from the present shackles of neocolonialism? Many scholars have made several suggestions to this effect.[53] I would add my voice and say that there is no other road but a revolutionary pedagogy that will both heal and raise the epistemological consciousness of the developing nations to the contemporary conduits of colonialism. As Grande noted, 'Revolutionary pedagogies have the potential to provide such a structure as they have the analytical robustness and ideological inclination needed to sort through the underlying power manipulations of colonialist forces.'[54] One such pedagogy is *reconfiliation*, a word and idea brought into theological lexicon by Archbishop Anthony J. V. Obinna. We shall now consider this theology and what pathway to healing it can afford us.

---

52 Yancy, *What White Looks Like*, 7.

53 John McLaren, 'Globalization and Vertical Structure', *American Economic Review* 990, no. 5 (2000): 1239–1252. See also Yancy, *What White Looks Like* (Ruck-Simmons, 2006). Spencer, 2006, p. 118. Yancy, *What White Looks Like* (West, 1999).

54 Grande, 2004, 88.

Reconfiliation: A Way to Heal from Slavery, Colonialism, and Ancillary Discriminatory Practices

The theology of reconfiliation stems from the theology of God becoming man and assuming our human nature in order to raise us to the divine nature. It is the theology of our adoption in Christ. The coming into the world by Christ, accomplished through the collaborative agency of Father, Son, and Holy Spirit, was to redignify fallen humanity, breaking down alienating barriers and cleavages and building up the kingdom of God and the 'family of God in which every man or every woman becomes a fellow son or fellow daughter of God'.[55] Jesus. by assuming our human flesh and making himself like us in all things but sin. made possible the union between God and humanity and between heaven and earth. In the same way, we are all joined into one family of God and brothers and sisters in all respects. This union breaks down all barriers and divisions that people erect between them and others. 'There is definitely a divine persuasiveness in being exposed more and more prayerfully and sacrificing mission of our Lord Jesus Christ geared towards making all of humanity one family.'[56] This understanding of humanity as belonging to one family of God would help immensely to heal the divisions and barriers that people erect between them and others. It will hopefully help people to see one another as one and consequently accord one to the other the respect and dignity they expect from others.

This theology of reconfiliation necessitates the need to forgive the past humiliation and abuse of the Western world on the African people. The Africans have every reason to be angry due to the level of abuse, as highlighted above, that they endured in the hands of the whites and yet every reason to forgive because of what God has done for us in Christ—reconciling the fallen humanity with God. 'This is the essence of refiliation and reconfiliation which more concisely say so. For if "the lamb of God who takes away the sins of the world" can join the company of sinners on their pilgrimage to repentance and purification no one who comes into Jesus'

---

55 Obinna, 'Confilitory Collaboration between the Church in Africa and Europe: A Theo-filio-logical Background', 9.

56 Obinna, 'Confilitory Collaboration between the Church in Africa and Europe: A Theo-filio-logical Background', 10.

company can honestly dare to keep aloof from penitential humanity.'[57] This healing process is not just for the crimes committed against Africans by the West but also crimes committed against Africans by their own people. This will include all forms of discriminations that are still extant today. For instance, the *diala-osu* practice among the Igbos of Nigeria is a very strong discriminatory practice even today, which has created a complicated social phenomenon among the Igbos. This caste system has in more ways than one dehumanized fellow Africans, regarding and treating them differently as people who are not worthy for intermarriage or relationship. This has injected a lot of venom in the bloodstream of some Igbos in Nigeria. This form of discrimination is damaging the social fabric and relationship among the people. It has created an atmosphere of suspicion and disregard one to the other.

The call to this penitential process is for both victims and perpetrators and should be a catharsis for the historical wounds on the African spirit. Reconfiliation is an invitation to this healing process where we all see ourselves as brothers and sisters interlinked in some mysterious fashion through our adoption in Christ. The coming of Christ into the world built the bridge of oneness across the different cultures and nationalities. It is Christ who is the healer and the fulcrum of that human relationship that will restore the sense of dignity and respect for all humans. The idea of reconfiliation is a powerful remedy to the ills of humanity. Archbishop Anthony J. V. Obinna has been in the forefront of the fight against indignities perpetrated by the colonialists and some African cultural practices, especially in the Igbo culture and religion. The current war he is waging against the *diala-osu* caste system comes readily to mind. According to him, he began this fight as far back as a teenager when he didn't know much about this cultural discrimination among the Igbos.

Now that he has read much and understood the frivolity and baselessness of the caste system, he feels both better equipped and positioned to confront it head-on. He has intervened in some cases where parents have disowned their children because of their choices of who to marry. He has insisted on the rights of people to marry a man or woman of their choice based on mutual love and not on some discriminatory cultural practice such as the *diala-osu* system. He has handled many difficult marriage cases, and the

---

57   Obinna, 'Confilitory Collaboration between the Church in Africa and Europe: A Theo-filio-logical Background', 8.

outcome for the couples has been heart-warming. Though it appeared to be an upstream battle, he seemed not to renege on his conviction to accord every human person the dignity and respect he or she deserves as a child of God reconfiliated in Christ. He has taken the crusade to the pulpit, and from there he, is re-educating the Igbos in order to intellectually and spiritually empower them to stand against the fetish for the unholy practices of discrimination and worship of idols. This is a step in the right direction since it will, over time, bring great transformation and healing to the Igbo culture.

This movement towards healing and reconciliation should not be reserved to Archbishop Obinna or the willing few but our collective fight against anything cultural or otherwise that dehumanizes us, enslaves us, or creates barriers between us. Reconfiliation is a positive step towards bringing humanity back to its original beauty and dignity endowed by the Creator. In essence, it is the responsibility of all of us to work for the restoration of humanity's lost dignity occasioned by slave trading of Africans by the West and the discriminatory practices in Africa and beyond the frontiers. This is the hope and possibility that reconfiliation holds out to both Africans and the Western world.

References

- Abbot, M. Walter, ed. *The Documents of Vatican II*. Translation editor Msgr. Joseph Gallagher. New York, NY: American Press Association Press, 1966.
- Alim, H. S. 'Hearing What's Not Said and Missing What Is: Black Language in White Public Space.' In *Intercultural Discourse and Communication: The Essential Readings*, edited by S. F. Kiesling and C. Bratt Paulston. Malden: Blackwell Publishing, 2004.
- Altbach, P. A. 'Education and Neocolonialism.' *Teachers College Record* 72, no. 4 (1971): 543–558.
- Cole, Michael and Sheila R. Cole. *The Development of Children*. 4th edition. New York, NY: Worth Publishers, 2000.
- Davidson, A. L. *Making and Molding Identity in Schools*. New York, NY: State University of New York Press, 1996.

- Dewey, John. *Experience & Education*. New York, NY: Touchstone, 1938.
- Garrett, B. Paul and Patricia Baquedano-Lopez. 'Language Socialization: Reproduction and Continuity, Transformation and Change.' *Annual Review of Anthropology* 31, no. 1 (2002): 339–61.
- Donnelly, D. A., et al. 'White Privilege and Color Blindness.' *Violence Against Women* 11, no. 1 (2005).
- Fanon, Frantz. *The Wretched of the Earth*. Translated by Richard Philcox. New York, NY: Groove Press, 1963.
- Frankenberg, R. *White Women, Race Matters: The Social Construction of Whiteness*. Minneapolis, MN: University of Minnesota Press, 1993.
- Garcia, E. Eugene. *Teaching and Learning in Two Languages. Bilingualism and Schooling in the United States*. New York, NY: Teachers College Press, 2005.
- Garner, S. 'The Uses of Whiteness: What Sociologist Working on Europe Can Draw from US Research on Whiteness.' *Sociology* 40, no. 2 (2006): 257–275.
- Gee, J. Paul. *Situated Language and Learning*. New York, NY: Routledge, 2004.
- Grande, Sandy. *Red Pedagogy: Native American Social and Political Thought*. USA: Rowman & Littlefield Publishers Inc., 2004.
- Heath, B. Shirley. *Ways with Words: Language, Life, and Work in Communities and Classrooms*. New York, NY: Cambridge University Press, 1983.
- Heath, B. Shirley. 'What No Bedtime Story Means: Narrative Skills at Home and School.' In *Linguistic Anthropology*, edited by D. Alessandro. Boston: Blackwell, 1983.
- Hill Collins, P. *Black Feminist Thought: Knowledge, Consciousness, and the Politics of Empowerment*. 2nd ed. New York, NY: Routledge, 2000.
- Lippi-Green, R. *English with an Accent*. New York, NY: Routledge, 1997.

- Maina, F. 'Disrupting Preconceptions: Postcolonialism and Education.' *Teachers College Record* 106, no. 12 (2004): 2304–2311.
- Manglitz, E. 'Challenging White Privilege in Adult Education: A Critical Review of the Literature.' *Adult Education Quarterly* 53, no. 2 (2003): 119–134.
- McIntosh, P. 'White Privilege: Unpacking the Invisible Knapsack.' *Peace and Freedom* (July/August 1989): 10–12.
- McIntosh, P. 'White Privilege and Male Privilege: Apersonal Account of Coming to See Correspondences through Work in Women's Studies.' In *Race, Class and Gender*, edited by M. Andersen and P. Hill Collins, 70–81. Belmont, CA: Wadsworth, 1995.
- McLaren, P. *Che Guevara, Paulo Freire, and the Pedagogy of Revolution*. New York, NY: Rowman & Littlefield Publishers Inc., 2000.
- Mercer, Neil. *Words and Minds*. New York, NY: Routledge, 2000.
- Ngugi wa Thiong'O. *Barrel of a Pen: Resistance to Repression in Neo-Colonial Kenya*. New Jersey, NJ: Africa World Press, 1983.
- Obinna, A. J. V. 'Confiliatory Collaboration between the Church in Africa and Europe.' Paper presentation at a conference, 2004.
- Rogoff, B. et al. 'Firsthand Learning through Intent Participation.' *Annual Review of Psychology* 54 (2003): 175–203.
- Ruck-Simmons, M. 'Invisible Violence and Spiritual Injury with Post-Secondary Institutions: An Anti-Colonial Interrogation and Response.' In *Anti-Colonialism and Education*, edited by G. J. S. Dei and A. Kempf. The Netherlands: Sense Publishers, 2006.
- Shimahara, N. 'Education as Cultural Imperialism.' *Teachers College Record* 76, no. 4 (1975): 688–690.
- Spencer, E. A. B. 'Spiritual Politics: Politicizing the Black Church Tradition in Anti-Colonial Praxis.' In *Anti-Colonialism and Education*, edited by G. J. S. Dei and A. Kempf. The Netherlands: Sense Publishers, 2006.
- Tse, L. *Why Don't They Learn English?* New York, NY: Teachers College Press, 2001.
- Wane, N. N. 'Is Decolonization Possible?' In *Anti-Colonialism and Education*, edited by G. J. S. Dei and A. Kempf. The Netherlands: Sense Publishers, 2006.

- West, T. C. *Wounds of the Spirit: Black Women, Violence and Resistance Ethics.* New York, NY: New York University Press, 1999.
- Yancy, G., ed. *What White Looks Like.* New York, NY: Routledge, 2004.
- Zentella, A. C., ed. *Building on Strength: Language and Literacy in Latino Families and Communities.* New York, NY: Teachers College, 2005.

Chapter Sixteen

Erik Erikson's Concept of
Generativity Applied to Priests

Edmund Aku

How do we rate success? Our people consider successful those with either financial and/or political influence in the community, those who have attained high academic prominence, and parents who have raised their children to these standards. Do these same standards of accomplishment hold for the priest? If success depended solely on these markers, then priests would hardly be counted as successful. They cannot be financially influential as they tend to depend on others for financial support. They are not politicians. So though they may have political opinions, they may not have the instruments that would afford them true political influence in the society. (On the wake of commercialized evangelism, many may question the above positions on success for priests. Priests have adopted evangelical- or Pentecostal-style ministry to gain political and financial equity for themselves. This will be discussed further later.) Priests are celibate. So their vocation is not compatible with biological parenthood. Well, they are usually educated people. But is that the criterion for success for the priest? Where does their success lie?

In this paper, I will attempt an answer, examining the concept of generativity, a quality that, following Erik Erikson's psychosocial stages of development, is expected of people in their middle adult life—a time when most priests would have put in enough years in the ministry to warrant an evaluation of their productivity. Does the length of commitment to the priestly vocation count as a successful accomplishment? What constitutes the success, the years spent in service or how well they have been spent in service, the *chronos* or *kyros*? Before honing into the concept of generativity, which I think will help in answering this question, I will like to quickly run through Erikson's stages of development.

Erikson's Psychosocial Stages of Development

Erikson's theory of personality development is termed psychosocial because it examines where the individual intersects with society in the process of development,[1] conceptualizing, as Marcia, et al. put it, 'the links between inner and outer reality'.[2] Erikson sees personality development as occurring in the process of the resolution of the conflicts between individual psychological needs and the needs of society. Our personality depends on how well we resolve the conflicts at the various stages of our development.

He creates eight stages of development in a lifespan. Successful resolution of the crisis of each stage corresponds to a healthy personality and the acquisition of basic virtues or characteristic strengths helpful in resolving subsequent crises.[3] Failure to deal successfully with the challenge of each stage results in an unhealthy personality. There is, however, room to repair in a later stage some of the lapses of previous ones. In other words, Erikson endorses the possibility for continued growth and development throughout one's lifespan.[4] Furthermore, authors have instructed that the psychosocial diagram should not be seen as only

---

1   E. Douvan, 'Erik Erikson: Critical Times, Critical Theory', *Child Psychiatry and Human Development* 28, no. 1 (1997): 15–21.

2   J. Marcia and R. Josselson, 'Eriksonian Personality Research and Its Implications for Psychotherapy', *Journal of Personality* 81, no. 6 (2012): 617–629.

3   S. A. McLeod, 'Erik Erikson', retrieved from [accessed 2018].
    See also P. H. Munley, 'Erik Erikson's Theory of Psychosocial Development and Vocational Behavior', *Journal of Counseling Psychology* 22, no. 4 (1975): 14–319.

4   Douvan, 'Erik Erikson: Critical Times, Critical Theory', 15–21.

a staircase of achievements. The negative poles are also important in psychosocial resolutions and hence relevant to personal stability. 'In old age, for instance, it is necessary to experience both the thesis of integrity and the antithesis of despair in order to formulate one's own synthesis,' they write[5].

It should be made clear that Erikson never intended any stage to stand in isolation. The formation and development of the person that begins from day 1 of the person's birth is epigenetic. Epigenetics, in this context, includes both the psychosocial implication of a 'synchrony between individual growth and social expectations'[6] and the sense that emergent characteristics of the person build on the ones developed in the preceding stages.[7] As could be gleaned from the following review of the various stages, there is a 'predetermined order' that interacts with the social environment.[8] Marcia and others express this very eloquently that 'at each of the eight chronological periods in the lifespan, there are physical changes to which one's social environment responds with particular expectations and supports in the form of cultural practices and institutions'.[9]

For example, a child of school age, with the right physical, mental, and emotional capability is expected in applicable societies to begin learning to read, write, and add up numbers. This learning process is supported by the provision of the proper schools. Whereas in the previous stage the child interacted with its social environment through 'play', now it does so by 'learning to work'. According to Erikson, everyone goes through these eight stages of development in a lifespan.

The discussion of the stages that follow was extracted from McLeod's article on the topic. We are reviewing the entire stages because of their interconnectedness. It has repeatedly been stated that unresolved issues in the previous stages impact the later ones. This means, for example, as Donald Capps has indicated, that 'the human strengths (virtues) that develop in childhood are critically important to the formation of a

---

5   Marcia, et al., "Eriksonian Personality Research and Its Implications for Psychology', 617–629.

6   Marcia, et al., 'Eriksonian Personality Research and Its Implications for Psychology', 617–629.

7   McLeod, 'Erik Erikson'.

8   McLeod, 'Erik Erikson'.

9   Marcia, et al., 'Eriksonian Personality Research and Its Implications for Psychology', 617–629.

resourceful self'.[10] Hence, 'vocational development takes place within the broader framework of psychosocial development'. Success and fulfilment in the priesthood does not just depend on length of service. It incorporates adaptive skills that the priest has demonstrated from the earlier stages of development.

Trust vs. Mistrust

The first stage corresponds with the first year of life. The crisis in this stage of development is between trust and mistrust. At this stage, the role of primary caregivers is critical. A stable and consistent care enables a healthy development for the infant. It develops a sense of trust. Such a child grows to feel secure and confident in other relationships. On the other hand, when raised in a harsh and unpredictable environment, the infant develops mistrust. Uncertain about its surrounding world, it grows to be fearful, lacking in confidence and ability to influence events. Hope is the virtue or strength acquired at this stage of development.

Autonomy vs. Shame and Doubt

Between eighteen months and three years of age, the child enters the second stage of development where the challenge is that of autonomy versus shame and doubt. At this stage, the child is developing physically and becoming mobile. The child's independence is expressed in various ways. For instance, it is able to move about away from the hands of the caregiver and play with toys of its choice. It is also able to show preference of what to wear or eat and attempts self-dressing and feeding. When parents or caregivers encourage and support the child in these efforts, tolerating failure but not to the degree of losing self-confidence, the child grows to be more confident and secure. Nurtured in such a healthy environment, it is able to explore the limits of its abilities. An unhealthy environment, where the child is overly criticized and controlled, creates a feeling of inadequacy

---

10 Donald Capps, 'Erikson's Schedule of Human Strengths and the Childhood Origins of the Resourceful Self', *Pastoral Psychol* 61 (2012): 269–283.

and a lack of self-esteem in the child. It becomes overdependent on others, not trusting its abilities. The healthy child acquires the virtue of will.

Initiative vs. Guilt

At this third stage, spanning ages three to five, the child plans and initiates games and activities with others. The child, very inquisitive at this stage, explores its interpersonal skills by initiating activities. The healthy child feels secure to lead others and make decisions. The unhealthy one develops a sense of guilt and lack of self-initiatives. Such a child simply follows others. How those around the child treat its curiosity determines how it copes with the crisis of this stage. Are its questions recognized or simply trivialized? That determines whether the child develops healthy or unhealthy tendencies at this stage. However, some level of guilt feeling is necessary to enable the child exercise self-control and have a conscience. The virtue of this stage is purpose.

Industry (Competence) vs. Inferiority

Between ages five and twelve, when the child is of school age, the challenge is between industry and inferiority. Here the child's teachers and peers are prominent in its development. Teachers and mentors teach the child academic skills and pertinent social norms. It learns reading, writing, and arithmetic. Interacting with its peers helps molds the child's self-esteem. It seeks their approval of its competencies and accomplishments. Peer acknowledgement leaves the child with a sense of pride. Encouragement and acknowledgement from mentors (parents, teachers, and their surrogates) and peers create a sense of confidence and industry in the child. Conversely, the child feels inferior and doubts its abilities if its initiatives are thwarted. Some degree of failure enables the child to be modest. Competence is the virtue here.

Identity vs. Role Confusion

When the child is between ages twelve and eighteen, transitioning to adulthood, the crisis it deals with is that of identity versus role confusion. Becoming more independent, the adolescent looks to the future. Concerned about belonging and fitting into society, career, relationships, and family are some of the elements that come into focus for the child of this age range. At this stage the individual develops sexual and occupational identities. It seeks to define its identity and learn the roles it will occupy as an adult. Failure to establish a sense of identity within society can cause role confusion, where the individual is not sure of itself and its place in society. The role confusion or identity crisis may set the adolescent out exploring different lifestyles (work, education, or political activities). Forcing the adolescent into an identity may result in rebellion, unhappiness, and the adoption of a negative identity. Successful integration at this stage portrays the virtue of fidelity, which involves the ability to commit one's self to others based on accepting them despite ideological differences.[11]

Intimacy vs. Isolation

Stage 6 occurs when the individual is between ages eighteen and forty. As a young adult, the individual deals with the crisis of intimacy and isolation. This is the period where the individual begins sharing itself more intimately with others, with the goal of establishing long-term commitments in relationships outside the family. When this stage is handled with success, the individual is comfortable in relationships and demonstrates safety, commitment, and care in the relationships. The maladjusted person will be avoiding intimacy and afraid of commitment in relationships. This could lead to isolation, loneliness, and possibly depression. Love is the virtue successfully attained here.

---

11   McLeod, 'Erik Erikson'.

Generativity vs. Stagnation

In middle adulthood, the individual between forty and sixty-five has the chance of being generative or stagnated. At this point in the lifespan, careers are already established; people are generally settled in their relationships and may also have begun their own families. They also have a sense of belonging to the larger world. There is a sense of giving back to society through raising children, being productive at work, and becoming involved in community activities and organizations. Failure here leads to stagnation and a feeling of unproductivity. Success here brings the virtue of care.

Ego Integrity vs. Despair

From age sixty-five and above, literally at the retirement age, people tend to slow down on productivity. They are wont to thinking of their accomplishments and feeling fulfiled with integrity if they considered themselves successful. However, if they felt they were not productive or successful enough to accomplish their life's goals, people become dissatisfied with life and end in despair, which may lead to depression and hopelessness. Wisdom is the virtue that accompanies the successful individual here. It enables people to look at their lives with a sense of closure and completeness. They accept death without fear.

After closely examining all eight stages, it is evident that by the time most priests are midway into the span of active ministry, their chronological ages will correspond with the seventh stage. It means their developmental challenge is that of generativity and stagnation. As a result, we shall explore this stage in greater details. It must, however, be acknowledged that generativity has been revealed as relevant outside the midlife stage[12] and as indeed a significant indicator of successful aging. In this vein, Erikson also talked of the dignified generative function of older people, e.g., the

---

12   H. Busch, J. Hofer, Au, Alma, I. P. Solcova, P. Tavel, and T. T. Wong, 'For the Benefit of Others: Generativity and Meaning in Life in the Elderly in Four Cultures', *Psychology and Aging* 29, no. 4 (2014): 764–775. See also S. K. Whitbourne and S. V. Penek, 'Young Adult Generativity and Parental Status as Midlife Generativity Predictors' (American Psychological Association 2008 Convention Presentation).

grand-generative function of grandparenthood.[13] Cleared about that, let us now take a closer look at the ramifications of the concept of generativity.

Understanding Generativity

As has already been indicated above, Erikson characterized generativity as the key developmental issue in middle adulthood. He defined it as 'the concern in establishing and guiding the next generation'.[14] It means that generative individuals are seriously committed to passing on knowledge and experiences to the younger generation to help it develop and thrive.[15] The idea of investing time and energy in caring for the next generation has direct implications for parenting one's biological children. But studies have shown that generative ideals are not limited to biological parenting. Erikson did indicate that though 'children are important for generativity', it is not achieved by 'the mere fact of having or even wanting children'.[16] Indeed, it is possible to be generative without having children.[17] Additionally, other theorists have expanded the idea to include concern about more general issues related to welfare of the community, such as volunteering for charities.[18]

If the intention behind generativity is to help the younger generation develop and thrive,[19] then it has to be altruistic and other regarding. Marcia et al. affirm this when they state that 'generativity refers to care for the life cycles of others'. The term *care for species* is also used by some authors. But in consonance with the biblical mandate to love your neighbor as yourself (Matt. 12:31; Mark 22:39), such care for others will not be fulfiling unless it goes with self-care. Hence Marcia and her team maintain that 'the criteria for the generativity statuses reflect involvement

---

13   A. Schoklitsch and U. Baumann, 'Measuring Generativity in Older Adults. The Development of New Scales', *GeroPsych* 24, no. 1 (2011): 31–43.

14   Eric H. Erikson, *Childhood and Society*, 2nd edition (New York, NY: Norton Inc., 1963).

15   Busch et al., 'For the Benefit of Others'.

16   Eric H. Erikson, *Childhood and Society* (New York, NY: Norton Inc., 1950).

17   Schoklitsch and Baumann, 'Measuring Generativity in Older Adults. The Development of New Scales'.

18   Whitbourne and Penek, 'Young Adult Generativity and Parental Status as Midlife Generativity Predictors'.

19   Busch et al., 'For the Benefit of Others'.

and inclusivity in care for self and others'.[20] This implies a balance of care for self and others, necessary in avoiding 'over functioning and burn out'.[21]

With such a balance in place, it is not surprising that 'generativity has been argued to be an important indicator of successful aging'.[22] Persons of this quality are likely to come to a positive balance in a life review, that is, achieve ego-integrity.[23] Schoklitsch and Bauman note in the same trend that 'generativity is indeed an important factor in maintaining one's psychological health in old age'.[24] Busch et al. identify 'minimizing the risk of disease and disability, maintaining physical and mental function, and continuing engagement with (social) life'[25] as essential components of successful aging, all of which are relevant elements of self-care. Peterson gives us various senses in which care, whether for self or the other are manifested. It includes 'to care to do' something, 'to care for' somebody or something, to 'take care of' that which needs protection and attention, and 'to take care not to' do something destructive.[26]

Relating generativity to these expressions of care that includes the desire to help those who are in need implies that Erikson didn't intend generativity as simply a biological construct. This is affirmed by Schoklitsch and Bauman's statement that 'midlife adults have the responsibility to bear, nurture, and guide subsequent generations as well as develop and maintain societal institutions and natural resources'.[27] They further refer to Kotre's expansion of Erikson's idea of generativity to include four distinct forms: 'biological, parental, technical, and cultural'.

Whereas 'biological generativity is about begetting, bearing, and nursing children', parental generativity has to do with 'feeding, clothing, sheltering, loving, and disciplining offspring (biological or not) and initiating them into the family's tradition'. Teachers, as educators, pass

---

20   Marcia et al., 'Eriksonian Personality Research and Its Implications for Psychology', 617–629.

21   Marcia, et al., 'Eriksonian Personality Research and Its Implications for Psychology', 617–629.

22   Schoklitsch and Baumann, 'Measuring Generativity in Older Adults. The Development of New Scales'.

23   Busch et al., 'For the Benefit of Others'.

24   Schoklitsch and Baumann, 'Measuring Generativity in Older Adults. The Development of New Scales'.

25   Busch et al., 'For the Benefit of Others'.

26   B. E. Peterson, 'Longitudinal Analysis of Midlife Generativity, Intergenerational Roles, and Caregiving', *Psychology and Aging* 17, no. 1 (2002): 161–168.

27   Schoklitsch and Baumann, 'Measuring Generativity in Older Adults. The Development of New Scales'.

on skills to pupils, who lack and need them. They exemplify technical generativity by teaching students 'how to read, how to program a computer, how to perform a healing ritual'. When they go from teaching skills to passing on meanings, teachers express cultural generativity. 'Societal generativity principally involves caring for other younger adults: serving as a mentor, providing leadership, and generally contributing to the strength and continuity of subsequent generations'.[28]

Schoklitsch and Bauman introduced the idea of ecological generativity that underscores the importance 'of passing the environment on to subsequent generations'.[29] The generative individual sees the same importance in a healthy environment as in healthy values and experiences for the future of humankind. Such individuals are devoted to leaving behind a healthy legacy. In other words, whatever is intended to improve the life and situations of others is generative.

That generative responsibility includes care of younger people presupposes intergenerational bonds. Peterson clearly states that 'any measure of generativity, if it is true to Erikson's formulation, must tap the importance of intergenerational bonds'. Generative individuals should recognize that they are part of a lineage of caregiving efforts. They were cared for as children, and now they are in turn caring for the next generation (Peterson). Faithful to the intergenerational roles, generative individuals should be disposed to help their aging parents, if they need help. The intergenerational cycle entails reciprocity in the caring experience. The implication here is that generativity does not involve just care of self and of others but also accepting care from others (Peterson). Peterson recalled that a study of generative individuals showed that they 'told stories in which they enjoyed an early family blessing (e.g., they felt cared for) and were sensitized to the suffering of others (e.g., they felt concern for others)'.[30]

Religion and spirituality are mentioned as also relevant to generativity. This is because they are 'among the few forces that counteract the social instability and moral insensitivity of today's secularized society'.[31] In

---

28   Schoklitsch and Baumann, 'Measuring Generativity in Older Adults. The Development of New Scales'.

29   Schoklitsch and Baumann, 'Measuring Generativity in Older Adults. The Development of New Scales'.

30   Peterson, 'Longitudinal Analysis of Midlife Generativity, Intergenerational Roles, and Caregiving'.

31   G. M. Brelsford, S. Marinelli, J. W. Ciarrochi, G, S. Dy-Liacco, 'Generativity and Spiritual

other words, they help to better society. Mahatma Gandhi, who pioneered nonviolence as tool of bettering society, is mentioned by Erikson as a model of generativity. Authors point to a plethora of generative souls in Christianity and the Western theology. They include people who followed the example of Jesus, who gave up his life for the salvation of all, and his teaching of love of neighbour.[32] Generative individuals show concern for the well-being of the future generation, and thereby focus on the betterment of human family, which includes a healthy and stable environment, religion, and spirituality, as implied by Brelsford and his colleagues, assist toward this end.[33] They further allude that 'those rating high on religiousness or spirituality tend to have generative concerns and actions'.[34]

According to Brelsfold and team, studies have shown a strong positive correlation between personality and spiritual disclosure. They admit a relationship between generativity and higher scores on positive personality traits like agreeableness, extraversion, conscientiousness, and openness to experience and lower scores on neuroticism,[35] which they said were all positively correlated to increased spiritual disclosure. Conversely, high levels of neuroticism correlated to lower levels of spiritual disclosure and negative to generativity.[36]

Generativity has also been associated with effective leadership, based probably on the understanding that good leaders are servants seeking the well-being of their subjects than their own personal gains. This is the position supported by Zacher and others. The generative leader, according to them, focuses more on the younger generation than on their own gains, careers, and accomplishments.[37] Peterson's emphasis on the link between generativity and prosocial personality characteristics like 'empathy, responsibility, self-control' or with 'satisfaction with work' that includes

---

Disclosure in Close Relationships', *Psychology of Religion and Spirituality* 1, no.3 (2009): 150–161.

32 Brelsford et al., 'Generativity and Spiritual Disclosure in Close Relationships'.

33 Brelsford et al., 'Generativity and Spiritual Disclosure in Close Relationships'. See also H. Zacher, K. Rosing, T. Henning, M. Frese, 'Establishing the Next Generation at Work: Leader Generativity as a Moderator of the Relationship between Leader Age, Leader-Member Exchange, and Leadership Success', *Psychology and Aging* 26, no. 1 (2011): 241–252.

34 Brelsford, et al., 'Generativity and Spiritual Disclosure in Close Relationships'.

35 Zacher et al., 'Establishing the Next Generation at Work: Leader Generativity as a Moderator of the Relationship between Leader Age, Leader-Member Exchange, and Leadership Success'.

36 Brelsford et al., 'Generativity and Spiritual Disclosure in Close Relationships'.

37 Zacher et al., 'Establishing the Next Generation at Work: Leader Generativity as a Moderator of the Relationship between Leader Age, Leader-Member Exchange, and Leadership Success'.

'a focus on helping others while downplaying monetary incentives' and 'healthy concern for others' corroborate this (Peterson).

Aberrations of Generativity

Having explored all these qualities of generativity, it is apt to point out at this juncture that there are also aberrations to generativity. This occurs when the right actions and behaviours are presented with the wrong motivations or intentions. Before delving into that, I would like to add that the direct antithesis of generativity is stagnation or self-absorption. To the extent that people fail to achieve generativity, they become stagnated. That is, they spend their later years focusing inward on their own concerns. There is nothing wrong with self-care or addressing personal concerns, but if those are our sole *raison d'etre*, then we are egotistic. We languish in some kind of sterility or stagnation. Such self-absorbed individuals, according to Erikson, readily lavish care on themselves as if they were their one and only beloved child. Stagnation is likely to produce depression, apathy, and emptiness.

As mentioned briefly above, the aberrations of generativity occur in people who are self-engulfed. Even when they pretend to show concern for others, their ultimate goal is self-aggrandizement. Marcia et al. mention two types of what they term pseudo-generative statuses: agentic and communal. Agentic pseudo-generative persons show care to only those individuals who are essential to the realization of their own goals or projects, those who follow the agentic person's own agenda. Those who are communally pseudo-generative only care when they receive compensation, gratitude, and appreciation for whatever good they do.[38] Jesus advises us not to be like such people.

These characteristics are not too different from what Busch and team describe as Machiavellianism. People with this personality trait 'readily manipulate others to achieve their goals and disprize other people's concerns because they see others as means rather than ends'. He further adds that people high in Machiavellianism have little interest in contributing to society. Any prosocial behaviour on their part is cloaked in the need for prestige and public recognition, he argues. Thus, ultimately,

---

38 Marcia et al., 'Eriksonian Personality Research and Its Implications for Psychology', 617–629.

even seemingly prosocial behaviours only serve their selfish agenda. Busch and colleagues therefore conclude that 'the cynical and self-centred Machiavellian perspective seems hardly compatible with the "hope on the advancement and betterment of human life in succeeding generation's characteristics of belief in species"'.

Having come thus far, we are in a better position to see what to look for or expect from a truly generative priest. This is discussed in the conclusion that follows.

Commercialized Evangelism: An Aberration of Generativity

Disappointedly, commercialized evangelism has creeped into the Catholic church thanks to priests who are today seeking popularity and fame by adopting the methodology of pastors of the Evangelical or Pentecostal denominations. These pastors prey on people's fear, threatening them with doom prophecies if they failed to do their biddings and promising them miracles and prosperity on obedience to their calls. Considering the difficulties people are living through today in Nigeria, it is no surprise that they are so gullible to the gimmicks of these preachers who pretend to be bearers of the magic wand that controls people's fortune, drawing loyalty and following with their prosperity baits. Recently, a Catholic priest was demanding patronage from politicians in exchange for favourable prophecies, threatening them with a spell of political doom on failure to donate to his satisfaction. On the surface value, such persons may appear successful, considering the mega crowds they pull. But their apparent productivity is more self-centred than altruistic. This does not meet the test for generativity. It is an aberration. They manipulate others, taking advantage of their weaknesses to serve their own selfish interests. The last time I checked, Christ was still the model for Catholic priests, not the Evangelical celebrity preachers.

Conclusion: Priests and Generativity

I would imagine that the opportunity of being a priest places one on a better path to generativity. This, however, does not imply an automatic correlation between the two. If generativity implies care for the future generation/s, care for our species and community, and that religion and spirituality, as was stated earlier, are one of the few forces that can support social stability and moral sensitivity in society, the minister of religion is definitely at the heart of this generous movement. The priest is one of such ministers. The priesthood is different from several other careers in life because it is a vocation of service. Most people work for profit and make a living by the profit they make through their services. The priesthood is principally a call to service.

This, however, does not make any priest a generative individual. Nevertheless, a priest who is truly devoted to his vocation, executing his services to the best of his abilities and knowledge is undoubtedly generative. Such a priest is inspired by the example of Christ who came to serve and not to be served and to give his life as a ransom (Matt. 20:28; Mark 10:45). Christ is a model of servant leadership. That is what priests are supposed to be doing, leading by serving. A generative leader focuses on improving the conditions of the people, not personal fame and popularity. This is the path the priest is expected to toe as the leader of God's people. Otherwise he will create a division among his flock, pushing his personal agenda, favouring those who subscribe to them, and exemplifying those aberrations of generativity we saw above, including Machiavellianism.

Christ's humanity was a sacrificial option. He gave up his divinity and embraced the human nature to the point of death on the cross. In many ways, answering the call to be a priest of God also involves personal sacrifices. However, unless these are rightly channelled, the sacrifices will be in vain. They will lead to aberrations of generativity than to generativity. Following this prayer of the psalmist— 'Not to us, Lord, not to us, but to your name be the glory' (Ps. 115:1)—the priest should dedicate his services to the greater glory of the Lord. Once our services and sacrifices are motivated by the zeal for personal glory and rewards, then we have drifted from the imitation of Christ and lost out on generativity.

Brelsford and team link spiritual disclosures with higher scores on positive personality traits and prosocial behaviours that have equally been associated with high marks of generativity. When the priest not only teaches and preaches the gospel values but also lives by them, he scores highly on the generativity scale. It wouldn't suffice to teach about love without complementing it with loving as Jesus taught us. Generativity involves positive personality traits that make us approachable to others. In that way, they can confide in us and trust us with their weaknesses and fears, trusting that we can support them with empathy.

Intergenerational concern is another characteristic of generative individuals. Generativity involves reciprocal concern across generations. We build and develop on the generosity of our predecessors. We also have to be generous towards those coming after us. This is good not only for the survival of the priestly ministry but also of the human family. Generosity to the human family also includes contributing towards a healthier sociopolitical environment and one that is ecologically sustainable. Freely you have received; freely you shall give (Matt. 10:8). This passage is very significant to the ministry of the priest as it refers to the Lord's commissioning of the apostles to their various ministries to his people. It points to a continuous caring and generous giving of self for the good of all. This sprit is often threatened by the pull of mundane pursuits, which often cause us to forget that what we do to the least ones we do for Christ (Matt. 25:45).

Importantly, this process cannot be seen as one-way traffic. In caring for the younger generation or recipient individual, the generative person develops too. The relationship and gains are bilateral. For example, teachers need students to confirm their experiences of identity and generativity, just as students need teachers for developing their senses of industry an identity (Marcia et al.). So the priest and the faithful need one another to satisfy their identities and respective callings in life.

Interestingly, in teaching about love, Jesus never encouraged self-atrophy. Love of self, not selfish love, was for him the backbone for love of others: love others as yourself (Matt. 22:39; Mark 12:31). It is part of the second greatest commandment. This love of self is not egotistic or narcissistic. It is complemented by love of others. Both go hand in hand. The way I love myself reflects the type of love am able to extend to others. Hence self-care is imperative to caring for others. A sound mind in a sound body, they say. By maintaining healthy mental and physical attitudes, we remain stable holistically and are better in place to care more meaningfully for others. As Marcia and others agreed above, generativity statuses involve and include a balance of care of self and others.

The generativity of Archbishop Obinna is obvious in no little way in his promotion of the use of the Igbo language through the Odenigbo lectures and his fight against the dehumanizing practice of *osu* discrimination. These legacies will survive him into the unforeseeable future.

References

- Brelsford, G. M., S. Marinelli, J. W. Ciarrochi, and G. S. Dy-Liacco. 'Generativity and Spiritual Disclosure in Close Relationships.' *Psychology of Religion and Spirituality*, 1, no. 3 (2009): 150–161.

- Busch, H, J. Hofer, Alma Au, I. P. Solcova, P. Tavel, and T. T. Wong. 'For the Benefit of Others: Generativity and Meaning in Life in the Elderly in Four Cultures.' *Psychology and Aging* 29, no. 4 (2014): 764–775.

- Capps, D. 'Erikson's Schedule of Human Strengths and the Childhood Origins of the Resourceful Self.' *Pastoral Psychol* 61 (2012): 269–283.

- Douvan, E. 'Erik Erikson: Critical Times, Critical Theory.' *Child Psychiatry and Human Development* 28, no. 1 (1997): 15–21.

- Erikson, E. H. *Childhood and Society*. New York, NY: Norton Inc., 1950.

- Erikson, E. H. *Childhood and Society*, 2nd edition. New York, NY: Norton Inc., 1963.

- Marcia, J. and R. Josselson. 'Eriksonian Personality Research and Its Implications for Psychotherapy.' *Journal of Personality* 81, no. 6 (2012): 617–629.

- McLeod, S. A. 'Erik Erikson.' 2008. Retrieved from http://www.simplypsychology.org/Erik-Erikson.html

- Munley, P. H. 'Erik Erikson's Theory of Psychosocial Development and Vocational Behaviour.' *Journal of Counselling Psychology* 22, no. 4 (1975): 14–319.

- Peterson, B. E. 'Longitudinal Analysis of Midlife Generativity, Intergenerational Roles, and Caregiving.' *Psychology and Aging* 17, no. 1 (2002): 161–168.
- Schoklitsch, A. and U. Baumann. 'Measuring Generativity in Older Adults. The Development of New Scales.' *GeroPsych* 24, no. 1 (2011): 31–43.
- Whitbourne, S. K. and S. V. Penek. 'Young Adult Generativity and Parental Status as Midlife Generativity Predictors.' American Psychological Association 2008 Convention Presentation.
- Zacher, H., K. Rosing, T. Henning, and M. Frese. (2011). 'Establishing the Next Generation at Work: Leader Generativity as a Moderator of the Relationship between Leader Age, Leader-Member Exchange, and Leadership Success.' *Psychology and Aging* 26, no. 1 (2011): 241–252.

Section Five

Moral Theology, Human Life and Liturgical Music

Chapter Seventeen

Laudato Si': Integral Ecology and the Restoration of Our Cultural Heritage in Africa

Kingsley Ndubueze

Introduction

The publication of *Laudato Si': On Care for Our Common Home* in 2015 by Pope Francis was an epoch-making event in the history of the Catholic social magisterium.[1] Not only was it the first time that the Bishop of Rome dedicated an encyclical exclusively in response to the social and ecological questions of our times but also, it was the first time an explicit recognition of 'intrinsic value' has been extended to the nonhuman creatures in the Roman Catholic Social Teaching.[2] As a result, the integral ecology that is conspicuously and commendably central in *Laudato Si'*

---

1   Pope Francis, *Laudato Si: On Care for Our Common Home*, available from http://w2.vatican.va/content/francesco/en/encyclicals/documents/papa-francesco_20150524_enciclica-laudato-si.html [[accessed November 3, 2018].

2   Kingsley Ndubueze, 'Responsible Environmental Stewardship for Sustainable Development in Africa: Edward Schillebeeck's Co-Humanity and Creaturality and Pope Francis' Integral Ecology', *African Ecclesial Review* 60, nos. 1 and 2 (2018): 119–139, 133.

seeks for a sustainable and integral human development of both human and nonhuman creatures in our natural and human environments.[3]

More so, Pope Francis' integral ecology incorporates the recognition of 'cultural ecology' that under all circumstances gives special prominence to the 'patrimony of nature' and the 'cultural patrimony'.[4] In that sense, he states that:

> This patrimony is a part of the shared identity of each place and a foundation upon which to build a habitable city. It is not a matter of tearing down and building new cites ... [but] rather, there is a need to incorporate the history, culture and architecture of each place, thus preserving its original identity. Ecology, then, also involves protecting the cultural treasures of humanity in the broadest sense. More specifically, it calls for greater attention to local cultures ... and the language of the people.[5]

It is imperative we protect, preserve, and restore our cultural heritage in Nigeria and in Africa at large. This is pertinent, since we appear to be at the verge of losing our rich cultural identities, history, traditions, folklores, values, sensitivities, and even our mode of dress and spoken languages in the midst of threats from modernity and religions.[6] This is with particular reference to those 'Christian Churches and pastors' who embark on cutting down our ancient community trees and demolishing our cultural monuments and artefacts in the name of 'community deliverance' under the pretence that peoples' progress, breakthroughs, fertility, rationality, vocation, peace, unity, and even that their eternal destiny are tied to those cultural memorabilia, ancient works of art, and ecological trees.[7] Albeit without any prejudice or

---

3   Francis, *Laudato Si'*, §13.

4   Francis, *Laudato Si'*, §143.

5   Francis, *Laudato Si'*, §143.

6   George Nwachukwu, 'Odenigbo Lecture of the Catholic Archdiocese of Owerri', available from https://www.owarch.org/odenigbo-lectures/ [accessed November 12, 2018]. See also E. O. Wahab et al., 'Causes and Consequences of Rapid Erosion of Cultural Values in a Traditional African Society', *Journal of Anthropology* (2012): 1–7. See also Deborah Yakubu Dangana, 'Nigeria: How Western Culture Erodes Values Among Nigerian Youth', *Daily Trust*, August 8, 2014, available from https://allafrica.com/stories/201408081141. html [accessed November 16, 2018].

7   I have seen some communities in Igboland where this development has taken place, and also, I have equally read of other incidences of its occurrences in many other places, like in Rivers State and Edo State. See also Simon Ebegbulem, 'Pastor Cut Sacred Iroko: "Vengeful

intent to downplay some perceived cases where demonic forces seem to cause havoc through various diabolical manifestations, nor do I intend to deny that some evil activities and fetish exploitations have been perpetuated in the name of culture and tradition in some places.

However, the attitude of indiscriminate and disproportionate chopping down of our community trees and the demolishing of monumental artefacts without any consideration to replacing them has some harmful ecological effects on our environment since trees serve as 'carbon sinks' that limit and mitigate the impact of greenhouse gases in the atmosphere.[8] More so, the attitude is equally perceived to be dangerous to our natural and human ecologies because it appears to affect adversely our human relationship with the natural environment and with other creatures,[9] whereby humanity tends to abuse and desacralize nature with impunity, leading to the current age of the ecological crisis and global warming.[10]

To that effect, this article explores how Pope Francis' integral ecology in *Laudato Si'*, as well as his cultural ecology that seeks the well-being of both human and nonhuman creatures, are relevant to the process of restoration and rehabilitating our dissipating rich cultural heritage in Africa. Therefore, I will underscore that respecting our cultural ecology, together with creating pride for our cultures and traditions, especially those that are not antithetical to the gospel message, results in our collective effort to preserve our cultural identity. This paper is divided into three parts. The first part provides a summary of what the paper intends to achieve, as well as the vision of a transparent cultural enlightenment through our language in the *Odenigbo* lecture series founded by the archbishop of Owerri Ecclesiastical Province. The second part explains the integral ecology of Pope Francis in relation to its integral involvement

---

Tree on Killing Spree": Benin Community Natives Flee', *Vanguard*, available from https://www.vanguardngr.com/2018/03/pastors-cut-sacred-iroko-vengeful-tree-killing-spree-benin-community-natives-flee/ [accessed November 16, 2018] and Sunday Onen, 'Africa: Pastor Cut Down Sacred Iroko, "Vengeful Tree on Killing Spree" Benin Community Native Flee', in *Africa Trade News*, March 27, 2018, available from http://www.atqnews.com/ng/pastor-cut-sacred-iroko-vengeful-tree-on-killing-spree-benin/ [accessed November 16, 2018].

8   Emeodilichi Mba, 'Assessment of Environmental Impact of Deforestation in Enugu, Nigeria', *Resources and Environment* 8, no. 2 (2018): 207–215.

9   Ndubueze, 'Responsible Environmental Stewardship', 119. See also Michael Northcott, *A Moral Climate: The Ethics of Global Warming* (Maryknoll, NY: Orbis Books, 2007), 16.

10 Francis, *Laudato Si'*, §2. See also Northcott, *A Moral Climate*, 16. Philip Sherrard, *Human Image: World Image: The Death and Resurrection of Sacred Cosmology* (Cambridge, UK: Golgonooza Press, 1992), 3.

with cultural ecology towards promoting our cultural heritage in Africa. The third part presents the effects of cutting down our ancient community trees and the ecological benefits resulting from having our environment respected and protected through promoting our cultural heritage. Finally, the conclusion states that our cultural heritage and identity speak more about who we are as a people.

The *Odenigbo* Lecture Series: Towards a Transparent Cultural Engagement

It is evident and remarkable that the silver jubilee celebration of the Owerri Ecclesiastical Province is a huge blessing to the province. The celebration is equally an honour for His Grace, Most Rev. Anthony John Valentine Obinna, the archbishop of Owerri Ecclesiastical Province—an outstanding educator and one of the prominent and important pillars of our Catholic faith in Owerri Province. In addition, there is no doubt that on this jubilee, the first archbishop of Owerri Province calls for a deep reflection in order to raise our consciousness towards restoring our cultural engagement as a people and as Christians. To that effect, we need to have a careful look at our cultural heritage in a 'confiliatory spirit'[11] using a *theo-filio*-logical understanding that promotes freedom and involves a 'life-engaging', 'life-orienting', 'thought provoking' conversation over our actions and activities in order "to be capable of adding a qualitative value in our sense of human living" and relationship with others and with our environment.[12] This especially concerns a sustainable and integral human development that gives credence to our 'cultural ecology', as proposed

---

11   In the understanding of Archbishop Anthony Obinna, 'confiliatory spirit' denotes a genuine effort to internalize the unifying force and a collaborative love and mission of the almighty God the Father, the Son, Jesus Christ, and the Holy Spirit in our daily lifestyles as Christians in our natural environment. This is in line with Archbishop Obinna's theological exploration of 'confiliatory collaboration' from a *theo-filio*-logical dynamo. He employs key theological thought-provoking terms like 'filiation', 'infiliation', 'refiliation', 'confiliation', 're-conciliation' in order to evaluate our sense of solidarity, collaboration, unity of purpose, and mission in the world. Thus, he states that, 'his proposal is the Re-conciliation and Confiliatory collaboration to be our life-engaging and life-orienting dynamo in making headway and sense in the varied family settings of our lives in church and society, in Africa and in our relations with the rest of the world'. See Anthony Obinna, 'Confiliatory Collaboration between the Church in Africa and Europe: A *Theo-Filio*-Logical Background' (lecture text, June 3, 2004), 1–12.

12   Obinna, 'Confiliatory Collaboration between the Church in Africa and Europe', 1–2.

by Pope Francis, with regard to promoting our traditions and protecting our human and natural environments from degradation in the age of the ecological crisis. This presupposition, therefore, becomes essential and apposite since His Grace Archbishop Obinna has been an ardent admirer and promoter of African cultures and development.[13]

In particularly, his **Nkuzi Odenigbo** lecture series has featured so far twenty-two prominent and illustrious Igbo sons and daughter as its lecture presenters since its foundation in 1996 (see the chronology below).[14] The Nkuzi Odenigbo, all these years, has been commendably dedicated to the promotion of our **Igbo** language (**Asụsụ Igbo**) and has

---

13   Anthony Obinna, 'African Cultures and Development: The Rectifying Challenge' (a lecture presented at The First Colloquium—Culture and Development in African Theology, Abidjan, Ivory Coast, September 27 to October 1, 2010), 1–16.

14   Odenigbo lecture is the brainchild of Archbishop Anthony J. V. Obinna. From Nwachukwu's 'Odenigbo Lecture': 'The concept of ODENIGBO was chosen as a banner of the lecture series because we as Ndi Igbo are constantly praying that through Igbo Language and genius Christ will dwell in our various lives and families. According to the founding father, Odenigbo is meant to foster a harmonious relationship between the Igbo culture and the goodnews brought to Ndi Igbo by Jesus Christ. It is designed to spread the gospel and promote the good aspects of our culture. Therefore, all Igbos irrespective of our Christian belonging, are called upon to join hands with the Catholic Archdiocese of Owerri in her effort to salvage our mother tongue from annihilation. Let us with one heart embrace ODENIGBO–NKUZI OHA NA EZE.' Since 1996, when His Grace, Most Rev. Anthony Obinna founded the Odenigbo lecture series, the lecture has been an annual 'thought-provoking' and 'life-engaging' cultural festivity that comes up within the first week of the month of September. Significantly, it has featured so far twenty-two prominent and illustrious Igbo sons and daughters like Prof. Nolue Emenanjo: 'Olu m Efula' 'May My Language Not Be Lost' (1996), Monsignor Theophilus Okere: 'Chibundu: Ofe Chukwu na Ndu Ndi Igbo' (1997), Prof. Edmund Ikenga Metuh: 'Onyegbula: Ndi Igbo na Nsopuru Ndu' (1998), Prof. Chinua Achebe: 'Echi Di Ime Taa Bu Gboo' (1999), Archbishop Anthony J. V. Obinna: 'Ujunwa: Añuri Uwa Niile' (2000), Prof. John Egbulefu: 'Uwa Ohuru: Aka Mgba Chere Ndi Igbo' (2001), Dr. Mrs. Gabriella Ihuarugo Nwaozuzu: 'Agwa Bu Mma: Nzuzi Na Nzujo Umu Igbo' (2002), Prof. Godfrey Igwebuike Onah: 'Odoziobodo: Ochichi Maka Ezi Oganihu Ndi Igbo' (2003), Dr. Barnabas Anaelechi Chukwuezi: 'Ahuike: Ike Ogwu Na Ike Ekpere' (2004), Prof. Victor Okereke: 'Akobundu: Amamihe Na Ebute Oganihu' (2005), Rev. Fr. Dr. Innocent Maduakolam Osuagwu: 'Ijeoma: Ofo Ndi Igbo Na Ago' (2006), Prof. Dora Akunyili: 'Ogwudi Ire: Ezi Nka Na Nruru Aka' (2007), Dr. Iheanacho Emeruwa: 'Oke Chi Nyere Igbo: Kedu Ebe Anyi Nozi' (2008), Rev. Fr. Dr. Ernest Munachi Ezeogu: 'Jesu Onye Afrika: Ozioma Maka Uwa Niile' (2009), Dr. Florence Obiageri Anugom: 'Ahu Mmadu: Nsopuru Kwesiriya' (2010), Monsignor Prof. Francis Obiora Ike: 'Ntohapu: Oru Oma Nke Ozioma' (2011), Most. Rev. Lucius Iwejuru Ugorji: 'Nzuko Nso Kristi: Nzukota Chukwu Na Mmadu' (2012), Prof. Peter Ejiofor: 'Oganihu Igbo: Onodu Asusu Igbo' (2013), Prof. Chinedum Nwajiuba: 'Ochichi Oma: Olileanya Ohanaeze' (2014), Rev. Fr. Prof. John Obilor: 'Obe Jesu Kristi: Ofo Ndu, Ogu Ndu' (2015), Prof. Barth Nnaji: 'Omenka: Nchuputa Na Mmeputa' (2016), Most. Rev. John Okoye: 'Uwadiegwu: Mma Na Njo Di N'uwa' (2017), and Dr. Mrs. Patricia Uloaku: 'Isuzi, Idezi Na Ikpozi Igbo: Mmasi Na Akamgba Di Na Ha' (2018).

facilitated a transparent cultural engagement and enlightenment with the view to empowering the people of my generation.[15] This surely will enable us to promote our cultural identity by upholding our *Asụsụ Igbo* in order to inculcate the quintessence of our rich cultural heritage and therefore work for its restoration, through clarifications, communication, and its implementation in all walks of life and especially in our school curricular. What this presupposes is that there is a crucial challenge that confronts every one of us in our different academic specialties towards integrating, assimilating, and expanding Igbo language. This significantly proposes making our *Asụsụ Igbo* to become a more '**scientific language**' whereby it can be used to learn and, at the same time, to teach different subjects in our academic environment.

As a matter of fact, it will be extremely fascinating whenever Igbo language is employed in studying mathematics, economics, agricultural science, biology, and the other sciences without excluding philosophy and theology in our school system. In this sense, the effort is channelled towards making sure that our *Asụsụ Igbo*, which is "in danger of becoming extinct in spite of the prime status the language enjoys in the company of other major languages in Nigeria",[16] can effectively continue to be spoken undiluted, written correctly and properly, read fluently, and at the same time promote its communication with meaning, authority, emancipation, significance, and reverence to our present and future generations with a high sense of pride and passion within and beyond our geo-social and political space in the community of nations. This demonstration implies that language goes beyond simple communication,[17] and our Igbo language

---

15   Nwachukwu, 'Odenigbo Lecture': 'The concept of ODENIGBO was chosen as a banner of the lecture series because we as Ndi Igbo are constantly praying that through Igbo Language and genius Christ will dwell in our various lives and families. According to the founding father, Odenigbo is meant to foster a harmonious relationship between the Igbo culture and the goodnews brought to Ndi Igbo by Jesus Christ. It is designed to spread the gospel and promote the good aspects of our culture. Therefore, all Igbos irrespective of our Christian belonging, are called upon to join hands with the Catholic Archdiocese of Owerri in her effort to salvage our mother tongue from annihilation. Let us with one heart embrace ODENIGBO–NKUZI OHA NA EZE'. Since 1996, when His Grace, Most Rev. Anthony Obinna founded the Odenigbo lecture series, the lecture has been an annual 'thought-provoking' and 'life-engaging' cultural festivity that comes up within the first week of the month of September.

16   Nwachukwu, 'Odenigbo Lecture'.

17   Lawrence Nchekwube Nwankwo, '"Onwe M Ozo"—My Other Self: A Discourse Analytical Approach to Rooting Marriage in Igboland More Deeply into the Christian Soil', (lecture text, 2018): 1–18, 1.

is not an exception. Therefore, our **Asụsụ Igbo** can equally contribute
much more than anyone of us can measure towards the formulation of
cultural ecological relationships with God the Creator, with our fellow
human beings, and with the natural environment in our common home.

Laudato Si': A Collaborative Dialogue for All People of Good Will

According to cultural anthropologists, culture gives identity to all
humanity irrespective of his/her background.[18] However, to engage in a
culture of collaboration, it is only possible in the framework of a team
spirit, communication, and a collaborative dialogue.[19] This is because
collaboration and dialogue are integrally connected and have the ability
to carry everyone along in order to improve the existence of people in
a given environment.[20] It suffices to say that the integral connectivity
and precision in the tone of writing in relation to the promulgation of
Laudato Si' points to the fact that the encyclical may have been prepared
in a culture of collaboration. Pope Francis' contribution is unique, since
he tries to incorporate and collaborate in order to carry everyone with
him in *Laudato Si'*. It is evident that he understands that "dialogue is
the key."[21] To that effect, 'he dialogues with theologians, philosophers,
scientists, national and continental episcopal conferences, governments
and all those who want and can contribute to care for our common home.'[22]
His collaborative understanding even extends to citing a ninth-century
Muslim mystic and Sufi poet, Ali al-Khawas.[23]

Furthermore, like previous papal encyclicals and documents since
Pacem in Terris (1963), Pope Francis calls for a dialogue to engage 'all

---

18   Anthony Cohen, 'Culture as Identity: An Anthropologist's View', *New Literary History* 24,
     no. 1 (1993): 195–209.

19   Kris D. Gutiérrez, Patricia Baquedano-López, Héctor H. Alvarez, and Ming Ming Chiu,
     'Building a Culture of Collaboration through Hybrid Language Practices', *Theory into
     Practice* 38, no. 2 (1999): 87–93.

20   Caroline Clark et al., 'Collaboration as Dialogue: Teachers and Researchers Engaged in
     Conversation and Professional Development', *American Educational Research Journal*
     33, no. 1 (1996): 193–231.

21   Alexandre Martins, '*Laudato Si'*: Integral Ecology and Preferential Option for the Poor',
     Journal of Religious Ethics 46, no. 3 (2018): 410–424, 417.

22   Martins, '*Laudato Si'*: Integral Ecology,' 417.

23   Francis, *Laudato Si'*, §233.

people of good will' in a conversation that determines the well-being of all creation.[24] As a matter of fact, this call for a special dialogue demonstrates an important step towards collaboration with all humanity. It implies that "he wants a broad participation."[25] This collaborative gesture is characteristic of his papal ministry. In choosing a name for himself after the election, as the first Jesuit and the first Latin American Pope, he preferred to choose Francis in honour of Saint Francis of Assisi, the patron saint of "those who promote ecology" and an epitome of care for all creatures.[26] However, more specifically, he wants to collaborate and identify with "both the cry of the earth and the cry of the poor," whom Saint Francis of Assisi also represents.[27] There is no doubt that he intends to incorporate the poor earth and the excluded to participate at the table of dialogue because they are among the most neglected, marginalized, "and maltreated of the poor."[28]

It was little wonder that during the homily of the inaugural Mass of his Petrine ministry, the Solemnity of Saint Joseph on March 19, 2013, he started calling for the protection of all of God's creation. He states that all of us have the vocation to protect all creatures of the natural environment.

---

24 Francis, *Laudato Si'*, §62. When the church speaks of 'men and women of good will', she intends to address something that is 'basic' and 'common' to all humanity, which invariably goes beyond religion, nationality, walks of life, and gender and also when the message is of course designed to achieve a wider coverage. The encyclical *Pacem in Terris* (April 11, 1963), by Saint Pope John XXIII, happens to be the first official document to use 'all people [men and women] of good will' (§168) to address all humanity in the international setting, with regard to emphasising the essence of upholding peace and justice in the natural world. See also *Compendium of the Social Doctrine of the Church* (2006) where the expression is used twelve times. Most specifically, like in matters concerning the care for our common home for which Pope Francis invites us to dialogue with one another, Saint Pope John Paul II had earlier in *Ecclesial in America* (1999) called for a collaborative dialogue and action by all humanity with regard to the well-being of the natural environment. Pope John Paul II, *Ecclesial in America*, §25, available from http://w2.vatican.va/content/john-paul-ii/en/apost_exhortations/documents/hf_jp-ii_exh_22011999_ecclesia-in-america.html [accessed November 3, 2018]. He stated that 'all people of good will must work to ensure the effective protection of the natural environment ... because the Creator entrusts the care of the earth into the hands of men and women since they are the crown of the process of creation'.

25 Martins, 'Laudato Si': Integral Ecology', 417.

26 It was in 1979 that St. Francis of Assisi was declared the heavenly patron for ecology and care for creation. Pope John Paul II, *Apostolic Letter 1979*, 1509. See also Pope John Paul II, 'Peace With God the Creator: Peace With All of Creation: World Day of Peace Message, January 1, 1990', §16, available from http://w2.vatican.va/content/john-paul-ii/en/messages/peace/documents/hf_jp-ii_mes_19891208_xxiii-world-day-for-peace.html [accessed November 3, 2018].

27 Francis, *Laudato Si'*, §49.

28 Francis, *Laudato Si'*, §2.

This is because "everything has been entrusted to our protection, and all of us are responsible ... [therefore], let us be 'protectors' of creation, protectors of God's plan inscribed in nature, protectors of one another and the environment".[29] This implies that Pope Francis even started earlier than *Laudato Si'* to demand that everybody on this planet, irrespective of religion, race, and walks of life, should be protected and as well be involved in the dialogue towards care for our common home, especially in the age of the Anthropocene.[30] More so, it is our 'common patrimony' and duty to care for what 'all humanity and nonhuman creatures own in common.[31] To that effect, in order to be more effective, authentic, and comprehensive in his collaborative dialogue, Pope Francis incorporates other nonhuman creatures in current debates towards promoting environmental stewardship and sustainability that includes the interests of all creation. Additionally, another reason for such collaborative action, with regard to *Laudato Si'*, is that Pope Francis, in his remarkable way, wants to contribute to the social teaching of his predecessors on integral ecology in order to show how connected human beings are with the natural environment around them.

---

29   Pope Francis, 'Be Protectors of God's Creation: Homily of the Inaugural Mass of the Pope Francis' Petrine Ministry, March 19, 2013', available from http://w2.vatican.va/content/francesco/en/homilies/2013/documents/papa-francesco_20130319_omelia-inizio-pontificato.html [accessed November 3, 2018].

30   The word 'Anthropocene' is not mentioned in the whole of *Laudato Si'*. Nevertheless, all that the encyclical highlights address what and how humans' unprecedented activities are destabilizing our common home, which calls for humanity to rethink their lifestyles before they are too late. The term 'Anthropocene' refers to the epoch that follows the Holocene (that is, the last 12,000 to 10,000 years again). It is generally called the human age. This means the age when anthropogenic/human activities are changing the earth systems in an extraordinary way. Unlike the Holocene epoch, which promoted a relative stability and civilization that encouraged agricultural production, see these articles, Will Steffen et al., 'The Anthropocene: From Global Change to Planetary Stewardship', *Ambio* 40 (2011): 739–761; Rockström et al., 'A Safe Operating Space for Humanity', *Nature* 461 (2009): 472–475; Will Steffen et al., 'The Trajectory of the Anthropocene: The Great Acceleration', *The Anthropocene Review* 2, no. 1 (2015): 81–98; Johan Rockström, 'The Anthropocene, Control and Responsibility: A Reply to Andy Stirling', *Steps Centre: Path to Sustainability* (2015), available from https://steps-centre.org/blog/johan-rockstrom-on-the-anthropocene/ [accessed November 17, 2018].

31   Francis, *Laudato Si'*, §156.

The Notion of Integral Ecology in
Pope Francis' *Laudato Si'*

The notion of Pope Francis' integral ecology is pivotal in *Laudato Si'*. It is an additional milestone in the social thought and the magisterial teaching of the Roman Catholic Church. This is because its passionate appeal is towards an "urgent challenge in order to protect our common home",32 from 'the harm we [human beings] have inflicted on her by our irresponsible use and abuse of the goods with which God has endowed her".[32] Therefore, Pope Francis' integral ecology is advocating for an integral relationship and collaboration whereby both human and natural ecologies are considered to be essential in all their dimensions as our conscientious means to bring about well-being in our society.[33]

It is noteworthy to observe that Pope Francis' concept of integral ecology is drawn from the long tradition of 'integral humanism' introduced by Jacques Maritain (1882–1973). This is a fundamental scenario where every aspect of humanity is taken into consideration as integral when dealing with human beings and the natural order.[34] Thus, following this tradition that has been developed by his predecessors since Pope Paul VI, Pope Francis, as a matter of fact, promotes an integral ecology that integrates every aspect of God's creation as being integral and connected in our common home.[35] To that effect, according to Pope Francis, integral ecology is simply living in harmony with all creation, which must combine the 'concern for nature, justice for the poor, commitment to society, and interior peace', and he calls this an 'inseparable bond'.[36]

Furthermore, in *Laudato Si'*, Pope Francis demonstrates that both human and natural ecologies should be accorded respect in order to not inflict more harm on our common home, since everything in creation is mutually interrelated and interconnected but not separated.[37] Despite the fact that the notion of integral ecology forms the background of this unique papal document, in chapter 4 of *Laudato Si'*, *integral ecology* is

---

32 Francis, *Laudato Si'*, §2.
33 Ndubueze, 'Responsible Environmental Stewardship', 129.
34 Jacques Maritain, 'Integral Humanism and the Crisis of Modern Times', *The Review of Politics* vol. 1, no. 1 (1939): 1–17.
35 Francis, *Laudato Si'*, §137, 138, 155.
36 Francis, *Laudato Si'*, §10.
37 Francis, *Laudato Si'*, §70,137, 240.

discussed in more detail. Pope Francis demonstrates the centrality of the integral nature of our ecology.[38] The necessity to respond to and rethink our indifferent behaviour towards nature and to understand, along with Pope Benedict XVI, that "the book of nature is one and indivisible"[39] becomes inevitable and imperative. Pope Francis defines ecology as the study of the "relationship between living organisms and the environment in which they develop".[40]

Thus, the position of Pope Francis is that the term *integral ecology* is of great importance in all ramifications. Here he goes beyond the boundaries of the scientific framework by initiating a substantial acknowledgement that ecology becoming integral demonstrates a recognition and "respect of its human and social dimensions."[41] Pope Francis integrates ecology with concrete social justice matters that affect the life of the people from attaining their potential, especially the poor communities and the natural environment they inhabit. This grounds ecological discussions on human ecology, natural ecology, social ecology, and other forms of ecology that encourage true sustainability of God's creation. Thus, the assimilation of ecology, into both environmental and social aspects, cannot be seen in isolation or as something separate in themselves. In fact, according to Pope Francis, "we are faced not with two separate crises, one environmental and the other social, but rather with one complex crisis which is both social and environmental".[42]

Integral Ecology as Integral Human Development

The understanding of Pope Francis' *Laudato Si'* demonstrates that the promotion of integral ecology gives the enabling environment for

---

38   In talking about ecology, it is noteworthy to say that Leonardo Boff has what appears to trace the root of ecology. In his opinion, he demonstrates that ecology as a word was formulated by a German biologist Ernst Haeckel (1834–1919) in 1866. Thus, he opines that ecology is 'derived from two Greek words, *oikos*, which means "house" or logos, meaning "reflection" or "study". Therefore, ecology means the study of the conditions and relations that make up the habitat (the house) of each and every person and, indeed, organism in nature.' Leonardo Boff, *Ecology and Liberation: A New Paradigm* (Maryknoll, NY: Orbis Books, 1989), 9.

39   Francis, *Laudato Si'*, §6.

40   Francis, *Laudato Si'*, §138.

41   Francis, *Laudato Si'*, §137.

42   Francis, *Laudato Si'*, §139.

an integral human development to flourish.[43] Thus, as indicated above, drawing from the 'integral humanism' of Maritain which "considers man in the wholeness of his natural and supernatural being, and which sets no a priori limit to the descent of the divine into man, we may call the humanism of the Incarnation. It is an "integral" and "progressive" Christian position which I believe conforms to representative principles of the genuine spirit of Thomism."[44] Pope Paul VI in his *Populorum Progressio*, in 1967, developed and reformulated 'integral humanism' into 'transcendent humanism' as 'integral' and 'true development for all peoples'.[45]

Twenty years later, Pope John Paul II updated the teaching of *Populorum Progressio* in his *Sollicitudo Rei Socialis* (1987) by offering a nuanced concept of development.[46] According to John Paul II, for development to be integral and authentic, it must have a moral character that considers the good of the individual as well as the whole of humanity and "does not exclude respect for the beings which constitute the natural world which is called thecosmos".[47] John Paul II situates integral ecology along with authentic human development to the extent that development and progress in a society is shared in common by all humanity with no exclusion towards the entire creation.

Furthermore, Pope Benedict XVI, following the teachings of Catholic Social Thought in his *Caritas in Veritate* (2009), modified what is now accepted as integral ecology in *Laudato Si'*. For Benedict XVI, the concept of human ecology and that of environmental ecology are not separated and cannot be divided; otherwise, it would lead to an absolute contradiction. Because we are talking about something that is "one and indivisible: it takes in not only the environment but also life, sexuality, marriage, the family, social relations: in a word, integral human development".[48] Here the issue

---

43 Francis, *Laudato Si'*, §46, 50, 109, 141.

44 Maritain, 'Integral Humanism and the Crisis of Modern Times', 8.

45 Pope Paul VI, *Populorum Progressio*, available from http://w2.vatican.va/content/paul-vi/en/encyclicals/documents/hf_p-vi_enc_26031967_populorum.html [accessed November 17, 2018].

46 Pope John Paul II, *Sollicitudo Rei Socialis*, §43, available from http://w2.vatican.va/content/john-paul-ii/en/encyclicals/documents/hf_jp-ii_enc_30121987_sollicitudo-rei-socialis.html [accessed November 17, 2018].

47 John Paul II, *Sollicitudo Rei Socialis*, §43.

48 Pope Benedict XVI, *Caritas in Veritate*, §51, available from http://w2.vatican.va/content/benedict-xvi/en/encyclicals/documents/hf_ben-xvi_enc_20090629_caritas-in-veritate.html [accessed November 17, 2018].

of environment coexists with every human constituent dimension without exclusion. This implies that once human ecology is neglected, the natural ecology is also disrespected. What it means, according to Pope Benedict XVI, is that the 'human ecology', 'social ecology,' and the 'natural ecology' are interwoven and inseparable.[49] Thus, whatever affects the environment has great impact on the human and nonhuman creatures of the natural world, just like the weakest link of every strong chain makes it vulnerable to a fault. Likewise, whatever benefits the ecology of the environment will at the same time enrich and benefit the human and social ecology.

In addition, integral ecology demonstrates that everything in creation is interrelated, so it calls for an integrated approach towards having a correlation between our relationships with one another. This should be expressed by our eagerness to help those who are excluded by securing a befitting and dignified existence for them and, at the same time, protecting nature.[50] This involves having a true ecological disposition. Pope Francis asserts that "it must integrate questions of justice in debates on the environment, so as to hear both the cry of the earth and the cry of the poor".[51] The simple reason for such serious consideration is that when the environment is destroyed, the people who are most affected are the poor of the planet since their communities, livelihood, and resources are depleted and degraded.[52] If these people are neglected, it greatly impacts on the protection of human ecology and the ecology of nature. Thus, Pope Francis in his *Evangelii Gaudium* (2013) infers that the protection of the environment and the "inclusion of the poor in our society is the basis for the integral [human] development of society's most neglected members."[53] For him, this inclusion should equally be extended to nonhuman creatures in our natural environment.

---

49   Pope Benedict XVI, 'The Human Person: The Heart of Peace', §8, available from http://
      w2.vatican.va/content/benedict-xvi/en/messages/peace/documents/hf_ben-xvi_mes_
      20061208_xl-world-day-peace.html [accessed November 17, 2018].
50   Francis, *Laudato Si'*, §139.
51   Francis, *Laudato Si'*, §49.
52   Francis, *Laudato Si'*, §48.
53   Pope Francis, *Evangelii Gaudium*, §188, available from http://w2.vatican.va/content/
      francesco/en/apost_exhortations/documents/papa-francesco_esortazione-ap_20131124_
      evangelii-gaudium.html [accessed November 17, 2018].

Laudato Si' and the Intrinsic Value
of Nonhuman Creatures

Unequivocally, Pope Francis, in *Laudato Si'*, demonstrates that it is indispensable and timeous for this genuine interaction. As a matter of fact, he refers to all nonhuman creatures of the natural environment as our "fellow creatures."[54] In this sense, I will assert that by referring to other nonhuman creatures as 'fellow creatures', Pope Francis establishes a commendably compassionate gesture of a sincere and in-depth solidarity with all of God's creation. He acknowledges that all creation belongs to one community. Therefore, he appeals to the kinship or community of creation model, whereby all creatures come together to see themselves as members of the same community and as fellow creatures in one common earthly home.

Furthermore, what he postulates resonates with the admission to "extend 'intrinsic value' to all non-human creatures, which is a new teaching, and at the same time a radical shift, in the Catholic Social Teachings."[55] According to Michael Northcott, this shift is one of Pope Francis' remarkable "interventions in the Church's response to the ecological crisis."[56] At the same time, Northcott further opines that this radical move is very significant since it constitutes a departure from the "five hundred long years tradition of the Latin Church, taking its lead from Thomas Aquinas,"[57] with regard to the relationship between human beings and the rest of creation.

This is pertinent because Aquinas stipulates that God's creation is channelled towards attaining the good and is of the benefit of humanity. Thus, Aquinas argues that there is the absence of "intellective soul" in other creatures, and as such, their purpose is that "they are designed by God for human use, provided that their instrumental use is not excessively cruel, especially to animals."[58] To that effect, this courageous contribution

---

54 Francis, *Laudato Si'*, §92, 140.
55 Ndubueze, 'Responsible Environmental Stewardship', 133.
56 Michael Northcott, 'Planetary Moral Economy and Creaturely Redemption in *Laudato Si'*, *Theological Studies* 77, no. 4 (2016): 886–904, 898.
57 Northcott, 'Planetary Moral Economy', 898.
58 Thomas Aquinas, *Summa Theologiae* III XP, q. 91, a. 5, trans. Fathers of the English Dominican Province (New Nork: Benzinger Bros, 1947), 6644. See also Francisco Benzoni, 'Thomas Aquinas and Environmental Ethics: A Reconsideration of Providence and Salvation',

of Pope Francis, no doubt, opens a prominent horizon for what Denis Edwards calls a "new theology of the natural world."[59] In fact, this theology gives pride of place to the value of the natural world. What it means is that the natural world has "an intrinsic value independent of its usefulness [because] each organism, as a creature of God, is good and admirable in itself."[60]

Thus, it could equally be said that all of God's creation "have value in themselves,"[61] and as such they have a purpose for which they were being created since they also "have their own value in God's eyes."[62] If nonhuman creatures do not have value in themselves before God, the psalmist would not have invited them to praise God with us: "Praise him, sun and moon, praise him, all you shining stars! Praise him, you highest heavens, and you waters above the heavens! Let them praise the name of the Lord, for he commanded and they were created' (Ps. 148:3-5)."[63] Even the famous *Canticle of the Creatures* of Saint Francis of Assisi equally testifies to the intrinsic value of nonhuman creatures.[64] But it is unfortunate that because of our greed and our drastic consumption and overexploitation of the natural environment, many creatures and "thousands of species of plants and animals are already extinct and will not give praise to God by their existence."[65] According to Pope Francis, one of the major problems that militate against the intrinsic value of nonhuman creatures in modernity is "the culture of consumerism" that is equally a fundamental concern coupled with "the loss of cultural values."[66]

Journal of Religion 85 (2005): 446–476. Northcott, 'Planetary Moral Economy', 898.

59 Denis Edwards, "'Sublime Communion": The Theology of the Natural in *Laudato Si*" *Theological Studies* 77, no. 2 (2016): 377–391. See also, Denis Edwards, *The Natural World and God: Theological Explorations* (Hindmarsh: SA, ATF Press, 2017).

60 Francis, *Laudato Si'*, §140. See also Lucius Ugorji, *Care for Your Environment: 1995 Lenten Pastoral Letter Umuahia Diocese* (Enugu: Snaap, 1995), 16.

61 Francis, *Laudato Si'*, §33, 76.

62 Francis, *Laudato Si'*, §69.

63 Francis, *Laudato Si'*, §72.

64 Francis, *Laudato Si'*, §1, 87.

65 Francis, *Laudato Si'*, §33.

66 Francis, *Laudato Si'*, §184.

Laudato Si' and Cultural Ecology

The promotion of integral ecology is closely linked with the recognition of cultural ecology in *Laudato Si'*. It is impossible to have one without the other because "together with the patrimony of nature, there is also an historic, artistic and cultural patrimony."[67] This cultural patrimony upholds our identity as humans who come from a particular natural environment with our values, customs, norms, and traditions, which in themselves define whom we are in mutual harmony with all creation. What Pope Francis demonstrates is that for integral ecology to be reflected in the lifestyle of all human beings, it must spring from their own cultures, patterns of existence, and in ways they relate with fellow humanity and other nonhuman creatures.

Therefore, it must have to "preserve the peoples' history, culture, architecture, language, their original identity, and indeed protect the cultural treasures of humanity in the broadest sense."[68] The initiative of this ecology welcomes and appreciates the effort of the indigenous communities, especially in their threats and pressures to abandon their cultures and traditions.[69] On the contrary, their cultures should never be suppressed but, rather, ought to be protected, since they "instill a greater sense of responsibility, a strong sense of community, a readiness to protect others, a spirit of creativity and a deep love for the land, and are equally concerned about what they will leave to their next generations."[70]

Furthermore, the essence of the cultural ecology in *Laudato Si'* is to give value and recognition to local cultures in the process of a collaborative dialogue. This is because "there is a need to respect the rights of peoples and cultures."[71] What it implies is that we bear in mind that culture is "a living dynamic and participatory present reality, which cannot be excluded as we rethink the relationship between human beings and the environment."[72] To that effect, caution should be adequately observed never to forcefully impose any reality or attempt to destroy the peoples' culture in order to not destroy their cultural heritage and identity since

---

67 Francis, *Laudato Si'*, §143.
68 Francis, *Laudato Si'*, §143.
69 Francis, *Laudato Si'*, §146.
70 Francis, *Laudato Si'*, §179.
71 Francis, *Laudato Si'*, §144.
72 Francis, *Laudato Si'*, §143.

such a distortion is as dangerous as the extinction of species.[73] Rather, every culture ought to be accompanied patently and meticulously so that everybody would be carried along towards transformation and assimilation. That should be the method of the Christian churches with regard to our cultural heritage in Africa.

The Church and the Preservation of Our Cultural Heritage

There is a particular need to preserve our cultural heritage because it defines who we are and where we come from in the community of nations.[74] Our African cultural restoration and its enrichment should always be our commitment.[75] More so, it is imperative for us to rethink any effort that is predisposed to destroying our cultural heritage, folklores, history, traditions, and sensitivities as a people. Those that are not antithetical to the Good News should never be demolished or burned down. Rather, it is our collective project to discern in a sincere dialogue with our culture and traditions in order to make them more relevant through our language in our time without losing their essence.

Instead of destroying our rich cultures and traditions, the church enjoins her members, especially in Africa and beyond, to find a conscientious way to explore their cultural heritage in the spirit of inculturation and evangelization in line with the wisdom of the Synod Fathers in the *Ecclesia in Africa*.[76] This committed effort has to do with the promotion of our cultural heritage in Africa so that it may "encourage an ever more effective and credible witness to Christ in every local Church, every nation, every region, and in the entire African Continent."[77] Furthermore, the words of Saint Pope John Paul II are indispensable and are as vividly fresh as

---

73 Francis, *Laudato Si'*, §143.

74 Cohen, 'Culture as Identity', 195.

75 Francois Dube, 'Cultural Restoration on the Agenda of Sino-African Cooperation', *ChinAfrica* (May 5, 2018), available from http://www.chinafrica.cn/Homepage/201805/t20180510_ 800129143.html [accessed November 23, 2018].

76 Pope John Paul II, *Ecclesia in Africa*, §127, available from http://w2.vatican.va/content/ john-paul-ii/en/apost_exhortations/documents/hf_jp-ii_exh_14091995_ecclesia-in-africa. html [accessed November 23, 2018].

77 John Paul II, *Ecclesia in Africa*, §127.

ever with regard to the significance of rehabilitating our cultural heritage. Therefore, he states that:

> 'By respecting, preserving and fostering the particular values and riches of your people's cultural heritage, you will be in a position to lead them to a better understanding of the mystery of Christ, which is also to be lived in the noble, concrete and daily experiences of African life. There is no question of adulterating the word of God, or of emptying the Cross of its power (Cf. *1 Cor* 1:17), but rather of bringing Christ into the very centre of African life and of lifting up all African life to Christ. Thus, not only is Christianity relevant to Africa, but Christ, in the members of his Body, is himself African.[78]

If Christianity is, as expected, to be relevant in our cultures and traditions and if it is equally anticipated to be African, whereby her members are Christlike in nature and in truth, as expressed by Saint Pope John Paul II, it must promote our rich cultural heritage and values at the same time. What this means, according to Emefie Ikenga Metuh, is that Christian spirituality has a lot of work to perform in Africa in order to continue to be unquestionably relevant with regard to the African cultures. This duty is for her to always try, as much as possible, to "enrich the Christian life of Africans in a way that it will enable them to remain truly Christian and truly African."[79]

Furthermore, even before John Paul II, Pope Paul VI had earlier addressed the Ugandan parliament during his visit in 1969, that the Catholic Church, while performing her mission and evangelization in Africa, should not in any way impose Western culture on African cultures at the detriment of good cultural values in Africa.[80] In trying to explain how the church should engage in her evangelization in Africa through language and the mode of expressing the faith in order to be systematic and integral to the life of the people, Paul VI states that:

---

78 John Paul II, *Ecclesia in Africa*, §127.

79 Emefie Ikenga Metuh, 'The Revival of African Spirituality: The Experience of African Independent Churches', *Mission Studies* VII, no. 2–14 (1990): 151–171, 152.

80 Pope Paul VI, 'Address of Pope Paul VI to the Parliament of Uganda in Kampala, Friday, 1 August, 1969', available at http://w2.vatican.va/content/paul-vi/en/speeches/1969/august/documents/hf_p-vi_spe_19690801_parlamento-uganda.html [accessed November 16, 2018].

The language and mode of manifesting this one Faith, may
be manifold; hence, it may be original, suited to the tongue,
the style, the character, the genius, and the culture, of the one
who professes this one Faith. From this point of view, a certain
pluralism is not only legitimate, but desirable. An adaptation
of the Christian life in the fields of pastoral, ritual, didactic
and spiritual activities is not only possible, it is even favoured
by the Church. The liturgical renewal is a living example
of this. And in this sense, you may, and you must, have an
African Christianity. Indeed, you possess human values and
characteristic forms of culture which can rise up to perfection
such as to find in Christianity, and for Christianity, a true
superior fulness, and prove to be capable of a richness of
expression all its own, and genuinely African.[81]

But whether the call of Paul VI, John Paul II, and indeed Ikenga
Metuh with regard to the method of evangelization in Africa and the project
of Christian spirituality have been carried out as they suggested is an
important debate for another day. However, in promoting contextualization
in the missionary activity of the church, Ikenga Metuh indicates that
contextual theology has the responsibility, while evangelizing, of taking
into consideration the "place, time, culture and the context of the
evangelized."[82] This is in consonance with the fact that the church can
also enrich herself by "borrowing some elements of human culture or
cultures, even though the Gospel and the evangelization are certainly not
identical with all culture."[83]

Nevertheless, in order to be more effective toward meeting the
expectations, together with the possibility of attaining a positive outcome
while being Africans with regard to preserving our cultural heritage and
at the same time being truly Christians, we have to embrace our cultural

---

81 Pope Paul VI, 'Homily of Paul VI: Eucharistic Celebration at the Conclusion of the Symposium
Organized by the Bishop of Africa in Kampala, July 31, 1969', §2, available at https://
w2.vatican.va/content/paul-vi/en/homilies/1969/documents/hf_p-vi_hom_19690731.html
[accessed November 16, 2018].

82 Emefie Ikenga Metuh, 'Contextualization: A Missiological Imperative for the Church in
Africa in the Third Millennium', *Mission Studies* 6, no. 1 (1989): 3–16, 4. See also, Pope
Paul VI, *Evangelii Nuntiandi*, §40, available at http://w2.vatican.va/content/paul-vi/en/
apost_exhortations/documents/ hf_pvi_exh_19751208_evangelii-nuntiandi.html [accessed
November 16, 2018].

83 Paul VI, *Evangelii Nuntiandi*, §20.

identities ourselves and at the same time strive to elevate the level and quality of our Christian conversation with our cultures and traditions. According to Pope Benedict XVI, in *Africae Munus §36,* there is the urgency to engage in an "in-depth study of African tradition and cultures,"[84] in order to be more effective. This will, no doubt, facilitate our eagerness to have "a through discernment in order to identify those aspects of the culture which represent an obstacle to the incarnation of Gospel values, as well as those aspects which promote them."[85]

In addition, we as a Church should acknowledge that African Traditional Religions (ATR) are still very much alive in our midst. Despite the fact that many of our brothers and sisters appear to be committed Christians, we have to understand that a good number of them, directly or indirectly, are at the same time still practicing ATRs. Some will secretly consult with their 'native medicine man/woman for seeming immediate remedies and solutions.' One of the reasons is that "with their reference to ancestors and to a form of mediation between man and Immanence, these religions are the cultural and spiritual soil from which most Christian converts spring and with which they continue to have daily contact."[86] This therefore implies that it is very difficult for one to completely be disconnected with what he or she has already connected to or lived with, even before Christianity. Another problem borders on the questions surrounding uncertainties such as disasters, calamities, deaths, catastrophes, and other unfortunate circumstances in the families and communities.[87] All these go a long way to challenge the faith of Christians in Africa, and elsewhere.

Furthermore, Benedict XVI is of the opinion that the church has the responsibility to look for and collaborate with the people, especially ATR, who know the culture very well to gain greater insight. To that effect, he states that:

> It is worth singling out knowledgeable individual converts, who could provide the Church with guidance in gaining a deeper and more accurate knowledge of the traditions, the culture and

84 Pope Benedict XVI, *Africae Munus*, §36, available at http://w2.vatican.va/content/benedict-xvi/en/apost_exhortations/documents/hf_ben-xvi_exh_20111119_africae-munus.html [accessed November 16, 2018].

85 Benedict XVI, *Africae Munus*, §36.

86 Benedict XVI, *Africae Munus*, §92.

87 Gabriel Idang, 'African Culture and Values', *Phronimon* 16, no. 2 (2015): 97–111, 107.

the traditional religions. This would make it easier to identify points of real divergence. It would also help to clarify the vital distinction between culture and cult and to discard those magical elements which cause division and ruin for families and societies.[88]

The position of Benedict XVI is in line with the teaching of the Second Vatican Council's, *Nostra Aetate*: Declaration on the Relation of the Church to Non-Christian Religions, with regard to respect and some level of tolerance towards other religions. Thus, the Council asserts that, "the Church, therefore, urges her sons [and daughters] to enter with prudence and charity into discussion and collaboration with members of other religions. Let Christians, while witnessing to their own faith and way of life, acknowledge, preserve and encourage the spiritual and moral truths found among non-Christians, also their social life and culture."[89] This means that, no matter how difficult it is to gather around the table of dialogue in order to understand our core differences, we should never be tired of doing so provided it underpins "openness and respect that is devoid of prejudices, and unnecessary misunderstanding towards enriching each other's ignorance for the good of religion and society."[90]

Cutting Down of Our Ecological Trees and 'Community or Family Deliverance'

Our cultural heritage tells us more about our cultural identity, origin, and foundation, especially with regard to our monumental artefacts, history, and traditions.[91] In the case of our community trees, they are also part of our heritage. Most of them are planted, strategically, within the communities by our community's forebears, bearing in mind that some of

---

88   Benedict XVI, *Africae Munus*, §92.

89   Vatican Council II, '*Nostra Aetate*: Declaration on the Relation of the Church to Non-Christian Religions', §2, in *Vatican Council II: The Conciliar and Post Conciliar Documents*, ed. Austin Flannery (Northport, NY: Costello Publishing Company, 1975), 738. See also Benedict XVI, *Africae Munus*, §92.

90   Emefie Ikenga Metuh, 'Reconciliation: The Path to True Peace and Authentic Progress for Nigeria and Africa', *Mission Studies* XVII, no. 1–35 (2001): 12–22, 16.

91   Idang, 'African Culture and Values', 97.

those trees are over five hundred years old.[92] Albeit, history has it that, some of them came into being on their own, especially with particular reference to Iroko tree, which is generally seen as a gift by the ancestors.[93] To that effect, some of our community trees stand as visible signs of the community's ancestral presence and bond of connectivity between the old and the present generations. Therefore, they are regarded as ancestral community trees and are also considered to be 'sacred'.[94]

However, in recent times, as our cultural values have been subject to many attacks by modernity and religious fundamentalism,[95] our community trees are equally affected. In this scenario, the cutting down of some of our community trees in the name of 'community deliverance' calls for our immediate attention.[96] Because it indirectly encourages the eroding of our cultural heritage, identity, and values in Nigeria and beyond. This attitude is seen among some 'radical Christian Churches' who perceive all cultural monuments and artefacts as fetish, unChristian, out of fashion, and unworthy of a place in our natural environment.

More so, the cutting down of our ancient, ancestral community and ecological trees, like we have seen in some communities in Igboland, South-East, South South of Nigeria, and beyond, in the name of 'community deliverance' is done in the understanding that some peoples' progress,

---

92 Sunday Onen, 'Africa: Pastor Cut Down Sacred Iroko'.

93 In Igboland, Iroko tree (*Osisi Ọrji*) is generally known as not being planted by anyone because it springs on its own like a small mustard tree in a family compound, village, and community square; and it grows into a very big and mighty tree. *Osisi Ọrji* is held in high esteem as the best among the trees in the cultural setting and also because of its socioeconomic value.

94 Andrew Gurstelle, 'Sacred Trees of the Savè Hills Cultural Landscape', *University of Michigan Working Papers in Museum in Studies*, no. 10 (2013): 1–18, available at https://deepblue.lib.umich.edu/bitstream/handle/2027.42/102522/Gurstelle_working_paper_Final.pdf?sequence=1 [accessed November 16, 2018].

95 Chitra Nagarajan, 'Religious Fundamentalism and the Erasure of African Cultures, Religions and Traditions', *African Identity* (2016), available at https://thisisafrica.me/religious-fundamentalism-erasure-african-cultures-religions-traditions/. See also, Nwachukwu, 'Odenigbo Lecture' [accessed November 16, 201].

96 As indicated in the introduction, I have seen some communities in Igboland where this development has taken place, and also, I have equally read of other incidences of its occurrences in many other places, like in Rivers State and Edo State. See also Ebegbulem, 'Pastor Cut Sacred Iroko'. More so, the destruction of cultural monuments, shrines, temples, historical statues, and memorabilia in Africa, Asia, Syria, in the Middle East, and other places are mostly carried out in the name of religion. They could equally be seen in line with the demolition of our ancient monuments and artefacts in recent times all over the world since they are also seen as sacred by some custodians of cultures.

breakthroughs, fertility, rationality, riches, employment opportunities, unity, and peace are tied to their ancestral spirits and some "cosmic forces."[97] This is something that is so worrisome in our time. Nevertheless, there are some pertinent questions and uncertain assumptions that need to be asked and clarified. However, spiritual things are not found on the surface. Therefore, I implore for a sincere collaborative dialogue between those Christian churches who cut down our ecological trees suspiciously without replacing them and the custodians of our cultures towards finding better ways to address this worrying development.

Apparently, in many places, the whole process surrounding the felling down of those ancient community trees appears to be ill-conceived and uncivilized since the trees are disproportionately chopped down without any intention of replacing them in order to mitigate the effects of drastic weather conditions in the age of climate change.

Furthermore, some of those ancient community trees serve as huge umbrellas for community, village, and family meetings; cultural dances; and market squares. And they are even used in some places for school curricula activities, such as handworks and skills acquisition empowerment. They also serve as places where our folklores and oral traditions are properly transmitted and passed on to the next generation. They offer communities grounds to comprehend and contemplate the reason for being and existence and for solidarity. They serve as a place of 'live and let live', where John Mbiti could comfortably say that "I am because we are and since we are, therefore I am."[98] In addition, those community trees serve as our natural canopies for both human beings, animals, and birds of the air. People usually stay under them for relaxation as well as receive gratuitously fresh and undiluted oxygen that is unquestionably healthy and essential for all living creatures, while they naturally and freely remove our carbon dioxide and pollution in a mutual exchange.

Consequently, this emerging scenario of cutting down our ancient community trees is disturbing because it appears to encourage the destruction of our communitarian spirit by demolishing our community

---

97   Lawrence Nchekwube Nwankwo, 'Olu Ezinauno and Neo-Christianity: A Critical Reflection on a Practice in Igboland' (lecture text, 2018), 1–16. It suffices to say that the 'community or family deliverance' is equally referred to as Olu Ezinaulo in some places. It started becoming common since 1990 as one of the ways towards the interpretation of negative spirits and their evil manifestations on the lives of many individuals, families, and communities.

98   John Mbiti, *Concepts of God in Africa* (London: SCK, 1979), 108.

and family meeting grounds. Anything that affects the family also undermines the sociocultural cradle of the African heritage, identities, cultures, and traditions.[99] In fact, it is one of the quickest ways of killing the peoples' cultures in Africa since it sets people apart from themselves, thereby denying the community a cultural space where cultural and family bonds are generated. This is because it forcefully destroys the peoples' communitarian life and their cultural centres where families, villages, and communities gather to reconcile conflicts and differences in a traditional cultural setting.[100]

However, it has been reported that a few communities have been exploited, where some of these ancient ecological trees have been felled down in the name of 'community deliverance'.[101] The communities have been lured to pay huge amount of money in order to settle the so-called prayer warriors' and 'prosperity pastors who go about inflicting fear, division, and deception. And they manipulate innocent, gullible people under the guise that they are organizing 'community or family deliverance' in order to 'liberate' and set them free from their 'ancestry causes'.[102] Yet in most cases, the situation has actually turned out to be the opposite, while considerable problems and misunderstanding still exist.

Nevertheless, it suffices to say that the situation is completely different for those genuine cases where indeed there appear to be palpable incidences of wicked actions and diabolical and evil manipulations in the name of culture.[103] As a result, some people are perceived to be in bondage and seemingly suffering without progress and development, and indeed, there are frequent deaths, calamities, and some mysterious accidents.[104] These communities are evident to the fact that I do not intend to downplay or deny that some people in cultural and traditional practices are themselves seeming to be demonic and as such need to be totally redeemed by the Christian message. Significantly, there are testimonies where such

---

99   Ikenga Metuh, 'Reconciliation', 17.

100 Ikenga Metuh, 'Reconciliation', 17.

101 Some of the communities in South East and South South of Nigeria where this incident has taken place are meant to contribute huge amount of money in the form of levy among the groups who champion the course in order to hire, to settle the 'pastors' with regard to their payment, and if the need arises, to lodge them in hotels (and other places) as well as their 'men and women prayer warriors'.

102 Onen, 'Africa: Pastor Cut Down Sacred Iroko'.

103 Emefie Ikenga Metuh, *God and Man in African Religion* (Enugu: Snaap, 1999).

104 Idang, 'African Culture and Values', 107.

'liberation and freedom' have taken place, with particular reference, appreciation, and acknowledgment to those priests, men, and women of prayer who are authentic, genuine, and self-sacrificing towards family and community deliverance, cleansing, healing, and reconciliation.[105]

Ecological Benefits of Our Community Trees

Over and above the cultural bond, history, and tradition attached to our cultural heritage and community identity, the fostering of communitarian spirit, the sense of respect, recognition, aesthetics, and for their socioeconomic benefits,[106] the presence of our community trees in our natural environment has other values and benefits with regard to the well-being of both the human and nonhuman creatures. However, we pay particular reference to the ecological value of our community trees and their ecological benefits, especially in the age of climate change and global warming. It suffices to say that as the effects of the climate change become more evident and for the fact that human factors in modernity are perceived to have been causing unprecedented alteration to the earth system and that we humans are moving towards a tipping point because of our harmful attitude against the natural environment,[107] the ecological need for having our trees and forests protected is apposite. Thus, it is necessary that we rethink the suffering our harmful actions against the natural environment are causing to all of God's creation.[108]

To that effect, according to *Laudato Si'*, which acknowledges important findings of sciences on climate change, the mitigation of the negative impacts of global warming can never be attained without having

---

105 Stephen Njoku, *Curses, Effects and Release* (Enugu: Christian Living Publications, 1993).

106 Folaranmi Babalola, Temitope Borokini, and Alfred Onefeli, 'Socio-Economic Benefits of Iroko Trees (Milicia excelsa Welw C.C. Berg) in Ibadan Metropolis, Oyo State, Nigeria', *International Journal of African and Asian Studies* 1 (2013): 11–17.

107 Johan Rockström et al., 'Planetary Boundaries: Exploring the Safe Operating Space for Humanity', *Ecology and Society* 14, no. 2 (2009): 32, available at https://ced.agro.uba.ar/gran-chaco/sites/default/files/pdf/sem6/Rockstorm%20et%20al%202009.pdf [accessed November 16, 2018]. See also, Johan Rockström, 'Bounding the Planetary Future: Why we need a Great Transition', Great Transition Initiative: Towards a Transformative Vision and Praxis (2015), available at https://www.greattransition.org/publication/bounding-the-planetary-future-why-we-need-a-great-transition [accessed November 16, 2018].

108 Ferdinand Nwaigbo, 'Pope Francis and the Programme of Ecology in a Time of Change', *African Ecclesial Review* 58, nos. 3 and 4 (2016): 214–233, 216.

our ecological trees and forests in place to assist in absorbing the emissions of carbon dioxide (CO_2) and other greenhouse gases.[109] Trees are very effective in the protection and sustainability of our natural environment since they serve as 'carbon sinks'.[110] While they release fresh oxygen for our healthy living, they absorb the CO_2 we generate into the atmosphere through combustion of fossil fuel from our generators, industrial plants, and automobiles. This implies that trees help to maintain important services in our environment like purification, cleaning up, and filtering the air and the ecosystem of odour and pollution.[111] They equally have a cooling effect on the ecosystem by modifying the high temperatures and the excruciating heat of the scorching sun by preserving the humidity of our surroundings.

Furthermore, our community trees contribute enormously in preventing the loss of biodiversity and the extinction of species because these trees are habitats to a lot of biodiversity.[112] Yet it is evident that we take for granted what we have and possess as a people, and little by little, we lose them. Beauty, they say, lies in the eye of the beholder. But what of the melodious cry of those beautiful coloured species of birds on those trees, the squirrels that have their playing field on them, those magnificent butterflies, ants, bees, and other insects that cross pollinate our plants in the gardens and farms in order to have good yields? One of the side effects with the extinction of certain species of plants, reptiles, and animals is that it has 'irreversible consequences'.[113] Whatever we lose as a result of our harmful attitude to the nonhuman creatures, we may not have them back again.[114] According to Bishop Lucius Ugorji, another danger with species extinction is that if it continues, "the ecosystem would be put to tremendous strain and

---

109 Francis, *Laudato Si'*, §23.

110 Melanie Friedel, 'Forests as Carbon Sinks', *American Forests* (July 18, 2017), available at https://www.americanforests.org/blog/forests-carbon-sinks/ [accessed November 16, 2018].

111 Anders Wijkman and Johan Rockström, *Bankrupting Nature: Denying our Planetary Boundaries* (London: Routledge Taylor & Francis Group, 2011), 133.

112 Megan Nichols, 'What Is Biodiversity Loss and Why Is It a Problem?', *Science, Energy & Environment* (June 4, 2018), available at https://interestingengineering.com/what-is-biodiversity-loss-and-why-is-it-a-problem [accessed November 16, 2018].

113 Rockström et al., 'Planetary Boundaries: Exploring the Safe Operating Space'.

114 Francis, *Laudato Si'*, §32–42. It is noteworthy to stress that the dangers in losing our biodiversity are drastically enormous, while the significance to care for our entire ecosystem are immeasurable and can never be underestimated. As a matter of fact, some of the importance of biodiversity is aptly and carefully captured in chapter 1 of *Laudato Si'* under the subtitle *Loss of Biodiversity*.

humans may have great difficulty surviving."[115] Because we are at risk of losing those plants and reptiles that are very healthy and medicinal with regard to our well-being.[116]

More so, our community trees are very effective in creating an optimal flow of rainwaters and as well serve as pressure breakers to runoff water. In a remarkable way, they protect the topsoil from porous effects and, at the same time, with their natural capacity to bind the soil, they contribute immensely in the prevention of soil erosion, which is a major problem in many communities in the South-East of Nigeria.[117] In addition, with their imposing heights and statures, our community trees are always there as 'wind breakers and shelterbelts' that shield the natural environment from being adversely affected and the soil from being blown away in the face of drastic weather conditions and tornadoes.[118]

Therefore, because of the aforementioned essential ecological benefits, it is worrisome whenever our community trees are chopped down for any reasons, especially in the name of 'community deliverance'. However, if it is ascertained beyond every reasonable doubt that a particular tree in any community is being used for diabolical manipulations in order to halt progress, prosperity, well-being, and even to cast deadly spells on some targeted individuals and persons, then our moral discretion has to be judiciously applied. This is because human life is always sacred and must be treated as such under all ramifications. Humans are ends in themselves and must not be used as means to promote wickedness in the name of cultural heritage. To that effect, anything that hinders the means and proficiency for a human person to attain his/her God-given potential has to be condemned and rejected outright.

As a matter of fact, anytime we engage ourselves in cutting down our ecological community trees, we end up endangering our lives as human

---

115 Lucius Ugorji, 'Sustaining the Environment: Towards Facing the Moral Challenges of the Ecological Crisis', in *Words from the Heart of a Shepherd: Selected Homilies, Addresses and Lectures of Bishop Lucius Iwejuru Ugorji*, ed. Lucius Ugorji (Enugu: Snaap, 2015), 378–393, 382.

116 Johan Rockström and Mattias Klum, *Big World Small Planet: Abundance within Planetary Boundaries* (Sweden: Bokförlaget Max Ström, 2015), 21.

117 Toma Buba, 'Impacts of Different Tree Species of Different Sizes on Spatial Distribution of Herbaceous Plants in the Nigerian Guinea Savannah Ecological Zone', *Scientifica* (2015): 1–8, 2.

118 Molla Mekonnen Alemu, 'Ecological Benefits of Trees as Windbreaks and Shelterbelts', *International Journal of Ecosystem* 6, no. 1 (2016): 10–13.

beings and as well as the natural environment. What it means is that we are exposing ourselves and our common home to harm, thereby making it and all of God's creation vulnerable to drastic effects of the global warming. Because there is no "dichotomy between human and natural ecologies."[119] That is, "everything is indeed 'interrelated' and at the same time 'interconnected' as well as interdependent."[120] More still, those ecological trees in themselves have their 'value', 'usefulness', and "their place of worth in the eyes of God."[121]

Nevertheless, in the current ecological crisis, we should not embark on cutting down our community trees, unless it is a last resort. But more specifically, we need to rethink rash judgement, pointing accusing fingers towards one another, and shifting responsibility away from any misfortune and undesirable circumstances that arise. Above all, "we need a mind-shift to connect and reconnect people with nature, societies with the biosphere, the human world with Earth."[122] One of the admirable ways to achieve this is by restoring our cultural heritage in Africa. It calls for a renewed commitment to respect our community trees and see them as having the pride of place for which they have been regarded for many years now. Such recognition has helped to conserve and protect them.

Furthermore, we need to resonate with our neglected commendable tradition of tree planting once again.[123] This will enable us to continue to be at the forefront to promote and pray for all of God's creation in our families, communities, churches, and schools alike. In that sense, I remember with great joy my primary school years in the 1980s when the values of taking good care of our environment was held in high repute. It was a sense of duty and responsibility for every classroom to have a flower bed properly decorated with different beautiful flowers. In most cases, the teachers and the school authorities supervised them and awards were given out at the end of the school year for the most outstanding flower beds. Pupils were able to learn how to connect with beauty and nature. But nowadays, it is alarming that some primary and secondary schools cannot even boast of having a green space, let alone talk of teaching our children the joy of

---

119 Ndubueze, 'Responsible Environmental Stewardship', 119.
120 Ndubueze, 'Responsible Environmental Stewardship', 119. See also Francis, *Laudato Si'*, §120, 137, 138, 24.
121 Francis, *Laudato Si'*, §140, 69.
122 Rockström and Klum, *Big World Small Planet*, 21.
123 Francis, *Laudato Si'*, §211.

planting their own flowers and trees. To be precise, the attention of these schools needs to be drawn to the need to recover this custom. This implies that we need also an ecological education that will bring us closer to the earth by "establishing a harmony within ourselves, with others, with nature and other creatures, and with God."[124] In addition, according to Pope Francis, those in government are equally reminded that some of our cities and housing estates are also "lacking in sufficient green space since we are not meant to be inundated by cement, asphalt, glass and deprived of physical contact with nature."[125]

Conclusion

The restoration of our cultural heritage in Africa can never be more necessary now than at any other time, because the publication of Pope Francis' *Laudato Si'* promotes an integral ecology that seeks for a cultural ecology. Significantly, there is no better way to promote our cultures than to ensure that they are integral to promoting ecology, which incorporates the well-being of both the human and nonhuman ecologies in their broadest sense, where respect should be accorded to all of God's creation. In order to be true Christians, we must not deny being Africans, let alone deny our cultures since they give identity to where we come from. As a matter of fact, there is no contradiction in being both Christians and Africans and,

---

124   Francis, *Laudato Si'*, §210. This type of education is very necessary in our time. According to Saint Pope John Paul II, it is very much needed. Pope John Paul II, 'Peace with God the Creator, Peace with All of Creation: World Day of Peace Message, 1990', §13, available at http://w2.vatican.va/content/john-paul-ii/en/messages/peace/documents/hf_jp-ii_mes_19891208_xxiii-world-day-for-peace.html [accessed November 16, 2018]. To that effect, he states: 'An education in ecological responsibility is urgent: responsibility for oneself, for others, and for the earth. This education cannot be rooted in mere sentiment or empty wishes. Its purpose cannot be ideological or political. It must not be based on a rejection of the modern world or a vague desire to return to some "paradise lost." Instead, a true education in responsibility entails a genuine conversion in ways of thought and behaviour. Churches and religious bodies, non-governmental and governmental organizations, indeed all members of society, have a precise role to play in such education. The first educator, however, is the family, where the child learns to respect his neighbour and to love nature.'

125   Francis, *Laudato Si'*, §44. Furthermore, Bishop Lucius Ugorji of Umuahia diocese requests those in government to use their authority to execute and implement good environmental policies for the safety of the planet earth and for the fact that all God's creation is our common patrimony for care. Lucius Ugorji, *Political and Social Ethics: Issues of the Moment* (Enugu: Snaap, 2008), 59.

at the same time promoting our cultures and traditions, provided they are not antithetical to the gospel message.

Thus, while the church should be open to recognizing local cultures and the language of the peoples, the custodians of our cultures should equally be transparent towards engaging in a collaborative dialogue leading to an authentic assimilation, clarification, and elucidation of those practices that are in conflict with Christianity. This demonstration underscores that we have to be thoughtful and conscientious, knowing full well that our cultural heritage defines our identity and speaks more about whom we are as Africans and what our cultural relationship with nature entails. Therefore, everybody is called upon to engage in ecological initiatives that will promote our integral ecology, as well as our cultural ecology, while restoring our cultural heritage.

Bibliography

Alemu, Molla. 'Ecological Benefits of Trees as Windbreaks and Shelterbelts.' *International Journal of Ecosystem* 6, no. 1 (2016): 10–13.

Aquinas, Thomas. *Summa Theologiae* III XP, translated by Fathers of the English Dominican Province. New Nork: Benzinger Bros, 1947.

Babalola et al. 'Socio-Economic Benefits of Iroko Trees (Milicia excelsa Welw C.C. Berg) in Ibadan Metropolis, Oyo State, Nigeria.' *International Journal of African and Asian Studies* 1 (2013): 11–17.

Benedict XVI. *Africae Munus.* http://w2.vatican.va/content/benedict-xvi/en/apost_exhortations/documents/hf_ben-xvi_exh_20111119_africae-munus.html.

———. *Caritas in Veritate.* http://w2.vatican.va/content/benedict-xvi/en/encyclicals/documents/hf_ben-xvi_enc_20090629_caritas-in-veritate.html.

———. 'The Human Person: The Heart of Peace.' http://w2.vatican.va/content/benedict-xvi/en/messages/peace/documents/hf_ben-xvi_mes_20061208_xl-world-day-peace.html.

Benzoni, Francisco. 'Thomas Aquinas and Environmental Ethics: A Reconsideration of Providence and Salvation.' *Journal of Religion* 85 (2005): 446–476.

Boff, Leonardo. *Ecology and Liberation: A New Paradigm.* Maryknoll, NY: Orbis Books, 1989.

Buba, Toma. 'Impacts of Different Tree Species of Different Sizes on Spatial Distribution of Herbaceous Plants in the Nigerian Guinea Savannah Ecological Zone.' *Scientifica* (2015): 1–8.

Clark et al. 'Collaboration as Dialogue: Teachers and Researchers Engaged in Conversation and Professional Development.' *American Educational Research Journal* 33, no. 1 (1996): 193–231.

Cohen, Anthony. 'Culture as Identity: An Anthropologist's View.' *New Literary History* 24, no. 1 (1993): 195–209.

Council II, Vatican. '*Nostra Aetate*: Declaration on the Relation of the Church to Non-Christian Religions.' In *Vatican Council II: The Conciliar and Post Conciliar Documents*, edited by Austin Flannery. Northport, NY: Costello Publishing Company, 1975.

Dangana, Deborah. 'Nigeria: How Western Culture Erodes Values Among Nigerian Youth.'

Daily Trust, August 8, 2014. https://allafrica.com/stories/201408081141. html.

Dube, Francis. 'Cultural Restoration on the Agenda of Sino-African Cooperation.' *ChinAfrica*, May 5, 2018. http://www.chinafrica. cn/Homepage/201805/t20180510_800129143.html.

Ebegbulem, Simon. 'Pastor Cut Sacred Iroko: "Vengeful Tree on Killing Spree": Benin Community Natives Flee.' *Vanguard.* https://www. vanguardngr.com/2018/03/pastors-cut-sacred-iroko-vengeful-tree-killing-spree-benin-community-natives-flee/.

Edwards, Denis. *The Natural World and God: Theological Explorations.* Hindmarsh, SA: ATF Press, 2017.

———. '"Sublime Communion": The Theology of the Natural in *Laudato Si'.' Theological Studies* 77, no. 2 (2016): 377–391.

Francis. 'Be Protectors of God's Creation: Homily of the Inaugural Mass of the Pope Francis' Petrine Ministry, March 19, 2013.' http:// w2.vatican.va/content/francesco/en/homilies/2013/documents/ papa-francesco_20130319_omelia-inizio-pontificato.html.

————. *Evangelii Gaudium.* http://w2.vatican.va/content/francesco/en/apost_exhortations/documents/papa-francesco_esortazione-ap_20131124_evangelii-gaudium.html.

————. *Laudato Si': On Care for Our Common Home.* http://w2.vatican.va/content/francesco/en/encyclicals/documents/papa-francesco_20150524_enciclica-laudato-si.html.

Friedel, Melanie. 'Forests as Carbon Sinks.' *American Forests,* July 18, 2017. https://www.americanforests.org/blog/forests-carbon-sinks/.

Gurstelle, Andrew. 'Sacred Trees of the Savè Hills Cultural Landscape.' *University of Michigan Working Papers in Museum in Studies,* no. 10 (2013): 1–18. https://deepblue.lib.umich.edu/bitstream/handle/2027.42/102522/Gurstelle_working_paper_Final.pdf?sequence=1.

Gutiérrez et al. 'Building a Culture of Collaboration through Hybrid Language Practices.' *Theory into Practice* 38, no. 2 (1999): 87–93.

Idang, Gabriel. 'African Culture and Values.' *Phronimon* 16, no. 2 (2015): 97–111.

Ikenga Metuh, Emefie. 'Contextualization: A Missiological Imperative for the Church in Africa in the Third Millennium.' *Mission Studies* 6, no. 1 (1989): 3–16.

————. *God and Man in African Religion.* Enugu: Snaap, 1999.

————. 'Reconciliation: The Path to True Peace and Authentic Progress for Nigeria and Africa.' *Mission Studies* XVII, no. 1–35 (2001): 12–22

————. 'The Revival of African Spirituality: The Experience of African Independent Churches.' *Mission Studies* VII, no. 2–14 (1990): 151–171.

John Paul II. *Ecclesia in Africa.* http://w2.vatican.va/content/john-paul-ii/en/apost_exhortations/documents/hf_jp-ii_exh_14091995_ecclesia-in-africa.html.

————. *Ecclesial in America.* http://w2.vatican.va/content/john-paul-ii/en/apost_exhortations/documents/hf_jp-ii_exh_22011999_ecclesia-in-america.html.

————. 'Peace with God the Creator: Peace with All of Creation: World Day of Peace Message, January 1, 1990.' http://w2.vatican.va/

content/john-paul-ii/en/messages/peace/documents/hf_jp-ii_
mes_19891208_xxiii-world-day-for-peace.html.

————. *Sollicitudo Rei Socialis.* http://w2.vatican.va/content/john-paul-ii/en/encyclicals/documents/hf_jp-ii_enc_30121987_
sollicitudo-rei-socialis.html.

Martins, Alexandre. '*Laudato Si'*: Integral Ecology and Preferential Option for the Poor.' *Journal of Religious Ethics* 46, no. 3 (2018): 410–424.

Maritain, Jacques. 'Integral Humanism and the Crisis of Modern Times.' *The Review of Politics* 1, no. 1 (1939): 1–17.

Mba, Emeodilichi. 'Assessment of Environmental Impact of Deforestation in Enugu, Nigeria.' *Resources and Environment* 8, no. 2 (2018): 207–215.

Mbiti, John. *Concept of God in Africa.* London: SCK, 1979.

Nagarajan, Chitra. 'Religious Fundamentalism and the Erasure of African Cultures, Religions and Traditions.' In *African Identity* (2016). https://thisisafrica.me/religious-fundamentalism-erasure-african-cultures-religions-traditions/.

Ndubueze, Kingsley. 'Responsible Environmental Stewardship for Sustainable Development in Africa: Edward Schillebeeck's Co-Humanity and Creaturality and Pope Francis' Integral Ecology.' *African Ecclesial Review* 60, nos. 1 and 2 (2018): 119–139.

Nichols, Megan. 'What Is Biodiversity Loss and Why Is It a Problem?' *Science, Energy & Environment* (June 4, 2018). https://interestingengineering.com/what-is-biodiversity-loss-and-why-is-it-a-problem.

Njoku, Stephen. *Curses, Effects and Release.* Enugu: Christian Living Publications, 1993.

Northcott, Michael. *A Moral Climate: The Ethics of Global Warming.* Maryknoll, NY: Orbis Books, 2007.

————. 'Planetary Moral Economy and Creaturely Redemption in *Laudato Si'.' Theological Studies* 77, no. 4 (2016): 886–904.

Nwachukwu, George. 'Odenigbo Lecture of the Catholic Archdiocese of Owerri.' https://www.owarch.org/odenigbo-lectures/.

Nwaigbo, Ferdinand. 'Pope Francis and the Programme of Ecology in a Time of Change.' *African Ecclesial Review* 58, nos. 3 and 4 (2016): 214–233.

Nwankwo, Lawrence. 'Olu Ezinauno and Neo-Christianity: A Critical Reflection on a Practice in Igboland.' Lecture text (2018): 1–16.

―――. '"Onwe M Ozo"—My Other Self: A Discourse Analytical Approach to Rooting Marriage in Igboland More Deeply into the Christian Soil.' Lecture text (2018): 1–18.

Obinna, Anthony. 'African Cultures and Development: The Rectifying Challenge.' A lecture presented at The First Colloquium—Culture and Development in African Theology, Abidjan, Ivory Coast, September 27 to October 1, 2010, 1–16.

―――――. 'Confiliatory Collaboration between the Church in Africa and Europe: A *Theo-Filio*-Logical Background.' A lecture delivered on June 3, 2004, by Archbishop Anthony Obinna, 1–12.

Onen, Sunday. 'Africa: Pastor Cut Down Sacred Iroko, "Vengeful Tree on Killing Spree" Benin Community Native Flee.' In *Africa Trade News*, March 27, 2018. http://www.atqnews.com/ng/pastor-cut-sacred-iroko-vengeful-tree-on-killing-spree-benin/.

Paul VI. 'Address of Pope Paul VI to the Parliament of Uganda in Kampala, Friday, 1 August 1969.' http://w2.vatican.va/content/paul-vi/en/speeches/1969/august/documents/hf_p-vi_spe_19690801_parlamento-uganda.html.

―――. 'Homily of Paul VI: Eucharistic Celebration at the Conclusion of the Symposium Organized by the Bishop of Africa in Kampala, July 31, 1969.' https://w2.vatican.va/content/paul-vi/en/homilies/1969/documents/hf_p-vi_hom_19690731.html.

Rockström *et al.* 'A Safe Operating Space for Humanity.' *Nature* 461 (2009): 472–475.

―――. 'Planetary Boundaries: Exploring the Safe Operating Space for Humanity.' *Ecology and Society* 14, no. 2 (2009): 32. https://ced.agro.uba.ar/gran-chaco/sites/default/files/pdf/sem6/Rockstorm%20et%20al%202009.pdf.

Rockström, Johan. 'Bounding the Planetary Future: Why We Need a Great Transition.' Great Transition Initiative: Towards a Transformative Vision and Praxis (2015). https://www.greattransition.org/publication/bounding-the-planetary-future-why-we-need-a-great-transition.

―――. 'The Anthropocene, Control and Responsibility: A Reply to Andy Stirling.' *Steps Centre: Path to Sustainability* (2015). https://steps-centre.org/blog/johan-rockstrom-on-the-anthropocene/.

Rockström, Johan and Mattias Klum. *Big World Small Planet: Abundance within Planetary Boundaries.* Sweden: Bokförlaget Max Ström, 2015.

Steffen et al. 'The Anthropocene: From Global Change to Planetary Stewardship.' *Ambio* 40 (2011): 739–761.

———. 'The Trajectory of the Anthropocene: The Great Acceleration.' *The Anthropocene Review* 2, no. 1 (2015): 81–98.

Ugorji, Lucius. *Care for Your Environment: 1995 Lenten Pastoral Letter Umuahia Diocese.* Enugu: Snaap, 1995.

———. *Political and Social Ethics: Issues of the Moment.* Enugu: Snaap, 2008.

———. 'Sustaining the Environment: Towards Facing the Moral Challenges of the Ecological Crisis.' In *Words from the Heart of a Shepherd: Selected Homilies, Addresses and Lectures of Bishop Lucius Iwejuru Ugorji*, edited by Lucius Ugorji, 378–393. Enugu: Snaap, 2015.

Wahab et al. 'Causes and Consequences of Rapid Erosion of Cultural Values in a Traditional African Society.' *Journal of Anthropology* (2012): 1–7.

Wijkman, Anders and Johan Rockström. *Bankrupting Nature: Denying our Planetary Boundaries.* London: Routledge Taylor & Francis Group, 2011.

Chapter Eighteen

Universal 'Right to Life' and the Concerns of Theological Rationality

Ikenna Paschal Okpaleke

Introduction

In a world that is filled with paradoxes concerning life, the right to life, the duty to protect and preserve it, as well as the claims to control and even take it away, a review of the right to life comes to the fore. Faced with the ethical choices of abortion and euthanasia, the moral questions surrounding wars and migration, a theological assessment of the threat faced by life from both the liberals and conservatives becomes the needful. It is therefore necessary to theologically revisit the fundamental arguments that secured the 'right to life' within the thirty-point list of United Nation's Universal Declaration of Human Rights (1948) and the Igbo stance on life in the concept of *Chi-Nwe-Ndu* (God owns life).[1] This is all the more

---

1   See Archbishop Obinna's statement after the defeat of the bill to legalize abortion in Imo State, where he argues for the Africans to uphold and defend life irrespective of the neo-imperial ideological intimidations and imposition of morality incompatible to the African minds. Cf. Anthony J. V. Obinna, 'Upholding African's Godly Life-State', press release on June 7, 2010, p. 2.

expedient in the light of the seventieth anniversary of the Declaration. To attempt this theological task, therefore, I shall proceed in three steps. Step 1: I shall make a close reading of the UN 'right to life' to determine the fundamental nature of life to any other right. I shall dialogue here briefly with Kenneth M. Boyd, who challenges the self-evident claims to the 'right to life' in creation accounts. Step 2: I shall delve deeper from the Christian perspective to trace a fundamental right to life that need not be declared but only to be affirmed. Step 3: I shall then look at few examples of affirmation of the value of life (Benedict XVI and Francis) in the light of contemporary challenges. I will then make demands for the reformulation of UNDHR in which life is primarily recognized as a gift, while at once constituting a fundamental right. At the end of this investigation, I shall add a postscript that reflects on the 'culture of life' with Archbishop A. J. V. Obinna's profile on the defense of life as its starting point.

I: UN Declaration on Human Rights: Necessary but Nonoriginal

From the purely political perspective, the UN Declaration cannot stand as an original idea. The government of the United States of America, who helped to form the UN following the post-World War II events, seems to have integrated their pre-existing political principles into the canons of the UN. The human rights were already part of the American Declaration of Independence of 1776. Right to life in a politically endorsed format first appeared in this declaration:

> We hold these truths to be *self-evident* that all men are created equal, that are endowed by the Creator with certain inalienable rights, that among these are Life, Liberty and the pursuit of Happiness.[2]

This declaration, which is the most prominent in terms of the appearance of the right to life within the field of positive law, is predated by some others. Puritan migrants from England had in many of their pre-revolutionary American documents reflected on the right to life. Vivid

---

2 Declaration of Independence: A Transcription, https://www.archives.gov/founding-docs/declaration-transcript. Italics mine [accessed December 4, 2018].

examples could be found in the December 10, 1641, statement of the Massachusetts Body of Liberties that, on the basis of the right to life, argues that no person's life should be taken away.[3] Another is George Mason's Virginia Declaration of Rights (June 12, 1776), which actually influenced Thomas Jefferson in his drafting of the US Declaration of Independence. The Virginia Declaration in its section 1 talks of 'enjoyment of life' as part of 'inherent rights' of all human beings.[4] These examples, limited to positive law, do not clarify the fundamental nature of this right. It is just presumed rather than proven.

In his article, 'The Right to Life', the Scottish scholar Kenneth M. Boyd dismissed any claim that the right to life is self-evident. He attempts an interpretation of the Gilgamesh epic and the Genesis story to establish the fact that perhaps the idea that the right to life is fundamental might be wrongly defended. Boyd argues that the stories of Adam and Eve and Gilgamesh highlight that knowledge/power and everlasting life are mutually exclusive alternatives.[5] From the very beginnings, human beings were presented with the pristine choice between life and knowledge/power and the option of knowledge/power has irrevocably been made by human beings. Life was not therefore a matter of right but of choice. Life in this case points to an everlasting life and not to the type of life that the 'right to life' addresses.[6] Surprisingly, the everlasting life they refer to is not the life beyond death, which according to him the Old Testament often paints in horrific images,[7] but rather to the quality of life. According to Boyd, what is more evident in these early stories about the origin of human life is a certain intuition that grounds the contemporary agitation for right to life.

This intuition that grounds the right to life, Boyd argues, is based on a certain covenantal relationship among human beings. As a symbolic exchange of promises, a covenant serves for the mutual protection of an ideal by both parties. It is unconditional and non-legalistic-like contract. It does not really aim at gaining anything in return but commits itself

---

3   R. Perry and J. Cooper, *Sources of Our Liberties* (Washington: America Bar Association, 1952), 148. The statement, however, gave some legal conditions under which the taking of any person's life might be tolerated.

4   The Virginia Declaration of Rights, http://www.gunstonhall.org/georgemason/human_rights/vdr_final.html [accessed June 4, 2018].

5   Kenneth M. Boyd, 'The Right to Life', *Journal of Medical Ethics* 7 (1981): 132–136; 133.

6   Boyd, 'The Right to Life', 133.

7   Psalm 88: 4–5. He also references Homeric epics as presenting such despicable pictures of the life beyond.

to the protection of such an ideal. This ideal might be in the divine-human relationship or in the context of marriage. One cannot doubt the contractual elements that are found in marriage, but the idea of covenant appeals more to the unconditionally and self-offering character of love. It is this covenantal relationship that secures the right to life. In this context, therefore, the covenantal aspect of the terrible conflicts that led either to the US Declaration of Independence and the UN Declaration of Human Rights are behind the claim to the right to life. It is thus quite interesting that the claim to the right to life only emerges at the end of wars. Little wonder that Boyd would rather opt for 'responsibility to life'.[8] Is our attempt here better served by a rephrasing of the question from a concern for 'right to life' to that of 'responsibility to life'? Is this a question either/or both/and?

II: Right to Life and the Judeo-Christian Foundation

Much as Boyd's arguments reaffirm the need for a communal responsibility towards protecting life, its questioning of the right to life appears to have taken off from a wrong starting point. To begin from the choice between knowledge/power and everlasting life is to skip what came before it, namely life. The first creation account that contains no story about the choice simply presents us with the creation of man and woman in the image and likeness of God. Both, having given life, were blessed to continue procreating life (Gen. 1:27–28). Meanwhile, in the second account of creation, the creating of the Tree of Life and the Tree of Knowledge is placed right after the creation of the first man (Gen. 2:7–9), whom thereafter was saddled with some responsibility (Gen. 2:15). Now the question of choice and responsibility presupposes the existence of life, which forms the basis for any execution of choice and responsibility. Boyd seemed to have miscalculated on two grounds by (a) not differentiating the primary gift of life from the Tree of Life and (b) not establishing the right to life as a necessary condition for any responsibility to defend it.

But if the scripture portrays life as a *donum*, a gift from God, where then does the idea of life as a right emanate in the same scripture? One might argue that before God, the giver of life, the right to life does not

---

8   Boyd, 'The Right to Life', 136.

apply since life comes from Him and returns to Him (Deut. 32:39; Job 33:4; Neh. 9:6; Ezek. 37: 1–14; Eccles. 12:7). God is life *per excellence* (John 14:6). The right to life, therefore, finds its best perspective within the community of human beings, interacting together as beneficiaries of God's gift of life. Each person thus has an inalienable right to life, which has its foundation in the gift given by God rather than from any human person. Life belongs to the individual as a justified gift that cannot be taken away by anyone who did not give it in the first place.

Giving life as the privileged and indivisible preserve of God should be distinguished from giving birth. Creation is fundamentally different from procreation. To give life is an act of creation, while to give birth belongs to procreation. As aforementioned, procreation is a responsibility that is given by God. It is a form of human participation in the creational activity of God, who out of love invites us to fellowship with Him. Any attempt therefore to interpret the procreative act as creational is fundamentally misguided. Even the recent vocabulary of cocreationism in eco-theology ought to be understood in its participatory character and not beyond that. It expands the debate on 'right to life' to the entire created cosmos and falsifies the exclusive human claim to this right. Such exclusivity is based on a theology that interprets human dominion over creation as human domination. The divine responsibility to humans over creation should be properly understood as a responsibility of stewardship and not a dominion of exploitation.[9]

To return to our earlier argument, the right to life becomes then an exercise of primary justice. Justice not understood simply as 'giving each one his or her due' but rather respecting and not interfering with that which belongs to an individual by virtue of his or her existence as a gift from God. Granted that the modern individual might dismiss the idea of God, the fact remains that life was not given to human beings by fellow humans. Technology in its attempts have experienced its limitations, and so if humans created life, then the first human would not only have been self-created but also would have been technologically superior to contemporary humans. In the failure to establish such a claim, justice in the human

---

9   For further insights in this debate, see Theodore Hiebert, 'Rethinking Dominion Theology', *Direction* 25, no. 2 (1996): 16–25; Celia Deane-Drummond, *Eco-Theology* (London: Darton, Longman and Todd, 2008); Ernst M. Conradie, *Christianity and Ecological Theology: Resources for Further Research* (Stellenbosch: Sun Press, 2006).

society should therefore identify life as a *right* that inherently belongs to every individual and which must be respected, protected, preserved, and even nourished.

Placed as the third item in the list of UNDHR, the drafters seem therefore to exhibit a lack of attention to the fundamental nature of the right to life.[10] Their inclusion of the right to property (UNDHR §17) in the list, which places it at the same level as the right to life, is largely misguided.[11] For without life, we cannot talk of any other right. And where this right is not protected and highlighted, then every other right becomes vulnerable to abuses or neglect, often without consequences. Or is the appearance of this right in the list merely for political reasons as was the case in the US Declaration of Independence with its aim at appeasing the South? Debates that relate to the nonabsolutization of this right in contemporary culture would likely dismiss the fundamental character of this right in order not to play into the hands of pro-lifers whose arguments are often deeply faith-based, namely on the sacrality of life. But for most people today, the vocabulary of the 'sacred' amounts to nothing real or tangible. It evokes the idea of antiquated religiosity, which seeks to preserve *something* based on commands of a 'transcendent' God that has no meaning to concrete existence. Having limited existential reflections to that which is immediately accessible to human senses, that which transcends human intellect is best rejected or sustained in a future that works assiduously to discover '*the hidden*' rather than ascribe it to the power beyond human intellect. With such reasoning, everything becomes subject to human

---

10 One might argue whether we should even talk of the right to life as this suggests that it is given (as a favour) by a person (perhaps, a superior human being) who has the authority over another's life. While this right seeks to protect the 'weak', it risks conferring an exaggerated authority on the 'strong'. But who is the weak, and who is the strong? Is the life not a gift that shared commonly by all? Perhaps it is better to talk about the 'gift of life' rather than the 'right to life', and in this instance, I will agree with Boyd in talking about responsibility towards protecting this 'gift of life'. I agree that the concept of 'gift of life' does not really belong to the positive law. Finding a better vocabulary to express the reality of this gift and the responsibility to protect it, while avoiding imposing the right over it on human beings, is yet a problem to be solved. Or should the 'right to life' be expunged from the UNDHR list and the 'gift of life' given a special position above it?

11 The right to private property cannot be considered as fundamental or absolute in itself. It is at the service of common good (Leo XIII, *Rerum Novarum*, 47). The same idea is found in Paul VI's *Populorum Progressio*, John Paul II's *Laborem Exercens*, *Centesimus Annus*, and Benedict XVI's *Caritas in Veritate*. And it is at the root of the principle of the *universal destination of earthly goods and the preferential option for the poor*, which constitute a pillar of Catholic social teachings.

manipulation and experimentation. Everything, including life, can then be experimented upon; and as a result, the right to life remains only a political compensation severed from its root in divine creativity. Hence, there are many threats it faces today, some of which we shall outline below.

III: Threats to Life and the Magisterial Gospel of Life

One of the major threats to life is suicide, which could be described as the taking of one's life on the basis of one's right over it. Available statistics show that suicide is on the increase in most parts of the world today.[12] In the context of right to life, can one argue that anyone who takes his or her life had just exercised a fundamental right? If this right is one's inalienable right, is suicide not therefore a justified action, the reasons behind it notwithstanding? With much sympathy to victims of 'right to (take one's) life', I think that the best way to understand the right to life is to highlight the individual ownership or possession of this right as that which he or she has received as a primary and fundamental gift from God.

Thus, *I have right to life not because I earned it by myself but because it is given to me. And as long as it relates to other human beings who are cobeneficiaries of this same gift, it remains my exclusive reserve to which no other person (as cobeneficiary) has a supervening authority. But its character as a right with respect to my possession of it, nevertheless, is limited such that I cannot extend such right to the extent of taking out my life since I did not give it to myself in the first place. My 'ownership' of life becomes, as it were, a secondary ownership that can only be exercised in preserving the life and not in either the giving or the taking of it.* Giving the innumerable abuses of human 'ownership' of life, one wonders what has become of the right to life today. Does the juridical nature of its formulation not justify the problems associated with it today?

My argument for a reframing of this idea serves to underline concretely the teachings of the Roman Catholic Church concerning life. Curiously, the very concept of right to life is hardly found in the papal encyclicals. John Paul II, however, applies it in *Centesimus Annus* (1991) in an appraisal

---

12   American Foundation for Suicide Prevention, 'Suicide Statistics', https://afsp.org/about-suicide/suicide-statistics/ [accessed July 3, 2018].

of the UNDHR but links it immediately to discredit abortion. According to him, this right includes 'an integral part of which is the right of the child to develop in the mother's womb from the moment of conception' (CA, 47). Hardly does any other document refer to 'right to life' as such since such references are always qualified with the idea of human dignity. The church undertakes the responsibility of ensuring the dignity of the gift of life and, on the basis of the value of life, strives to defend the (moral and legal) rights that human persons should enjoy in the society.

By way of illustrating the church's commitment, popes Benedict XVI and Francis demonstrate this consistency in their social teachings. Benedict XVI, in his discussion on human development, instead of referring to right to life rather talks of 'respect for life' and 'openness for life'. Such attitude of respect and openness to life is critical and fundamental to *true development*. It is a sign of absolute receptivity to a primary gift from God, who gives us that which is primary to any form of development, namely life. Without life, there is no development. Benedict XVI argues,

> ***Openness to life is at the centre of true development.***
> When a society moves towards the denial or suppression of life, it ends up no longer finding the necessary motivation and energy to strive for man's true good. If personal and social sensitivity towards the acceptance of a new life is lost, then other forms of acceptance that are valuable for society also wither away. The acceptance of life strengthens moral fibre and makes people capable of mutual help. By cultivating openness to life, wealthy peoples can better understand the needs of poor ones, they can avoid employing huge economic and intellectual resources to satisfy the selfish desires of their own citizens, and instead, they can promote virtuous action within the perspective of production that is morally sound and marked by solidarity, respecting the fundamental right to life of every people and every individual. (CV, 28)

Pope Francis, in the same line, reasserts the church's responsibility to defend life and carefully distinguishes it from the defense of human and civil rights (***Evangelii Gaudium*** [EG], 65). Here specific reference is made to the dignity of the defenseless and the vulnerable of the society and especially the life of the unborn. Francis further argues that 'this defense of unborn life is closely linked to the defense of each and every other human right. It involves the conviction that a human being is always sacred and inviolable, in any situation and at every stage of development. Human beings are ends in themselves and never a means of resolving other problems. Once this conviction disappears, so do solid and lasting foundations for the defense of human rights, which would always be subject to the passing whims of the powers that be' (EG, 213). He sharply dismisses any suggestion that attempts to eliminate human life in any form and for any reason could be seem as a 'progressive' agenda (EG, 214).

What is perhaps insightful is that the pope gives a broader perspective to the church's care for life. Life is much more than human life. Human beings therefore are not the only beneficiaries of the gift of life. Our openness to life not only demands that we protect the dignity and value of human life but also that we become 'stewards of other creatures' (EG, 215). Francis expands this message in his highly acclaimed *Laudato Si'*, calling for human responsibility of care over other created things. Other created things are not to be abused or exploited: *'Our insistence that each human being is an image of God should not make us overlook the fact that each creature has its own purpose. None is superfluous. The entire material universe speaks of God's love, his boundless affection for us'* (LS, 84). The mentality that exploits other created things has the tendency of extending such exploitation to human life. A conceptual framework that finds it difficult to affirm the inviolable value and dignity of life, except in legal formulary, will also find it difficult, by association, to affirm the purpose of other created things. Regrettably, Francis asserts the following:

> All too often, as we know from experience, people do not choose life, they do not accept the 'Gospel of Life' but let themselves be led by ideologies and ways of thinking that block life, that do not respect life, because they are dictated by selfishness, self-interest, profit, power and pleasure, and not by love, by concern for the good of others. ... As a result, the living God is replaced by fleeting human idols which offer the intoxication of a flash of freedom, but in the end bring new forms of slavery and death.[13]

---

13 Pope Francis, *Homily at Mass for 'Evangelium Vitae' Day*, June 16, 2013, no. 3, http://w2.vatican.va/content/francesco/en/homilies/2013/documents/papa-francesco_20130616_

Conclusively, there is an undergirding narrative of relativity in the very concept of 'right to life'—a narrative that opens up the possibility to justify any infringement on this right. Despite the consideration of such rights as fundamental, the very word 'right' already evokes the meaning of a nonabsolute character. Now, while this might be valid in reference to the One who is responsible for giving life, it remains a language that cannot be validly applied by cobeneficiaries of the same gift. However, it may exclusively refer, as we have earlier argued, to the individual's claim to the gift of life as his or hers in the midst of other cobeneficiaries, yet it makes little sense to give it a legalistic character as the UNDHR does. A possible way out is to reformulate the Declaration, and therein first assert the absolute nature of life as a gift, and thereafter assert the rights that are necessary for human life to thrive in the society. Life is a given, thus a gift, which cannot therefore be taken away by anyone, including the beneficiary. It is exactly in constituting a primary gift that life becomes then a right that stands above every other right.

Postscript: Archbishop Obinna and the 'Culture of Life'

It is on record that the first Nigerian March for Life took place in June 2009 and was also repeated on the fourth of June 2013. Both marches were led by Archbishop Anthony J. V. Obinna of Owerri.[14] The 2013 march, which came at the end of a two-day pro-life conference with the theme *Protecting Human Life from Conception to Natural Death*, attracted thousands of participations from across the many denominations in the state. Indeed, this march was popularized by the intention of the then Rochas Okorocha–led government's attempt to legalize abortion in the state. Of course, the news of the planned legalization of abortion was well in the public domain, and lobby groups were already convinced that nothing was going to stop it, despite the fact that it was not coming from the

---

omelia-evangelium-vitae.html [accessed June 10, 2018].

14 The Catholic Bishops' Conference of Nigeria would later emulate this act of Obinna to stage a national march for life the next year in 2014. In fact, from 2013, there has been the campaign of '40 Days for Life', which is championed by the pro-lifers. But quite significantly was the May 22, 2018, national protest in defense of life by Catholics all over Nigeria, which focused on the many killings of innocent citizens by criminal elements, particularly the April 24 massacre of two priests and seventeen parishioners by Fulani herdsmen while at Mass.

people. It is, thus, rational that only a huge event that seriously registers the citizen's opposition to the law is capable of truncating the plan. This is exactly what Obinna succeeded in accomplishing together with the people.

At the end of the successful rally, Obinna, together with Justin Okoro (chaplain of Pro-life Owerri) and Obianuju Ekeocha (founder of Culture of Life Africa) signed a communique titled 'United in God for Life'.[15] The document 'United in God for Life' was built on a fundamental, scriptural, and theological conviction that every life 'is formed and perfected in the image and likeness of God'. In fact, its argument on the sanctity and sacrality of life is not restricted to the often-limited focus on conception but equally extends to the entire process of life till natural death. As such, 'United in God for Life' had a wider scope and was intended to accomplish a much-ambitious task of strengthening the grievously threatened culture of life. As the introduction laments, 'our society is experiencing the dangerous encroachment of the culture of death from without and within.' This truth remains radically evident even today. The seriousness of the tragedy faced by the culture of life is created on the one hand by the external actors—influences, sponsors, lobbyists, agents, and interest groups—who for political and economic reasons find ways of compromising the value that our society attaches to life, and on the other hand by the decadence in the value system of our society, which downplays morals and ethical codes, making it possible for people to become irresponsible for their actions and to even collaborate with the opposing agents in the war against the culture of life.

Now, the 'culture of life' is a loaded concept not just because of its content—such as human dignity, development, prosperity, health, and general well-being—but also because of its connotation within the African context. 'Culture of life' draws its meaning mostly from the African worldview in which life (even if considered as a private property) and community intersect. Of course, there is no culture without a community of persons. Variously described as vital force (Placide Tempels), Ubuntu (Zulu), Ujamaa (Julius Nyerere), and so on, the culture of life is the culture of community, in which there is a 'vital participation' of all for the sake of each one of all.

Nigerian theologian at DePaul University Stan Chu Ilo argues that the sort of participation being advanced here is not a certain form of *social*

---

15   Obianuju Ekeocha, 'A Call to Unite for Life', *Culture of Life Africa* (June 24, 2013), http://cultureoflifeafrica.com/tag/pro-life-event [accessed March 22, 2019].

fellowship but a sharing in a vital union. Vital union expresses the African understanding of life and represents the God-willed 'bond that joins the living and the dead in a vertical and horizontal relationship; it is the life-giving principle in all'. It reflects 'the result of communion, of participation in the one reality, the one vital principle that unites all things'.[16] *Vital participation* refers simply to a life-giving action. In other words, from an ethical perspective, 'anything that diminished vital participation in the community, locally or globally, should be considered evil because it diminishes God and impoverishes the community'. Invariably, any 'failure to participate in the community or exclusion of the voices of those on the margins or the voices of the 'other' is evil for the same reason'.[17]

Indeed, on the fourth of June 2013, the community, led by Obinna, defined once again what *vital participation* really is, as they rose in defense of life and the culture of life in which the dignity of everyone is protected from conception to natural death. The government had no option than to retrace its steps even when this was prompted by mere political reasons.[18] As stated earlier, today, six years after this famous march, the culture of death has had its ominous shadow over Imo state and even over the entire Nigeria. From the many deaths that have been recorded in the state due to kidnappings to the inhuman acts of the state government, it has been an unending season of 'tears and blood', to use the expression of the popular political visionary and Afrobeat king Fela Anikulapo Kuti. Since 2013, never have we seen such disregard for the culture of life, which is stated in flow of blood in Nigeria, particularly during the 2019 elections and in the killings by Boko Haram and herdsmen in places like Kaduna, Nasarawa, Adamawa, Sokoto, Yobe, Borno, to mention a few.

As someone at the forefront of 'speaking truth to power' in defense of the culture of life, Obinna remains one of the few voices that regulate the plots of both the state and nonstate actors when it comes to the promotion of the culture of life. Hence, the task of caring for life is basically embedded in Obinna's theology of confiliation,[19] which contends against the politically

---

16   Stan Chu Ilo, 'Africa's Place in the World Christianity: Towards a Theology of Intercultural Friendship,' *Toronto Journal of Theology* 29, no. 1 (2013): 125–142; 138.

17   Ilo, 'Africa's Place,' 138.

18   *The Leader News Online*, 'Rochas Reverses Position on Abortion Law as Catholic Church Remains Cautious', (September 8, 2013), https://theleaderassumpta.com/rochas-reverses-position-on-abortion-law-as-catholic-church-remains-cautious/ [accessed March 22, 2019].

19   Anthony J. V. Obinna, 'Confiliating Americans: Recti-valuing One Another, A Theology and

motivated de-filiation tendencies that claim to treat the gift of life as secondary and under human choice. But as the threats increase in its complexity, multiplicity, and depth, then we need more voices and more actions on the defense of life.[20]

Practice of Reconfiliation,' a lecture delivered by Archbishop Anthony J. V. Obinna at Beeson Divinity School on the Campus of Sanford University, Birmingham, Alabama, USA (2016), 2.

20 Far from being a critique on Obinna, he himself recognizes this need. In a conference paper he gave on June 13, 2014 at the *International Conference on Family and Pro-Life* organized by the Catholic Bishops' Conference of Nigeria (CBCN) in conjunction with Culture of Life Africa and Action Family Foundation of Nigeria titled 'Consolidating and Scaling-Up the Successes of Pro-Life Activism in Nigeria', Archbishop Obinna reiterated that the role of the family as fundamental in every African culture and tradition as contained in the *Apostolic Exhortation: Ecclesia in Africa* (no. 53). In this presentation, Obinna states thus, 'Beyond reactive responses to anti-life, anti-family, anti-sexuality, and anti-health issues, it is necessary to integrate into our Church and public formation programmes, seriously prepared messages that draw from the authentic, doctrinal and moral teachings of the Church.'

Chapter Nineteen

'Jubilate Gaudio'— 'Sing Aloud With Joy' Archbishop Anthony J. V. Obinna's Use of Music for Pastoral Outreach

Ignatius Nwachinemere Nze

Archbishop Anthony J. V. Obinna has demonstrated amiable pastoral prowess by using different mediums in his pastoral outreach. For instance, some of these are the Whelan Research Academy for Religion, Culture, and Society, an institution that organizes a symposium that addresses, showcases, and promotes the rich values of religion, culture, and society; the Odenigbo lecture that showcases great Igbo values and identity and promotes Igbo language; the EU-Care Ministry, an outreach that provides assistance and welfare for the poor and needy. He has also devoted time to promoting his thoughtful theology through public lectures. Prominent among these is 'A Theology and Practice of Reconfiliation'.[1] This not all! Archbishop Obinna is also known for his love for music and the use of it for his pastoral outreach. This is the focus of this reflection. It is a reflection because unlike some other articles that may be published alongside this, it does not engage in a detailed research format.

---

1   A video of this lecture can be found on YouTube: https://youtu.be/TSssTQoKANw.

This reflection abides by the simplicity and humility of Archbishop Anthony J. V. Obinna as it does not seek to extol his merits and accomplishments in the world of music and pastoral leadership. It is rather a brief reflection of his application of music in discharging his pastoral duties and in communicating his thoughtful theological teachings. His love for music is evident from his activities that promote the use of music in evangelization. For instance, the music cantata organized at the archdiocesan level, as well the singing competitions organized at the archdiocesan and zonal levels in the Catholic archdiocese of Owerri are traced back to his interest and love for music.

Among the Igbo community where Archbishop Obinna comes from, there is a common expression of curiosity and wonderment when someone excels in virtues of morals and responsibilities or exhibits some admirable talents. Such curiosity could also be expressed when one performs below expectations. When any of such occurs, one may hear someone ask, '*O shi ya onye?*' or '*Kedu onye o si n'aka ya muta ya?*' ('How did he/she learn this?' or 'Who inspired him/her to such greatness?'). A close understanding to this is a similar expression of curiosity among the Jews in the time of Jesus. In Mark 6:1–3, Jesus began to teach in the synagogue on the Sabbath. Many people were there, and when they heard him, they were all amazed. 'Where did he get all this?' they asked. Considering Archbishop Obinna's proclivity to music in his pastoral outreach, one may wonder, 'From where did Archbishop Obinna learn the art of music?' A quick answer would be, 'From the seminary, of course!' He could have as well learnt the art of music out of personal interest and through some other ways.

However, there is something more to the above speculations. Archbishop Anthony John Valentine Obinna was born into a family of music lovers and renowned musicians of their time. His father, Mr Michael Obinna of blessed memory, was a catechist and headmaster. He was also a choirmaster and an organist. He had his personal keyboard and would take it to churches, mostly when he visited churches that did not have one. He inspired many youngsters to develop interest in music. When he eventually married, he married a woman who was good and interested in music too, Mrs Grace Obinna. Mrs Obinna developed interest in the husband's talent and was able to play a few musical instruments. She was so popular in singing and was considered to be the Florence Nightingale within the old

Emekuku parish. Her singing prowess attracted the attention of someone who promised her a harmonium. But before the gift of the harmonium could reach her, she died singing for Christ. While singing during choir practice at Mount Carmel Catholic Parish, Emekuku, she slumped and was rushed to Holy Rosary Hospital, Emekuku, where she died. The promised harmonium was later delivered and is still with the Obinnas as a *memorabile* up till this day.[2] Suffice it to say that Archbishop Obinna's interest in music was primarily developed and nurtured by the musical excellence of his parents and family. The fact that one of his brothers, Mr Gerald Obinna of blessed memory, was a renowned vocalist buttresses the point that *music runs in his blood.*

Archbishop Obinna's love and devotion to the Blessed Virgin Mary is also reflected in his recurring use of Marian hymns during his pastoral visits to parishes and chaplaincies in the archdiocese of Owerri. One of the most common Marian hymns that *even the babe and suckling* could predict his use of is this:

> *Mary, Mary Nne anyi Mary eh!*
> *Nwanyi Obioma, Mary eh!*
> *Were anyi nye Chukwu n'aka.*

Translation:

> Mary, Mary our Mother, Oh Mary!
> Most good-hearted woman, O Mary!
> Entrust us to God's care.

Archbishop Obinna participates actively in singing during liturgical celebrations. He vets liturgical songs rendered during celebrations and would not allow compositions with doctrinal and theological errors to be sung in the gathering of the people of God. One can literally gain insight into his spirituality by paying attention to the songs that move him most. For instance, his spirituality is well captured in this liturgical hymn, which he loves so much and would excitingly sing along audibly with the congregation—joy!

> *Onyenweanyi mee ka ime uche gi buru nrim,*

---

2   This account was provided by Mr Paddy Obinna, Archbishop Obinna's older brother.

Ka aguru ime uche gi chubem ura
Ka ime uche gi nyebe m afo ojuju
Jeso, Vejin Maria na ndi Nso nine
Mere uche Nna, ha hujuru anya.
Mana ha nozi n'otito ugbua!
Nna mee, mee, ka anyi si n'ahuhu mezuo uche Gi,
Wee keta anuri, anuri gi di ebighiebi.

Translation:

O Lord, may the task of doing your will be my food,
Let me sleeplessly hunger to do your will,
Grant that I may derive satisfaction by doing your will.
Jesus, the Virgin Mary, and All the Saints
Who did the will of the Father suffered tremendously.
But now they live in glory!
Father, may we accomplish your will through suffering
And gain everlasting joy, your everlasting

Just as the human body derives strength and nourishment from food, Archbishop Obinna yearns ceaselessly to derive strength and nourishment from doing the will of God. His love for this hymn is consistent and reflective of his episcopal motto: 'To serve God and his people.' Demonstratively, in his ever readiness in serving God and his people, he selflessly subscribes to doing the will of God, which he perceives as the bedrock of successful pastoral care for the people of God entrusted to his care. St. Augustine teaches that 'he who sings prays twice'. By repeatedly personalizing this hymn, Archbishop Obinna continues to pray for the grace to be focused in doing the will of God. As the above hymn highlights the sufferings endured by Jesus, Virgin Mary, and all the saints, he advocates for steadfastness and persistence in everyone's struggles and desires for doing the will of God. In his reflection on 'The Menace of Hate-Prone Cleavages: Creation in Ruins', he decries the sufferings of the people, intensified by religious persecutions and community clashes in Nigeria as well other parts of Africa, like Ivory Coast, Liberia, and Sierra Leone. He contemplates and unearths the evils of humanity in 'Igbo-Nigerian-African world along with the evil imported and spread beyond Africa by Arab and European imperialists'.[3]

One can see in this some similarities between Archbishop Obinna and St. Oscar Arnulfo Romero, an archbishop from El Salvador, who spoke out against poverty, social injustice, assassinations, and torture. Archbishop Obinna relentlessly continues to speak out against the evils and insensitivities of political leaders who inflict hardship on the vulnerable people they lead. He proposes *confiliance*, in its understanding as 'appreciative regard for fellow humans and a healing dynamic for humanity', as a resource for 'standing tall' against oppression. He expressively notes, 'In the face of humanity's ontological and anthropological crisis I see Confiliance—Confiliation as a possible theistic-human principle and action guide in resolving these crises.'[4] One may wonder where Archbishop Obinna's use of music comes to play in this discussion. Having expressed his hope in *confiliance*, one can see his unflinching encouragement for the downtrodden in one of his compositions inspired by Luke 18:1, thus:

> Keep on praying, keep on praying,
> Keep on praying, and never loose heart!
>
> Keep on hoping, keep on hoping,
> Keep on hoping, and never loose heart!
>
> Keep on keep on, keep on keep,
> Keep on keep on, and never loose heart!

Although the race to salvation and journey to the kingdom of God requires individual efforts and commitments, Archbishop Obinna advocates for a communal effort in the salvation race, that the people of God should be in solidarity with one another. This is reflected in his ***theological dictum*** of ***Onyeaghalanwanneya*** (Literarily: ***Nobody should leave a brother/sister behind***). This concept has been devotionally promoted in one of his compositions, thus:

> ***Chineke kere anyi wee si***

---

3   Anthony Obinna, 'Confiliatory Collaboration between the Church in Africa and Europe: A Theo-Filio-Logical Background', June 3, 2004, 5.

4   Anthony Obinna, 'Confiliance: Humanity's Healing Kinship'.

Onye, onye aghala nwanne ya!

Translation:

God our Creator enjoins us
Let no one leave another behind!

This piece, which is family and community-oriented, has become like an anthem each time he goes on a pastoral visit to one of the parishes in the archdiocese, St. Peter's Onyeaghalanwanneya. In this *theological dictum,* he invites every one of us to be 'Our brother's/sister's keeper.' It is an invitation to encourage one another in the task of excelling in virtues of morals and responsibilities. This reflects his claim, 'Long before the 1994 Synod of Bishops of the Church in Africa which took up the theme of "Family" as a principal framework for building the Church in Africa, I had between 1979 and 1984 devoted research time and energy to developing a positive family principle for educating Nigerians morally and religiously in a volatile, pluralistic context. The principles of life-enhancement and convivalism are the outcomes of that research.'[5] This is one of the numerous instances of Archbishop Obinna's thoughts, which he theologically communicated in songs. One can relate his exhortation for all to be welcoming, protective, and friendly with one another in St. Paul's declaration to the Corinthians, thus, 'None of you should be looking to your own interests, but to the interests of others' (1 Corinthians 10:24). His systematic *reconfiliation dynamo,* which he often conveys through music, is targeted at nudging 'Nigerians and Africans into a more proactive and programmatic stance in relating with ourselves, with Europeans and with others with whom we share a more familial world'.[6]

Archbishop Obinna's use of music in communicating theological realities exhumes his prowess as a teacher of religious studies, where he excelled in *driving home* every desired knowledge to his students. Being an archbishop and shepherd of the people of God, he understands the he has a larger diversified *flock* with different levels of comprehensions and assimilations. Thus, he uses music, which permeates the hearts of listeners

---

5   Anthony Obinna, 'Confiliatory Collaboration between the Church in Africa and Europe: A Theo-Filio-Logical Background', 1–2.

6   Obinna, 'Confiliatory Collaboration between the Church in Africa and Europe: A Theo-Filio-Logical Background', 2.

and helps them to memorize and recall what is being communicated to **nail down** his message. His composition of **Onyeaghalanwanneya** simplifies and draws his message of **confiliance** to every other mind that is not academically inclined. This song is a **digestive veritable tool** for understanding his **confiliance**, 'the unifying sense of kinship that invites and challenges us humans to recognize, respect, and treat all humans as fellow sons and daughters of God and of this universe'.[7]

Archbishop Obinna believes that by recognizing, respecting, and treating all humans 'as fellow sons and daughters of God and of this universe', we truly become alive in Christ. For him, to be alive in Christ is to adhere meticulously to the good news of Jesus Christ, which invites us to love God and love our neighbors as ourselves. His Grace the Archbishop presents this in one of his compositions, with which he encouraged and inspired his seminarians during his first 'Re-Union' session with them after becoming the bishop of the Catholic Diocese of Owerri:

> Alive in Christ with the good news,
> Alive in Christ with the good news.
> Alive in Christ with the good news,
> Alive with the good news!
>
> Alive in Christ with the Father,
> Alive in Christ with the Father.
> Alive in Christ with the Father,
> Alive with the Father!
>
> Alive in Christ with the Spirit,
> Alive in Christ with the Spirit.
> Alive in Christ with the Spirit,
> Alive with the Spirit!

How may we appreciate Archbishop Obinna's contributions to the practice of evangelization and pastoral leadership through music? It would be worth doing if his compositions are put together and preserved for the future generation. I call on those entrusted with the liturgical music of the Catholic Archdiocese of Owerri to start the process of collecting the compositions of Archbishop Anthony Obinna and putting them together in

---

7   Anthony Obinna, 'Confiliance: Humanity's Healing Kinship'.

formats that will be accessible to all who would wish to listen and benefit from them. On this note, I enjoin priests and all entrusted with the pastoral care of the people of God to join in Archbishop John Valentine Obinna's endeavor of proclaiming the good news and shepherding the people of God through the use of music. 'Jubilate Gaudio!' Sing aloud with joy!

About the Contributors

Rev. Fr Prof. Bede Ukwuije, CSSp, is the first assistant to the superior general of Spiritans in Rome. He holds a doctorate in theology (ThD) from the Institut Catholique de Paris and a PhD in theology and religious studies from the Catholic University of Leuven, Belgium. He became a missionary in France for twelve years, serving as students' chaplain at the University of Rennes, chaplain of African Migrants' Community in the dioceses of Rennes and Nanterre, and formator at the Spiritan Formation Community in Clamart. He is a member of the Theological Commission of the Union of Superiors General, Rome. His books include *Trinité et Inculturation* (Desclée, Paris, 2008); *The Memory of Self-Donation. Meeting the Challenges of Mission* (Paulines Africa, Nairobi, 2009); *God, Bible and African Traditional Religion* (SNAAP Press, Enugu 2009); *The Trinitarian God: Contemporary Challenges and Relevance* (Paulines, Mumbai 2013); and *Grace and Contradiction. Letter to an Impatient Friend* (SAN Press, Enugu, 2011).

Rev. Fr John O. Egbulefu, CCE, has a doctorate in philospohy (1979, Innsbruck), a doctorate in theology (1982, Münster, Germany), is a lecturer in dogmatic theology (1983/84, CIWA Port Harcourt) and habilitation (postdoctoral research, 1984–1988, Bonn), a professor of dogmatic theology for thirty years from 1989 (Rome), and the founder of the Priestly Religious Congregation of Christ the Emmanuel with the Apostolate of Technoscientific Theological Research since 1983 (Ohuru-Aba, Nigeria).

Ikenna Paschal Okpaleke is of the Catholic diocese of Aba and currently a PhD researcher at KU Leuven, Belgium.

Rev. Fr Donald Mark C. Ude, CSSp, is an FWO Research Fellow at the Institute of Philosophy KU Leuven, Belgium.

Rev. Fr Andrew Chukwurozie Nkwocha is a priest of Catholic Archdiocese of Owerri. He is a native of Umuohie Ngor in Ngor Okpala, a local government area or Imo State. He was ordained in 1996 at Maria Assumpta Cathedral Owerri. Before his ordination, he studied both philosophy and theology at St. Joseph Seminary Ikot Ekpene and Seat of Wisdom Seminary Owerri respectively. After more than a decade of pastoral experience as a priest, he was sent to study in Boston College, Massachusetts, USA, where he obtained master's degree in pastoral theology and ministry. Presently, he is a chaplain at Boston Medical Center USA.

Rev. Fr Dr Innocent Osuagwu is a Catholic priest of Owerri Archdiocese of Owerri, Imo State. He holds a licentiate in ecclesiastical sciences and a doctorate in philosophy. He is a member of the Theology Commission, Inculturation Commission, and is a pastor.

Rev. Fr Dr Boniface Nkem Anusiem is an indigenous priest of Obazu Mbieri Imo State but was ordained for the Catholic Diocese of Aba, Nigeria. He is a professional writer, dynamic and motivational speaker, preacher, and an erudite media and communication scholar, mentor, and consultant. He lives and works in the United States of America.

Rev. Fr Kenneth Nnaemeka Ameke is a Catholic priest of the Archdiocese of Owerri and a researcher at the department of systematic theology KU Leuven, Belgium. He specializes in Christology and development of ecumenical models for interecclesial relation.

Rev. Fr Dr Stephen Egwim is a Catholic priest of the Archdiocese of Owerri and a biblical scholar with a special interest in the book of Psalms.

Rev. Fr Dr Alexander Izuchukwu Abasili, SMMM, specialises in the Old Testament biblical exegesis. He earned, among others, a masters of advanced studies in theology and religious studies, a licentiate and STD in sacred theology, and a PhD in theology and religious studies (biblical studies dept. Old Testament) from KU Leuven, Belgium. His research interests include the meaning and role of human sexuality in the Hebrew Bible, the book of Samuel, and contextual biblical exegesis. He is the author of a number of the books, including *The Understanding of Adultery in the Hebrew Bible* (2016, pp. 417) and *Marriage and Adultery in the Old Testament: An Igbo African Contextual Reading* (2018, pp.608).

Rev. Fr Kingsley Ndubueze is a priest of Umuahia Diocese. He holds a Licentiate Degree in Sacred Theology (S.T.L.) from the Catholic University of Louvain (KU Leuven). His doctorial research is on how to take care for our common home in the Anthropocene in search of a new anthropological stance towards creation (KU Leuven). He has special interest in theological ethics, environmental ethics, and ecology.

Rev. Fr Patrick Mbarah' is a priest of the Archdiocese of Owerri Nigeria. He holds a licentiate degree in Arabic and Islamic studies from the Pontifical Institute of Arabic and Islamic Studies (PISAI) Rome and a doctorate with specialties on interreligious dialogue from the Pontifical Angelicum University Rome. He has special interest in dialogue of world religions.

Rev. Fr Edmund Aku is a priest of the Catholic archdiocese of Owerri. He holds master's degrees in both educational administration and psychology and a PhD in moral theology. For several years, he taught sociology, psychology, and ethics in the state of Connecticut community colleges system. He is currently the director of pastoral care with Catholic Health Services in Miami, Florida.

Rev. Fr Vincent Onwukwe is a Catholic priest of Okigwe diocese. He is a researcher at the Old Testament Biblical Studies KU Leuven. He specializes in the book of Genesis, narrative criticism of the Hebrew Bible, and African contextual biblical hermeneutics.

Rev. Fr Samuel Uzoukwu is a priest of the Catholic Archdiocese of Owerri, ordained in 2007. He holds an MBA in management (Marshall, Minnesota) and an STL in sacred theology (Dominican House of Studies, Washington, DC). He works as priest-chaplain for Archdiocese of Baltimore at the University of Maryland Medical Centre in Baltimore, Maryland (USA), and is a doctoral student of moral theology at the Angelicum (Rome).

Rev. Fr Moses Eziukwu Chikwe is a priest of the Archdiocese of Owerri and the director of education in the archdiocese. Fr Chikwe's education peregrination took him to the United States of America, where he bagged his master's degree in education administration from Loyola Marymount University, Los Angeles, and his PhD in education from University of California at Los Angeles. His research centres on school leadership and the use of data for equity and social justice work in high schools. This is aimed at finding policy solutions to the perennial unequal educational opportunity prevalent in our high schools.

Rev. Fr Ignatius Nwachinemere Nze is a one-time vice chairman of the Music Commission of the Catholic Archdiocese of Owerri (under Rev. Fr Dr Julius Mmegwa) and was a radio producer and presenter with the Federal Radio Corporation of Nigeria at Radio Nigeria Heartland FM 100.5 Owerri. He holds a master's degree in theology and ministry and a master's degree in social work (MSW) with a concentration in health and mental health. He is the coordinator of Catholic Pastoral Services for the Roman Catholic Archdiocese of Boston at Boston Medical Center, USA. Fr Nze is currently researching into the topic of Catholic hospital chaplain at the intersection of contention on the dignity of human person, focusing on the task of providing ethical response to the conflicts of end-of-life care.

Glossary

Acculturation: Refers to the meeting of cultures and the changes it generates. Acculturation is proposed as a multidimensional process consisting of the confluence among heritage-cultural and receiving-cultural practices, values, and identifications.

African (Igbo) Cosmology: The concept of the world, whether sensible or supra-sensible, held by a people in a given culture has a vital influence on their attitude to and evaluation of life and death. These notions necessarily, though sometimes covertly, shape our behaviour and, thus, guide our actions. There are four components of Igbo cosmology: *Okike* (refers to creation), *Alusi* (deals with the supernatural forces and deities), *Mmuo* (spirit), and the *Uwa* (means the world).

Chifiliation: This is theofiliation with an Igbo prefix *Chi*.

Christi-filiation: Designates the Christly and Christlike sonship to sonship relation of humanity with God in the paradigm of the Church family. Christi-filiation remains the channel of theofiliation in creation.

Christophobia: This is the irrational fear or hatred of Christianity or Christians.

Churchianity: Refers to the devolution of Christianity into a mutual admiration society that embraces the church's subculture with an emphasis on the social aspects as well as adaptation to the modern world. It suggests a form of a religious system that attempts to confine Christ to an enclosed space.

Cofiliation: Refers to the basic appreciation that human beings across all differences and divides are fellow sons and daughters in the human family.

Colonialism: Forced change in which one culture, society, or nation dominates another.

Confiliance: This is seen as a local and global humanization imperative with which and toward which to move in the face of humanity's lingering hurts and fresh atrocities. It is regarded as the dynamics to discern humanity's healing kinship.

Confiliation: Refers to the rediscovered and recovered sense of the human kinship with one another that cuts across contexts, cultures, differences, and convictions of the one human family. It is also a theistic human principle and action guide in resolving human crisis that recognizes the reciprocal, equal sonship and daughtership of all human beings.

Confiliality/Cofiliality: Pertains to the sociological and religious extension of brotherhood and sisterhood in which fraternity and sorority are secondary to the primacy of filiality.

Covivance: This is derived from the traditional social structure that alludes to the living together in harmony of human beings in the spirit of sharing life and its gifts communally. It becomes a practical measuring index for mutual coexistence of human beings.

Cross-cultural: May refer to cross-cultural studies, a comparative tendency in various fields of cultural analysis. It also deals with the cross-cultural communication, a field of study that looks at how people from differing cultural backgrounds communicate. It also refers to any of various forms of interactivity between members of disparate cultural groups.

Crucifiliation: Opens the anthropological aspect that indicates that to be human is to be a creature united in the sufferings of Christ and sheltered in God's love. This understanding does not confuse the idea of suffering as consequence of sin that separates us from God but as what unites us in the suffering of Christ. Julian of Norwich termed this understanding as the 'cruciform anthropology'.

Culture: This is the set of means used by mankind to become more virtuous and reasonable in order to become fully human.

De-filiation: Means a refusal or denial of sonship or daughtership.

Divine Filiation: Refers to the new integral kinship of creation in Christ. It designates the completion of the filiation by creation to a new way of being in order to participate in the full parentage that belongs to God in the manner of the mysterious relationship in and within the Godhead.

Eco Filiation: Relates to the recognition, care, and acknowledgment of the nonhuman creation by human beings.

Ecumenical filiation: Applies to the communion of all the sons and daughters of Christ severed by the wounds of division of the Christian family of God founded by Christ. It also concerns itself with the returning to the true belief and the common leadership of Christ of the heretics, syncretist, schism, and church proliferators

Enculturation: This is the process whereby an individual learns the requirements of the culture in which he or she is steeped. It is also the process by which culture is passed from one generation to the next. It is synonymous with socialization.

Filiation: Refers to the intimate or legal relationship that exist between the child and the parents, between sons/daughters and the mother/father. It is an all-gender inclusive term.

Humanization: This is a process that recognizes the inherent dignity and the inalienable rights of one as member of the human family. It is also a matter of recognizing the common humanity of the other people one encounters and thus includes them in one's moral scope. Through humanization, one breaks down the enemy image about the other person but considers the person as one who deserves a moral consideration.

Inculturation: Deals with the intimate transfer of authentic cultural values through their integrity in Christianity and the insertion of Christianity in various human cultures. It is basically an evangelization of the cultural pluralism, for instance, modern world, scientific development and the emerging social sciences, industrialization and urbanization that are shaping the new form of mass culture (GS, 53)

Interculturality: refers to the cross-cultural dialogue and challenging self-segregation tendencies within culture. It also deals with the human attitude that penetrates the system of the other people in order to see things from their perspective, which opens one up for relation.

Pro-filiation: Designates the filiation in God's mind and providential plan since eternity. Cf. Ephesians 1:4 'God chose humans and destined them for adoption in Christ before creation.'

Re-Christofiliation: Alludes to the reconciliatory work of Christ in/ through Him to restore the human person to God to a state of being an *imago Christi*.

Reconfiliate: Describes the fact of effecting and regaining the right of sonship and daughtership in a family in fellowship with other sons and daughters of the family. This verb form of reconfiliation shares similar meaning with refiliate and confiliate.

Reconfiliation: This is the liberative illumination by which the entire creation is reanchored in God in which Jesus Christ is the roots and who provides the interconnecting branches to all humanity through His blood. Reconfiliation also adds an absolute dimension to the peacemaking and harmonizing thrust of reconciliation by emphasizing the equal dignity of all humans from creation and by redemption.

Re-con-filiation: This means the reconstitution or the re-establishment of the status of son or daughter to any person whosoever. It would also mean the new joining or conjoining or new-kinning of humans into fellow sons and daughters in equal dignity.

Reconfiliator: Points to Jesus Christ as the universal person who redignifies and reglorifies the broken humanity.

Reconfiliatory: The computer mistakes this for 'reconciliation'. It may be unfamiliar, but it is not totally strange. It has a relationship with the words 'filial' and 'affiliate', both of which evoke a sense of belonging that approximate that of a son or daughter in a family. Reconfiliatory constitutes the divinizing-humanizing thrust that will hopefully engage and challenge each of us celebrants and participants.

Recti-filiation: This is the corrective inclusion of excluded humans into the one family of sons and daughters.

Refiliation: With its verb form, *refiliate, confiliate,* and *reconfiliate* defines the fact of effecting and regaining the right of sonship and daughtership in a family in fellowship with other sons and daughters of the family.

ReinGodment: Refers to the human re-experience of the Incarnation of Christ who continuously perfuse creation with the grace of God from the human state of nothingness to the beauty and splendour of God.

Retheofiliation: Applies to reconciliation of the human person to the initial creation filiation after de-filiation by sin.

Theofiliance: This is definable as creation's new and integral sense of kinship with God derived from its relationship with the Son of God who has become the Son of Man. Cf. *divine filiation.*

Theofiliation: This is the filiation of the humanity and creation to God into the Trinitarian communion and life. Cf. *divine filiation.*

Transculturation: Deals with a set of elements present in all cultures or the ethnocentric and unidirectional transfer of some elements from one culture to another.

Index

CPSIA information can be obtained
at www.ICGtesting.com
Printed in the USA
BVHW031037181019
561476BV00006B/53/P

9 781796 061123